The Orphaned Land

THE ORPHANED LAND

NEW MEXICO'S ENVIRONMENT SINCE THE MANHATTAN PROJECT

V. B. PRICE

Photographs by Nell Farrell

University of New Mexico Press
Albuquerque

Library of Congress Cataloging-in-Publication Data

Price, V. B. (Vincent Barrett)
The orphaned land : New Mexico's environment since the
Manhattan Project / V. B. Price ; photographs by Nell Farrell.
p. cm.
Includes bibliographical references and index.
ISBN 978-0-8263-5049-7 (pbk. : alk. paper)
ISBN 978-0-8263-5051-0 (electronic)
1. New Mexico—Environmental conditions—Case studies.
I. Title.
GE155.N6P75 2011
577.2709789—dc22
                                        2011009569

The photographs in this book were shot in color and
can be viewed as intended at www.nellfarrell.com.

||||||||||||||||||||||||||||||||||||||||||||||||||||||||||||||||

For Rini and our family, far and wide,
and for the children of New Mexico

In memoriam
Clifford Brook
Rosalie Buddington
Patrick Chester Henderson
Warren Russell Martin
Winfield Townley Scott
Sandra Rae Greenwald
Edith Barrett Price
James Michael Jenkinson
Marjorie H. Rini
Helen K. Herman
Milas Hurley
Anne Seymore
Vincent Leonard Price, Jr.
Dudley Wynn
Katherine Simons
Mark Douglas Acuff
Mildred and John Gifford
Reg Williams
Florence and Bev Watts
Joan Hodes
Mary Grant Price
Susie Henderson
Paula Hocks
George Clayton Pearl
S. Jack Rini
Cecil Robert Lloyd

What we do anywhere matters, but especially here. It matters very much. Mesas, mountains, rivers and trees, winds and rains are as sensitive to the actions and thoughts of humans as we are to their forces. They take into themselves what we give off, and give it out again.

—Edith Warner, *In the Shadow of Los Alamos:*
Selected Writings of Edith Warner

And they were sawing off the branches on which they were sitting, while shouting across their experiences to one another how to saw more efficiently. And they went crashing down into the deep. And those who watched them shook their heads and continued sawing vigorously.

—Bertolt Brecht, *Exile III*

"For the New Mexico Reservation," he said. "I had the same idea as you. . . . Wanted to have a look at the savages. Got a permit to New Mexico. . . . I actually dream about it sometimes. . . ." They slept that night in Santa Fe. The hotel was excellent. . . . "Five hundred and sixty thousand square kilometers, divided into four distinct Sub-Reservations, each surrounded by a tension wire fence. . . . Upwards of five thousand kilometers of fencing at sixty thousand volts. . . . To touch the fence is instant death," pronounced the Warden solemnly. "There's no escape from a Savage Reservation. . . . Those, I repeat, who are born in the Reservation are destined to die there."

—Aldous Huxley, *Brave New World*

Contents

PREFACE

Laypeople can sometimes go where professionals fear to tread, but even the enthusiastic have to rein themselves in. When I began this book, I thought I was going to write an environmental history of New Mexico from the start to when I finished. I soon realized that I was not equipped to undertake that enormous task. I am a journalist, not a historian or a geographer. My interests lie primarily in the present. Reading Kevin Fernlund's *The Cold War in the American West* made it clear to me that my starting point should be the Manhattan Project. But the subject remained overwhelming, so I decided to focus on environmental justice, water, toxic waste, and the complicated interactions of urban and rural life.

Fernlund asks "whether the cold war transformed or deformed the American West."[1] A good portion of my environmental accounting of New Mexico since the middle of the twentieth century deals with that question. The Cold War is intimately connected with New Mexico's modern history because of the importance of nuclear weaponry to our state's intellectual culture and economy and because, during the period of the Cold War and after, an amazing amount of damage was done to our environment.

In every chapter of this book, readers will encounter questions that have to do with knowledge. How do we know what we know? Who is credible and who is not? Whose account deserves suspicion? What is a scientific "fact," what is biased spin, and how do you tell the difference?

Information on the history and condition of our environment over the last seventy years is, paradoxically, both abundant and extremely difficult to come by. One of the challenges of trying to write about the subject is the lack of publicly available scientific data, and that is partly because so much of the information in question has been gathered and interpreted by public and private entities with political or profit motives.

Often the best a researcher can do is build a broad picture from circumstantial evidence reported in the mainstream press and by nongovernmental organizations. When it's possible to compare interpretations and data on a significant event from various sources, it's always revealing to see what's been left out and by whom. This book is in part a history of the way the press has reported on environmental issues. In the seven years it took to write it and to verify as best I could the information I presented, the availability on the Internet of primary documents from reliable federal agencies, like the Centers for Disease Control and Prevention, and from the New Mexico state government increased dramatically. Such sources, though, do not appear to have generated much news in the mainstream print and television media.

The chilling effect that legal and financial pressure, coupled with bureaucratic impenetrability, can have on gathering and publishing environmental information has become almost a deep freeze in the twenty-first century. Even media powerhouses are not immune. Companies like General Motors, BP, and Morgan Stanley demand advertising contracts allowing them to pull ads from publications that run stories reflecting badly on them. Developers can still direct strategic litigation against public participation, known as SLAPP suits, at environmental activists, even though many states have sought to outlaw such suits. Information from government often flows so sluggishly that the public's right to know is overridden by national security concerns or just a reflexive love of secrecy. In 2005 here in New Mexico, vital information on a uranium enrichment plant proposed near Eunice was withheld, not just from the general public, but from state government. Dow Chemical, Monsanto, Goodrich, Goodyear, Uniroyal, and other corporations are suing the publisher and authors of a University of California Press book, *The Deadly Politics of Industrial Pollution*, that charges chemical companies with deceiving the government about the potential carcinogenic effects of vinyl chloride monomer, a key ingredient in automobile tire manufacture. Even animal rights activists are being charged under federal terrorism laws.

The biggest environmental lawsuit in New Mexico's history was effectively kept out of the news for more than two years before a federal court of appeals dismissed the case in 2006. A $4 billion dollar lawsuit against General Electric and other corporations is hard to hide, but New Mexico's newspapers and television stations did just that, not wanting to give credence to the allegation that the military and a major national company had been dumping toxic waste into the water supply of Albuquerque's South Valley, even though GE had spent millions of dollars trying to clean up what had already been designated a Superfund site by the Environmental Protection Agency. The state's suit contended the contaminated water would never be drinkable again. GE is involved with other corporations in more than eighty Superfund sites across the country.

Even if the big stories aren't always covered by the press, reams of information about environmental issues are still leaked, gathered covertly, and reported from public documents and open meetings by local papers around New Mexico and by radio stations and wire services. I can testify that the back issues of the *Albuquerque Journal,* the *Albuquerque Tribune* (before it closed), and the *Santa Fe New Mexican,* combined with small town papers and occasional enterprising reporters from big papers in the West, can provide enough clippings on the environment to fill several large accordion files a year.

Many of the other questions on which this book turns can be phrased as simple reminders. First, there's a lot we don't know. When it comes to establishing environmental cause-and-effect relationships, for example, it is extremely difficult to go beyond suspicious correlations, anecdotes, and common sense. The ease of overturning statistics in court makes it simple for corporations and military contractors to avoid owning up to responsibility for health problems that seem directly related to their activities. An egregious case in point is the response of mining companies to the dramatic presence of lung disease among Navajo and Pueblo uranium miners. Even though lung cancer was virtually unknown in this population before they began to work in radioactive surroundings, some corporations suggested that the miners' lung problems were caused by smoking.

Determining cause-and-effect relationships between environmental pollutants and long-term change in the biota may be an interminably slow process, but common sense tells us that dumping solvents, nuclear waste, and other noxious substances into our air and water and topsoil isn't a good idea. If you're downstream from a herd of cattle, let's say, you don't drink the water. You don't need scientific proof beyond the shadow of a doubt that cow excrement is bad for you. On the face of it alone, littering pollutants into the commons is a social crime of which any of us could be the victim. The precautionary principle, a notion that underlies sensible approaches to dangerous substances in our daily lives, applies to military and corporate science, too. When in doubt about potential harm, err on the side of caution—when in doubt, don't do it. In addition to using common sense, though, we need to remember that scientific knowledge is inherently controversial. Just because we don't have standard proof of the relationship between a cause and an effect does not mean that it isn't there. A reluctance of the guardians of the status quo to accept challenging ideas is a major theme in the history of science. Today such guardians use relatively subtle tactics that label those who question them as crackpots.

Many corporations and defense agencies, and their scientists and technicians, are driven by a philosophy that permits any means to achieve strategic or business goals. When positive ends are used to justify dishonorable means, disaster almost always ensues. Just as it is important to keep morality in mind rather than letting profit and loss determine our view of the environment, I think we need to apply moral fortitude to the challenging process of educating ourselves about the environment. In reading this book you will learn, as I did in researching it, more than you might want to know about a lot of extremely unpleasant subjects. It is understandable to react with feelings of hopelessness, and I don't pretend that I haven't been deeply saddened by much of what I have discovered. But the more I explored the ways that our environment has been changed over the last half century, the more convinced I became that we don't really know enough to be depressed. Our knowledge is still in the early stages—our knowledge, that is, of how the living world works as a whole, how its various hierarchies and feedback loops interact, and the nature of its self-corrections, adjustments, breakdowns, and renewals. And we don't have the big picture when it comes to unintended consequences and tradeoffs. We have to keep learning if only because we can't afford to let fear and depression immobilize us. We can't tell our children and grandchildren that the world is a hopeless mess. We can't think that way ourselves if we mean to help our planet and those we love. Given the provisional nature of environmental science at this moment in history, despair must be converted to curiosity that will not only generate the research to help us survive, but that will break down the barriers of denial and obfuscation.

Even though I feel an activist's passion for New Mexico, I am not an "investigative reporter," journalism's equivalent of a prosecutor. I'm not out to prove anything. In this book, I set out to see what was there. Naturally, I have a slant. Like the overwhelming majority of

Americans, I belong to the environmental camp. It's self-evident to me that all living organisms are inseparably linked to their surroundings. Their health and well-being depend on the health and well-being of the places they inhabit. This is also true emotionally and aesthetically for humans. We thrive in places we consider beautiful and wither in the midst of the ugly and degraded. My slant holds that soiling our nests, extravagantly overusing our resources, and being unmindful of the basic and determining environmental conditions under which we live threatens our well-being.

Finishing this book has been difficult because more and more information is becoming available every week and every day. In 2010, for example, the Centers for Disease Control and Prevention released a major report on radioactive contamination from operations at the Los Alamos National Laboratories, presenting findings that make it clear the lab has been underestimating its environmental impact for years. New data like this make me wonder if I am writing this book five or ten years too early. Perhaps in the next decade young scholars interested in regional environments will assemble a deeper and more complex knowledge base from their own research and help us to find ways to overcome and compensate for the dangerous habits of the past.

ACKNOWLEDGMENTS

My view of human interaction with the environment is strongly influenced by the pragmatic design concepts described by Ian McHarg in his groundbreaking 1969 book *Design with Nature*. McHarg understands that designing against nature, or trying to overcome natural constraints, is in the long run a fruitless, wasteful, and impractical endeavor. Though McHarg's focus is on planning and the built environment, his central metaphor of cooperation with nature in the form of an early version of biomimicry is the underlying ethic in all ecologically prudent human activity.

Wes Jackson's line of thought in his book *Becoming Native to This Place* amplifies my own interests in the natural forces that underlay the spiritual and economic life of Ancient Puebloan peoples. Working with an ecological landscape, modifying it in respectful ways where possible, and adjusting to its natural limits and constraints when necessary, rather than trying to overpower it and reshape it, are enduring principles of cultural and social sustainability.

My thinking in these matters also has been influenced by the work of southwestern archaeologist David Stuart and his book *Anasazi America*, in which excessive use of short-term power techniques and grandiosity of intentions are contrasted with efficient long-term living strategies in the arid Southwest. The Anasazi—or Ancestral Puebloans, as many descendants prefer to be called—dramatically and indelibly altered their natural surroundings in ways that were not sustainable.

The cautious yet definitive tone of environmental historian J. R. McNeill in his magisterial *Something New Under the Sun: An Environmental History of the Twentieth-Century World* allowed me to understand more deeply the enormous range of interconnected social and natural phenomena that comprise the formal discipline of environmental history. McNeill's emphasis on the intensity of change in the twentieth century and on the "unintended consequences of social, political, economic, and intellectual patterns" has been a restraining influence on my sense of outrage over the unnecessary and disrespectful contamination of New Mexico's natural resources.

I am also indebted to the perspective of historian William Cronon, whose view on "nature as a human idea" in his book *Uncommon Ground* makes the clear point about the relativity of environmental politics, even as it deals with the precise, but always provisional, descriptions of reality afforded us by science. In his essay "Modes of Prophecy and Production: Placing Nature in History," Cronon describes environmental historians as performing "a delicate interdisciplinary balancing act in trying to reconcile the insights of their colleagues in history, ecology, geography, anthropology, and several other fields."

It's not possible to think about environmental history in the United States today without acknowledging a debt of gratitude to Carolyn Merchant, whose introduction to American environmental history and analysis of major problems in the discipline are foundational works. Her books *Radical Ecology* and *Reinventing Eden* root the study of human interaction with the natural world in a moral context of care and sympathetic nurture.

And of course, when dealing with the environment of New Mexico, it's impossible not to be instructed by the invaluable work of William deBuys, Valerie Kuletz, Alfonso Ortiz, Gregory Cajete, Mark Reisner, Jerry Williams, Gary Nabhan, Paul Horgan, Ross Calvin, Dan Scurlock, Greg Mello, Marc Simmons, Gerald Nash, Ferenc Szasz, and Courtney White, to name a prominent few among many dedicated workers and thinkers in this field.

William deBuys's *Enchantment and Exploitation: The Life and Hard Times of a New Mexico Mountain Range* joins Dan Scurlock's *From the Rio to the Sierra: An Environmental History of the Middle Rio Grande Basin* as the major environmental histories I know of written in a New Mexico setting. I am, of course, contrasting here environmental history with the multitudinous accounts of the natural history of our state and region. DeBuys's insight that "in an unforgiving environment, small errors yield large consequences" is central to my thinking in this book.

In the long run, people do not knowingly despoil environments they identify with and love. Love and respect normally go hand in hand. Political, cultural, corporate, and military colonization by outsiders who do not respect the land or people they exploit is the major source of the pollution and ruination of local environments. Motivated by their affection for New Mexico, local activists, from farmers to bird watchers, from NGOs to idealists of all stripes, have often brought polluters to a standstill and even reversed their negative impact. It is this local energy, based on a love of place, that is the major source of hope for the future.

I also have many friends and associates to thank who've lifted the burden of quixotic isolation from this effort. Armed with no research grants, no funding from big foundations or even small ones, I have been encouraged, advised, and allowed to talk through many of the most difficult questions and conundrums by my friends in New Mexico.

I have relied on numerous "readers" to keep me from making a fool of myself while writing the text. They are the artist Rini Price, poet and naturalist Mary Beath, photographer Nell Farrell, whose photographs grace this book, physician and novelist Francis Roe, political scientist and writer Richard Fox, troubleshooter and advisor John J. Cordova, and longtime water observer and independent environmental scholar Lisa Robert. I owe a profound debt of gratitude to them all.

I have been blessed with the talent and curiosities of a number of friends who followed the trails of many complicated matters and opened my mind countless times. Chief among them are poet, writer, and environmental artist Mary Beath, who focused on endangered and invasive species and has been my consultant on the natural sciences; Elizabeth Wolf, who excavated and put together a mountain of information on groundwater pollution in Albuquerque's South Valley; Micaela Siedel, who did vital exploratory research on the South Valley; Armando Lamadrid, who independently explored the South Valley and amassed an archive of up-to-date information; Lynne Reeve, who explored mining history, the ecology of mining, and mining technology in New Mexico; Maria Santelli, who was so generous with her expertise in matters pertaining to the Waste Isolation Pilot Project near Carlsbad, to depleted uranium ammunition, and to uranium mining, including the Church Rock spill; Lisa Robert, whose detailed and holistic views of agricultural, water, and urban development were a constant source of insight and inspiration; and physicist Spencer Campbell, who, over many lunches, gently straightened out my confusions about hard science, physics, and engineering. I am particularly indebted to Mikaela Renz-Whitmore, who not only organized more than thirty years of newspaper clippings and endless file folders full of information, but also helped me make sense of my many drafts and footnotes over the seven years it took to write this book. She was indispensable. I am also grateful to University of New Mexico environmental historian Virginia Scharff, who helped me think through thorny matters concerning global warming and who gave me consistently encouraging energy and wise advice throughout this effort.

Longtime friend and historian Marc Simmons spent time with me at his "camp" on land near the old mining town of Cerrillos and over lunch at the San Marcos Café and feedstore, helping me come to grips with some of the essentials of historical research and what it takes to follow through a project like this to some useful conclusion. Marc was writing his thirty-eighth book at the time. Artists Allan and Gloria Graham and their completely "off the grid" way of life on edge of the Pecos Wilderness have inspired me for more than forty years. *Albuquerque's Environmental Story*, which Hy and Joan Rosner began in the 1970s, is an exemplary model for anyone writing about the environment in New Mexico. My brother-in-law, Jim Rini, the cartoonist and naturalist, has broadened my perspective on politics, economics, and the environment for well over a quarter of a century. His insights have been invaluable. Political scientist Richard Fox has talked with me for decades about the political ramifications of environmental scrutiny. His advice always hits the mark. Likewise, John Cordova has opened his bottomless files on water and environmental racism to me and has helped me explore many issues regarding generic corporate views of the environment. His intelligence and friendship have been catalytic. Historian, writer, and archivist Michael Miller and tireless public advocates Don Hancock, Chris Shuey, and Paul Robinson have been unfailingly generous with their knowledge. Neighborhood activist and legal scholar Ruth Koury's in-depth research and generosity of interpretation cleared my head about many issues of the law. I've been helped greatly by the openness and expertise of four physicians—Marty Kantrowitz, Ben Daitz, Robert George, and Francis Roe—who have helped me understand the health risks associated with certain environmental contaminants. The late historian Ferenc Szasz, archaeologists Mike Marshall and David Stuart, landscape architect Baker Morrow, and biologist Carol Brandt have helped and guided me in many fruitful directions. I give special thanks to Rosalie Otero, director of UNM's University Honors Program, where I've taught for the last twenty-six years, and to my faculty colleagues and students, who have kept me energized and comforted in the extended family and community of our program.

This book owes its existence to the welcoming enthusiasm, insight, and patience of former UNM Press director Luther Wilson. Without the editorial advice of former UNM Press director Beth Hadas, it would have been next to impossible for me to complete this project. Her wise counsel, her sensitivity to context, and her brilliant understanding of the English language have been a sustaining blessing over many years of work on this book and others. I am grateful as well to editor Diana Rico for her clarity and precision.

I could never have contemplated a project like this without the tireless support and editorial insight of my wife, the artist Rini Price, who has worked with everything I've written over the last forty-two years and consistently made it better. The clarity of her values and unerring moral compass have informed and inspired me for over half my life.

The Orphaned Land

NEW MEXICO'S ENVIRONMENT SINCE THE MANHATTAN PROJECT

INTRODUCTION

One of the essential questions of the Information Age is: Whom do you believe? Answering that question when confronting environmental pronouncements is especially perplexing. Whom do you believe when you hear from governments and corporations with almost comic monotony that their releases of contaminants into the environment are not a threat to public health? Do you believe them, or are you suspicious? And on what are your suspicions based? Whom do you believe in debates over New Mexico's endangered species? Is the Rio Grande's silvery minnow a worthless bait fish, a canary in the mineshaft warning of impending disaster, or a prodigious algae eater and food supply for larger fish that has helped keep the river clean and full of life for centuries? Is it possible that the invasive species known as both salt cedar and tamarisk sucks up so much of the Rio Grande's water that eradicating it would provide enough water for farming, or is urban and industrial conservation also required? Did

◄ Petroleum tanks across the canal from GE in Albuquerque's
South Valley (see page 128). December 2006.

global warming, and its local manifestations in New Mexico, cause the record-breaking heat waves in the drought years of 2003 and 2010? Does diluting polluted groundwater make it potable? If not, what use is treated water that is undrinkable? Is it really possible to remove industrial solvents from water and make it clean enough to safely recharge aquifers if reverse osmosis technology isn't used?

Fact or Propaganda

Environmental information may be, in fact, one of the more controversial and contested categories of knowledge in the modern world. It's a category of knowledge cobbled together from experts in a variety fields and intellectual traditions, not to be confused with ecology. In the debate over the Waste Isolation Pilot Project (WIPP) outside Carlsbad, New Mexico, for instance, Department of Energy officials, military strategists, nuclear physicists, the Carlsbad business community, and a wide range of antinuclear and conservation activists have been at odds with each other since the late 1960s about the safety of storing nuclear waste in the potash fields of southeastern New Mexico. To make a long story short for the moment, one side contends that the plutonium and other nuclear wastes to be buried at the WIPP site aren't really all that dangerous, just "stuff" like contaminated gloves and hammers and some sludge. The people of Carlsbad get good jobs, nuclear safety is served, and it's all as risk free as anything can be in this life. Opponents of WIPP counter by asking: If this stuff isn't so dangerous, why is it being moved in high-tech trucks, along secretly scheduled routes, frequently in unmarked canisters, to be buried more than two thousand feet below the surface of the earth in a salt mine catacomb that is wedged between two aquifers, and that will have on top of it, when it's full of nuclear debris, signage meant to convey the warning of extreme danger for at least ten thousand years so drillers and miners will stay far away? And there are always the questions about what is really in those barrels to be stored at WIPP and why the nuclear weapons community has been so imprecise over the years about what kinds of wastes it's accumulated. Whom would you believe here? Whose questions and assertions appear to be the most reliable?

I find certain reporters more credible than the news organizations they work for and follow their writing wherever it appears. All writers have a slant, as E. B. White used to say, but a slant is far different from a bias, a party line, or a piece of corporate or governmental propaganda. Chuck McCutcheon is always a reliable source. His book *Nuclear Reactions: The Politics of Opening a Radioactive Waste Disposal Site*, for instance, is handsomely readable and full of useful information. When he writes that plutonium's alpha particles "travel only inches and cannot penetrate skin or even a sheet of paper, [but] if it is inhaled, swallowed, or absorbed into the bloodstream through a cut, any amount of plutonium as small as one-millionth of a gram can cause cancer,"[1] you know he's giving the real picture. Tony Davis, an environmental writer for nearly thirty years, first broke the story that put an end to the myth of Albuquerque's inexhaustible aquifer. U.S. Geological Survey data showed that it was not the size of Lake Superior, but far smaller and more complex than suspected. His handling of the USGS report in the *Albuquerque Tribune* gave credibility to the need to create a water conservation program in the city. Davis now writes for the *Arizona Daily Star* in Tucson. John Fleck, an environmental writer for the *Albuquerque Journal*, has become one of the most trusted voices in the state when it comes to explaining issues of environmental science and the politics that surround them. In a piece on heavy snows in New Mexico in 2009, he explains how hot, dry spring winds can cause even a substantial snowpack to "simply evaporate before it has a chance to make it into our rivers."[2] In a time of climate change and drought, Fleck put such snows into the kind of perspective that anyone can understand. Laura Paskus, a freelance environment writer published widely and in the *High Country News* in Paonia, Colorado, was the first reporter to focus on the racial animosity surrounding an effort of several Pueblo tribes and the Navajo Nation to protect sacred lands on Mount Taylor from uranium mining. She did the gutsy, trustworthy work of a seasoned reporter, assembling quotes from interviews with people of violently opposing views. McCutcheon, Davis, Fleck, and Paskus have credibility in my eyes. They are not selling anyone's party line, they rise above publisher reticence when necessary, and they present clear information that even opposing views cannot and do not try to refute.

Commodity or Habitat

My own feelings and slant on the environment are probably obvious. But I am a skeptic by nature and find myself increasingly unconvinced by anyone's dogma, even my own. I'm especially wary of the environmental community's tendency toward absolute pronouncements, born from years of marginalization and the need to be heard, as well as the tendency of various scientists for hire to pontificate about objectivity and statistical relevancy. An underlying theme in this book will be the ever-present conflict of interpretations between those who see the environment as a commodity and those who view it more broadly as a habitat for both nonhumans and humans. My slant leans toward the habitat side of the ledger. I tend to oppose anything that damages and heedlessly exploits the terrain on which we depend both on practical grounds and, I have to say, on aesthetic and spiritual grounds as well. Is allowing the air above oil and natural gas fields in the San Juan Basin to fill up with noxious fumes from gasoline-powered compressors—creating a situation as bad as any smoggy day in Los Angeles—really an acceptable environmental cost to produce energy, when pollution-control devices could mitigate emissions? What does it mean that an extractive industry and its government regulators are so cavalier about the detrimental side effects of their operations that they won't even consider spending a few dollars more in their quest to make billions?

The reasoning that permits those ugly and dangerous emissions affects a good deal of Albuquerque-area real estate. Let's say you are planning to buy a house in semirural Corrales on the old floodplain of the Rio Grande. Right above that idyllic village is the largest manufacturing facility of the largest computer chip maker in the world—Intel. And since its opening in the mid-1990s, more and more Corraleseños have been experiencing chronic headaches, respiratory troubles, and other symptoms familiar to people exposed over long periods of times to toxic fumes. Corrales residents contend these problems are caused by Intel's smokestack emissions. Intel denies it. Both marshal armadas of "facts" and interpretations. Whom do you believe?

Or let's say you are about to invest in some property in the newly developing subdivision near Kirtland Air Force Base and Sandia National Laboratories. Would you be satisfied to hear from the DOE that the mixed-waste landfill near the development is too dangerous to move, but safe enough to keep near your proposed neighborhood? Human impacts on New Mexico's environment lead people repeatedly to such risky reasoning. They're what make the subject so interesting and so frustrating, and the reality of these issues so potentially dangerous.

Carson and Commoner

The ethical roots of this book are grounded in three credible, commonsense inspirations that apply as much locally as they do globally: the work of Rachel Carson and Barry Commoner and the precautionary principle.

Branded as a hysteric and other things unfit to print, Rachel Carson attracted the wrath of misogynists when she refused to mince words about the "chain of evil" that pollution causes through the natural and human world. She was the first popular writer to face this subject and make American readers face it, too. The degradation Carson describes in her 1962 classic *Silent Spring* is as serious in New Mexico as anywhere else on the planet.

> The history of life on earth has been a history of interaction between living things and their surroundings. Only within the moment in time represented by the present century has one species—man—acquired significant power to alter the nature of his world. ... The most alarming of all man's assaults upon the environment is the contamination of air, earth, rivers, and sea with dangerous and even lethal materials. This pollution is for the most part unrecoverable; the chain of evil it initiates not only in the world that must support life but in living tissues is for the most part irreversible. In this now universal contamination of the environment, chemicals are the sinister and little recognized partners of radiation in changing the very nature of the world—the very nature of life.[3]

Much, though not all, of New Mexico's environmental history in the last sixty years mirrors ongoing ecological processes in an increasingly globalized world, a world that still ignores the four commonsense "laws of ecology" set forth by Barry Commoner in his 1971 book *The Closing Circle*.[4] These four laws, though virtually self-evident, are beyond the awareness of major polluters and their regulators, the military, corporate manufacturers, and government agencies. They are, first, "Everything is connected to everything else"; second, "Everything must go somewhere"; third, "Nature knows best," or, as Commoner explains, "Stated baldly, the third law of ecology holds that any major man-made change in a natural system is likely to be *detrimental* to that system"; and fourth, "There is no such thing as a free lunch," or, as he explains, "In ecology, as in economics, the law is intended to warn that every gain is won at some cost."[5]

Precaution

The precautionary principle, an idea apparently unknown to everyone but good parents, businesses of good conscience, and people who strive to make the proverbial campsite cleaner than they found it, is wrapped up in the old slogan "Better safe than sorry."

The Center for Health, Environment, and Justice, along with the e-newsletter *Rachel's Environment and Health News* and its editor, New Mexican Peter Montague, want to try to "prevent pollution and environmental destruction before it happens." They advocate for this precautionary approach "because it is preventive medicine for our environment and health." What they call their "BE SAFE Platform" has four principles: First, "heed early warnings"; as they say, "government and industry have a duty to prevent harm . . . *even when the exact nature and full magnitude of harm is not yet proven* [emphasis mine]; second, "put safety first" by studying the potential harm of new materials and technologies "rather than assume it is harmless until proven otherwise"; third, "exercise democracy" by making sure that government and industry decisions are based on meaningful citizen input and mutual respect and by ensuring that "uncompromised science" informs public policy; and fourth, "choose the safest solution," or, as they emphasize, "the safest, technically feasible solutions."[6]

Carson, Commoner, and those who advocate for precaution represent to some people the height of rationality. Others see them as meddlers and crazy idealists, trying to disrupt the natural flow of innovation and profit. Probably most Americans know which side they are on, but when it comes to individual issues backed by disputed scientific data, most of us don't know how to evaluate the credibility of an argument. President George W. Bush's administration tried to do away with the credibility issue by declaring that "sound science" is characterized by an absence of any dispute at all, a kind of science that does not exist and cannot exist in an absolute form. Controversial scientific findings, or noncorporate science, were labeled by the White House as junk science. For the Bush administration all science was fundamentally political; either it was on their side or it was wrong.

Mindscapes

Trying to get a handle on the environmental conditions of a political entity like a state, one finds a complicated set of laws and policies, as well as a full range of lobbying and advocacy groups, whose actions become almost part of the environment itself. Even though a state is merely a legal fabrication, its invisible borders, as J. B. Jackson remarked about the line separating New Mexico from Mexico in the Chihuahuan Desert, have a mysterious but recognizable impact on ground level truth, even if that ground is only in the mind of the beholder. It's a matter of mindscape and landscape combined. As William James writes about consciousness and the "fusion of thought and feeling," the "mixture of things is so pervasive" that you can hardly tell them apart.[7] Whether the mindscape of New Mexico's environment, known to us through art, politics, law, and science, is different from the landscape without us, we'll never know. But while we're here, we are alive to the physical underpinnings of our mental habitat; we exercise our analytical abilities, our sensitivity to faulty logic, our political savvy, and a nose for "no brainer dangers" and the smooth hypocrisies of corporate and military press releases. When we can't see Shiprock for the haze, our mind's instinct is to try to do something about it. When we expand our local mindscape to embrace the planet, no place becomes unimportant to us, because all places create our ultimate habitat and stimulate our survival instincts.

Nowhere are such instincts needed more than when trying to comprehend, let's say, the realities of global warming's effects on a specific locality. This is particularly true now, with record temperatures around the world, and a possible turning point in world consciousness about the effects modern human beings have on their global and local environments, largely thanks to former Vice

President Al Gore's persuasive film about global warming, *An Inconvenient Truth*.

In the rich coal veins of northwest New Mexico and neighboring Arizona, the connections among fossil fuels, greenhouse gases, and the degrading of virtually nonrenewable groundwater supplies are particularly clear. Peabody Energy mines coal on Black Mesa, near Hopi land in the middle of the Navajo Reservation. The same company mines coal outside of Grants, New Mexico. Peabody sends its coal from Black Mesa to Laughlin, Nevada, via a pipeline full of coat dust and water, known as slurry. It's the only slurry operation left in the country; coal is transported by train everywhere else. Some Hopis and Navajos contend Peabody's use of thirty-eight hundred acre-feet a year of the Navajo aquifer under parched Black Mesa has dried up springs crucial to farming and grazing south of Peabody's operation. The company, of course, denies the connection, citing its own hydrological studies. Peabody, the largest private coal company in the world, uses water from the Blue Water Lake aquifer outside of Grants to clean the coal, not transport it. This aquifer is a potential water source for Albuquerque and therefore could provide a financial windfall for Grants if a water pipeline is established between the two towns. Peabody's coal, along with coal mined all over the world, makes its contribution, of course, to the greenhouse effect. Coal mining in the Southwest is linked to chaotic weather patterns that may, in fact, contribute to our latest drought cycle, which in turn has a role to play, along with population expansion, in draining aquifers of fossil water that cannot be replenished in a drought cycle, nor replenished rapidly even in a wet spell. Coal mining cannot be seen as environmentally friendly, despite its current necessity owing to American foot-dragging over developing alternative energy sources and fuel-efficient transportation technologies.

Conscience and Context

At no time is a nose for credibility more needed by citizens of New Mexico than in the early years of the new century, when many experts consider the current drought to be as bad or worse than those of the Dust Bowl years of the 1920s and '30s. With water tables sinking and reservoirs drying up, despite the occasional wet winter, the consciousness of the state's electorate has turned to environmental issues with an intensity and breadth of concern unusual in a military and resources-extraction economy like New Mexico's. And many moderate and even conservative voters are showing alarm over the state's loosely applied environmental regulations and its absence of a working strategic water plan. But despite a rise in awareness, despite unaccounted for and seemingly ever-present environmental upheavals, the prevailing mind-set about the environment is one of mildly inquisitive apathy, like that of someone who speed reads blurbs on the back of a book and feels satisfied he or she has mastered the author's salient points.

Though no one to my knowledge has yet developed equations that allow people to apply global warming statistics to local conditions, direct observation tells most New Mexicans that the 1990s and early years of the twenty-first century have brought increasingly hot and dry weather to the state. Even remote New Mexico can't avoid the wake of the world's greenhouse heat wave. All of us contribute to it and suffer from it. As J. R. McNeill wrote in his *Something New Under the Sun: An Environmental History of the Twentieth-Century World*, owing to fossil fuels and economic activity in general, "We have created a regime of perpetual ecological disturbance. . . . This perpetual disturbance is an accidental byproduct of billions of human ambitions, and efforts, of unconscious social evolution."[8]

And yet *The Economist* magazine's *The World in 2003*, its annual business and political rundown on global conditions, offers not a single word about climate change, a looming gasoline shortage, or, for that matter, any environmental issue crucial to our economic and physical security.[9] And the 2006 edition of *Censored: The Top 25 Censored Stories* mentions one environmental story: mountaintop-removal coal mining in West Virginia.[10] With much of Europe having the hottest summers on record in 2003 and 2005 and New Mexico suffering through the hottest July and August ever, with local water scarcities looming in the eighth year of a drought in New Mexico and the Southern Rockies, with heat-sparked forest fires all over northern Europe and the American West, you'd think *The Economist,* the world's greatest business magazine, might factor into its analysis of contemporary economic and political reality something about the weather, at least, not to mention a vast array of other environmental concerns.

But the staff of *The Economist,* like so many other business backers, still treat the world we live in, our habitat, as a thing of no worth, financially and politically speaking, until it is developed or put to use.

Such is true, and has been true, for years in New Mexico and the rest of the United States. Environmental conditions are not factored into cost-benefit analyses. Natural resources are owned and are therefore private assets that can be turned into cash, and the consequences of their use are only marginally accounted for by regulation when compensation for damages undercuts profits. The world is treated by traditional economists as an externality, as something outside the system, positive when it turns into an asset, negative when it becomes a cost center, such as a corporate Superfund site.

Externalities and the "Savage Reservation"

Reading *The Economist* left me with the sensation that I'd been reading reports from a science-fiction world, a dystopian fantasy, a world not unlike that Aldous Huxley imagined where civilization organized its calendars by the "year of our Ford." The more I think about New Mexico's environment, the more eerily similar current conditions are to Huxley's classic in which the state is characterized as "the Savage Reservation."

When I first read *Brave New World* in the summer of 1958, I had only a vague idea where New Mexico was and no idea at all about the cultural and aesthetic fascination it held for so many Americans. I was two months away from moving to New Mexico myself, as a barely eighteen-year-old freshman at the University of New Mexico in Albuquerque, where I've lived ever since. So when I read about the state's curious status in Huxley's imagination, as a place fenced off from the rest of the world by a high-tech, electrocution-quality chain-link barrier, to keep the world out and to keep the inmates in, I was fascinated, but troubled, that he called New Mexico "the Savage Reservation."[11] For Huxley, the future of the Land of Enchantment, as we're officially known, was as a place run by a Warden for misfits and outcasts, with "no communication whatever with the civilized world," whose people "still preserve[d] their repulsive habits and customs," amid "pumas, porcupines, and other ferocious animals . . . infectious diseases . . . priests . . . venomous lizards," in the desert far away from a surreal future society chillingly like our own, an addictively upbeat, totalitarian fun park in which happiness was mandatory and prescribed for all, and where consumerism was considered the highest social good. Is that what New Mexico is really like? I wondered.

It wasn't until nearly forty years later, as I began research for this book, that I understood Huxley's dystopian description of New Mexico as a powerful metaphor for how members of the United States' military and high-tech cultures have tended to view our state since World War II—as a place beyond the pale, where weapons of mass destruction can be built and some of civilization's most dangerous debris can be thrown away, out of sight, out of mind.

Dystopian New Mexico

New Mexico is among the poorest states in the union and has the eighteenth worst industrial pollution, according to the EPA's 2001 Toxic Release Inventory,[12] which doesn't keep tabs on the nuclear defense industry and its toxic and nuclear dumping. With New Mexico being the home of the two nuclear research and development facilities and the first underground nuclear waste depository in the country, as well as the home of the nation's first uranium enrichment centrifuge, you'd think our ranking would be much higher. We're eighteenth, as opposed to third or fourth, only because we have a population of under two million people in a state that has a huge land area of 121,356 square miles,[13] the fifth largest in the country.

Seeing New Mexico as the Savage Reservation and, along with the rest of the arid West, as a national sacrifice zone helps us to understand environmental racism. We who live in this overlooked region are the only ones who can assess the largely hidden quantity and variety of environmental hazards in the state. Such knowledge is hard to come by even for the experts. In October 2001, for instance, the Department of Energy reported that the nation's most contaminated nuclear sites, which include the Los Alamos National Laboratory (LANL), "don't have a firm grasp on what is buried in their soil."[14] Though newspapers are full of stories, large and small, relating to the environment, no attempt has been made, that I'm aware of, to accumulate a coherent overview of current conditions, much less of their historical origins.

Even the briefest sampling of stories, however, reveals the need for an overarching perspective:

▶ a dangerously unstable mountain of slag from the Molycorp molybdenum mine near Questa that state engineers say could crash down on Molycorp offices, the Red River, and parts of the town of Questa itself;

▶ the testing of munitions made from depleted uranium behind the campus of New Mexico Tech in the town of Socorro from the mid-1970s to the 1990s;

▶ the existence of some twenty-one hundred hazardous waste storage sites at LANL discovered after the 2005 Cerro Grande fire in the Jemez Mountains;

▶ the Centers for Disease Control and Prevention's Los Alamos Historic Document Retrieval and Assessment report of 2009 confirming that LANL consistently released radioactive emissions into the air and water of northern New Mexico;

▶ the DOE's study in October 2000 that reported the amount of plutonium and other radioactive debris buried near nuclear plants (including LANL) might be ten times greater than previously believed;

▶ the rare victory to preserve the sacred Pueblo pilgrimage site of Zuni Salt Lake, which was endangered by coal mining for a power plant outside Phoenix;

▶ the city of Rio Rancho discharging large quantities of untreated feces into the Rio Grande;

▶ Cochiti Lake, whose bottom is reputedly the destination of radioactive sediments from LANL, seeping water into Cochiti Pueblo farmlands and causing them to become too saline, and perhaps too polluted, for planting;

▶ a controversy over a fifty-year-old unlined mixed-waste and nuclear dump site on Sandia Base, close to the massive Mesa del Sol development;

▶ the Sparton Superfund site from the 1980s being turned into a used car lot;

▶ increasing worries over the ongoing draining of Albuquerque's aquifer;

▶ looming struggles for vital San Juan–Chama water between the cities of Santa Fe and Albuquerque and the Navajo Nation, and worries that the protracted drought in the Colorado River basin will force New Mexico to curtail its use of the San Juan, a tributary of the Colorado;

▶ the threat to the cottonwood bosque of an increasingly dirty and depleted Rio Grande;

▶ underground oil and fuel pipelines crisscrossing populated areas in the state, such as the village of Placitas, a bedroom community for wealthy Albuquerqueans;

▶ a natural gas underground pipeline explosion that killed twelve members of the same family picnicking in a backcountry campground near Carlsbad;

▶ continued underground septic tank and gasoline storage tank leaks throughout the Middle Rio Grande Valley;

▶ lawsuits brought by the families of Navajo uranium miners who are alleged to have died of job-related cancers, including the issue of a massive leak at the Church Rock uranium tailings dam, which dumped ninety-four million gallons of yellow-brown radioactive water into the Puerco River in 1979;

▶ proposed natural gas drilling in the pristine Valle Vidal and efforts to drill for oil and gas on south central New Mexico's Otero Mesa, with its vast expanses of native grasslands, wildlife, and literally oceans of pure, clear fossil water, enough to serve the needs of more than a million people for a hundred years, by some estimates;

▶ the revelation in 2008 of a gigantic jet fuel spill at Kirtland Air Force Base in the groundwater under a prosperous Southeast Heights Albuquerque neighborhood;

▶ and myriad other stories indicating that New Mexico's natural environment could well be more endangered by military, corporate, and urban polluters and consumers than anyone imagines.

Mining Reality

Regulators and the media take a piecemeal approach to the seemingly countless environmental degradations that have been reported here over the last decades. It is difficult to accumulate statistically reliable scientific data establishing patterns or trends, especially since the military and corporate communities are usually less than forthcoming with unbiased and straightforward information about their activities.

I see it as my job, in this book, to attempt to make sense of these scattered bits of information, which form a litany of environmental abuse, and assess what they mean—if they are reliable, if they add up to anything, or if they are isolated and dispersed events that may be true and even tragic in their own regard, but which have little combined impact on the state as a whole.

My aim is to give the general public a realistic perspective from which to view, and politically engage, the issues surrounding New Mexico's environmental health and resources. Trying to get a handle on the realities of what Kevin Fernlund calls a "staging area for global war"[15] is a great challenge. We're dealing with contested data that we're not equipped to assess, so we must rely on examination of the consistency of the arguments involved. That also means, in some sense, examining the quality of rhetoric, the use of hyperbole, and conclusions that either do or do not follow from premises. It means as well dealing with risk assessment and determining who is arguing from the precautionary "Better safe than sorry" perspective and who is arguing from the "We don't know enough, so don't sweat it and damn the torpedoes" perspective. When it comes to global warming, let's say, one argument goes, "Well, the experts are still out on global warming, so worries about our weather here and what to do about it are really unnecessary and premature." In other words, if the world picture might turn out to be OK, but local conditions are changing, then somehow the future abstraction becomes the reality, and the daily truth we know from the ground up becomes a politically unacceptable aberration. It's like arguing against local conservation efforts and managed growth by saying that, after all, nationwide residential use of water amounts to a measly 2 or 3 percent and is insignificant compared to agricultural usage, even though in Bernalillo County residential use accounts for more than 70 percent of all water uses. It is easy to be caught between things we know are real but don't want to believe and spins we don't trust but that take the edge off action by seeding doubt.

Obfuscation and confusion notwithstanding, one has to start somewhere. I originally subtitled this book "Notes for an Environmental Accounting of New Mexico Since the Manhattan Project," first, because no such overall assessment currently exists, and, second, because as a journalist I realize that a full description of the subject requires the attention of many environmental historians with not only a devotion to New Mexico, but the financial and institutional support to give years of concentrated effort to unraveling this complicated subject.

Slant

My efforts here will be guided by four journalistic approaches: a reportorial overview of issues in the present; case studies of pertinent examples of those issues; surveys of positive steps taken to ameliorate current conditions and analyses of what else might be done in the future; and concluding commentaries on the implications of these findings.

My reportorial interest is in, first, how human activity has affected the natural environment and, second, how environmental degradation in turn influences human decision making and well-being. I will focus on the pollution of natural and human habitats; the waste of nonrenewable resources; the consequences of short-term thinking, secrecy, denial, and sometimes arbitrarily contradictory viewpoints; and the lessons to be learned from benign cooperation with natural forces. I'll be most concerned with the environmental impact of economic and military activity; technology of all sorts; population growth and demographic change; expansion of the built environment; and the possible effects of global climate change. I will chronicle water quality and quantity; air pollution; toxic and nuclear waste dumping; environmental racism; open land and urban sprawl; importation of diseases and hazardous conditions; intrusive plant and animal species; endangered species; agriculture and ranching; manufacturing and transportation; and extractive industries.

As an environmental and human rights columnist, I am used to commenting on and chronicling the present. But my sense of political realism is rooted in a long-range view of historical cause and effect. And though visionary authors such as Paul Hawken, Amory Lovins, and L. Hunter Lovins in their book *Natural Capitalism* admonish us to "see the world as it can be, not merely as it is," I believe we still haven't begun to record the mere basics of environmental reality in New Mexico, or anywhere else for that matter.

I am not by nature or profession a value-neutral observer. My slant in forty years as a columnist has been against unresponsive, insensitive, and arrogant power. I detest careless and disrespectful change as much as I abhor waste. But I am interested, as well, in seeing through ideologies and beyond rote responses and entrenched antagonisms. I remain fascinated by multiple descriptions of the same reality that can, and often do, differ greatly.

Throughout this book I will be making a distinction between human action and nonhuman nature. This dichotomy goes against my predisposition to view humankind as a completely integrated part of the natural world. The point is, however, that human beings are fully natural creatures engaging in activities that have an incalculably more powerful impact on the natural environment than the activities of other creatures. This is a prime part of the human condition and comes about because of our sciences, inventions, technologies, and inabilities to concern ourselves with, or predict, the long-term consequences of the impact we have on our surroundings.

CHAPTER ONE

KEY HUMAN IMPACTS ON THE NEW MEXICO ENVIRONMENT

While human activity has been changing the landscape of what is now New Mexico, often dramatically, since migrants arrived in the Americas some fifteen to twenty thousand years ago, nothing in the past—not even the coming of the railroad in 1879 or the dawn of the automobile culture in the 1930s—comes close to the impacts humans have made on New Mexico's environment since World War II. Many of these effects have proven to be dangerous to the physical and social health of the human community in New Mexico and the biotic world upon which it depends. They fall into five broad categories: pollution of air, water, and soil; accelerated depletion, sometimes to extinction, of species of flora and fauna; disruption of natural habitats and processes; alteration of forests, grasslands, and countrysides

◄   This mill was established in Hurley, ten miles from the Santa Rita mine, because there is sufficient water there. Now trucks drive in the opposite direction over the pipes, carrying the old tailings back to the mine in order to leach more copper from them. One miner recounts that in the old days you would smoke a cigarette in this town and it would taste sweet. "Like sucking on a penny," adds Terry Humble. March 2008.

by overharvesting, overuse, and improvident development; and scarring of landscapes by extractive industries and energy and transportation technologies. Environmental degradation has often taken place during the last sixty years in close proximity to marginalized populations, the urban and rural poor of all races and cultures. Most environmental problems result from economic and military activity, and in New Mexico they usually result from both, owing to the extent to which the state's economy depends on the military.

Geographers and biologists emphasize the sheer speed of change in our lifetimes and the sense of future shock people in relatively wealthy societies have been feeling since the seventeenth century. As one scholar puts it, "Most of the [environmental transformation] of the past three hundred years has been at the hands of humankind, intentionally or otherwise. Our ever-growing role in this continuing metamorphosis has itself essentially changed. Transformation has escalated through time, and in some instances the scales of change have shifted from the [local] and the regional to the earth as a whole. Whereas humankind once acted primarily upon the visible 'faces' or 'states' of the earth, such as forest cover, we are now also altering the fundamental flows of chemicals and energy that sustain life on the only inhabited planet we know."[1]

Continuous Degradation

To be sure, human history can be seen as a series of degradations since the beginning: annihilation of species; genocidal assaults, large and small, on marginalized humans; deforestation; overgrazing; soil depletion and erosion; mining pollution; introduction of invasive species; soil-damaging misuse of water technologies; and the scars left by mass human migrations and road building. Many of these historical trends run all the way into the present. But much human

activity in the environment has been directly beneficial to human existence. Such efforts as small-scale farm irrigation from rivers, streams,
arroyos, and reservoirs, large and small (not from aquifers); well-
contained towns and roadways; harvesting of renewable resources;
levee building, alkaline drainage, and flood protection; preservation
of wilderness and historic sites; community grazing on commons
land; soil conservation and replenishment; urban tree planting; and
many other environmentally respectful and savvy activities fall into
this category. The use of fossil fuels, which took off with the coming
of the railroad and accelerated as automobiles grew to dominate the
economy, led to a gradual accumulation of petrochemical pollution.
Further contamination came with radioactive toxic waste and with
the pest-control toxins and plastics that were byproducts of industrial farming, feed lot ranching, and the expansion of suburbia in the
1950s. The long-term effects of pollutants have no precursors in the
pre-Conquest or colonial Hispanic past in New Mexico.

Blindsided by the Future

What's happened in New Mexico since World War II has happened
to most other localities on the planet: increased population, increased
pollution, increased warming. Because New Mexico was an isolated, thinly populated state that attracted some brilliant scientists, it
proved unexpectedly useful during the Cold War. Six months before
the explosion in 1945 of the first atomic bomb at Trinity Site in New
Mexico, the University of New Mexico Press published an analysis
of the state's economic prospects after the war. It was called *New
Mexico's Future*, written by E. L. Moulton. Usefully organized and
reasoned, Moulton's careful examination of employment, manufacturing, and service industry trends in wartime New Mexico displays,
of course, no knowledge at all of the secret nuclear labs in Los Alamos,
and therefore no clue as to the role that Sandia Labs and Kirtland Air
Force Base would play in Albuquerque's and New Mexico's future.
Moulton also, of course, did not know that the interstate highway
system, which was initiated during the Eisenhower administration,
would stimulate suburban sprawl in New Mexico. Even in 1945,
however, economists were predicting that the United States would
be using more petroleum by 1960 than it could discover in domestic oil fields. Moulton's provisional solution was innovative—the

hydrogenation of subbituminous coal, turning one hundred pounds of coal into eight gallons of fairly high-grade gasoline. But Moulton failed to predict the long-range impact the use of fossil fuels would have on our atmosphere and climate.[2] Reading Moulton, it seems clear now that the actual postwar future caught even the brightest minds in the state completely by surprise.

Like much of the rest of the world, New Mexico in the twenty-first century looks superficially the same as it did fifty or sixty years ago, with the addition, of course, of miles of power lines and super-highways, gigantic billboards, and other accoutrements of commerce and communication. But all is not well with New Mexico beneath the surface, nor with the rest of earth. It's not the literal earth I worry about. Like many others, I feel certain that natural processes will endure, even though altered by our presence. It's us I worry about, and the other life-forms that interact with us.

Rachel Carson wrote prophetically and so clearly about these concerns in the 1960s. The corporate and governmental worlds ridiculed her at first, eventually paying grudging attention when isolated facts bore out her general perception of degradation from industrial and Cold War nuclear waste. And though a political subculture has arisen in the United States around her environmental insights, it appears so dangerous to corporate and military interests that its more fervent activists are labeled "ecoterrorists."

Carson wrote in *Silent Spring*, "Only within the moment of time represented by the present century has one species—man—acquired significant power to alter the nature of his world."[3]

> During the past quarter century this power has not only increased to one of disturbing magnitude but it has changed in character. The most alarming of all man's assaults upon the environment is the contamination of air, earth, rivers, and sea with dangerous and even lethal materials. This pollution is for the most part irrecoverable; the chain of evil it initiates not only in the world that must support life but in living tissues is for the most part irreversible. In this now universal contamination of the environment, chemicals are the sinister and little recognized partners of radiation in changing the very nature of the world—and the very nature of its life.[4]

Since the test of the first nuclear bomb on July 16, 1945, at Trinity Site near Carrizozo, New Mexico's environment has been assaulted repeatedly by nuclear and industrial contamination stemming from military research and development and from manufacturing and mining activities. Post–World War II New Mexico may still look like the Land of Enchantment, but significant parts of its natural environment may have been corrupted beyond repair.

Human Impacts

To make matters worse for every locality on the planet, including New Mexico, of course, four trends dominate the "human manipulation of the environment . . . in the modern era," according to geographer Andrew Goudie. "The first of these is that the ways in which humans are affecting the environment are proliferating. . . . Secondly, environmental issues that were once locally confined have become regional or even global problems. . . . The complexity, magnitude, and frequency of impacts are probably increasing. . . . Finally, compounding the effects of rapidly expanding populations is a general increase in per capita consumption and environmental impact. . . . One index of this is world commercial energy consumption, which trebled in size between the 1950s and 1980."[5] Owing to population growth and the increasing use of technology, human impacts on the environment "will be greatly magnified," Goudie observed.[6]

It's not that humans were a benign presence in the natural world in New Mexico and elsewhere before the industrial revolution and World War II. Culpable in part perhaps for a mass extinction of megafauna at the end of the Pleistocene in New Mexico's general region some ten thousand years ago and capable of making lasting alterations, scars, and disruptions—even with only stone and wood tools—on surface landscape features with urban developments in Chaco Canyon and other Ancestral Puebloan sites, humans have mined, hunted, cultivated, carved roads, and developed built environments all across the New Mexican habitat, never failing to leave their markings. But consider the differences between a digging stick and a plow, a plow and a tractor, a tractor and a bulldozer, a bulldozer and a steam shovel, a midden and a toxic dump, a flint quarry and a nuclear waste pit, stone-lined ritual roadways and a state crisscrossed by asphalt and concrete highways and underground pipelines—these give a clear picture of how persistent humans have always been at not only adapting to environments but making environments themselves adapt as far as possible to human wants and needs.

What follows is a brief overview of human impacts on the environment of our state.

Early Migrations

The first appearance of *Homo sapiens* as an exotic and then an invasive species in the New World is said to have occurred anywhere from seven thousand to twenty-five thousand years ago. In the long run, nothing has had a greater environmental impact than that early migration of people, probably from Asia for the most part, by a variety of routes into what is now New Mexico and beyond. The cause of the extinction of megafauna in New Mexico and elsewhere in the Americas—creatures such as saber-toothed tigers, *Bison taylori*, great ground sloths, woolly mammoths, and dire wolves, ungulates such as the native camel and horse—is the source of considerable controversy. Was it primarily climate change that wiped out such formidable creatures, or was it the relentless efforts and ingenuity of human hunters? Perhaps it was a combination of both. The extent of megafauna populations is unclear. But it is not mere coincidence that megafauna died out after humans had established themselves as the dominant predators armed with stone-tipped weapons and fire, which may have been used in hunting strategies at the end of the Ice Age. "Don't underestimate the role of man," cautions archaeologist Mike Marshall. Human hunters "could have been lighting wildfires all over the place" as a hunting strategy and "could have introduced micro organisms that helped kill off megafauna."[7]

From the time they arrived, human communities were engaged in surface and shallow subsurface mining of agate, chalcedony, and chert with which to fashion spear points and other tools. In 1942, University of New Mexico geologist Stuart Northrop commented on the "imposing array of evidence for the prehistoric use of minerals in New Mexico."[8] But no trace remains of the leavings and tailings of these mining enterprises, though humans are capable of startling rearrangements of landscape using wooden and stone tools or just their bare hands.

The Genius of Sensitivity

The first signs of maize agriculture, migrating from central Mexico, appear in New Mexico between 1700 BC and 1100 BC,[9] and then, slightly later, beans and squash arrive, also from the south. Well-known sites of early agriculture in New Mexico include Bat Cave, on the southern edge of the Plains of San Augustin in Catron County, and the Fresnal Rock Shelter site southeast of Alamagordo.[10] Maize was domesticated in central Mexico around 3500 BC. Corn may have arrived with Basketmaker II populations that migrated north into the Southwest. This ancient agriculture seems not to have harmed the environment. The protection of water resources, the channeling of rain runoff, and the situating of garden plots in the mouths of canyons and arroyos watered by floodplain irrigation did not disfigure the landscape. Soil depletion may have been a problem, but studies of recent Puebloan agricultural practices show that flood irrigation provides natural compost and humus, which has a restorative fertilizing effect on sandy soils.

Puebloan Engineering

A major detectable human impact on the natural world came from mining by the Puebloan ancestors, whose mineral artifacts in Chaco Canyon date from as early as AD 900. Mining enterprises were prodigious relative to the hand technology of times, and the accumulation of imported minerals was equally impressive. A total of some forty minerals have been found in Chaco sites, including alabaster, jet, quartz, pyrite, jasper, onyx, petrified wood, and sulphur. Garnets, copper, galena, malachite, talc, and turquoise were probably brought to Chaco from the Cerrillos area southwest of Santa Fe, along with red spiny oyster shell from Baja California with its beautiful red coloration.[11] Hand mining operations appear not to have scarified the landscape, despite extensive salt mining near Zuni, around Estancia, and at other sites. Puebloan ancestors mined coal, but not in landscape-marring quantities. And their mining of turquoise around Cerrillos, near Santa Fe, while extensive, was environmentally discreet. Cerrillos turquoise was exported all through Mexico, including into the Mayan provinces, starting as early as AD 900.

From about AD 1250 on, we see the full flowering of pre-Conquest Pueblo road building in the Chacoan province, from Chaco Canyon to Aztec, Mesa Verde, and countless ceremonial sites as far south as Casas Grandes, or Paquime, in northern Mexico.[12] Sometimes rock lined, sometimes stone paved, often dug into rock, and usually straight as an arrow, these roads are still detectable more than seven hundred years after their construction.

This period also saw the flourishing of Chacoan agriculture and the creation of various waterworks, including runoff catchment basins, dams, weirs, and canals. The cultivation of the entire Chaco Canyon floor may have resulted from this massive agricultural and irrigation effort. This efflorescence of agriculture made possible massive building projects that Chacoan culture is known for. Chacoan great houses required the hand working of millions of pieces of sandstone and the lumbering of more than a quarter million pieces of timber, many of them massive, some fifty miles away in the Chuska mountains. One Chacoan outlier, Pueblo Pintado, appears to have timber from a single stand of pine trees, evidence perhaps of the first instance of clear-cutting in the region.

After the great drought circa AD 1150 had emptied out the Chacoan province, Ancient Puebloan people suffered a hundred and fifty years of turmoil, marked by frequent migration and periodic warfare. It wasn't until around 1300 that Pueblo peoples settled in the Middle Rio Grande Valley and began the irrigation system that was to become the foundation of all future New Mexican waterways. Some two hundred and fifty years before the Spanish arrived, the Middle Rio Grande Valley had as many as forty pueblos and more than fifteen thousand inhabitants. Sizable pre-Conquest Puebloesque town sites were also constructed all over the northern New Mexico highlands and in the Gila-Mogollon area at this time, often accompanied by extensive logging, stone hauling, and excavations for dirt, sand, and clay from which to make adobe, mud, and plaster. Considerable mining operations were ongoing for generations.[13] Though most pueblos had clay quarries for pottery, they don't seem to have left environmental scars, despite the nearly industrial-level production of pottery in the Puebloan area.

Colonization and Exchange

With the arrival in the New Mexico area of the Coronado Expedition (1539–42), the Spanish Conquest of the Americas north of the Rio Grande, along with the Columbian Exchange of plants, animals, and disease, began. Horses, for instance, were a major part of fauna in the pre-Conquest Americas, roamed to Eurasia and possibly to Africa, became extinct in the Americas at the end of the Pleistocene,[14] and then were reintroduced on Columbus's second voyage, in 1493. They were bred in the Caribbean and taken to the mainland by Cortez to be used in warfare. Following the arrival of Juan de Oñate in New Mexico, after he opened the Camino Real in 1598 with his four thousand sheep, one thousand cattle, one thousand goats, and one hundred and fifty mares and colts,[15] wild mustang herds of escaped or stolen domesticated horses migrated onto the Great Plains and south into what is now Texas.

In addition to horses, the Spanish brought oxen, mules, burros, wheeled vehicles, sheep, chickens, goats, pigs, and steel implements, including saws, shovels, axes, traps, and guns, along with devastating diseases like influenza, smallpox, whooping cough, typhoid, and measles, into territory formerly controlled by the Pueblos, Apaches, Navajos, Comanches, Utes, and Shoshones and then up the Camino Real. The Columbian Exchange in New Mexico saw the Spanish cultivating Pueblo maize, squash, and beans. The Spanish also brought up from Mexico tomatoes and chile peppers, as well as various melons, grapes, wheat, and fruit trees, including apples and peaches. The peach orchards cultivated by Zuni and Navajo people descend from those times. Though Spanish settlers and Pueblo farmers worked the land extensively, they made little use of the iron plow. Iron was scarce and expensive, and the pliable desert soils were easily worked in traditional ways by hand,[16] with labor provided by Pueblo slave workers. Sheep, goats, and cattle, on the other hand, caused great damage almost from the start. They denuded the soil of its shallow-rooted brush and grass, leaving the topsoil exposed to wind and water erosion.[17]

The first recorded European mining operation in New Mexico was carried out by Coronado's men in the Jemez Mountain area when they excavated for sulphur from which to make gunpowder. Coronado also mined salt near Zuni and sent large quantities of it to Chihuahua by burro.[18]

The Pueblo Revolt of 1680 more or less expelled the Spanish from New Mexico for a dozen years. Drought, religious persecution, and what amounted to agricultural slavery are often cited as reasons for the revolt. Some say, however, that it was more directly precipitated by a fatal cave-in at the ancient, but then Spanish-run, turquoise mine at Mount Chalchihuitl near Cerrillos and San Marcos Pueblo.[19] After the reconquest by Diego de Vargas in 1692–93, the Spanish province of New Mexico continued to be a cultural as well as a geographical outback in the Spanish empire, its peoples continuing to use wooden tools and other local technologies.

During the Pueblo Revolt, horses began to be used by Native Americans in New Mexico. Pueblo peoples before the revolt were forbidden to ride, train, or own horses. When Spanish settlers fled the Pueblo uprising, they left behind many of their horses, and the Pueblos raised large herds while the Spanish were gone, selling or trading them to Kiowa, Comanches, and Apaches, who used them and traded them onto the midwestern and Texas plains. It took less than seventy years to convert the Plains tribes to a horse culture. The Cheyenne were observed by the French in 1745 to be using horses for migration, hunting, and warfare.[20]

Invasive disease took a terrible toll on Pueblo peoples in the Middle and Upper Rio Grande Valley from the beginning of the Conquest right through to the opening of the Santa Fe Trail in 1821 and the start of the Mexican period. The Pueblo population was reduced by smallpox and other plagues from something close to fifty thousand people in more than one hundred pueblos to somewhere around seven thousand people in eighteen pueblos.[21] That's an 86 percent drop in population, a die-off of genocidal proportions.

Even with more than thirty thousand acres under cultivation,[22] Pueblo farmers had a marginal impact on natural systems compared to European farmers. Pueblo farmers preferred to irrigate with river overflow and diversions from tributaries. Although Pueblo builders were used to harvesting and transporting large quantities of wood for construction, they mostly used dead fall for cooking and heating, until forced to do otherwise by the Spanish and missionary authorities.[23]

This was a period of increased settlement and grazing and of intensified irrigation agriculture. Much productive effort in this period was disturbed by violent conflicts with nomadic tribes, including a major Comanche attack of sixteen hundred mounted warriors wreaking havoc up and down the Middle Rio Grande Valley in 1742, just thirty-six years after Albuquerque was founded. Deforestation was severe in the eighteenth and nineteenth centuries in New Mexico, often requiring villages and settlements to collect firewood from as far as twenty miles away.[24] Movement of enormous herds of livestock, settlers, and soldiers, not to mention goods and raw materials, to and from Mexico along the Camino Real caused disastrous overgrazing, soil degradation, and arroyo gullying. Irrigation agriculture without proper drainage resulted in alkaline buildups in the soils, and invasive weeds like dandelions and a variety of clovers began to take hold.[25] Elk, bison, and pronghorns were threatened by the spread of invasive brucellosis from Spanish cattle herds.[26] Spanish copper mining at Santa Rita in the southwest corner of the state began in 1804. Vast mule trains took the ore south to Mexico and then to the royal mint in Spain.[27] The open pits of the Santa Rita could send as many as twenty thousand mule loads south a year.[28]

Gringoization

The opening of the Santa Fe Trail in 1821 marked the beginning of the Americanization of New Mexico's economy and way of life. The vast trade in beaver and river otter hides in the early- to mid-nineteenth century had a considerable impact on the New Mexico woodland landscape, all but ending the creation of ponds and marshes by the nearly extinct beaver. Much pressure was also placed on bison, elk, deer, and bighorn sheep by trappers and travelers along the Santa Fe Trail, who profited from a seemingly bottomless market for meat and hides. By 1888, hunters had killed the last elk in the Pecos. Fifteen years later, bighorn sheep were gone from the New Mexico Rockies, and the last grizzly bear became a trophy for a hunter in 1923.[29]

The western American gold rush did not start in California, but in the Ortiz Mountains in New Mexico around 1828, twenty-one years before the forty-niners. The Ortiz, behind the Sandia Mountains and near the San Pedros, are still worked occasionally today, but with minor success owing to the scarcity of water. The early impact on water quality of the sudden influx of rags-to-riches miners with high hopes and a total disregard for the natural context of their mining operations is hard to assess. But the roots of many mining issues today having to do with excessive and dangerous tailings in proximity to natural waterways can be found in those early gold rush days.

When General Stephen Kearny annexed the New Mexico Territory during the Mexican-American War in 1846,[30] east coast and midwestern Americans followed the early pathfinders and began the long and constant "gringo" migration into the Southwest. They encountered a mix of Spanish-speaking and indigenous cultures that embraced nearly twenty languages and had worked out a cultural stalemate in the course of three hundred years of tumultuous interaction. The Anglo migration to the Sunbelt began with wagon trains. The whole territory ran on mule, oxen, and horse power. Grazing problems were endemic with huge herds of draft animals as well as cattle, sheep, and goats. In the Rio Puerco Valley, southwest of the town of Cuba, grazing so denuded the land that cattle trails became conduits for rainwater, eroding into deep, sometimes impassable, arroyos that ended up ruining not only the grazing but the farming lands as well. Other longhorn cattle drives crossed the dry plains, including the Goodnight-Loving and Chisum trails around 1866, which sent cattle from Texas to Navajos and Apaches in captivity at the Bosque Redondo, as well as into the Great Plains.

Land Abuse

Around the late 1870s, land and grazing wars, such as that waged in Lincoln County in 1877, began heating up between cattle ranchers, sheepherders, and homesteaders who had been filtering, in ever greater numbers, into the territory since the Homestead Act of 1862.[31] This stimulated New Mexico's population explosion not sixteen years after American forces first arrived and proclaimed annexation from the rooftops of Las Vegas, New Mexico. A year later, the New Mexico Territory was split into the separate regions of New Mexico and Arizona. The Santa Fe Trail from Missouri to Santa Fe and the older Spanish Trail from California to Santa Fe continued to expand trade into the territory from American and west coast Spanish sources. The territory was invaded by new species of weeds, notably Russian thistle, or tumbleweed, which started its endless migration around the West when a shipment of flaxseed containing tumbleweed seeds reached South Dakota in 1873.

Two of the major extirpations of animal species in America—the bison massacre from the 1850s to about 1889 and the extinction of the passenger pigeon a year later, in 1900—were felt in New Mexico's high plains east of the Rocky Mountains. Millions of bison—estimates range from twenty million to sixty million—were hunted into near extinction until the last herd of fewer than six hundred was eventually preserved in Yellowstone National Park in 1902.[32] Perhaps as many as five billion passenger pigeons overforaged their habitat and were hunted into extinction by 1900, primarily on the East Coast and in the Ohio Valley, but also in New Mexico, where fossil remains show that they were part of the local fauna since the Pleistocene.[33] That these vast numbers of birds and animals could be extinguished so quickly gives us a sense of how plausible it is for human hunters to have been a major cause of megafauna extinction after the last Ice Age. Those early hunters lacked firearms but were able to use fire as technology for killing.

Railroad and Floods of Change

The coming of the railroad in 1879 opened New Mexico to full Americanization. Heavy logging for railroad ties began in the northern New Mexico forests and in the Zuni Mountains. Strip-mining and deep rock mining for coal to fire steam engines flourished at major points along the train routes, including Raton, Gallup, and, near Santa Fe and Albuquerque, around Madrid and Los Cerrillos. By the 1890s, the irrigation system of the Rio Grande—or the American Nile, as it was called by boomers—created such excellent growing conditions that farmers in the region regularly exported fruits and vegetables to California. Farming in the Mesilla Valley and on the land along the Pecos River was flourishing a decade later, producing nuts and other agricultural bounty. The wool industry was booming all over the north in the 1880s, with heavy impact on grazing lands. Wool-laden wagon trains could line up for as many as five miles on their approach to the train center of Las Vegas, New Mexico. Sheep ranching thrived in Mora County, which had some of the finest grasslands in the state.[34]

In 1902, the U.S. Reclamation Service, later known as the Bureau of Reclamation, was formed to prevent deforestation and overgrazing. At almost the same time, vast stretches of former Spanish land grants were bought up through shady real estate dealings in which inconsistencies and loopholes in Spanish and Anglo law were used to swindle Hispanic landholders out of lands that they had owned and used for generations. These communal lands were converted to nationally owned lands that would eventually become national forests.

Mining boomed in Magdalena, southwest of Socorro, after World War I, when Sherwin-Williams Paint Company mined the area's lead and zinc deposits, creating paints that harmed, unwittingly at the time, who knows how many American children.[35] Also at the end of World War I, molybdenum mining began on the Red River.[36] Near the end of that war, coal mining in New Mexico was employing over five thousand people at more than sixty mines.

Oil and Water

Elephant Butte Dam was under construction from 1911 to 1916, and other dams, such as Sumner, Caballo, El Vado, and Avalon, would follow during the Works Progress Administration (WPA) in the mid-1930s. In partnership with the federal government, the Middle Rio Grande, starting in 1925, was leveed, and drainage ditches were established along the river to clear fields of unused water that were leaching salts onto agricultural land and ruining crop yields. This momentous development, along with the creation of the Middle Rio Grande Conservancy District, was equaled in importance by the discovery and early working of enormous potash veins near Carlsbad around 1921 by oil drillers in the Permian Basin. In 1923–24, a vast treasure of oil and natural gas was discovered on the Navajo Reservation and in the San Juan Basin. In 1924, another economic and natural boon was added to New Mexico's public treasury in the form of the Gila Wilderness in southwest New Mexico. It was the first federal wilderness area established in the nation.

Invasive Overkill

Early in the 1920s, erosion along the Rio Grande, Rio Puerco, and San Juan floodplains was so severe, threatening crops and even homes, that well-meaning government naturalists looked to biological solutions to anchor the rivers' edges. Unhappily for the bosque today, they chose to plant tamarisk, or salt cedar trees, known today as "water vampires," on the banks of the Rio Grande and Rio Puerco. Along with the Russian olive, which found its way from gardens and nurseries to the bosques of both the Rio Grande and the San Juan,[37] the tamarisk has become a menace to intermittently drought-stricken New Mexico.

With overgrazing about to turn much of the West into a dust bowl, the Taylor Grazing Act was established in 1934 to regulate grazing on public lands. Dust storms had devastated sizable portions of northeastern and southeastern New Mexico as well as Kansas, Oklahoma, Texas, and eastern Colorado. The Navajo and Zuni livestock reduction program, designed to alleviate the ferocity of dust storms, ended in the slaughter of tens of thousands of sheep, severely damaging the tribes' economies and cultures. It could be contended that Navajo and Zuni sheep fell victim to the long and frequently violent struggle between sheep and cattle growers and those who came to be known as "stockmen" because they ran both species on their ranches. There was, of course, no thought of a stock reduction program off reservation.

Far from denuding the landscape, the Siberian elm, the most successful of all exotic species of trees in the Southwest, was introduced into Albuquerque by the New Deal mayor and soon-to-be New Mexico governor, Clyde Tingley, in the early 1930s. The unstoppable Siberian elm, a stately tree when properly pruned, makes so many seedpods—"Tingley flakes," they're called—that a whole garden could be hidden under them, or they could pile up into drifts two feet high. The seed flakes sprout with the slightest amount of water. Tingley's Folly did what the mayor had planned—it brought summer shade to the hot, dry neighborhoods of desert Albuquerque. It also proved extremely allergenic, an unintended consequence that many Albuquerqueans believe outweighed its usefulness.

Social Altruism

Besides the Native American livestock reduction program and the Taylor Grazing Act in the early- to mid-1930s, the New Deal program that most affected New Mexico was the Civilian Conservation Corps (CCC), which hired some thirty-two thousand people in the state over twelve years to create the state park system, among other conservation tasks.[38] The CCC was the first and greatest conservation effort in U.S. history. CCC crews planted as many as three billion trees around the country until the corps was ended after Pearl Harbor.[39] But while CCC men were conserving New Mexico's environment, hunter and latter-day mountain man Ben Lilly killed the state's last grizzly bear in the Gila Wilderness in 1932, after spending a lifetime eradicating wolves, mountain lions, and bears in southwestern New Mexico. Coincidentally, as the last great wild predators were being wiped out, the early 1930s saw the modern version of the Camino

Real, the Spanish Trail, and the Santa Fe Trail, known as Route 66, or the Mother Road, symbolically tame the wildness and end the isolation of the state. Extending more than two thousand miles from Santa Monica, California, through Gallup and Albuquerque to Santa Fe and on to Chicago, Illinois, Route 66 signaled the beginning of the car age in New Mexico. Few man-made objects have had as vast an impact on the West as the Mother Road. It stimulated car travel, sightseeing, and general adventuring. And Albuquerque, some eight hundred miles from the Pacific, was the first serious midsized downtown to develop along its route.

New Mexico in the 1930s was an overwhelmingly agrarian state, mostly rural in population, with a few small cities built up around universities and other branches of state government. Although the air, soil, and groundwater pollution brought on by the automobile was growing, chemical fertilizers and pesticides were already present, and the resource depletion caused by population growth had already started, albeit imperceptibly, New Mexicans still conceived the future of the state as being one in which agricultural, livestock, and mining products could be put to use by local workers and manufacturers rather than shipped out of state for development and profit.

Nuclear Colonization

But New Mexico's future was radically changed in 1943 when the United States military bought land near the Pajarito Plateau in the Jemez Mountains to create the Manhattan Project, causing the boys' school of Los Alamos to become an intellectual boomtown like none other in the nation. The years since 1943 have seen the greatest, most dangerous, and longest lasting impacts of human activity on the natural and human worlds of the New Mexico environment. Nuclear research and manufacture began to undermine natural systems early in the war. Nuclear waste has gone from zero to staggering density in many parts of the state. Industrial toxic waste associated with the military-industrial complex has been deposited, by and large, indiscriminately in Los Alamos and surrounding areas and in Albuquerque around Kirtland Air Force Base and Sandia National Laboratories (SNL) since the 1940s. Uranium mining began on Navajo and Laguna Pueblo land near Gallup and Grants in the early 1950s, when one of the largest uranium discoveries in the world was made. Nearly fifty years later, as many as four hundred miners or members of their families have died of suspicious cancers. Uranium mining brought with it massive earthmoving equipment, huge toxic leaching ponds, and open pit mines sending uranium dust sailing eastward to the population centers along the Middle Rio Grande Valley. These invasive attacks coincide with the change Albuquerque experienced from its heyday as an ideal location for the healing of tuberculosis in the early twentieth century to a city whose clean air and water is coming increasingly under suspicion.

Molybdenum, a national security mineral, used to harden iron, was long mined in the Red River area. Molybdenum mining got new life in the 1950s when even larger quantities were found around Questa. Fifty years later, tailing piles from the mine were so huge they'd become unstable, threatening to avalanche into the Red River and on parts of the town of Questa itself. By 2006, Molycorp, the mining company responsible for the precarious tailings, had reported them stabilized.

Managing Wide Open Spaces

A year after Trinity, in 1946, the Bureau of Land Management was established to manage public rangelands in the western states and oversee the Taylor Grazing Act. In New Mexico, rangeland and grazing controversies were still prone to erupting in violence, more than eighty years after the cattle wars. BLM's creation did little to quiet conflicts, other than refocus stockmen's animosities toward the federal government. In the late 1960s, with rangeland scarce and major predators all but hunted out, the New Mexico Game Commission curiously approved the importing of exotic game animals. One such animal, the oryx gazelle from the Atlas Mountains in Africa, was introduced into southern New Mexico in 1969, and the herd grew to some five thousand animals, most of them living on the White Sands Missile Range.

Early in the post-Trinity years, Kirtland Field in Albuquerque and Sandia Base nearby were turned into sites that engineered and tested delivery vehicles for the nuclear weapons designed in Los Alamos. For years, much of the nation's nuclear stockpile was stored in the super-secret Manzano Base, a hill at the foot of the Manzano Mountains south of Albuquerque that was hollowed out to hold the weapons and protected with the highest security engineering then available.

Kirtland and Sandia are located near the edge of the massive Tijeras Arroyo, a major recharge area for the aquifer that until 2008 supplied all of Albuquerque's drinking water, and a conduit for water runoff into the Rio Grande that runs through a portion of Albuquerque's heavily populated South Valley, north of Isleta Pueblo. From the end of World War II through the Cold War and into the present, military dumping of toxic and nuclear waste into the city's water supply has contaminated a good part of southern Albuquerque.

Another Boom

The disastrous droughts of the 1950s, which saw Elephant Butte Reservoir and other water catchments dry up completely, managed to stunt New Mexico's burgeoning sprawl development for a while. But by the early 1960s, a New York Company called AMREP was building its first house on the fifty-five thousand acres it owned in what would one day become Rio Rancho, destined to grow to be the third largest city in the state in less than fifty years. And in 1962 work was begun on a major interstate crossing in Albuquerque called the Big I, the intersection of I-40 and I-25.

New Mexico's sonic environment changed dramatically in 1945 when White Sands Missile Range opened for business. Testing of early rocketry, fighter jets, and various missile programs dominated southeastern New Mexico's skies through the Cold War and beyond. And on at least three occasions in the 1950s, air force bombers accidentally dropped, or crashed with, unarmed hydrogen bombs around Albuquerque and west of the city. To my knowledge, the extent of environmental damage caused by the nonnuclear explosions of those bombs, along with the dispersal of radioactive debris, has never been examined.

Errant Thinking

Two awkward nuclear moments occurred in New Mexico in the 1960s, both under the auspices of Project Ploughshare, an Atoms for Peace initiative started by President Eisenhower. Project Gnome near Carlsbad in 1961 and Project Gasbuggy near Dulce in 1967 involved underground explosions of nuclear bombs, the former to create a pocket of thermal energy, the latter to make an underground catchment for natural gas. In both cases, experimenters appeared to be unaware of the political and economic implications of the radioactive residue of the explosions. The gas hole near Dulce, for instance, did indeed accumulate gas, but it was too radioactive for gas companies to market.

In 1964, the beginning of the construction of the Azotea Tunnel heralded the start of a new era in Middle Rio Grande water management. The Azotea Tunnel, completed in 1970, is the major conduit for what is known as the San Juan–Chama Project, diverting water from the San Juan Basin to serve water users from Taos to Albuquerque and Navajo land. That new water, meant to diminish Albuquerque's reliance on its shrinking aquifer, soon became an impetus for new growth on Albuquerque's West Side. Heron Dam, built to hold and disperse the new water as well as to maintain Cochiti Lake 120 miles downstream, was completed in 1971.

Environmental Inspiration

The 1960s were important years for New Mexico's environment. Not only did the Wilderness Act of 1964 establish the legal basis for conserving such areas as the Chama River Canyon, Bandelier National Monument, and the Sandia, Manzano, and Capitan mountains, but the Wild and Scenic Rivers Act of 1968 helped the state preserve its only designated wild river, the fifty-three miles of the Rio Grande from the Colorado border through the Rio Grande Gorge.[40]

Just before the end of the 1960s, Albuquerque experienced two moments of environmental sanity. The Albuquerque Chamber of Commerce and other business leaders put the kibosh on a paper mill proposed for the Rio Grande Valley just above the diversion at Angostura, not far north of Bernalillo. Their opposition came on environmental grounds, as they saw the mill as a major polluter. That same year, 1969, saw the development of La Luz, a revolutionary cluster development on the West Side of Albuquerque. This enclave of condominiums that conserved the open space around it was financially successful and won architectural awards but never proved to be a model for viable alternatives to sprawl development.

A national climate of environmental regulation began with the Clean Air Act of 1970, the Clean Water Act of 1972, and the Endangered Species Act of 1973. All three would play roles in the lives of New Mexicans. The Clean Air Act, enforced via highway funds, motivated Albuquerque to instigate auto-emission standards and testing to clean up the haze and smog that were starting to make the city's skies look like those of Los Angeles, Phoenix, and Denver. The Clean Water Act, along with the EPA, mandated the cleanup of most of New Mexico's seventeen or so Superfund sites, including three in Albuquerque's downtown and South Valley areas. The Endangered Species Act continues to play a vital role in maintaining wildlife habitats. Preserving the endangered silvery minnow, often described as the canary in the mineshaft for riparian habitats along the Rio Grande, has made urban, state, and federal planners think through the complications of maintaining the Rio Grande as the semiwild irrigation river that most of New Mexico's farmers and environmentalists want it to be.

Dubious Regs

Another innovation of the Nixon administration, the Environmental Policy Act of 1970, which requires an environmental impact statement (EIS) for all federal projects, has had a positive impact on New Mexico's environment as well, no matter how much developers, investors, and politicians may hate it. Still, the power and influence of

Retired diesel mechanic Terry Humble worked in the mines for more than thirty years. Now the self-appointed local historian in Bayard, he takes me to the shed behind his house to gift me some native copper and show me his old mining equipment. May 2007.

The Santa Rita open-pit copper mine, also known as the Chino, is one of the oldest and largest in the world. It is now owned by Freeport-McMoRan. May 2007.

The Amalgamated United Steel Workers of America Local 890 union hall in the town of Bayard. Murals by Bob Ames. May 2007.

A chapel near the mine, with a posted prayer to the Patroness of Impossible Cases, Saint Rita. May 2007.

One of the retired miners showing me around tells me that the statue of Jesus and Mary inside this stone chapel behind Saint Anthony's church in Fierro was transferred here from the church that used to be in Santa Rita, a town that became an island in the middle of the mine, before being closed and mined itself. Just beyond the parking lot outside are the headframes of a copper mine. March 2008.

The Hurley Cemetery. March 2008.

Tailings pile seen from the lookout over Santa Rita mine. March 2008.

Louisiana Energy Services' uranium enrichment facility in Eunice, halfway through its four-year construction (see page 211). March 2008.

The Sandia Mountains from Highway 550 north of Albuquerque and Rio Rancho, near the Santa Ana Star Casino. Note that preparations for development are already in place (see page 57). February 2007.

Looking north along the Rio Grande from a housing development on Albuquerque's West Side (see page 57). April 2007.

The New Mexico Wind Energy Center near House, in northeastern New Mexico, consists of 136 turbines, each 210 feet tall, with blades 110 feet long. PNM, the state's largest electric company, buys all of the power generated here, which replaces the same amount generated by coal and gas (see page 52). March 2008.

impact statements is entirely dependent on the politics of the moment. The two most heated controversies in urban New Mexico—over the building of the Montaño Road Bridge in Albuquerque's North Valley and the extension of Paseo del Norte through the Petroglyph National Monument on Albuquerque's West Side—were fully vetted via many EIS efforts and were still built and funded despite vigorous citizen opposition.

As environmentalism became institutionalized in the federal government in the form of the Environmental Protection Agency, a vigorous antienvironmental movement grew in the American West. In New Mexico, embattled ranchers, oil and gas producers, mining lobbies, and the energy industry are the most visible opponents of environmentalism. Catron County, the largest and most sparsely populated county in New Mexico, and one of the few counties in America that requires each adult resident to own a gun, has harbored what might be called an extension of the cattle wars of the nineteenth century. Ranchers and environmentalists struggle over grazing, soil erosion, logging, and degradation of riparian habitats on federal lands, sometimes with dramatic, near-violent results. The Catron County government even tried to pass laws that contested the legality of many national environmental laws. This dire situation in Catron County and other places in rural New Mexico prompted one of the most innovative and successful environmental partnerships in the country. Composed of conservationist ranchers and environmentalists, the Quivira Coalition is helping to defuse the near-autonomic distrust between the two factions.

In the forty years since the celebration of the first Earth Day, a remarkable, if largely unnoticed, outpouring of environmental reporting has taken place. Thousands of stories covering natural constraints on human activity and the impacts of human carelessness, ignorance, and malice have been published, most of them in the back pages of newspapers; few are given prominent play. Many more such stories never make the mainstream press at all, and those that do are read and digested mostly by people on the political margins.

Befouling Power

The air pollution in the San Juan Basin, which often is so bad one can't see Shiprock from the ideal viewing areas in Mesa Verde National Park, is caused not only by the two coal-power plants already in place there—the Four Corners Power Plant and the San Juan Generating Station—but also by the gasoline engines and compressors pumping oil and gas from tens of thousands of wells in the region. Coal is so plentiful in and around the basin that a new coal-fired power plant, a giant 1,500-megawatt facility known as the Desert Rock Energy Project, was being planned in 2006 for northwestern New Mexico on the Navajo Reservation. In the face of growing usage, two other plants in what the New West Network calls New Mexico's national sacrifice area, one near Farmington and one near Grants, are also being proposed.[41]

With nuclear energy being promoted anew as a useful technique to reduce greenhouse gases and global warming, uranium mining is casting a fresh shadow on New Mexico. Uranium was first discovered in the state near Grants in 1950, at the height of the Cold War. The Soviet Union had exploded its first atom bomb in 1949. Uranium soon displaced carrots as the leading product of the area.[42] In 1979, just over a month after the nuclear accident at Three Mile Island in Pennsylvania, a much more serious radioactive disaster took place along the Puerco River north of Gallup. A United Nuclear Corporation uranium evaporation pond near Church Rock broke though its dam and sent more than ninety million gallons of what was referred to as "liquor," or radioactive liquid, along with some eleven hundred tons of radioactive mill wastes, surging toward Arizona. Along the way, the spill was so powerful it ran into sewer lines and blew off manhole covers in Gallup, twenty miles south. Full of radioactive waste, the spill "degraded the western Puerco River as a water source. And it raised the specter that uranium mining in the Colorado River Basin might be endangering Arizona's Lake Mead, and with it the drinking water of Las Vegas, Los Angeles, and much of Arizona."[43] More than thirty years later, despite lengthy and strenuous protests from the Navajo Nation and other interested parties,[44] uranium mining companies are gearing up again, this time not planning to dig open pit and underground mines, but to use a process called *in situ leaching*, in which chemicals are injected into underground water to loosen uranium ore from gravel and sands so it can be pumped out of the ground. This process, like the Church Rock spill, could ruin the water supply in the immediate area and render the groundwater permanently toxic.[45]

Land Grabs

Ever since the first Europeans set foot in New Mexico, government agencies have been appropriating land from the people who live on it and use it. A variety of land grabs have caused controversy since World War II. After the Trinity explosion, the U.S. military appropriated huge tracts of ranch land to create what is today the White Sands Missile Range. Historian Marc Simmons tells the story of eighty-two-year-old John Prather, a tough-minded rancher who'd worked his land for fifty years before the government came after it. He refused to sell and succeeded in keeping his house and a small portion of his spread so he could "die at home."[46] Other property owners have not succeeded in hanging onto their land. Despite the defeat of the Bursum Bill in 1922, a bill that would have made legal various land grabs on Pueblo reservations by non-Native farmers who just moved in and wouldn't go away, the federal government managed to take over a vast lava flow on ancestral lands belonging to Acoma Pueblo, turning it into El Malpais National Monument, which opened in 1987. The Acomas objected and won concessions but couldn't stop the appropriation of the land. The pueblo of Acoma has worked consistently to buy up ancestral lands that have fallen into other hands, from far south of the pueblo and north to Mount Taylor.[47]

In the late 1960s, land grant activist Reyes Lopez Tijerina, a charismatic Tejano preacher, caused a furor in northern New Mexico by claiming that New Mexican Hispanics had been swindled out of lands granted to them by the Spanish Crown in colonial times, lands that were sold to the federal government or had fallen into the public domain and become national forests and grasslands. Tijerina and his followers provoked armed conflict with local and national law enforcement with their infamous Courthouse Raid in Tierra Amarilla and the brief takeover of the Echo Amphitheater in the Carson National Forest. Land grant activism has subsided in the last forty years but legitimized the cause, with Tijerina donating some eighty cubic feet of papers to the University of New Mexico Center for Southwest Research at the beginning of the twenty-first century.

The wisdom of selling off public lands once acquired is always in question. Ted Turner, the state's single largest land owner, is an environmental conservator, but between 1950 and the early 1980s, for instance, the New Mexico State Land Office, which manages state lands to raise money for education, had sold off more than two million acres to ranchers like Robert O. Anderson, Tom Catron, H. Yeats, the Skeen family, and Tom Bolack; developers like Bellamah, Falls, Berger-Briggs, Calvin Horn, Walker-Hinkle, and Heights Realty; and mining interests like Molycorp, Phelps Dodge, Kennecott, and United Nuclear.[48] One wonders if the sale prices compensated for the years of lease returns that were lost, not to mention the environmental consequences.

Metastasizing Growth

Population growth in New Mexico since the end of World War II has been something of a mixed blessing. The state's population was at 951,023 in 1960.[49] Forty years later, it had almost doubled. This phenomenal growth spurt coincided with one of the wettest periods in the state's history, which was preceded by one of the worst droughts on record, culminating in 1956 when Elephant Butte Lake was quite literally dry. The '50s saw a major die-off of piñons and junipers around northern New Mexico, much like the one in the early twenty-first century. In 1957, a year after Elephant Butte went dry, the drought appeared to lift with a gigantic snowstorm, but both the storm and the wet years were masking the true climatological nature of our region. New Mexico is a mixture of deserts. Drought is its normal condition. The forty years of recent growth has occurred mostly in cities, particularly in Albuquerque, which at the time was thought to be situated on top of an underground lake the size of Lake Superior.

It was only in the early 1990s that Albuquerque Mayor Louis Saavedra decided to use city wells to gather data on the size of the aquifer. Eventually, the U.S. Geological Survey expanded the measurement program and concluded that Albuquerque's aquifer was drastically smaller than had been thought and was diminishing with alarming speed. Despite these findings, the Albuquerque metro area continued to sprawl westward, gobbling up land, water or no water. Terrible struggles between the city and Pueblo governments over the extension of Paseo del Norte through the Petroglyph National Monument lasted until 2005. The San Juan–Chama Diversion Project began to bring water to Albuquerque in 2008, causing some serious concern about the quality of the city's drinking water. Albuquerque residents had always used exclusively fossil water from the aquifer. San Juan–Chama water would flow down the Rio Grande and into Cochiti Lake, being treated before residents would drink it. Citizens worry that the water will be contaminated by industrial solvents and radioactive seepage and debris from Los Alamos. The municipal water supply of Santa Fe was found in 2006 to contain chromium, uranium, and traces of plutonium from Los Alamos.

No one knows exactly how many radioactive and other toxic dumps exist on the military land in New Mexico. In addition to the so-called mixed-waste landfill, an unlined hole near Sandia Labs containing industrial waste, radioactive cobalt, and other toxic substances that according to the government are too dangerous to move, some observers say the Kirtland Base area has around four hundred waste sites of unknown size and contents. We know there are some two thousand waste sites associated with Los Alamos National Labs, because after the Cerro Grande forest fire in Los Alamos, reports maintained that none of the waste sites were damaged.

In September 2006, an editorial writer in the *Albuquerque Journal* expressed concern about living sixty miles downstream from Los Alamos, arguing for a public hearing in Albuquerque on the DOE's plan to quadruple the production of plutonium pits, the triggers for hydrogen bombs that used to be made near Denver at Rocky Flats, one of the most radioactive industrial sites in the United States.[50] The *Journal* and a prominent local NGO, Citizen Action, wanted the Albuquerque public to at least have a chance to voice questions and concerns. But despite calls for such a hearing from New Mexico's senator Jeff Bingaman and from the state's attorney general, Patricia Madrid, as of this writing, no hearing in Albuquerque had been scheduled.

The Bearer of Life and Poison

Water and water safety are always crucial questions in New Mexico. The drought of the early twenty-first century caused great hardship in Santa Fe and almost brought the city of Las Vegas, New Mexico, to a standstill, requiring stringent water rationing. In the very wet summer of 2006, however, Las Vegas received more than seven inches of rain in a two-month period. But while residents were grateful and even euphoric at times, they knew such downpours were an anomaly.

When erratic heavy rains do hit New Mexico, they often are accompanied by flash floods that send walls of water down dry arroyos, big and small. When heavy rains hit Albuquerque, the major drainage of the Sandia Mountains, known as Tijeras Arroyo, sends water coursing down past Kirtland Air Force Base and Sandia Labs into the South Valley a little north of the barrio of Mountain View. Unfortunately for the South Valley, no one has kept track of everything that's been dumped into the arroyo since Kirtland Air Force Base and Sandia Labs were built right next to it in the late 1940s. We do know that a major landfill was placed right next to the arroyo, and that a large outdoor concert venue near I-25 and the soon-to-be residential portions of the Mesa del Sol development was placed nearby. We also know from published accounts that defense contractors and perhaps the Atomic Energy Commission dumped toxic liquids into the arroyo for many years, and many unconfirmed reports strongly suggest that the military did, too. From Mountain View, near the Isleta turnoff, north to the neighborhood of East San Jose, between Broadway and Second Street, is perhaps the most environmentally compromised area in the state. Wells at either end of the area have been closed because of pollution. Two Superfund sites—one at a former Atomic Energy Commission weapons components manufacturing site, now owned by General Electric, and the other at a Santa Fe Railroad creosote treatment facility—are located there, as well as at least three major brownfields, gasoline storage tanks and underground pipelines, animal waste with antibiotic residue from a feedlot, automobile junkyards, the city waste treatment plant, and thirty-four of the city's thirty-six EPA-monitored manufacturing sites. More on this and other toxic sites will follow in later chapters.

Corporate Culpability

Like most environmental issues, air and water pollution usually involve either the economy or the military or, in New Mexico, both. In 2008, the air force revealed the existence of a massive leak of jet fuel at its Kirtland base in Albuquerque. Estimated by the air force to be two million gallons but by the New Mexico State Environment Department to be eight million gallons, it's a grave threat to Albuquerque's aquifer. The leak could have started in the 1970s, and it went undetected until 1999. A plume of the fuel is in the water table not a mile away from the city's major drinking water wells. Remediation began in 2010. One of the more fractious environmental disputes in the Albuquerque metro area involves the Intel Corporation, the largest computer chip manufacturer in the world. Its biggest production plant is on the outskirts of the fast-growing city of Rio Rancho, west of Albuquerque, on bluffs overlooking portions of the village of Corrales, a community of farmers and people who like the rural life. Some six hundred of those people have lodged protests for over a decade charging that Intel's smokestack emissions are making them sick, that the smell of acetone is often nauseating. They complain of a wide range of pulmonary ills, headaches, dizziness, sleeplessness, general lassitude, and suppressed immune systems. Intel vociferously denies it's to blame and comes close to denying the residents are sick at all.

In Albuquerque's South Valley, GE, Univar Corporation, Chevron and Texaco, Whitfield Tank Lines, and ATA Pipelines are all involved in cleaning up volatile organic compounds from both shallow- and deep-water aquifers. Two public wells in the community of East San Jose, nearby, were plugged in 1995 due to contamination. GE and other corporations were the defendants in the largest environmental lawsuit ever brought in New Mexico when state attorney general Patricia Madrid sued them for $4 billion, alleging their remediation efforts, scheduled to go on through 2010, would never restore the drinkability of the contaminated aquifer. Though a major portion of the suit's allegations were dismissed, it worked its way through federal court for years.[51]

In the first years of the twenty-first century, New Mexico was experiencing an ongoing controversy over drilling for oil and natural gas on the 332,000 acres of pristine grasslands known as Otero Mesa, south of Alamagordo. It is thought that there is enough fresh water in the aquifer under the mesa to supply all of southern New Mexico and El Paso for the better part of a hundred years. The Bureau of Land Management cleared the way for oil and gas exploration and production on the mesa. After fourteen years of litigation, however, the Tenth Circuit Court of Appeals ruled against the BLM. Environmentalists considered this a major victory. Litigation continues as of this writing in 2010. Farther north, the outdoors person's paradise of the Valle Vidal, some 100,000 acres of streams and mountain meadows, had been earmarked by El Paso Corporation, a natural gas company, for 191 cold-bed methane gas wells, with pumps camouflaged to coexist with the Valle Vidal's elk herds and magnificent scenery. Hunters, campers, and fishing aficionados were outraged at the idea and, according to U.S. representative Tom Udall from New Mexico's northern district, besieged the U.S. Forest Service with more than 55,000 public comments that "overwhelmingly argue gas development is incompatible with other uses of the Valle Vidal." With the support of New Mexico senators Pete Domenici and Jeff Bingaman, the U.S. Senate unanimously passed legislation in 2006 banning oil and gas drilling and development in the area.

Rescues and Mixed Bags

One of the most magnificent habitats and natural wonders in the state, the Valles Caldera National Preserve in the Jemez Mountains, fifteen miles west of Los Alamos, has been saved from development. The crater of a supervolcano that exploded more than a million years ago, the Valles Caldera used to belong to the Baca Ranch and was known by New Mexicans and tourists as an untouchable but very visible natural wonder. Its great volcanic bowl could be seen from the road to Los Alamos, but no entry was possible for years. The congressional act that saved the Caldera was signed in 2000. Ten years later, in May 2010, Tom Udall, now a U.S. senator from New Mexico, and Senator Jeff Bingaman introduced a bill to turn over the management of the Valles Caldera to the U.S. National Park Service.

In another positive political development, Zuni Pueblo won a historic victory over a proposed coal mine in its area that could have drained the Pueblo's sacred Salt Lake. Yet just weeks later, the BLM leased some 77,700 acres for oil and gas exploration nearby without researching the possible effects on groundwater in the area. A federal judge in 2003 ruled against the Public Service Company of New Mexico (PNM), the state's largest utility company, in its attempt to keep data from air monitors out of a lawsuit brought against the company by the Sierra Club and other groups. They charged PNM's plant near Farmington had violated its air quality permit sixty thousand times since 1990.

In October 2005, President Bush signed a bill creating the Ojito Wilderness, an eleven-thousand-acre badlands south of the town of San Isidro in Sandoval County. New Mexico's entire congressional delegation, in a rare moment of bipartisan unanimity, supported the bill, which also set into motion the sale of eleven thousand more wilderness acres from the BLM, adjacent to the Ojito, to Zia Pueblo nearby. Zia played a vital role in the negotiations.[52] Not fifteen miles away to the south and southwest, however, more suburban sprawl was engulfing the Albuquerque metro area and draining water from its already endangered aquifer. Driving out New Mexico Highway 550 to get to the Ojito Wilderness, one passes by an increasingly large number of new homes in the city of Rio Rancho on land that five years ago was empty. Southwest of Rio Rancho, along the eastern Rio Puerco, a new subdivision is planned in which some thirty thousand homes would get water, the developers promise, via the desalination of the brackish aquifer beneath the Rio Puerco Valley, thereby tripling water costs, according to some estimates.

Nuke Disputes

The prices of gasoline and natural gas in the summer of 2006 seemed to validate the renewed interest in the production of nuclear energy. Still, both nuclear weapons and nuclear energy raised major questions and continue to cause political heat. New Mexicans along major truck routes were contemplating the possibility of a higher level of nuclear waste being stored in the Waste Isolation Pilot Project (WIPP) near Carlsbad in the southeastern part of the state. This is a situation federal agencies and regulators said would never happen. WIPP is a huge underground facility dug by potash miners, with a flawless safety record, into salt beds some twenty-one hundred feet below the surface. It was designed to contain "transuranic radioactive waste," or materials like clothing and tools used in plutonium production, some of it from Rocky Flats, contained in large drums. Opponents of WIPP have argued in the past that hotter nuclear wastes would eventually melt the salts and attract water, corroding the drums and potentially damaging aquifers both below and above the WIPP site.[53]

Though some residents of Socorro remain concerned about the long-lasting health impacts of depleted uranium testing carried out there from the early 1970s to the early 1990s, depleted uranium (DU) remains a subject shunned by politicians and physicians alike. More than forty tons of DU shells were tested at a firing range behind the New Mexico Institute of Mining and Technology, a state university that has been very successful in attracting federal dollars. New

Mexico Tech is right in the middle of Socorro, a small town where everything is in close proximity to everything else.[54] DU, an extremely effective armor-piercing metal used in munitions, also appears to be a highly toxic substance. Children and others in Iraq, especially near areas where large quantities of DU munitions were used, have suffered what seem to be radioactively induced diseases. New Mexicans are concerned about the health impact of DU testing on children living near test sites here.

Depleted uranium is stored as a solid when fissionable isotopes have been removed by uranium enrichment processes. Eunice, a tiny oil patch town in southeastern New Mexico fallen on hard times, successfully lobbied in 2005 to become the site of the nation's first gas-centrifuge uranium enrichment plant, after the international consortium of energy companies that own and operate the plant were turned down in Louisiana and Tennessee.[55] The $1.5 billion National Enrichment Facility[56] will have to contend with the gaseous UF6 waste product, which is highly toxic, explosive and pyrophoric when in contact with water, and corrosive to most metals.[57] Chances are the waste materials will be stored five miles away from the plant, just across the border in Texas.

Not far from Eunice, the towns of Hobbs and Carlsbad were bidding in 2006 to host a pilot project for recycling spent commercial uranium fuel rods. This practice had been rejected by every presidential administration since Jimmy Carter's on the grounds that it could make weapons-grade uranium available to terrorists.

New Energy for Old

It seems more than likely that, as the world moves away from reliance on fossil fuels to alternative energies, New Mexico's scientific community will find itself both hard-pressed for and responsive to opportunity. As petroleum products are used less and less for transportation, as natural gas succumbs to cleaner coal in electric power generation, and as nuclear technology gains ever-increasing political and financial support, New Mexico's centers of economic power will shift dramatically. There's a chance that eventually the state will move away from toxic-waste-producing nuclear power and greenhouse-gas-emitting coal-fired plants as it successfully pursues a larger share of the nation's wind and solar energy markets. As of 2006, New

Mexico had a total of 407 megawatts of wind power capacity, with four major plants, the power from which is all bought and used by PNM, according to the New Mexico Energy, Minerals, and Natural Resources Department.[58] New Mexico still lags far behind Texas and California, with 2,370 and 2,323 megawatts of wind power, respectively, in 2006. But New Mexico could do quite well for itself in the mountain West, if the wind industry is given anything like the incentives delivered to the oil and gas industry. And innovative small-scale solar power operations have long flourished in New Mexico, both as entrepreneurial enterprises and as offshoots of the Sandia National Laboratories. Clearly the great conflict will be between a struggling fossil fuel business and the cities and towns whose lifeblood is the clean surface and underground water that petroleum drilling so often degrades. In many ways, the fate of Otero Mesa's pristine aquifer will tell the tale.

CHAPTER TWO

WATER
A DESERT AMONG EONS OF OCEANS

Finding McCauley Hot Springs for the first time, after a long hike above Battleship Rock in the Jemez Mountains, one gets a sense of the preciousness of water in New Mexico and of its mysterious and sacred nature. Water, the mother substance of us all, is the vitalizing force of all natural processes and the most vulnerable to misuse. Polluted waters kill wildlife, livestock, and people who are caught unaware. Learning your waters have been polluted feels like a desecration and a betrayal. Because there is no life without it, water has a numinous quality, as anything irreplaceably important does. It is a core metaphor in Pueblo mythology. And San Isidro, saint of the rain, is the patron of both Hispanic and Pueblo farmers. When you reach McCauley Hot Springs, the sense of wonder is overwhelming. Looking into the clear, hot depths you see water bubbling up

◄   Dead carp at McAllister Lake near Las Vegas, New Mexico.
     November 2007.

from the deep through a gentle turbulence of roiling white sand. The gods of the wild are surely there. The water appears seemingly out of nowhere, warm with life, a gift from the rocks and trees. Underground waters in the Jemez are heated by magma still close to the surface even millions of years since the great eruption that blew the top off the mountain and created the landforms of the vast, beautiful Valles Caldera, one of the largest such depressions on earth.

Not forty miles from the Jemez, however, all up and down the Middle Rio Grande Valley, more than seven hundred fifty thousand people depend on a diminishing underground water source. Sand, gravel, and clay hold deep, ancient waters that are minimally replenished by the high desert's infrequent rains and snows, by seepage from unlined irrigation canals, and by the river itself. The Rio Jemez empties into the Rio Grande, along with the water of the Rio Salado, near Bernalillo. Underground waters are what 90 percent of New Mexicans drink. And for its entire life as a city prior to 2008, Albuquerque has supplied its residents with nothing but pure water from that aquifer. In the last twenty-five years, however, it's become increasingly evident to water managers and conservationists all over the state, especially in Albuquerque, that there's more paper water than real water in New Mexico. The New Mexico state engineer, who oversees state water, made it clear in 2006 that "the state's surface water supply and most of the groundwater supply is fully or over appropriated. If all the water right permits, licenses, and declarations were fully exercised today, the current supply would not likely meet the demand."[1]

Before the Future Happened

How different it was when I first crossed Central Avenue at Fourth Street in bustling downtown Albuquerque in early September 1958, when the city was flush with federal Cold War dollars and the engineering expertise that Sandia National Laboratories employees could bring to its growth and prosperity. At Fourth and Central, I had no idea that the components for the Trinity bomb, which marked the start of the atomic age, had passed through the same intersection in the dead of night some thirteen years before, headed to what's now White Sands Missile Range in south central New Mexico. Before the July 16, 1945, detonation of the "gadget," as the bomb was called, Albuquerque was just a college town, with a busy downtown shopping center filled with novel historic architecture of many styles and buildings using Hispanic and Pueblo motifs. By 1955, when the Soviet Union had fired its first true hydrogen bomb, Albuquerque might well have been on the Kremlin's list of first-strike targets, making it one of the world's most vulnerable, and possibly valuable, places in Cold War terms. Not only was Albuquerque the transportation axis for the nuclear weapons industry, but Sandia Labs on Kirtland Air Force Base was the design center for nuclear weapons delivery systems and other highly secret military work. An influential handful of engineers at the labs, including future mayor Harry Kinney, played a key role in growing Albuquerque from a compact, distinctive southwestern city into a miniature version of a sprawling American metroplex in keeping with the national postwar suburban boom.

First Strike Target

It still seems half-crazy to me that Santa Fe and Albuquerque, rich in idiosyncratic tradition, literature, and art, should also be where one of the greatest human follies originated. The highest strata of science and technology colonized New Mexico with the same ferocity and persistence as did the Europeans to the Americas in the sixteenth and seventeenth centuries. That modern occupation eventually resulted in a mental chain reaction that almost risked destroying civilization during the Cuban missile crisis, and still could. Starting with one explosion in the New Mexico desert, a relatively small one—but big enough to flatten whole cities—the nuclear arms race produced seventy thousand nuclear weapons. Even today, the threat of ultimate nuclear chaos persists, with some twenty-five thousand warheads in the world's arsenals, eleven thousand of which are "on alert," ready for use "in minutes or hours."[2] Even at the beginning of the twenty-first century, a sizable but undisclosed number of nuclear warheads are still stored deep underground south of Albuquerque, having been moved in the 1990s from the former top-secret storage facility carved into the Manzano Mountains known as Manzano Base. The Albuquerque–Los Alamos–Santa Fe research triangle is probably still on some enemy's first-strike list.

Manhattan Project Poison

The impact of the nuclear arms race is global in scope, but it also has serious local ramifications. Only now, more than sixty years after the Trinity explosion, are the people of northern and central New Mexico beginning to realize that the nuclear arms race may have been polluting their drinking water for decades. This one fact, deeply buried in bureaucratic and public relations spin-doctoring, may prove to be the determining limitation on the futures of the major population centers in the Upper and Middle Rio Grande Valley. Along with the end of inexpensive gasoline and natural gas, as well as increased demand for water intensified by normal drought cycles and global warming, polluted water could add a burden that might ruin New Mexico's competitive edge in attracting its share of the immigration from water-starved Los Angeles, San Diego, Las Vegas, and Phoenix.

Rio Rancho

While the state's second-largest city, Las Cruces, has grown slowly, Albuquerque's geographic size and population have been expanding in boomtown fashion for most of its modern life, spreading east to the mountains and west over the river almost as far as the eye can see. In these days of global warming consciousness, carbon footprint awareness, and green building, the westward expansion of the Albuquerque metro area seems more and more like an economic and social disaster, isolating people from their jobs and requiring expensive city services in order for growth to continue into the open range of the West Mesa, perhaps the area hardest hit by water scarcity. The dire economic realities of the great recession of 2008–10 will undermine the financial well-being of the residents of Rio Rancho the worst. It's now the third-largest city in the state, but is still dependent on Albuquerque and Santa Fe for many jobs. In 1961, the AMREP Corporation bought about 55,000 acres north and west of Albuquerque, platted it, and sold some seventy-seven thousand lots to about forty thousand buyers using mail-order advertising for less than $1,500 an acre. From that beginning, AMREP parlayed its sales into the city of Rio Rancho, growing from some ten thousand residents in 1980 to well over sixty-three thousand people today. While Rio Rancho has never had enough water to warrant its growth and is always scrambling to buy up water rights from farmers, it dumps its treated municipal effluent into the Rio Grande. Its discharge is just upstream from Albuquerque's main diversion channel for drinking water from the San Juan–Chama Project. Rio Rancho has been known to dump raw sewage into the river, too, when its treatment plant breaks down. Rio Rancho is considered by its neighbors in Corrales, eastward down the bluff, to be a source of traffic congestion and pollution. The antipollution devices on Intel's gigantic factory, for instance, break down from time to time, a situation that has raised the ire of many Corraleseños who accuse the massive corporation of causing hundreds of people to become seriously and often chronically ill.

As the world heats up and the Club of Rome's 1960s predictions of resource depletion start proving true, continued sprawl in Albuquerque has the feeling of madness to it, something like what the Hopi call *Koyaanisqatsi*, "crazy life," or a world out of balance. When New Mexican Godfrey Reggio, with the aid of composer Philip Glass, directed a world-famous montage documentary by the same name in 1982, the film, with its time-lapse photography of urban life, became iconographic of a culture that was disintegrating before our eyes.

The End of Route 66 and the Beginning of Sprawl

Perhaps the best way to get a handle on Albuquerque's growth is to look briefly at its boosterism following my arrival in 1958, when Albuquerque was still a beautiful, self-contained little city. I traveled east to Albuquerque on Route 66, a federal highway that went right through downtown as Central Avenue and east through Tijeras Canyon, a dozen or so miles away. Route 66 was the road of dreams for many people migrating from the Midwest to the Pacific Coast, especially during the Dust Bowl and Depression era of the 1930s. The Mother Road, as it was known, reached Albuquerque in 1926, traveling from Santa Fe through the town of Bernalillo and down Fourth Street. In 1937, Route 66 changed its course into the east-west road that I and so many others knew so well. Downtown Albuquerque flourished for nearly thirty years but changed forever when I-40 and I-25 were pushed through the city on the sand hills above the historic business center, extending out to major shopping centers in the northeast heights, an area called Uptown today. By the mid-1960s, Route 66 was almost a thing of the past in New Mexico, lingering only around Tucumcari, where wrangling about bypasses and loss of business continued for years. The decommissioning of Route 66 was the start of Albuquerque's years of sprawl.

L.A. in the Desert

The Californication of Albuquerque was well underway before Earth Day, 1970. No one but struggling downtown business owners could quite believe it was happening—and happening so fast. Albuquerque was a one-momentum town. If a business surge moved to one place, it pretty much killed off the place it had left. When business moved northeast to two major shopping centers, downtown dried up. Government and the courts stayed downtown in a kind of judicial and administrative ghost town defined by parking structures. Despite many valiant efforts to revive it, downtown didn't really start a sustained comeback until Albuquerque grew large enough to support multiple retail momentums. The environmental impact of the interstates and the Uptown shopping centers is obvious today—millions of commuting miles, countless gallons of gasoline, heavy traffic, and a carbon footprint as unmanageable as that of any other big city in the West.

Even today, at almost a million people, it's still hard for many Americans and many New Mexicans to consider Albuquerque a major city. But Albuquerque is squarely in the company of Tucson, Phoenix, Amarillo, Salt Lake City, Las Vegas, and Denver, the major metro areas in the region. From 1940 to 2007, the Albuquerque metro area, which includes Bernalillo County and parts of Sandoval, Valencia, Torrance, and Cibola counties, grew from a population of 69,631 to approximately 950,000, with 1.2 million people predicted by boosters for 2010, presuming the water holds out.[3] In 1958, Albuquerque had fewer than 210,000 people. Contained though it was, it was the first actual downtown—with modest high-rises, swank neighborhoods, a university district with all the trimmings—that a driver would encounter coming the eight hundred miles east from Los Angeles, and that still holds true today on I-40. The immense urban sprawl that covered the entire Los Angeles Basin even fifty years ago was without a comparable urban center. After one crossed the Mojave Desert and climbed through the woodlands of northern Arizona to traverse the oceanic desert landscape of western New Mexico, Albuquerque felt like a cosmopolitan oasis. The differences between then and now are stark reminders of the ravages of uncontrolled development permitted by civic leaders who saw population growth, rather than growth in per capita income, as the leading indicator of prosperity. The same can be said, of course, for virtually every burgeoning city in the country, particularly in the West.

Santa Fe

Even though I might be accused of espousing New Mexico exception-alism, population growth manifested as sprawl has always seemed to me to be out of place in New Mexico's unique natural landscape. The state's major cities have all allowed themselves to sprawl on the pattern of a standard American car town, some more egregiously than others. Santa Fe, the state's capital, was different for most of its modern existence, but it, too, has succumbed to water-profligate suburban growth. Because of its Spanish-Pueblo architectural design code, its highly successful, long-term economic development strategy based on the fine arts, tourism, and New Mexico traditional cultures, and its semirural location at the foot of the Sangre de Cristo Mountains, Santa Fe grew slowly but steadily for years, despite rampant gentrification. With Californians moving into Santa Fe, home prices soared in the early 2000s, reaching a median of some $358,000 by 2005.[4] Santa Fe's chronic lack of water and intense water rationing at the turn of the last century didn't seem to inhibit its reputation as a southwestern Beverly Hills, secluded and peaceful, rich with high culture, and free of the crowded drawbacks of Southern California.

The logic of the car culture and the technological sweetness of the automobile, with its pivotal role in the consumer economy, were unstoppable. Even in the face of OPEC-induced oil crises in the 1970s, transportation planning in Albuquerque was largely a sham. "Citizen participation in the planning process," as the catch phrase had it, was an exercise in futility for those who tried to buck the development community's dislike of anything other than the most rudimentary, and changeable, zoning. Even if neighborhood input was intense and got incorporated into sector plans, the planning bureaucracy frequently forgot the agreements and approved developments that went against the plans, a slap in the face to neighborhood activists. All the while, Albuquerque continued to expand out into the desert.

In the late 1950s, to stimulate its growth, Albuquerque started to sell itself as the most water-rich city in the desert mountain West. As time went on, extravagant images would reinforce the claim. At one time in the 1970s, it was a matter of civic pride to say that Albuquerque was sitting on an aquifer the size of Lake Superior. It wasn't until the 1990s that the image was debunked by the U.S. Geological Survey's investigation of the aquifer. The USGS found a very different reality—a diminishing aquifer that might come up brackish and cause subsidence in anywhere from five to fifty years.

Money or Law

Who gets the water, and when, are perennial questions in New Mexico. State Engineer John D'Antonio estimated in 2006 that about three-quarters of the state's water use of some 4 million acre-feet a year (an acre-foot is 325,851 gallons) goes to irrigated agriculture. Of the remaining quarter, a surprisingly small 5 percent (or 200,000 acre-feet) supplies livestock raising, mining, commercial interests, manufacturing, and power companies. Just about 10 percent of the state's water is used by municipalities and their residents, though in Bernalillo County, nearly 90 percent of water use is business and residential. The remaining 10 percent of the state's water is lost to evaporation, though some ingenious water entrepreneurs have tried to buy up paper water rights to the evaporated water before it vaporizes, so to speak. The idea hasn't floated.

Agricultural water, which also maintains wildlife habitats both in rivers and in ditches, is largely surface water from major rivers, the Rio Grande in the center of the state, San Juan in the north, the Pecos and Canadian in the east, and the Gila in the west. From time to time, however, to meet interstate compacts, underground water is pumped and dumped into rivers and their irrigation systems. While residential use of water is heavily regulated in most New Mexican cities, population growth is not. Many suburbs, like Corrales and Placitas around Albuquerque, take water from the Middle Rio Grande aquifer using unmonitored wells. In fact, most wells in New Mexico remain unmonitored, despite fledgling efforts by the Office of the State Engineer in 2006 to keep track of private well use in southern New Mexico. And although some 110,000 acre-feet of water gets to New Mexico via the San Juan–Chama Diversion Project, provided there's snowpack around Rio Blanco and other tributaries to the San Juan in southern Colorado, that's a small fraction of New Mexico's real annual use. It is important to note that the Office of the State Engineer's estimate of our water use is just that: an estimate. To my knowledge no comprehensive regional or statewide water use statistics exist, and no one is really sure how much water is contained in all the state's aquifers, some thirty-two in all. It was only in September 2006 that New Mexico's senators Pete Domenici and Jeff Bingaman successfully introduced legislation, called the New Mexico Aquifer Assessment Act, that funded the U.S. Geological Survey to help augment the 2001 USGS study of the Middle Rio Grande Basin. The act provides for inclusion of the Estancia Basin east of Albuquerque, Salt Basin under Otero Mesa in southeastern New Mexico, Tularosa Basin north of there, and Hueco Bolson near Las Cruces. The Blue Water Basin around Grants, once the water source for highly successful post–World War II carrot and broccoli farming and the uranium and coal mining that replaced it, is not included.

Crazy Weather, Crazy Growth

As the state in 2006 suffered through an early winter drought, aquifers continued to shrink, and snowpacks in the San Juan Mountains were still too thin to count. A week before Thanksgiving that year, Santa Fe Baldy and Truchas peaks, usually majestic in their white mantles, had no snow at all. A month later, however, the state had a record snowfall and then lapsed into a La Niña drought as the spring of 2007 approached. Weather watchers consider the 1990s and early twenty-first century drought to be comparable to the bad dry spells in the 1950s and the 1970s. Drought usually inhibits population growth. But New Mexico has experienced a steady climb in birthrate and in-migration from all of the United States and Mexico since the end of World War II. In times of scarcity, especially drought, most species, of course, cut back in population expansion. But New Mexico's human population spiraled upward through wet and dry spells.

New Mexico's aquifers are becoming stressed, especially around big cities. They are virtually nonrenewable resources to begin with, being used up much faster than they are replenished by runoff and other marginal sources. And in drought years, the recharge is a trickle. For the last fifty years or so, however, water here has been used with abandon. A uranium mine proposed in 2006 for the slopes of Mount Taylor west of Albuquerque, according to some experts, could use seven million gallons of water a day. Intel, the largest computer chip manufacturer in the world, uses some six million gallons of water a day to clean its products at its massive Rio Rancho plant in Sandoval County, just west of Albuquerque, on the bluffs above the river village of Corrales. Intel's water comes from the Middle Rio Grande aquifer under Albuquerque, Corrales, and Rio Rancho. The company estimates that around 75 percent of that water is cleaned by reverse osmosis, becoming as pure as distilled water by the time it's sent through the sewer system to the city of Albuquerque's waste treatment plant in the South Valley and then discharged into the Rio Grande. In 1985, the fastest of the city of Albuquerque's ninety water wells could pump 3,000 gallons a minute. The city itself had a pumping capacity of 220 million gallons per day. Intel uses 3.5 percent of that capacity.

The drought that all but wrecked the municipal water supplies of Santa Fe and Las Vegas, New Mexico, in the 1990s and early twenty-first century was brought on as much by population growth due to immigration and by a general ignorance of where water comes from and how much we have as by the vagaries of weather. By the late 1990s, Albuquerque's pumping capacity had jumped to 300 million gallons a day. At that rate, you'd think Albuquerque and surrounding towns were sitting on top of an underground Lake Superior. And that's what city boosters believed for years. When the city finally bothered to check to see how fast the water table was sinking and estimate in a realistic way how much water was actually in the aquifer, the findings were alarming. Not only was there no lake under the city, USGS scientists told us, but massive pumping was about to cause certain parts of the city to subside.

Despite the USGS findings, widely distributed in 2002, developers were still planning for huge tracts of housing. Up to seventy thousand people were expected to settle near the Rio Puerco, with its brackish aquifer west of the city, and perhaps that many on the old Westland property to the east of the Puerco running all the way to the Rio Grande, owned by a California developer, SunCal, formerly owned by Atrisco Land Grant heirs. In 2006, Belen annexed a large portion of land around Los Chavez, south of Los Lunas, for a new development called Rancho Cielo that might be as large as that on the Rio Puerco. That same year, the long-awaited Mesa Del Sol, a master planned residential and industrial complex just south of the Albuquerque airport, was gearing up for its first housing starts, which might attract as many as a hundred thousand people. Where was all the water going to come from for all those new people? It's a question no major newspaper or politician was asking. And these new developments are in addition to the projected growth of Rio Rancho. But the recession of 2008–11 in New Mexico changed all that.

Gambling the Aquifer Away

To look at the topography of the Middle Rio Grande Valley, you wouldn't think there could be any water under it. Sand hills and bluffs line both sides of the river, which even in wet years is greened only by a very thin line of cottonwood, Russian olive, willow, and tamarisk bosque, with modest farmlands in the old floodplain east of the river. The Rio Grande, the second-longest river in the country, stretches some nineteen hundred miles from the San Juan Mountains to the Gulf of Mexico. In the middle valley, it didn't cut a bed for itself, but rather filled a massive fifteen- to twenty-mile-long depression caused by the uplift of the Sandia and Manzano mountains millions of years ago. Used for a least a thousand years by early Pueblo and then Hispanic farmers, the floodplain of the river could be as much as a mile wide before it was leveed and controlled in the early 1930s by more than twelve hundred miles of irrigation and drainage ditches. But even leveeing the river didn't prevent massive flooding in towns all up and down the floodplain in wet years. Nowadays, the Rio Grande is frequently dry and reduced to a trickle, so much is used.

Both the Pueblos of New Mexico and the latecoming Navajo and Apache were masterful managers of water. Without their sensitivity to the landscape and its relationship to the weather, neither nomads nor village dwellers would have survived the harsh climate of the high desert Southwest. Regardless of the useless disputes over whether pre-Conquest Native Americans had a highly developed ecological awareness and conservation ethic, their millennium-long ingenuity with water defies doubt. They have survived. The necessities of efficient and sustainable uses of water inspired them to develop a series of strategies that hold true today. They allowed the landscape and the climate to tell them where and what to build.[5] Ancestral Puebloan peoples often cultivated huge areas, but all on a small scale, with multiple crop types and redundant planting to ensure some crop survival. They used waffle gardens, flood field and arroyo bench farming, sand orchards, wild plant cultivation, and multiple kinds of mulching, with fields located virtually everywhere water was.[6] In the nineteenth century, large pueblos such as Zuni were known to plant ten thousand acres in corn, using Pueblo water management techniques.

The most prolific parts of the Middle Rio Grande aquifer, which is still recharged to some degree by the river, are in southeast Albuquerque near Eubank Boulevard and Central Avenue, and on the West Side of the city in the Ladera area. Calculations show that an enormous cone of depression has been sinking in the aquifer in the Eubank area for years, creating an underground vortex that draws water slowly north from the South Valley. This means that plumes of Superfund site pollution are entering both the shallow and the deeper aquifer.[7] A similar cone of depression was discovered in 2002 in the Buckman well area west of Santa Fe and across the Rio Grande from the canyons that drain the Los Alamos National Laboratories. Forty percent of Santa Fe's water comes from those wells, and the vortex from the pumping is so powerful, a LANL study showed, that groundwater around Los Alamos was being sucked under the Rio Grande and up into the Buckman wells. Rivers, it turned out, were not barriers to pollution, which was plentiful around Los Alamos.[8]

Like El Paso and Juarez, Albuquerque depended entirely on its aquifer for drinking water as late as 2008. The city pumped so much water from the aquifer that water was sucked down from Sandia and Santa Ana pueblos to the cone of depression in the southeast heights, an inadvertent continuation of centuries of appropriation of Native American waters.

Water Wars

Drawing water across political barriers is dicey, too. Texas and New Mexico got into a legal donnybrook in 1980 when the Public Service Board of El Paso, Texas, filed suit alleging New Mexico's law against exporting groundwater across state borders violated the interstate commerce provisions of the U.S. Constitution. At issue was water in two aquifers—or bolsons, as they say in the south—the Mesilla and Hueco, which stretch into Texas from New Mexico. El Paso wanted to drill into New Mexico's deeper portions of the bolsons. A protracted struggle in federal court ended in 1983, when a U.S. district judge ruled that the economy of the region, including southern New Mexico, could best be served if fast-growing El Paso was allowed the water.[9] It was a highly controversial decision, much at odds with what New Mexico saw as its own best interests. Eventually, the New Mexico state engineer at the time, Steve Reynolds, made licensing for wells in the area so problematic that El Paso was never allowed to drill for water on New Mexico soil. Subsequent interstate agreements led New Mexico to start developing nineteen regional water plans in 2003, producing a state water plan that would, at some point, incorporate the regional plans. As of 2004, El Paso and Juarez, Mexico, with a combined population of more than 3.5 million, depended on both the Huego and the Mesilla bolsons for their drinking water. But New Mexico and Texas are still parlaying over old and new disputes at the Texas–New Mexico Water Commission. Relations among water users along the Texas–New Mexico border, which had been tense for years, grew even more complex in 1966 when Texas and New Mexico joined to sue Colorado for an alleged one million acre-feet of water undelivered to New Mexico, which resulted in some five hundred thousand acre-feet undelivered to Texas. The Rio Grande Compact among Colorado, New Mexico, and Texas almost fell apart. Colorado's water debt was canceled, according to compact agreements, when the Elephant Butte and Caballo reservoirs were full. After many wet years, both were at capacity in 1985. But New Mexico was still left with its heavy water responsibilities to Texas. In dry years, it's estimated that the state might be as much as eighty thousand acre-feet short on its bargain.

Water and the Constitution

Water administration in New Mexico has constitutional authority. Article XVI of the state constitution delineates "Irrigation and Water Rights," confirming all existing water rights for "useful or beneficial purpose." "Priority of appropriation [of water] shall give the better right."[10] On those few phrases hangs a history of water disputes that have pitted Pueblo, Navajo, and Hispanic farmers, with their traditional rural cultures, against the advances of urban, industrial-based society. As the New Mexico state engineer explains on his website, "Priority administration refers to the temporary curtailment of junior water rights in times of shortage, so that more senior water rights can be served by the available water supply." Making a "priority call" and shutting down junior water right use "should be a measure of last resort," the state engineer affirms. Only the waters of the Cimarron River and Costilla Creek in northern New Mexico were under a priority call at the turn of this century. It's generally agreed that senior water rights are held by Native Americans, acequias, and agricultural water users, while manufacturers and urban and recreational users have junior water rights.

Native American Water Rights

Issues of water priority never go away in the arid West. In 2006, two major longstanding priority lawsuits were resolved, and in a third case, a pueblo and a small mountain town contested the water rights of rapidly growing Rio Rancho. In 2004, the Keresan pueblo of Zia challenged the city of Rio Rancho's efforts to buy water rights from farmers in the village of San Ysidro, less than ten miles away from the pueblo at the foot of the Jemez Mountains. Both Zia, a conservative pueblo with a full ritual life and severe water conservation practices, and San Ysidro are located near U.S. Highway 550, as is Rio Rancho some fifteen miles southwest. Zia and farmers along the Rio Jemez, which feeds San Ysidro and Jemez Pueblo in the canyon as well, had been struggling since 1983 to agree among themselves to bear a common burden of water rationing in times of scarcity. They came to a historic agreement in 1996. But ten years later, newcomer Rio Rancho, having outgrown its existing water rights, cast its eye north to the Jemez. All parties agree that Zia and the other farming communities in the Rio Jemez Basin have priority water rights over Rio Rancho. But Rio Rancho's size, its economic clout, and its political aggressiveness give it a strong hand to play in the dispute. The pueblo of Zia, as of this writing, had filed a protest blocking Rio Rancho's water grab, claiming its agreement with the other farming communities has legal authority. If Rio Rancho wins this dispute and buys the agricultural water rights, irrigation along the Rio Jemez will be diminished, with potentially disastrous results to Zia, which needs the current full flow of the river for farming.[11]

In another water struggle involving Native American priority rights and the needs of big cities, the Navajo Nation has agreed to the language in a bill amending the Colorado River Storage Project Act of 1956, introduced to Congress in December 2006 by New Mexico representative Tom Udall and New Mexico senator Jeff Bingaman. As pre-Conquest irrigators, the Navajo claimed priority rights to the entire San Juan River, which runs through and adjacent to their reservation in New Mexico. Their claim threatened the San Juan–Chama Diversion Project, which was to disperse Colorado River waters, including some forty-eight thousand acre-feet of water a year to Albuquerque and smaller amounts to Santa Fe, Española, Los Alamos, Taos, Los Lunas, and other areas. The dispute was settled when the Bingaman-Udall bill mandated "such sums as are necessary" to get the Navajo-Gallup Pipeline Project (known in the bill as the Northwestern New Mexico Rural Water Supply Project) up and running, piping San Juan River water to Gallup via the Navajo Reservation and averting crisis as the city's groundwater is all but used up. Failing the passage of the Bingaman-Udall bill, the Navajo Nation could shut down the San Juan–Chama Project indefinitely as it pursues its senior water rights through the courts.[12]

Another major breakthrough agreement involving senior Native American water rights also depended on federal funding to be activated at this writing. In 2006, the Aamodt water dispute, named for the first of some twenty-five hundred parties in the federal suit, R. Lee Aamodt, was finally settled after more than forty years of litigation. Hailed as a "precedent-setting compromise,"[13] the deal calls for the federal government to finance new waterworks for the farmers along the Rio Pojoaque north of Santa Fe. Congress appropriated $56 million in December 2010 to make the agreement a reality.

The Aamodt suit was brought in 1966 by the state of New Mexico during the land grant struggles in northern New Mexico. The suit reflected the state's early water history involving parties who all thought they had legitimate claims to senior water rights, including Pojoaque, San Ildefonso, Nambé, and Tesuque pueblos; Hispanic acequia users who had been farming in the Pojoaque Valley for nearly two hundred years; and numerous non-Hispanic agricultural users.

The suit was prompted by fears of the pueblos making a priority call on area waters in dry years, leaving other users with nothing. It was the first major adjudication of Pueblo water rights in New Mexico since 1908, when the U.S. Supreme Court in *Winters v. United States* declared that Native American water rights were rooted in their ancient history and came with them when the U.S. government created reservations for the tribes.

As water lawyer Jane Marx writes in *Water Law Issues in New Mexico*, "What remains abundantly clear is that tribes are entitled to water in amounts sufficient to support their communities in perpetuity."[14] The Aamodt suit, however, was complicated by a subtle distinction in a ruling by U.S. District Judge Edwin Mechem in 1985. Mechem concluded that, while the Winters Doctrine applied to the pueblos, it was not the exclusive precedent governing pueblo water rights, as pueblos were not reservations created by the U.S. government but rather land grants from Spain and Mexico, and as such were protected under the 1848 Treaty of Guadalupe Hidalgo. While Pueblo water rights are protected, the amounts they may use, Mechem ruled, must be determined by the acreage under irrigation from 1846 to 1924, as stipulated in the 1924 Pueblo Lands Act. In 1995, however, the Tenth Circuit Court of Appeals complicated matters further by inadvertently endorsing the viability of the Winters Doctrine for quantifying Pueblo water rights, leaving a "cloud of uncertainty."[15] If the federal government refuses to fund the water infrastructure necessary to enact the historic compromise of 2006, in which all users agreed to share scarcity, and the pueblos vowed not to engage in priority call power plays, then the whole tangled mess of Aamodt will go back to federal courts. Early in 2006, New Mexico governor Bill Richardson vetoed, with no explanation, a $75 million state appropriation to implement the Aamodt agreement.

Isleta and Taos Sacred Waters

Although water quantity, not quality, is the major focus of this chapter, a clean water case involving the city of Albuquerque and Isleta Pueblo is relevant. It exemplifies the pueblos' astute handling of their senior water rights and their aggressive approach to environmental legislation. And this holds true for both casino pueblos like Isleta and noncasino pueblos like Zia. In 1992, the city of Albuquerque sued the EPA in federal court after the agency had given approval to the pueblo of Isleta's clean water standards, which were higher than the state of New Mexico's and which Albuquerque did not meet. Isleta is located some five miles south of the city's waste treatment plant on a slight rise in the old floodplain of the Rio Grande. To avoid using Albuquerque's treated wastewater, the Pueblo made its purity standards drastically more stringent. One reason Isleta gave for imposing the higher standards had to do with its ritual and religious use of Rio Grande waters.

The city of Albuquerque, the Goliath in the Middle Rio Grande Valley, seemed offended that a pueblo of some forty-five hundred members would dare challenge the cleanliness standards of a city of nearly half a million. It lost the challenge to Isleta and the EPA and took its case to the Tenth Circuit Court of Appeals. The city's most interesting arguments had to do with the "rationality" of the Pueblo's assertion that water from the waste treatment plant dumped into the Rio Grande must be pure for ritual use. The city contended that the claim of religious usage went counter to the Establishment Clause of the First Amendment in that it required Albuquerque city government to aid in the establishment of a religion. The appeals court threw out Albuquerque's arguments and allowed the EPA's approval of Isleta's standards. The court argued that as long as governmental action didn't foster "excessive entanglement with religion," it did not counter the First Amendment. This suit brought by the city edges toward a subtle kind of environmental discrimination, which I'll deal with more fully in another chapter. But why should any community, especially one in which religion plays a vital role, not have the right to question the cleanliness of water discharged from a waste treatment plant immediately upstream?

Religious contingencies in water conflicts are not uncommon in New Mexico. At almost the same time as the settlement of the Aamodt case, Taos Pueblo joined with the Taos Valley Acequia Association, comprising seven thousand irrigators, and with other non-Pueblo water users in the Taos and Arroyo Hondo water systems, in an agreement ending thirty-five years of legal battles over water rights in the area. The Pueblo agreed not to make priority calls in times of scarcity in return for the preservation of its sacred wetlands and the watershed known as the Buffalo Pasture. One of the most famous water cases in New Mexico history also involved waters sacred to the Taos Pueblo. Taos Blue Lake and its watershed in a forested valley in the Sangre de Cristo mountains was scooped up by the federal government into what would become the Carson National Forest in 1906. It took sixty-four years for the Pueblo to get it back. Blue Lake, the source of the Rio Pueblo de Taos, which intersects the pueblo, is the most sacred site in Taos Pueblo cosmology, its place of emergence into this world. The U.S. Forest Service not only took Taos Pueblo's ancient title to the land, but turned it into a multiple-use area, to be used by skiers, hikers, loggers, grazers, and miners. It was the ultimate insult. One Taos elder said, "If our land is not returned to us, if it is turned over to the government for its use, then it is the end of Indian life. Our people will scatter. . . . It is our religion that holds us together."[16] In 1970, with the endorsement of President Nixon, the Senate Subcommittee on Indian Affairs deeded to Taos 48,000 acres of the forest, including Blue Lake, and exclusive use of 1,640 acres around the lake. This was the first Indian land ever returned by the federal government.

William Gonzales and Ginny Johnson in their blossoming orchard in the valley of San Agustin, which lies southeast of Las Vegas and is irrigated by the Gallinas River. The village church can be seen across their garden. April 2008.

San Agustin church. April 2008.

William and Ginny's house in San Agustin. April 2008.

It is not uncommon to see road signs used for water control in the acequias; here William uses one of his old campaign signs. April 2008.

William on his "new" tractor attempting to fix a leak between two segments of culvert under a dirt bridge over the ditch. May 2008.

The village of San Agustin. The San Agustin community ditch has seven active members who water alfalfa, garden orchards, and livestock, though they no longer live in the community full time. May 2008.

Ditch day in Guadalupita, near Mora. March 2009.

Booster pump station at the Buckman well field outside Santa Fe. February 2007.

The Rio Grande at the end of Old Buckman Road outside Santa Fe. February 2007.

View over an irrigation ditch of land being plowed near Tomé. March 2007.

Peralta Ditch, the acequia madre, Tomé. March 2007.

Flood irrigation in Tomé. Upon the first watering of the season, a farmer notes the high spots in the land and shunts the water to those areas when he or she floods again. May 2007.

No Winners, No Losers

Local water disputes in New Mexico are complicated enough, but when interstate compacts are involved, their agreements supersede local laws and customs, and crisis often ensues. When it comes to water, there can be no winners and losers. We all need water. Not to have it is a calamity, and the appropriation of water amounts to an act of violence. The political realities of New Mexico don't permit priority calls, even if such calls are legal. The state's ethnic and cultural heterogeneity and the resulting complexity in the makeup of its legislature have created a political culture of negotiation unique to the state. No group or region has a consistent upper hand in the legislature, neither rural nor urban forces, not ranchers, farmers, miners, loggers, neither Hispanics, Native Americans, nor Anglos, neither the north nor the south, neither commercial nor environmental interests. There's always a shifting balance among these competing economies and worldviews. We can see this balancing act most clearly in struggles over water in general, and specifically in the convoluted legal battle between Texas and New Mexico over the waters of the Rio Pecos, beautifully described in University of New Mexico law professor Em Hall's book *High and Dry*, a fascinating account of the political tradeoffs, engineering and statistical conflicts, and rowdy politics involved in this protracted legal conflict, which New Mexico eventually lost.

Texas versus New Mexico

In 1974, Texas took New Mexico to the U.S. Supreme Court, charging that "upstream New Mexico had deprived downstream Texas of more than 1,000,000 acre-feet of Pecos River water"[17] and was defaulting on the compact with Texas negotiated nearly twenty-five years earlier. A million acre-feet of water, Hall points out, is "five to ten times more water than the whole Pecos River usually carried in a year." And Texas wanted a fantastic amount of money, almost a billion dollars, in compensation. Over the next dozen years, that sum was whittled away to $14 million as it was agreed that New Mexico owed Texas 344,000 acre-feet. In 1990, New Mexico was required to follow a Supreme Court–mandated procedure for supplying, on average, some 10,000 acre-feet of extra water to Texas, with spikes some years as high as 30,000 acre-feet. But where was all this water going to come from, given New Mexico's water law based on "priority appropriation," historical first users getting available water first? The answer shows the complexity of New Mexico water law, which is both politically volatile and as slow moving as cold lava.

Steve Reynolds, the state engineer at the time and New Mexico's most famous and influential water czar, moved aggressively to meet the Supreme Court's demand, even though, as Hall quotes him, he remained "convinced that New Mexico never failed to meet her Compact obligation."[18] The complications involved the Supreme Court blaming junior water wells used by irrigators in the Roswell area and a ticklish, long-term dispute between Roswell and the Carlsbad Irrigation District, almost at the Texas border, which some alleged was keeping back waters meant for Texas to take care of its own needs. To come up with an additional 10,000 acre-feet of water, or some forty billion gallons, Reynolds's first solution was to do what he had always done, according to Hall, to avoid making priority calls.

He wanted to replace diminishing surface water with groundwater, this time by drilling a $20 million to $30 million "super well field" near Roswell and pumping the water into the Pecos. But in 1979, the New Mexico State Legislature turned down funds for Reynolds's well field request and bowed to the Supreme Court, paying Texas its $14 million. The state wanted to explore other, less expensive options, like moving water from other basins into the Pecos, mandating conservation measures, retiring water rights, sending the unused water to Texas, and, if all else failed, making priority calls, which the present state engineer, John D'Antonio, described as a "draconian measure," in which those with historically junior water rights will have their water "shut off."[19]

What followed was years of acrimony between southern New Mexico and northern New Mexico legislators and interests, between farming interests in Roswell and Carlsbad, and between New Mexico and Texas. Eventually New Mexico appropriated funds to begin buying water rights along the Pecos and set conservation measures in place. No priority calls were made. From 1987 to 1999, New Mexico had actually accumulated 22,800 acre-feet in "overage" sent to Texas, despite the disastrous drought years of 1990, 1991, and 1995, in which New Mexico was more than 44,000 acre-feet short of its compact goal. "If the figures show anything, they show that New Mexico is doing okay with a compact obligation that's arbitrary and unpredictable," Em Hall wrote.[20] But by January 2007, after seven years of worsening drought, State Engineer D'Antonio told *Santa Fe New Mexican* reporter Staci Matlock that the "state has a window of opportunity to manage its water better. . . . If it doesn't, it faces a federal takeover of water management on the Pecos River and the Rio Grande."[21] That window of opportunity was what Governor Bill Richardson had designated as the Year of Water in 2007.

Food and Water

As the 2007 Year of Water began, the old patterns of New Mexico politics seemed to fuse with water issues. Rural legislators went against urban and commercial interests, and northern acequias and southern irrigation districts eyed each other with mistrust. But the year before had seen a major revolution in water cooperation among Pueblos,

Navajos, acequia users, and other farmers that set the tone for what was sure to be an ongoing struggle between expanding cities that desperately needed to buy up agricultural water rights and the prime targets of their interests—the agricultural owners of senior rights.

The conflict between urban developers and farmers was given another, much sharper focus after Christmas in 2006, when the state experienced a record-breaking snowstorm that closed both I-40 and I-25 off and on for five days. The snow piled up some eighteen inches in Albuquerque's northeast heights and nearly four feet in the Pecos watershed north of Glorieta Mesa between Santa Fe and Las Vegas, New Mexico. The upshot of the storm was a slowly dawning realization that New Mexico grocery stores usually have only a week's supply of food, according to the New Mexico Grocers Association.[22] A prolonged loss of trucking services due to bad weather, flu quarantines, or any other reason would be a disaster. In a report from the New Mexico Climate Change Advisory Group at the beginning of 2007, it was revealed, according to *Santa Fe New Mexican* reporter Wendy Brown, that "only 3 percent of the state's food is produced locally," and much of that is dairy products.[23] How much sense does it make to take water away from local farmers when what New Mexico needs is more locally grown food, not more imported people?

Such logic is not lost on the New Mexico Acequia Association (NMAA) and its executive director, Paula Garcia. While many acequia farmers are living on the economic margins, they are far better off in a crisis than middle-class and well-to-do urbanites who depend on the trucking industry to haul in their food. At least acequia farmers would have some food on the table in times of disaster. Should the economy ever get savvy about potential food shortages, acequia farmers and other agricultural water users would lead a renewal in the local growing of produce. As the record storm of 2006 showed us, this is not merely a romantic notion of the virtues of rural life. Local food could provide the margin of survival for many.

In addressing the Year of Water, Garcia put food and water in context, writing:

> Since virtually all the water in New Mexico is appropriated, new uses of water have to come from the transfer of water rights from an existing use. A prevailing assumption is that water for

new uses will come from agriculture. Acequias and agricultural communities are economically disadvantaged and are likely to experience a net loss of water rights from the communities as wealthier individuals, entities, and regions acquire water rights from a position of greater economic power. From the standpoint of social justice, state policy makers should be mindful that these rural communities will need a secure water rights supply for their growth and development, including revitalization of agriculture. Increasingly, our finite water and farmland will be crucial in meeting the growing demand for locally grown food. New Mexico would be well served by water policies that recognize the diverse values embodied in water as opposed to allowing the value of water to be determined by the highest bidder.[24]

Few people are more eloquent and insightful than Garcia when it comes to assessing the overall scope of New Mexico's water issues. "The current struggle over water in New Mexico is between two world views. In one, water is considered a community resource, and the sharing of water and agricultural traditions are vital to the survival of land-based culture and communities. In the other, water is considered a private property right to be bought and sold in a water market in which the value of water is determined with a narrow economic definition," she wrote in a piece called "Community and Culture versus Commodification" in the Winter 2000 edition of *Voices from the Earth*, published by the environmental think tank Southwest Research and Information Center in Albuquerque.[25]

Private and Public Waters

As if to make Garcia's point more clearly, an urban fight in Albuquerque between privatized and public water management was shaping up for a showdown in 2007 as well, and it found Albuquerque and Bernalillo County on the same side of the issue as Rio Rancho in Sandoval County. The seeds of the dispute between the Albuquerque Bernalillo County Water Utility Authority (ABCWUA) and a California-owned company, New Mexico Utilities Inc. (NMUI), were sown back in the days when Albuquerque's leadership thought the aquifer would supply its needs forever and support endless expansion. In 1973, the

Albuquerque City Commission cut a deal with NMUI to supply water and sewer services to Paradise Hills, then a burgeoning development on the city's western mesa. At the start, NMUI had some eight hundred hook-ups. But by 2007, it was serving nearly fifty-three thousand people and competing with Rio Rancho for agricultural water rights, while taking much more from the Middle Rio Grande aquifer than was ever anticipated. The deal made in 1973 became obsolete when the USGS analyzed Albuquerque's aquifer for the first time in the early 1990s and found it to be anything but a bottomless lake. When the big drought hit in the late 1990s, the ABCWUA accused NMUI of having no conservation program in place, of not having enough water rights for the water it used, and of doubling its water use in ten years, while Albuquerque was reducing its own use by 30 percent. The city also raised NMUI's sewer rates dramatically. The dispute ended up in the courts with multiple suits and countersuits. The city-county water authority tried to buy NMUI, but its California ownership, Southwest Water, didn't want to sell, so ABCWUA threatened to exercise its power of eminent domain and pay a fair market price of $37 million.

Lurking behind such legal machinations were the ongoing depredations of drought and the strain New Mexico's growing population was putting on the whole state's water supply, including its dwindling aquifers. What was needed was a streamlining of water management, not a proliferation of water jurisdictions. There simply wasn't enough water. It was hard enough for acequia farmers to fend off public water predators, like cities that use water as a growth device. Who needed an out-of-state private company making millions selling New Mexico water to New Mexicans?

Eminent Condemnation

A further complication surfaced at the turn of the century. In threatening to condemn NMUI, the city-county water authority might use the same power of eminent domain that gives it, according to the Metropolitan Redevelopment Act, the right to condemn and take anyone's water rights within and beyond its jurisdiction. But the concept of eminent domain came under attack in the 2007 legislature, part of a nationwide backlash against the U.S. Supreme Court's highly controversial 2005 opinion in *Kelo v. New London*. In *Kelo*, the court allowed a municipality to condemn the private property of home-owners in a nonslum area so a large private corporation could engage in a massive and highly profitable redevelopment project. Applied to water, such a scenario in New Mexico—a big city condemning, let's say, private agricultural water rights in a particular basin—could be a disaster for the state farming communities.

In 2007, a bipartisan effort in the New Mexico State Legislature aimed to remove eminent domain from the Metropolitan Redevelopment Code of 1978, which allowed municipalities to condemn any property within five miles of its boundaries, including such property as water rights and waterworks. In the *Kelo* decision, Justice Sandra Day O'Connor remarked, in dissent, that the specter of condemnation hangs over all property. "She was absolutely correct, and that property includes water rights," said Janet Jarrett, an independent water researcher and rural advocate, who served as president of the New Mexico Water Assembly in the mid-2000s. In a speech to the annual congress of the New Mexico Acequia Association in December 2006, Jarrett said that "in the state of New Mexico, water rights are private property, and they are explicitly subject to taking under eminent domain."[26]

Jarrett maintained:

> As demands increase and water becomes ever more scarce, we could face a free-for-all of water takings. . . . Given their present statutory power, municipalities would trump all other interests with their vast jurisdiction, assuming the upper hand over interstate compacts, smaller towns, agriculture, the environment, and historic and cultural water uses. Such takings would also complicate tribal water issues, since the very fluidity of water ensures there will be no isolated impacts. Municipal power of condemnation means that water used miles outside a city's boundaries can be commandeered for use *within* its boundaries, gutting the ability of counties and neighboring entities to pursue their own economic development, or follow the vision of their residents. Such supremacy effectively moots all water and land use planning, both regionally and statewide.[27]

It would have been entirely possible for such a condemnation to be issued by the Albuquerque Bernalillo County Water Utility Authority, if eminent domain over water had not been eliminated from the law by a unanimous decision in both houses of the New Mexico legislature in 2008. In the end, virtually every senior water rights holder in the state—including rural conservation districts, Pueblos, Navajos, acequia associations, and other farming and ranching interests—opposed condemnation. Only the Municipal League in New Mexico supported it.

With its population growing all the time, its aquifer shrinking, and snowpacks in Colorado on a steadily downward trajectory, Albuquerque is in serious water trouble. And its water math seems to be skewed toward delusion. Albuquerque draws down some 110,000 acre-feet a year from the Middle Rio Grande aquifer. The city has an annual recharge deficit that's estimated, interestingly, at the same amount: 110,000 acre-feet. City officials have been selling the use of 48,000 acre-feet of San Juan–Chama river water as a way to save the aquifer. But if Albuquerqueans drink up 48,000 acre-feet of river water, they'd still be pulling out more than 62,000 acre-feet of groundwater a year. If the city continues to grow at the same rate, where do you think the new water will come from? Not the Colorado River, that's for sure, with its historic eleven-year drought and every big city in the West drinking from it.

Albuquerque also charges its customers an astonishingly cheap price per gallon of water. Albuquerque's water users pay some 60 percent less than Santa Fe's. Both Santa Fe and Las Vegas, New Mexico, have been forced to ration water for close to a decade, but Albuquerque has chosen to ignore that lesson, close its eyes, and say, "It can't happen here." In 2004, Albuquerqueans used about 165 gallons per person a day, while citizens in Santa Fe were down to 125 gallons, Las Vegas at 90 gallons, and Silver City at 135 gallons.[28] It's not just that Albuquerque and surrounding communities have kept growing at a record pace or that Intel is using a lot of water, it's that Albuquerque has always been a boomtown, and it isn't about to stop just because of water—until, of course, the city starts pumping sand. Real estate is Albuquerque's biggest business. Housing's more politically powerful than water, as long as there is any. As water researcher Consuelo Bokum says, "If ever there was an argument for taking the public welfare into account" when it comes to allocating water, "it's in Albuquerque. The highest and best use of water has historically been defined as who has the most money, and anyone else be damned."[29]

Quantity Without Quality Equals Trouble

As the drought in New Mexico wore on through the turn of the twenty-first century, the New Mexico First town hall on water took place in arid Socorro in May 2002. A probusiness group founded by New Mexico senators Pete Domenici and Jeff Bingaman in 1986, New Mexico First's water town hall did a commendable job of laying out major business issues. Its executive summary acknowledged that New Mexico's water supply "is finite and highly variable" and "in many areas . . . is not sustainable given present use levels, much less future needs."[30] It called for the adjudication of all water rights in the state by 2018, for the creation of a state water plan by 2004, and for the state to "aggressively develop, preserve, and protect New Mexico's water resources" by, among other means, "developing technology in evaporation, sensor technology, real-time data collection, desalinization, reinjection, watershed rehabilitation, and weather modification."[31] Glaringly absent from the water town hall's deliberations was any mention of water quality and the pollution that is known to exist and threaten portions of the state's drinking supplies. No mention was made of leaking underground gasoline storage tanks in gas stations or of uncharted, but thought to be considerable, contamination from septic tanks, and no mention at all was made of Superfund sites around the state nor the quality of river water that residents of the Middle Rio Grande Valley were on their way to drinking by late 2008. New Mexico has seventeen Superfund sites. The Middle Rio Grande Valley's three sites have already contaminated the aquifer with plumes of toxins of various sorts. And, of course, no mention would ever be made by a mainstream group like New Mexico First of the dark secret of military-industrial complex wastes around Los Alamos and in Albuquerque's Kirtland Air Force Base and Sandia National Laboratories. But anecdotal, circumstantial, and much solid evidence abounds about such pollution.

We do know for sure that with runoff from oil and gas pumping in Colorado draining into tributaries that feed the Colorado River and the San Juan, river water and the groundwater it feeds may already be more polluted than anyone recognizes. In August 2004, the *Albuquerque Journal* reported that some 45 acres out of 113 acres of cottonwood bosque around the River's Edge development in Rio

Rancho was dying off. What a U.S. Fish and Wildlife Service hydrologist called "mortality in the bosque" was thought to be the result of groundwater contamination. Test wells in the area showed higher-than-normal levels of chloride, ammonia, uranium, lithium, strontium, boron, and other substances.[32] To my knowledge, there's been no other reporting on the subject.

Drinking Water Project: Hoax or Saviour?

The quality of metro Albuquerque and Rio Rancho's groundwater, along with the safety of river water, plays a major unspoken role in what's come to be called the Albuquerque Drinking Water Project, which relies on forty-eight thousand acre-feet of water a year diverted from the Rio Grande. Sold by Albuquerque Mayor Martin Chavez as the salvation to Albuquerque's water problems, the project was presented glowingly by the local media with little attention to a lawsuit that questioned the very validity and safety of the project. Brought by a coalition of irrigators, rate payers of the Middle Rio Grande Conservancy District, and environmentalists, the suit claimed that the drinking water project, which diverts San Juan–Chama water already flowing through the river, "plus an equal amount of native flow to transport it through the municipal distribution system," is "detrimental to existing water rights and public welfare," according to Lisa Robert, author and editor of *APA Watermark*, the conservancy's Assessment Payers Association newsletter.[33]

The protest coalition, as it called itself, opposed the drinking water project on the grounds, Robert wrote, "that it will impact vested water rights, riparian health, and groundwater levels in the Albuquerque reach, and that it could jeopardize New Mexico's ability to meet its Rio Grande Compact obligations. At issue in all instances is the debt to the Albuquerque basin aquifer created by past pumping."[34]

When Albuquerque originally contracted for San Juan–Chama water in the late 1960s, it was "to offset the effects of municipal groundwater pumping on the river,"[35] Robert observed. The "transbasin supply [from the San Juan to the Rio Grande] has actually been supplementing both the river and the aquifer all along. A 2003 study performed for the Interstate Stream Commission . . . confirms that groundwater in the middle basin is moving *away* from the river and *toward* cones of depression caused by municipal pumping. Also undisputed is the fact that the river, which for more than three decades has consisted of a blend of Rio Grande and San Juan–Chama water, is leaking to the tune of some seventy-five thousand acre-feet a year in the Albuquerque reach."[36]

Robert explains the logic of the coalition protest by saying, "The city's existing groundwater permit requires the use of municipal [San Juan–Chama] water as an offset of the residual effects of past, present, and future pumping. However, the new *diversion* permit designates that same water as the main supply for municipal customers, and as such, all of it will be fully consumed."[37]

The complexity of water issues in New Mexico is mirrored in this lawsuit, which as of this writing is on the docket of the New Mexico Court of Appeals. Because agricultural water diverted from the river into the conservancy district's ditches is not calculated as part of the flow of the river itself, it goes unprotected by permits and licensing. Still, it is accepted fact that "seepage from the conservancy channels and drains keeps groundwater levels constant in the Albuquerque reach," Robert says. "That means that agricultural water is being used to meet the recharge demands of the aquifer, and as with the river itself, such seepage will continue long after municipal pumping is reduced because past pumping effects cannot be immediately neutralized. . . . When the city begins to divert its full portion of San Juan–Chama water, only Rio Grande water and the annual allotments of San Juan–Chama water owned by the conservancy district, Bosque Farms, and Los Lunas will be left to feed the urban cones of depression. This can be likened to tapping the bank accounts of others to make up for one's own overdraft."[38]

Unhappily, the ABCWUA has chosen not to buy into this complexity, preferring to sell the San Juan–Chama Project with as little public debate as possible. The ABCWUA has even produced a "water conservation calendar," a kind of San Juan–Chama pinup calendar, with photographs of the engineering glories of the new water treatment plant. In the pages for the month of November 2007, the photograph of a gigantic pill-shaped white storage tank bears the caption "ROBUST: Plant Design and Construction Will Meet the Area Water Supply Demands Well into Our Future"—a questionable assertion given the rate at which ABCWUA is still pumping water out of the aquifer.[39] If the drought in the Colorado River Basin continues much past 2011, which seems likely given warming trends, a provision in the seven-state Colorado Compact of 1922 could cause New Mexico to curtail its use of San Juan–Chama water. The compact requires the "upper basin" states of New Mexico, Colorado, Utah, and Wyoming to send to the "lower basin" states of Arizona, Nevada, and California seventy-five million acre-feet of water over a ten-year period. If the upper basin can't fulfill that obligation, its four states must diminish or stop their own use until the lower basin states get all the water the compact requires.

Guzzler Numbers

In January 2002, the *Albuquerque Tribune* ran a list of the "city's biggest water users," in gallons, from January to October 2001.[40] Golf courses were near the top of the list, using from 199,938,692 gallons at the top end to around 89,000,000 at the lower end. That's in the *millions* of gallons in a ten-month period. Philips Semiconductor used 330,687,808 in the same period, but that's nothing to what I calculate Intel used at 6,000,000 gallons a day for 220 days. It comes out to a whopping 1,320,000,000—that's over one *billion* gallons. But, of course, Intel is in Sandoval County and isn't counted on the list of city water users. Even though city residents brought their water usage down to 165 gallons a day per person in 2006, that's still 60,225 gallons per person a year. At a half-million people, more or less, that's 30 billion plus gallons a year.

Can we believe these numbers? Trying to get official sources to reveal real numbers that tell the truth about how much water is used and how much water we have is not easy. Numbers and logic get tossed around like so much confetti. Some of the strangest concoctions have come from Albuquerque's progrowth mayor, Martin Chavez. In 2003, he told *Albuquerque Tribune* reporter Frank Zoretich that after 1993, when the aquifer was shown to be tiny in comparison to the old stories of an underground lake, "A lot of people said, 'Let's stop growing.' But it's really not a growth issue."[41] Then the confetti started flying. If the city continues to grow at its current rate, the mayor said, then the aquifer has enough water left for twenty-five years, and with no growth at all, there's thirty-five years of drinking water left in the aquifer. That's doesn't sound like something that's *not* a growth issue to me. In twenty-five years, my grandson will be thirty-seven. And if he's in Albuquerque, he'll have no water to drink, by the mayor's tally. Another Albuquerque mayor, Jim Baca, whom Chavez defeated in 2001, wrote an opinion piece in the *Albuquerque Journal* in 2000 describing the aquifer as a "drought reserve," which he defined as a "portion of the aquifer above the subsidence threshold that we are setting aside for dry years."[42] That reserve, he said, is meant to last Albuquerque ten years if the San Juan–Chama water is scarce in dry years. Baca wrote that the threshold was around 260 feet of lowered aquifer and that, in certain parts of town, the aquifer was already down 150 feet. Some subsidence already seems to be taking place. Stucco has been cracking and foundations settling, with minor consequences so far, in homes and businesses around the area.

Santa Fe and Las Vegas Droughts

Only when governments respond to shortages and try to make the water last can we believe our elected officials. And that's what's happened since 1995 in Santa Fe and Las Vegas, New Mexico. City governments have rationed water much more stringently there than in Albuquerque. Santa Fe has been spreading rapidly since the early 1990s into dry, open highland country to the north and south. In 1996, a major development south of town, Eldorado Estates, was forced to declare a moratorium on new housing starts and commercial development because of drought and low water quality in shallow wells.[43] The whole city of Santa Fe was under heavy water rationing from 1995 to 2006. Water stress was becoming so intolerable that in 2004 Santa Fe mayor Larry Delgado tried to buy seventy-five hundred acre-feet of water from the Estancia Basin, east of the Sandia Mountains, in an area of booming growth that needed the water for itself. Communities in the Estancia Basin put up a fight, and their opposition, along with the expense of piping the water uphill to Santa Fe for sixty-five miles, caused Santa Fe to back off.

Santa Fe, like Albuquerque, is hoping that its share of San Juan–Chama water, 5,605 acre-feet, will augment its aquifer pumping and other surface waters enough to keep the city modestly growing. Las Vegas, however, has no claim on San Juan–Chama water and has suffered a serious water shutdown since the mid-1990s. Some years, like 2006, Las Vegas had to go to a stage 3 water alert, in which all outdoor watering was forbidden, including watering lawns and trees in the city's historic district with its avenues of elms. In July 2006, Las Vegas experienced its first heavy rainfall in nearly five years, a torrential monsoon that the parched lawns and trees sucked up so fast, puddles were hard to find the next day. In the weeks before the storm, overheated Las Vegans felt their city succumb to a collective depression. When the rains came, the whole city's mood became buoyant overnight.

To protect the rights of downstream users, Las Vegas can draw only twenty-six hundred acre-feet a year from its primary water source, the Gallinas River, according to a 2005 decision by the New Mexico Supreme Court. Any additional water must come from its reservoir at Storey Lake, which itself has been severely depleted by drought. Even though the city enforces draconian rationing, well users in the rolling countryside to the south and east pump from the water table at will, using the unmetered wells typical of New Mexico.

Brackish Boon or Toxic Dust

Based on what amounts to vague speculation from hydrologists and politicians about the amount of brackish groundwater at deeper levels of many aquifers in the state, New Mexico towns and cities are entertaining the notion of desalinating their way out of the drought. In the September 2006 issue of *Chemical Engineering Progress*, desalinization is seen by some international companies as a major global profit center. Big companies like Dow are refining desalinization techniques, and New Mexicans and West Texans can look forward to drinking formerly salty water. A major development proposed in 2006 for the Rio Puerco, twenty miles west of Albuquerque on I-40, counts on desalinated water from the brine beneath the Puerco for its projected seventy thousand new residents. Most of the world's desalinization plants are in Israel and along the Persian Gulf, according to Water Desalinization International. Waste salt is simply dumped back into the ocean and diluted. But on dry land, especially in New Mexico with its arsenic-laced water, waste disposal poses problems similar to those of nuclear waste. Salts, combined with arsenic and other minerals, are deadly to living systems. Where do you put the mountains of poisoned waste that desalinization would bring? Do you pile it up with the potash tailings around the deep salt mines near Carlsbad?

If worst came to worst, Santa Fe, Las Vegas, and many other towns might have to resort to buying cleaned-up brackish water. That could raise the price of water by as much as 500 percent.[44] But at least remote towns like Las Vegas don't have to contend with the possibility of serious water contamination from industrial and military processes as Albuquerque, Santa Fe, and Las Cruces do. Although I'll deal with toxic waste and water pollution in detail in a later chapter, it must be said here that water planning in north, central, and southern New Mexico virtually never mentions issues of water quality. One gets the feeling that the state engineer and various municipal water czars around the state never consult with public health officials. It's such an absence of public knowledge and concern about the cleanliness of our water supply that allows oil and natural gas drillers to maintain with straight faces that drilling through the pristine freshwater aquifer of the Salt Basin under Otero Mesa will have no ill effects on the quality of that water. Drilling brings up brine and uses petroleum lubricants. Drill casings leak. And at each drill site, depending on the technology in use, one or more unlined sump pits are full of petroleum and brine debris.

The Reverse of Crying Wolf

Virtually every time any public admission is made that some radioactive isotope, toxic compound, or industrial solvent is found in the public drinking supply, it is accompanied by official assurances that the amounts are too small to be harmful or that the substance in question poses no risk to public health. A classic case in point was the appearance of cancer-causing cesium-137 leaking from Los Alamos into the Rio Grande, discovered in 2000. LANL, predictably, called the leakage "low level" and attributable to background amounts left over from nuclear weapons testing fallout in the 1950s and 1960s. But Concerned Citizens for Nuclear Safety, an independent group out of Washington state, conducted its own tests and found the cesium-137 levels were substantially higher than would be normal for mere background radiation from old fallout. It also found that over a two-year period, travel time for contaminated groundwater from LANL to the Rio Grande could be as fast as a year. A spokesperson for the group said that "leakage of cesium-137 from LANL into the Rio Grande warns the public of what is on the way. If travel times are only a few years, then it's essential that the public provide meaningful oversight of LANL's wastes now, before we're drinking them."[45]

Albuquerque's new San Juan–Chama drinking water, of course, flows down the Rio Grande past the canyons and springs that drain the Pajarito Plateau, Los Alamos, and LANL. Albuquerque has many other water quality issues, not the least of which is a hundred thousand cubic feet of radioactive and industrial waste at Sandia Labs, known as the mixed-waste landfill, that could reach Albuquerque's aquifer by 2015. And in Las Cruces, residents were assured by the EPA in 2004 that a major underground plume of contamination near the intersection of Griggs Avenue and Walnut Street contained perchloroethylene (PCE) at levels too low to be a health hazard, even from water used in swamp coolers. Is this a credible assessment? I'll explore this and related questions later in the book, but I remind the reader of a basic principle: Everything has to go somewhere. Hardly anything remains where it is unless it is contained.

Pumping Pressures

Here is one final cautionary tale about pumping too much too fast from the water table. Although the following remarks were made at the Tenth Annual Middle Rio Grande Water Assembly in 2004, they could apply to any underground water basin in the state. Jim Bartolino, a hydrologist with the U.S. Geological Survey, contends that Albuquerque civic leaders knew long before the 1990s that the city did not have an inexhaustible water supply. As early as the 1950s, he told the assembly, "some City of Albuquerque wells went dry and caught the city flat footed."

The USGS went to the Albuquerque Chamber of Commerce and "said basically that the city had gotten a notice that its bank account was overdrawn. . . . Yet even into the 1980s, we saw advertising saying Albuquerque was living over Lake Superior."

Bartolino listed four common effects of groundwater depletion, which he defined as "long-term water level declines caused by sustained groundwater pumping." As some parts of the aquifer under the city show water level declines of more than 160 feet, he said, "I think it's fair to say we're in a groundwater depletion situation." The four effects of depletion are "water well problems, reduced surface water flows, subsidence, [and] deterioration of water quality." The deeper the depletion, the deeper the wells have to be, and the more energy it costs to draw the water up. The farther down you go, the more chance you'll run into clay, from which it's next to impossible to extract water.

Before pumping, the aquifer was discharging itself into the river's surface water as an overflow mechanism. Pumping "intercepts" that water, Bartolino said, and keeps it off the surface and away from habitats and irrigation. If the surface water is a "losing stream" to begin with, that is, if it is recharging the aquifer instead of being augmented by it, pumping just makes the surface stream lose water to the aquifer faster.

Subsidence can become a major issue if the water table gets too low, causing subsurface materials to begin compacting and shrinking when dry. Although subsidence is a minor problem so far, the USGS did detect a widespread subsidence of about two and a half inches around Albuquerque and Rio Rancho using Interparametric Synthetic Aperture Radar from 1993 to 1995. Not a good sign.

The last of Bartolino's cautions concerns water quality, but not pollution from military and industrial waste. The rule of thumb is simply that "water quality declines with depth." Bartolino calls this "almost a hydrologic truism." It's possible to drill so deeply that "we can degrade the water quality in the aquifer by pulling stuff into the water table that wasn't there to begin with, or by causing changes in the water chemistry, adding from brackish, deeper waters." As of the early years of the twenty-first century, hydrologists were not sure if this had happened in parts of Albuquerque's aquifer so far.[46]

Principles and Private Wells

We end where we began, with some basic principles. First, once you start pumping groundwater, you change it, either by polluting it or by altering the quality of the sands, clays, and gravels that are its matrix. If that groundwater is potable, no change will be for the better. Once you start changing surface water flows, through damming, diverting, or pumping in the water table around it, you change everything it's connected to, including the water table. Inevitably, the results will affect plants, animals, and long-term environmental health.

The other basic principle goes back to water law. If there is less wet water than paper water, then law, custom, money, and power will clash, and the people with less power and less money will find their water rights compromised and perhaps even effectively erased.

Are there any signs of hope in this tangled struggle among natural, political, and cultural forces? Will we learn to grow in ways that won't compromise our groundwater? I find hope in the state engineer's efforts to monitor private wells. There must be thousands of them in the state, if not tens of thousands, and no one knows how much water they withdraw from their aquifers. Even though farmers in Sierra County and elsewhere are furious over the state engineer's efforts to meter their pumping and have them pay for it, without such precise knowledge of water use, no accurate statewide water planning seems possible.

Signs of Hope

Although it remains to be seen if the 2007 Year of Water was merely a rhetorical effort, it does seem that consciousness, at least, has been raised about a serious threat to the water supply from New Mexico's cities. As the Executive Summary of the Middle Rio Grande Regional Water Plan puts it, "Many groundwater users, including municipalities and industries in the Middle Rio Grande, were allowed to begin pumping without securing water rights. . . . The accumulated eventual need for groundwater users to acquire and transfer water rights is very large and exceeds the quantity of currently transferable water rights."[47] In the near future, I imagine, the legislature will require that developers, cities, and industries buy water rights before they use new water. And that is bound to cause, after the warfare has subsided, more mindful growth and conservation planning. Perhaps the most hopeful sign is the continued presence of dozens of private citizen water experts and NGOs who monitor water use in New Mexico with no ties to profit-making companies, the military, or business-oriented cities. Such groups include the Southwest Research and Information Center, Citizen Action, Concerned Citizens for Nuclear Safety, the Los Alamos Study Group, the Assessment Payers Association of the Middle Rio Grande Conservancy District, and many others. Attending virtually endless meetings, growing in sophistication with each major water battle, and working behind the scenes to craft sane and accountable legislation, citizen experts and their organizations have the depth and breadth of knowledge to see through the officious pronouncements of local and state governments.

CHAPTER THREE

ENVIRONMENTAL DISCRIMINATION
DUMPING ON THE POOR

S oil and groundwater pollution is ubiquitous but almost invisible in New Mexico, especially in areas occupied by people who are not well-to-do. Many poor people, lacking economic clout, are relatively voiceless and hence less troublesome to corporations and governments than better-heeled Americans are. In isolated and impoverished neighborhoods in Albuquerque, in mineral-rich desert lands around Native American communities in western New Mexico, in towns around military R&D operations, and in small cities in the southeastern New Mexico oil patch known as little Texas, dumping toxic waste on the lands of vulnerable people is a common practice. Mining and manufacturing companies and the military discharge carcinogenic substances into groundwater and soil, release radioactive

◄   Julio Dominguez of South Valley Partners points out a dead acequia across the railroad tracks from the GE plant. He says that these used to be irrigated lands but now they are junk lots: the water was polluted both by GE and by creosote pits used for soaking railroad ties, and the acequia was shut down. October 2006.

byproducts of uranium that leach into aquifers, and emit chemicals and soot into the air, all the while denying direct connections between pollution and disease.

The polluters who take advantage of the poor and marginalized aren't always consciously malicious. The practice is largely about money. Classical economics treats natural resources as externalities, free commodities that have no intrinsic value. If free resources like groundwater don't fit into a cost equation, creating pollution becomes part of doing business, a way to transform a cheap or free resource into a marketable commodity. If you're a corporation and can pollute without anyone knowing it, you've saved yourself a bundle. Even if you get caught, fines and cleanup costs are minimal relative to the income of many polluters. It doesn't matter which political party is in power. Discriminatory dumping goes on even during the watch of an environmentally inclined governor like Bill Richardson and even when businesses are trying to appear to do the right thing.

Pollution and Politics

The problems of environmental injustice are so entrenched in New Mexico that the 2007 legislature—despite the strong urging of Richardson, the Southwest Network for Environmental and Economic Justice, and the New Mexico Environmental Law Center—couldn't pass a House and Senate bill called the New Mexico Environmental Health Act. In its annual *Legislative Scorecard*, the nonpartisan Conservation Voters New Mexico (CVNM) addressed the bill's failure. "Unfortunately," observed CVNM, "many polluting facilities are concentrated in poor and minority neighborhoods and communities. This bill would have helped ensure that all communities, regardless of their ethnic, socioeconomic, or cultural makeup, are treated equally in decisions about where to locate pollution-causing industrial projects."[1]

In spite of the governor's good intentions, the New Mexico State Investment Council in 2007 bought more than $20 million in the stock of an ethanol refinery plant to be built near a low-income neighborhood in Clovis. Residents strenuously objected when the state granted an air quality construction permit. As Blake Prather, vice president of Concerned Citizens for Curry County, a coalition opposed to the plant, told the *Albuquerque Journal*, "It's a thing that Gov. Richardson is sitting there trying to push his environmental agenda but then at the same time he's desecrating it over here in the community where all these people live."[2] The plant was expected to discharge some 470 tons of chemicals a year into the atmosphere around Clovis, an amount of airborne debris that apparently does not violate state or federal clean air standards. The ethanol company, ConAgra, agreed to raise the plant's smokestack to 100 feet in hopes of circulating its emissions away from the neighborhood.[3] Such conflicts occur repeatedly in New Mexico, as they do all over the country. They are precisely the reason why Governor Richardson issued his 2005 environmental justice executive order in the first place.

Small victories lead to high hopes, which are often dashed. Residents of the rural Estancia Valley around Moriarty, east of Albuquerque, fought the building of a biomass power plant in their area in May 2007.[4] They won a reprieve when an air quality permit was denied so the state could gather further information. Residents voiced anger at a community meeting not only about the plant's potential emissions but also about being left out of the planning process. One community member was quoted as saying that "everything is on the back end. We won't know until afterwards. Where is the responsibility here?"[5]

The "biomass" would be culled from supposedly overgrown woodlands in the area as a forest fire prevention strategy. While seemingly on the cutting edge, biomass power generation, like ethanol fuel production, can have unforeseen economic and environmental consequences. The use of corn and other traditional food products to refine into ethanol has driven up the price of food itself in many parts of the developing world, sometimes to the point of causing food riots among urban and rural poor. Ethanol does not require corn ears to be produced, according to the Rocky Mountain Institute. Both biomass power and ethanol can use waste products, such as weeds and husks. But while biomass power generation could use any woody plants, including the oceans of weeds in New Mexico, as fuel, it is usually linked to a forest fire prevention program that involves thinning out undergrowth from woodlands. What worries many who work to conserve wildlife habitat is that such "thinning" could amount to clear-cutting.

Our Backyard

Environmental degradations can occur without visible consequences for years. My wife and I have a firsthand experience of this phenomenon. We've lived and gardened in Albuquerque's North Valley for nearly forty-two years, working a large garden patch with diminishing, but cherished, returns every spring and summer. In the early 1970s we experienced one of those marvels that give gardeners an extra share of delight. We found a cottonwood leaf sticking up out of the pea patch. At first we thought a leaf had just fallen on its stem in the mud. But no, the leaf was attached to roots; it was a cottonwood tree. We transplanted it to a bare spot in our garden and watched with pride the tree's vigorous growth over the next five or six years. One year, quite suddenly, after its leaves had appeared, the cottonwood tree dropped dead, losing its leaves practically overnight. We believed something was wrong with the tree, and we planted a globe willow in the same spot. Six years later, the same thing happened—good years of growth, then sudden death. Between plantings and mortalities, we'd dug post holes for a long fence and kept running into pockets of what must have been a midden site in the 1930s and '40s, with lots of rusted oil cans, car parts, and other auto-related debris. When the second tree died, it occurred to us that both trees could well have been killed off by an underground pocket of pollution.

Over the years, I've come to consider the sudden deaths of those trees as emblematic of what happens to neighborhoods where toxic waste is dumped. There are areas in Albuquerque and other New Mexican cities, for instance, that are so polluted with so many kinds of toxins, or so poisoned with radioactive debris, that their existence has met with official cover-ups and a refusal by the mainstream media to deal with them as a major social catastrophe and public health danger in the making. I'll discuss some of them later in this chapter. Many rural landowners in the past, with no public garbage collection, dug unlined trash pits for debris that could include used oil and paints and other toxins among miscellaneous household and agricultural trash. The practice continues in some places even now. Sometimes individuals and companies would dump their debris in rural places, or even arroyos, just as people still dump trash along the ditch system in Albuquerque's north and south valleys, as if it were populated by people who didn't matter. City landfills are usually placed at the edges of poorer or politically unrepresented parts of town, but some trash dumpers don't even go that far to get rid of their waste.

It was impossible, without great effort and deep pockets, to reconstruct the origin of the midden in the vicinity of our land. In the 1930s and '40s, the mid–North Valley hadn't been gentrified. It was rural, agricultural, and largely poor. We don't know what had killed our trees, but it could have been pollution, and the pollution could well represent an early example of what could happen to all of us in the future. While I don't think this was a case of purposeful environmental injustice, there's no question in my mind that putting dangerous waste out of sight, out of mind often means putting it in places and among people without political or economic clout.

Environmental Racism

Such practices became business and national defense policy in the post–World War II United States. The problem is so serious in New Mexico that when Governor Bill Richardson signed an executive order in November 2005 creating an Environmental Justice Task Force, its membership comprised representatives of every major land- and health-oriented department in state government. The executive order mandated that environmental justice considerations be addressed in all projects administered by any agency of the state. New Mexico is "committed," the order said, "to affording all of its residents, including communities of color and low income communities, fair treatment and meaningful involvement in the development, implementation, and enforce of environmental laws . . . regardless of race, color, ethnicity, religion, income, or education level."[6] While many of New Mexico's "third world communities" were heartened to some degree by

Richardson's recognition of the problem, I'm sure they are also taking the "we'll see" attitude of the skeptics in Clovis and the Estancia Valley.

New Mexicans have waited a very long time for the concept of environmental injustice to be accepted as an actual category of wrong-doing. Richardson's executive order is part of a movement in the mountain West that has gained momentum from two well-publicized nongovernmental evaluations of the environmental plight of the poor and disenfranchised. In 1987, the United Church of Christ issued a report entitled *Toxic Wastes and Race in the United States*, assert-ing "the existence of clear patterns which show that communities with greater minority percentages of the population are more likely to be the sites of commercial hazardous waste facilities. The possibil-ity that these patterns resulted by chance is virtually impossible." In 1990 (two years before a study by the EPA confirming environmental discrimination), the Southwest Organizing Project (SWOP), a tena-cious nonprofit watchdog group based in Albuquerque's South Valley, joined with Louisiana's Gulf Coast Tenant Leadership Development Project to send letters of protest to ten high-profile American envi-ronmental NGOs, including the Sierra Club, Friends of the Earth, the National Audubon Society, and the National Resources Defense Council, citing "years of neglect on environmental issues relevant to poor and minority peoples."[7]

The SWOP letter charged that, for centuries,

> people of color in our region have been subjected to racist and genocidal practices, including the theft of lands and water, the murder of innocent people, and the degradation of our environ-ment. Mining companies extract minerals, leaving economically depressed communities and poisoned soil and water. The U.S. military takes lands for weapons production, testing, and stor-age, contaminating surrounding communities and placing minor-ity workers in the most highly radioactive and toxic work sites. Industrial and municipal dumps are intentionally placed in com-munities of color, disrupting our cultural lifestyle and threatening our communities' futures. . . . There is a clear lack of account-ability by the Group of Ten environmental organizations towards Third World communities in the Southwest, in the United States as a whole, and internationally.[8]

Uncertainty as a Legal Weapon

These grassroots environmental groups were responding, in part, to the military-industrial propaganda that flourished in the 1980s, propaganda that temporarily beguiled many mainstream conservationists and environmental organizations. Companies created an image for themselves of being run by a new generation of somewhat reluctant but born-again green-thinking leaders. This image came in the form of a seemingly enlightened but patronizing agreement that dangerous pollutants were harming American communities, rather than the old scornful and outright denials. Their acceptance came with a caveat, however. Harm from pollution had to be substantiated by cold, hard facts. Fact-finding would often be funded by industry, in a gesture of magnanimity. But no remediation would be undertaken until the facts proved it was necessary. The unspoken reality, of course, was that industry-funded studies would find no hard data—anecdotal evidence perhaps, but nothing statistically relevant. As one Chevron executive put it in 1987, "The popular assumption . . . and too often one played up for political purposes . . . is that *any* detectable impurities have to be harmful, . . . that if we can measure it, we ought to get rid of it. . . . The point is not that we can afford to be complacent . . . or ignore toxics in our environment. It's simply that we should base our environmental policies on *facts*."[9]

Industry used the fundamental uncertainty of science to protect itself from public outrage. Any scientific assertion can be, and must be, contested before it can be considered a proven fact. And while it is being contested and is still "unproven," industry insists that it need not be accepted as "fact" by anyone.

What I call the revulsion standard is much safer. Communities are almost invariably disgusted if dangerous materials in any amount occur in their groundwater and soil. If neighbors can't prove that such impurities are harmful to the local environment, industry can't prove that they are not. And, of course, "*any* detectable impurities" have as good a chance of being harmful as harmless. The logic is simple. Look at any addition of synthetic materials to natural conditions as *potentially* harmful. Don't pollute any water or soil until you *know* the alien substance is not harmful. That's the basis of the precautionary principle: If you don't know an action or a substance is safe, then don't do it or release it. The precautionary principle is part of the scientific education and ethic of chemical engineers, whose professional societies hold that the best way to deal with toxic waste is to avoid releasing it in the first place. This is an idea that's apparently anathema to most polluting industries. They understand that environmental science for hire by industry produces results that go the way of the employer. Absolute certainty is next to impossible, and uncertainty of any kind can be used as an excuse to doubt "facts" trending in the "wrong" direction for the employer.

Environmental injustice in New Mexico has a sorrowful history that begins with the stealing and despoiling of tribal lands and water rights and encompasses the outright theft of Hispanic land grants, nuclear dumping in rural areas, environmental damage from the oil and natural gas fields in the San Juan and Permian basins, and massive uranium mining with its legacy of cancer and disease on Navajo land in northwest New Mexico.

Pueblo Water Rights

One of the strangest ironies of environmental injustice involves Pueblo water rights. Laws known by various obvious euphemisms but formally called the Indian Intercourse Act of 1834 and the Dawes Act of 1887 made a distinction between the "savage and uncivilized tribes"[10]—Navajos, Apaches, Comanches, Utes, and other nomadic groups—and the Pueblos, who as urban dwellers were considered to have achieved a higher level of culture. The Intercourse Act allowed the federal government to protect the water and lands of the so-called savage tribes but not those of the Pueblos, who "as citizens of Mexico became citizens of the United States on annexation [in 1846] and were entitled to the same constitutional rights and privileges as any other class of citizens."[11] The chronically poor Pueblos were "corporate bodies with perfect titles to their lands and with ample remedy to protect and defend their titles and to manage for themselves."[12]

"In return for the exalted status conferred on them by the territorial courts and acquiesced in by the Supreme Court of the United States, the Pueblo lost federal guardianship over their lands afforded under the Intercourse Act to all other Indians in the territory," writes Ira G. Clark in *Water in New Mexico*.[13] Territorial courts generally decided against Pueblo claimants in suits to oust squatters and land grant holders with conflicting claims. And the Dawes Act, which allowed individual Native Americans to sell common land, was a disaster in the making for the Pueblos. It wasn't until 1896 that the federal government funded a water rights attorney to help Pueblos protect their claims. The New Mexico Enabling Act of 1910, two years before statehood, prohibited outright the taking of Pueblo lands and waters and the sale of liquor on Pueblo property. A liquor dealer at one of the pueblos challenged the Enabling Act on the grounds that it conflicted with the Dawes Act. The suit went to the U.S. Supreme Court, which reconsidered Pueblo status and downgraded the official view of them as a "civilized" people, saying the Pueblos were "essentially a simple, uninformed, and inferior people" who needed to become, in effect, wards of the federal government.[14] The decision, Clark wrote, "not only marked the end of unrestrained encroachment on pueblo land and water rights but by implication placed in jeopardy all rights acquired in violation of the law."[15]

Not only did the Pueblos have to give up their legal recognition as "civilized" and superior urban dwellers, the federal protection of their waters caused virtually everyone who had appropriated or laid claim to their lands and resources, often with strong belief in their legitimate rights, to view the federal government and the Pueblos as usurping their ability to survive. Open conflicts arose and a crisis was looming when New Mexican Albert B. Fall, then secretary of the interior, tried to ease the situation in 1922 by having New Mexico's U.S. senator Holm O. Bursum introduce a federal bill that would, in effect, validate all squatters' claims, and the claims of others, against the Pueblos and their land and water.

The Bursum bill to limit Pueblos' water use to their diminished level of consumption in 1922 was strenuously opposed by the Pueblos, who created the All Indian Pueblo Council to fight it. Pueblos and their intellectual and artistic allies in northern New Mexico (including Mabel Dodge Luhan and John Collier, eventually commissioner of Indian affairs under Franklin D. Roosevelt) considered the Bursum bill a death threat to Pueblo culture, pointing out that the bill condoned gross tampering with Pueblo economies. "Aggressions, encroachments, and other decimating practices by settlers upon Indian lands, claiming title of one sort or another, have been in vogue for many years, principally since the advent of American sovereignty," historian Ralph Emerson Twitchell wrote in

1923, "and the Indian has always been the losing party. This should be stopped at once and for all time. Trespasses have been the rule rather than the exception in the use and occupancy of their pasture lands, and local courts and juries have yet, in my judgment, to show where the Indian has never received justice."[16]

The Bursum bill was defeated and replaced with the Pueblo Land Board Act of 1924, signed into law by Calvin Coolidge. The Pueblo Land Board over the next eight years examined more than five thousand claims to over a hundred thousand acres of Pueblo land (mostly open grazing land). The board succeeded in restoring many acres to Pueblo owners and helped them pursue compensation. Federal courts overturned the board on numerous occasions, and the Pueblos themselves maintained that compensation for lost lands was often inadequate.[17] Since the advent of the economic clout that came with casino revenue in the 1990s, many pueblos have simply resorted to buying back ancestral lands at the going rate. Still, outright land seizures continue.

Stealing Pueblo Lands

A case in point was the creation in 1986 of the El Malpais National Monument near Grants, over the strenuous objections of the pueblo of Acoma. The Malpais, a huge black-rock lava flow, borders on Acoma tribal lands. The Pueblo objected to the monument because it would encroach on its territory and because the tribe had bought several parcels of land in the lava flow to protect religious shrines that marked the way for rain clouds to travel across Zuni Salt Lake and through the Malpais to Acoma.[18] But because the uranium boom was over, Grants was hurting for revenue. The New Mexico congressional delegation turned a deaf ear to Acoma's opposition.

"Acoma is hurt by the fact that laws made by the dominant society continue to oppress native people," the Acoma Tribal Council told the New Mexico delegation. "We can no longer be pushed and required to yield to the injustice being done to us. We can only see how the white man's laws are so often used to the detriment of our sacred lands. We just insist that this act is unjust."[19]

Sandia Pueblo met strong opposition from conservative New Mexicans in Congress over its claim to the ownership of ten thousand acres on the northwest face of Sandia Mountain. Things were said that I am sure the Pueblo will never forget. In 2003, President Bush signed into law an agreement that ended the Pueblo's claim by giving it legal control of the land, not outright ownership. The Pueblo also retains its traditional hunting rights[20] and religious shrines.[21] To arrive at this solution, Sandia hired Jack Abramoff's lobbying company (well before he was indicted) and payed him as much as $2.75 million to secure the deal. According to Abramoff's plea agreement, he and publicist Jack Scanlon "pocketed 80 percent" of the money.[22] Three years before the settlement was signed by the president, Sandia Pueblo reached an agreement with the U.S. Forest Service that the wealthy homeowners in area objected to with all the political clout they could muster. They appealed to New Mexico representative Heather Wilson and New Mexico senator Pete Domenici, citing their fears that the Pueblo would jeopardize their property rights and even, one day, evict them. Though both Domenici and Wilson later signed onto the 2003 settlement, the 2000 agreement with the U.S. Forest Service met with their violent verbal reaction, accusing the tribe of working an "irrelevant" "back-deal" "reached in bad faith."[23] Such language would never have been directed toward a non-Indian from members of the Congressional delegation. (Domenici denied having been lobbied by Abramoff on the matter.)

Sandia Pueblo's claim to the mountain was first made in 1858, four years after the U.S. Office of Surveyor-General was given the task of sorting out Spanish and Mexican land titles under the 1848 Treaty of Guadalupe Hidalgo. The Pueblo argued that the surveyor and Congress erred in removing from their tribal holdings the ten thousand acres on the northwest face of the Sandias, which eventually became part of the Cibola National Forest.

Legal Non Sequiturs

The nineteenth century in New Mexico was a time when customary ways of doing business and managing land ownership were thrown into upheaval by the American conquest. Not only was the New Mexico Territory cut off from the Spanish and Mexican legal systems, but Indo-Hispano culture was inundated with American products and laws and the American ethos of cutthroat competition. As historian Marc Simmons explains, "Within a short time after establishment of the American legal system, complications arising from these Hispanic practices [land grant heirs holding individually owned small parcels while keeping most of the grant in common for grazing and wood gathering] produced a tangled web of claims and counter-claims and opened the way for speculators to obtain, often through deceit and fraud, a controlling interest in some of the most valuable grants."[24] Environmental historian William deBuys estimates that "over a fifth of the Carson and Santa Fe national forests was once part of extensive land grants conveyed to Hispanic settlers and ultimately confirmed by Congress and the U.S. courts. Still more forest land was claimed as grants by Hispanics but not confirmed by the government, which repeatedly failed to protect the property rights of land-grant heirs."[25] All told, such lands amount to hundreds of thousands of acres in national forests. Hispanic communities in northern New Mexico depended on what had been grazing and timber lands held in common by various land grants and their members. As the commons eroded, what came to be called pockets of poverty developed in Mora, Rio Arriba, San Miguel, and Taos counties.[26]

Tijerina

By the mid-1950s, the threat to small farms and ranches was severe and anger over lost lands intense. In response, legend has it, the Penitente Brotherhood invited a young activist preacher from Texas, Reies Lopez Tijerina, to come to northern New Mexico and investigate the possibility of massive land theft.[27] At that moment, one of New Mexico's most fascinating and colorful political figures was born. Tijerina gave up preaching and traveled to Mexico City to research in government archives the documentation that guaranteed title and protection of Hispano lands in the 1848 Treaty of Guadalupe Hildago. The University of New Mexico Center of Southwest Research has archived Tijerina's eighty cubic feet of papers, much of it, apparently, dealing with land grants.

In the 1960s, when I was working as a reporter for the *Albuquerque Tribune*, Tijerina's organization, the Alianza Federal de Mercedes, set out to organize dispossessed land grant heirs and make sure they knew their rights under the Treaty of Guadalupe Hidalgo. Tijerina and others maintained that a huge portion of the Tierra Amarilla Land Grant was taken to make the Carson National Forest. His appeals in the 1950s to President Eisenhower to restore stolen lands had been rebuffed. The U.S. Forest Service found Tijerina's claims and increasingly dramatic rhetoric worrisome and even frightening. Rangers and other Forest Service employees in the north eventually took to carrying sidearms and displaying rifles on racks of their trucks. By 1966, when Tijerina returned from Spain, where he'd been studying Spanish law, he and the Alianza were the object of intense interest. For years, Tijerina had been the subject of FBI surveillance, as I learned when I contacted a source in the local FBI office who allowed me to peruse boxes of clippings, wiretaps, and other information on Tijerina's activities covering some twenty years. As a so-called fiery Chicano activist, he'd been the victim of legal prejudice and negative press for years.

Tijerina was an extremely forceful and persuasive orator in both Spanish and English. I heard him many times, including an hour and a half session alone with him in the Alianza headquarters on Third Street in Albuquerque in early 1967. The headquarters was in an old grocery store that had a very large meat locker. It was in that space that Tijerina and I conversed, alone. I came away convinced of two things. First, land grant heirs had a legitimate and historically defensible position that had been ignored for more than a hundred years. (I also came to see that the issue was so complicated and so clouded in historical and legal documentation that even a gifted orator like Tijerina had a hard time explaining it.) Second, Tijerina and the land grant heirs might have been better served by a more scholarly, less bombastic approach in the public media. But that was not to be. Tijerina admired Dr. Martin Luther King, Jr., but Tijerina was not a pacifist. His righteous anger kept erupting through his speeches. In the meat locker, he spent most of his time elaborating his racial theories, dismissing Anglos, Asians, and Africans as members of old, tired-out races, with the only new race still full of hybrid vigor being the mestizo, the Indo-Hispano.

Tijerina's passion for social justice and his ability to attract and mesmerize large crowds frightened the mainstream community in New Mexico, both Anglo and Hispanic. "Of all the Hispanic activist organizations—farm labor, political, cultural, and civil rights movements," columnist José Armas wrote in the *Albuquerque Journal* in 1992, "the Alianza's activities were among the most volatile because they demanded enforcement of the international treaties that protected Hispanic land grants." Armas called Tijerina a "student of

Spanish history" who "championed the birth of the Hispanic culture to those of us active in the civil rights movement in the 1960s."[28]

Federal and state scrutiny of Tijerina's activities and associations intensified in 1967, when he and some three hundred members of the Alianza occupied the Echo Amphitheater near Abiquiu in the Carson National Forest because it had once been part of the San Joaquín del Río de Chama Land Grant. They created a land grant republic with its own government, issued visas to tourists, and even charged Forest Service rangers with trespassing (but let them go unharmed). After nearly a week of occupation and being constantly shadowed by the FBI, the Rio Arriba County sheriff's department, and the state police, the land grant heirs gave up. Five of their leaders, including Tijerina, were arrested for destroying government property (a Forest Service sign) and released on bond.

Tijerina and the Alianza were treated by the mainstream media as curiosities, and the whole land grant issue, in spite of its basis in legal claims and scholarship, was portrayed as little better than castles in the air. What was a profound injustice to thousands of northern New Mexicans was seen by most of the state as crackpot whining. Many New Mexicans had never heard of the Treaty of Guadalupe Hidalgo in 1967 and could not believe that the United States government would ever steal land from anyone.

Shortly after the Echo Amphitheater incident, Tijerina and others held a meeting in Coyote, New Mexico, to plan their next move. The district attorney of Rio Arriba County, Alfonso Sanchez, had the meeting disbanded and arrested many. Tijerina escaped. A few days later, Alianza members, led by Tijerina, stormed the county courthouse in Tierra Amarilla to make a citizen's arrest of Sanchez for wrongfully abridging their right to assemble and exercise their freedom of speech. The tale of the courthouse raid has been told many times. It's enough to say here that things went badly, and a state police officer was shot, as were a prison guard and a deputy sheriff. D.A. Sanchez wasn't in court that day, and the raiders took two hostages and fled into the hills. A huge armed contingent that included National Guard tanks tracked them down. Tijerina was initially acquitted of all charges stemming from the courthouse raid, but he was later tried again, convicted despite accusations of double jeopardy, and sentenced to two years in federal prison. I was in the *Tribune* newsroom the morning after the raid and saw what seemed at first to be identical photographs on the local and international wires. One showed Israeli tanks in the Seven Day War, taking the Golan Heights. The other showed tanks rumbling down the Chama Valley. It was a classic case of the government overreacting and making things worse by intimidating and disrespecting many innocent people.

The courthouse raid and the national attention it gained the Alianza did nothing in the long run to help the land grant heirs regain their stolen lands. Nor did it increase sensitivity on the part of the Forest Service to the land grant issue. The Alianza was not seen as a civil rights movement, but rather as a local group of malcontents—poor, Hispanic, and therefore dismissible. It's not that Tijerina was universally idolized in northern New Mexico as he was in East Los Angeles, where posters of his portrait were displayed in restaurants beside that of Cesar Chavez. Tijerina was a *tejano*, a Texan, and hence not welcome in the north by politicians and insiders like Rio Arriba County D.A. Sanchez and county sheriff and Democratic party chair Emilio Naranjo. Still, despite Tijerina's outsider status, many social justice advocates agreed with his assessment that land grant heirs had been victims of a major land grab. If Tijerina had not been such a volatile speaker, and if the Alianza hadn't been branded as a rural manifestation of the inner city unrest that had led to minority riots, perhaps more attention would have been paid to Tijerina's scholarship and claims.

Battles over Grazing

Two disputes, one in late 1967 involving cattle grazing in the Carson National Forest, the other some twenty-five years later over sheep grazing in wilderness areas in northern New Mexico, illustrate the complexity of environmental injustice in New Mexico. The *Albuquerque Tribune* in 1967, under my byline, called the cattle grazing troubles the Mora County Cattle Wars. That year, right in the middle of the land grant dispute, the Forest Service brought in as head ranger for the Carson National Forest an employee from Arizona who apparently had no inkling of the cultural and historical conflicts raging in New Mexico at the time. In retrospect, the story is reminiscent of John Nichols's famous novel *The Milagro Bean Field War*. In the little ranching communities of Amalia and Costilla, near the central border between New Mexico and

Colorado, small ranchers had been grazing cattle for centuries, and sometimes their herds would stray onto the Carson because there was no fence to keep them out. These ranchers considered much of the Carson to be theirs anyway by virtue of the Treaty of Guadalupe Hidalgo. The Arizona ranger, a man who liked to run things by the book, did the unthinkable and started impounding cattle that had "trespassed" onto the Carson, charging ranchers fines and fees that were often more than a steer was worth. Ranchers were literally up in arms, carrying Winchesters and sidearms. One Korean war vet, reputed to be the leader of the revolt, told me he'd shoot any Forest Service personnel who set foot on his land, which also bordered the Carson. It seemed as if the whole of northern New Mexico was armed and itching for a fight. One cattleman gave me a tour of the region, constantly and angrily pointing to the lush grass in the national forest and the barren, overgrazed land around it. He noted bitterly that no cattle could trespass on most of the Carson because most of it was fenced. Just when it seemed the shooting would start, the Forest Service reassigned the Arizona ranger and gave back the impounded cattle. It didn't take a day before the potential cattle war quieted down to a simmer.

"Those People"

Some twenty-five years later, the basic issues of land grants, grazing, and environmental discrimination erupted again. In the unusually dry August of 1989, Anglo environmentalists tried to keep a thousand head of Churro sheep owned by the Ganados del Valle Sheep Cooperative near Tierra Amarilla from grazing in the Humphries State Wildlife Area around the Chama Valley. The New Mexico Department of Game and Fish had put a moratorium on all grazing in wildlife areas, which had in the past been grazed by Anglo ranchers. Ganados shepherds were offered grazing space on Jicarilla Apache land. Shortly, however, because of pending lawsuits with the Department of Game and Fish, the Jicarilla had to withdraw the offer. It was only then that Ganados engaged in an act of civil disobedience and moved their herd into the Humphries wilderness. Certain environmental organizations took to calling the Ganados *pastores* "those people." It grew to be a very nasty situation, one where environmentalists acted directly against the interest of a local group.

Ganados del Valle was the first contemporary example in New Mexico of what a land-based community can do for itself. Ganados was founded in 1983 by Maria Varela and Antonio Manzanares in the small town of Los Ojos, a few miles from Tierra Amarilla. Like many other towns in the north, Tierra Amarilla seemed to be on its last legs economically. Los Ojos, on the other hand, continues to flourish. Its first business, under Ganados, was Tierra Wools, a weaving cooperative that grew to have an international clientele. Later Ganados produced custom meats at their processing plant and established other enterprises. The town looks prosperous. No buildings are abandoned. The church is well maintained. Opposition to the shepherds trespassing their herds in the wilderness, even though they practiced scientific grazing methods designed to enhance forage for wildlife, was a low point in modern New Mexico environmental history.

"Environmentalists, many of them new transplants to New Mexico, look at the ravages left by the industrialization of public lands and, perhaps to their credit, have decided to fix it. But it is unfathomable why environmentalists would not look to the people who have lived for hundreds of years in agropastoral communities, which buffer public lands, as the first to be consulted and as peers in this effort," wrote Maria Varela in a 2001 essay. "After all, Hispano villagers and Native Americans have lifelong knowledge of these lands and have fought extractive industries and the U.S. Forest Service [since] long before the modern environmental movement. By rendering people of color invisible, or vilifying them as 'violent' or 'tools of the livestock and lumber transnational corporations,' many environmentalists have, in their historical and cultural illiteracy, assumed the cloak of conqueror."[29]

A subplot to this story involved the Sierra Club, a patron of the arts and culture of New Mexico, and then–state attorney general Tom Udall. If things had gone the way Ray Graham III had intended in 1971 when he gave the Sierra Club Foundation $100,000 in Firestone stock to buy rangeland for sheep grazing in New Mexico, Ganados wouldn't have been forced to trespass in the wilderness area. Through a tangle of lawsuits and countersuits, it became clear that the Sierra Club had never bought the grazing land. More than twenty years later, in 1992, Attorney General Udall sued the Sierra Club Foundation, acting in the interests of Graham and Ganados del

Valle, charging that land should have been bought for Ganados. The Sierra Club settled out of court in 1995 for $900,000, which included twenty years' worth of interest and dividends on the Firestone stock.[30]

Albuquerque's South Valley

Environmental injustice is a huge problem in certain parts of Albuquerque's South Valley. Commuters cannot tell from the freeway that a ten-mile stretch from Bridge Boulevard to the Isleta curve, between Broadway and Second Street, is, next to Los Alamos, Sandia National Laboratories, and Kirtland Air Force Base and other military installations, the most polluted area in the state, as it has been since the 1950s. At first glance, this area seems like a wasteland of junkyards and small industries, but it is also residential. Just north of a residential and industrial area known as Mountain View is the heavily populated East San Jose neighborhood, and farther north the predominantly African American neighborhood called John Marshall. Just south of these neighborhoods, near Woodward and Broadway, was the location of the South Valley Works, the third point in New Mexico's nuclear research and manufacturing triangle, LANL and SNL being the other two. In the 1950s, scientists and engineers at the South Valley Works, operated by American Car and Foundry under a contract with the Atomic Energy Commission, did research and development on nuclear engines. This same site, now owned by General Electric, was the subject of the largest environmental lawsuit ever brought in New Mexico. In October 1999, the state attorney general, Patricia Madrid, sought some $4 billion in damages from GE and numerous other companies, alleging that the groundwater in the vicinity of the plant was permanently ruined and would never be potable again.

Into this area of the South Valley drains the massive Tijeras Arroyo, the natural runoff channel for nearly a hundred square miles of the Sandia and Manzano mountains. The arroyo runs right through Kirtland Air Force Base and down the southern end of Mountain View, emptying into the bosque and the Rio Grande. It is thought to have been a major illegal dumping site for the military and others over many decades. Mountain View and adjacent areas have long anecdotal and documented histories of health issues among their residents, but as of this writing, no government agency that I'm aware of has ever conducted a thorough sociomedical history of the area. As Annie P. Michaelis writes in the *Journal of Public Health Policy*, "In the United States, popular prejudices allow the health problems of those who are viewed as politically or socially less desirable to be given less attention than the problems of those who command power or sympathy within mainstream politics and society. Marginalized population groups are at risk of having their public health needs inadequately addressed."[31]

In 2004, New Mexico environment secretary Ron Curry told a meeting of the Mountain View Neighborhood Association, "We want to elevate the issues of the South Valley pollution so people across New Mexico can see this neighborhood as a microcosm of many problems found in New Mexico," according to the *Albuquerque Journal*.[32] While the remoteness of New Mexico on the national scene has made the state an easy dumping ground for waste from all over, within the state, local polluters have dumped more poisons in Mountain View, Los Padillas, Pajarito Mesa, San Jose, and environs than anywhere else. *The Albuquerque Journal* summed up the area's plight neatly:

> According to (Bernalillo) county Environmental Health Department Data, the South Valley . . . has three [*sic*] U.S. Environmental Protection Agency–identified Superfund sites, the majority of the county's "Brownfield sites" (abandoned industrial sites) as well as thirty-six polluting industries that are regulated by the EPA. Thirty-one of those polluting industries are in the Mountain View neighborhood. [Some of the major polluters in the Mountain View area] include Public Service Company of New Mexico's Persons Station, seven petroleum fuel bulk terminals, Rek Chemical, and thirty-five other hazardous waste facilities that include a water [sewer] treatment facility, a dairy, more than twenty-five auto recycling yards, five gravel and concrete companies, a solid waste landfill, a fertilizer factory facility, and a chicken farm. In addition, there are more than sixteen major air-polluting industries and sixty-six smaller polluting industries in the area.[33]

"Along with all of those problems," the *Journal* reports, the Mountain View area "is home of the largest underground nitrate plume in New Mexico. The plume is about three-quarters of a mile wide and thirty feet deep. The plume contaminated sixty-one private wells and two city wells. The plume is not considered a Superfund site. The EPA Superfund sites in the South Valley . . . area include a petroleum hydrocarbon plume from the Chevron, Texaco, and ATA Pipeline tank farms and the old GE plant site, which covers about one square mile in the San Jose area. . . . Industrial operations at the site contaminated the soil and ground water with chlorinated solvents and other pollutants."[34] The *Journal* made no mention of the other major Superfund site in the area—the creosote-soaking site for the Atchison, Topeka, and Santa Fe Railroad, where railroad ties were cured for more than sixty years.

Pollution as the Norm

As recently as 2003, some forty thousand gallons of unleaded gasoline spilled into a bermed containment area in the ConocoPhillips Products Terminal near Broadway and Woodward, the location three years earlier of a ten thousand gallon spill of diesel fuel. Cleanup efforts were expected to take decades, using vapor extraction and burn-off methods from soil, and groundwater if necessary.[35] The most reasonable explanation for the spills was human error. But why are the tanks there in the first place? Residents of the area have long wondered why their portion of the South Valley has such a history of environmental neglect and misfortune, especially when the city's sewage treatment plant, also in their neighborhood, makes life miserable with its noxious odors. It took nearly thirty years from when the plant was built in the 1970s to mitigate the stench to a bearable level, though many people say it isn't there yet.

The local press has paid close attention to pollution in the South Valley, but only sporadically. The 1980s brought particular attention to the subject. The Pronto PCB dump site is an example of craven toxic littering exposed by alert residents that actually garnered federal Superfund relief. As environmental scholar and consultant Paul Robinson of the Southwest Research and Information Center described it, waste oil full of PCBs, which are known carcinogens, was hauled from Texas between 1980 and 1982 and dumped into unlined pits on south Coors Boulevard, past the current Walmart on the western edge of the South Valley. According to Robinson, the "illegal dumping caused PCBs and volatile organic compounds to migrate as much as fourteen feet below the surface in less than two years. With the water table only some fifty-six feet below, emergency Superfund moneys were used to clean up the site, a rescue situation today that would not be possible with Superfund appropriations cut to the bare bones." The operator of the Pronto site was not indicted, but the company that transported the poisoned oil was indicted and fined.[36]

In the 1980s, 70 percent of the South Valley's nearly thirty-nine thousand residents were Hispanic, and almost 50 percent of them lived well below the poverty level.[37] The Pronto PCB incident was a classic case of the dumping of waste in poor neighborhoods being seen as a good business decision. Besides, the Texas company was dumping its waste in another state—out of sight, out of mind. This was nothing new in the South Valley. Since the 1950s, the area has been a sacrifice zone to the nuclear defense industry and its contractors, much like the Grants uranium belt on and around the Navajo, Acoma, and Laguna reservations.

Post-Trinity Pollution

The pollution of three major public wells—one at Mountain View Elementary School and two in San Jose—and numerous other private wells in the 1980s probably originated in post–Manhattan Project nuclear research in Albuquerque. Many South Valley residents were dependent on private wells. The city and county were notorious for endlessly postponing the development of water and sewer lines in the area and surcharging residents when they did finally get around to providing services. In 1979, two city wells serving some seventy thousand people, predominately black and Hispanic, in the San Jose area were found to contain chlorinated industrial solvents.[38] Chemicals such as benzene and trichloroethylene, or TCE, a known carcinogen, were found in as many as twenty private shallow wells and the two 912-foot-deep city wells in San Jose,[39] number 3 and number 6. The city wells were decommissioned in 1981.[40]

Cleaning up water pollution takes a long time. The two decommissioned city wells were not plugged and sealed until 1988, one year after a new city replacement well, called Burton number 4, had been drilled.[41] By 1988, however, the EPA claimed not to know who was responsible for the pollution.[42]

According to a 2007 EPA update on its Region Six, in the South Valley of Albuquerque/Bernalillo County, it took seven years after contamination was first spotted before cleanup of the shallow aquifer plume and polluted soil was begun. And it wasn't until 1996, fifteen years after the initial discovery, that pumping and treatment began in the deepwater aquifer.[43] The plume had been tracked moving east at a slow rate toward the great vortex, or cone of depression, caused by massive city pumping some ten miles away, near the corner of Central Avenue and Eubank NE. More than twenty years after the East San Jose wells were closed, the cleanup continues. The EPA estimates that some 4.9 billion gallons of water have been treated so far.[44] The principal pollutants are dichloroethene, trichloroethylene, tetrachloroethylene, benzene, ethylbenzene, and toluene xylene, all of them volatile organic compounds.[45] The EPA says that the volume of contaminated groundwater at the site remains "unknown,"[46] causing one to wonder how it will be determined when cleanup can stop.

The San Jose groundwater pollution is directly related to the industrial activity at the old South Valley Works at the edge of East San Jose. A plume of contamination some two square miles also contained petroleum products from variously owned gasoline storage tanks and pipelines just south of the GE site. This plume was the cause of the $4 billion suit brought by the state of New Mexico to compensate for the lost drinking water.

Tijeras Arroyo

About five miles south of the GE plant and the petroleum storage plants is the channel of the huge Tijeras Arroyo that cuts through Kirtland Air Force Base and flows to the river near Mountain View Elementary School. Until the early 1980s, no part of the arroyo through the South Valley was concrete lined. After a highly publicized incident of blue baby syndrome in the Mountain View neighborhood, followed by much political outrage on the part of both state and national officials and local residents, the Tijeras Arroyo channel through the valley was lined with cement.[47] Where it runs into the bosque, however, it remains unlined.

Mountain View's underground water had long been suspected of containing dangerous amounts of nitrates and other suspicious substances. Nitrates are known to cause blue baby syndrome and possibly some cancers. The same year that the San Jose wells were closed, a very high concentration of nitrates, some two hundred times higher than in safe drinking water, was detected in Mountain View.[48] Following the birth of the blue baby, public sentiment was adamant that the state immediately move to correct the problem.[49] Meetings of as many as three thousand people were accompanied by extensive newspaper coverage. Governor Toney Anaya and the legislature appropriated some $100,000 for a preliminary investigation of the problem. But neither the city nor the county was willing to contribute matching funds. The city didn't want to fund county efforts, and the county wouldn't fund work being done in the city's portion of Mountain View. In 1985, wrote Paul Robinson, "no ground water clean up has occurred, no alternative for domestic waste disposal has been provided, and no source of the nitrate problem has been identified."[50] The only good news in the neighborhood was that the blue baby had been restored to health.[51]

One of the more galling aspects of this situation is that this nitrate pollution had been identified many times before the 1980s, most recently in 1970. The *Albuquerque Tribune* reported in February that year that the "nitrate problem in Mountainview [*sic*] is serious enough that health officials are recommending that pregnant women in the area, and babies under one year old, drink only bottled water until the problem is solved."[52] A front-page story in the *Albuquerque Journal* a few days later reported that the nitrate levels in some Mountain View wells were ten times higher than safety standards would allow and made even stronger warnings about keeping children from drinking that water. This lengthy piece also stated that nitrates had been discovered in fifty-six private wells in 1963.[53]

Most Mountain View residents figured the nitrates came from the sewage treatment plant at the western edge of their neighborhood on Second Street, not far from the elementary school. The well there had been contaminated as early as 1958, and the county was forced to drill deeper into the aquifer for clean water.

In 1986, the state of New Mexico found so-called low levels of what the *Albuquerque Tribune* labeled as explosive chemicals in Mountain View's groundwater, including nitrobenzene.[54] A year later, a state health department study showed pollution from nitroglycerin, but not nitrobenzene.[55] In 1989, another test conducted by the state found traces of a plastic-based Dutch explosive in the groundwater.[56] A year after that, the EPA, using a private laboratory, claimed its results were "unusable," because the laboratory didn't follow EPA analytical procedures.[57]

Dumping in the Arroyo

Invariably an aura of uncertainty surrounds public information about the causes and health impacts of pollution. Rarely does a government news release mention public health danger. Disclosures of pollution generally end with phrases such as "poses no risk to public health." But in 1982, a story appeared in the *Albuquerque Journal* that clearly stated the magnitude of Cold War pollution in the South Valley. American Car Foundry (ACF), working as a contractor for the Atomic Energy Commission at what would one day become the GE Superfund site, regularly dumped industrial solvents and liquid plastics into Tijeras Arroyo on Kirtland Air Force Base property. From 1955 to 1967, 170,000 gallons of these hazardous liquids were dumped into the arroyo, which emptied out in the Mountain View neighborhood.[58]

An April 1982 story by *Albuquerque Journal* reporter Nolan Hester quoted Kirtland officials who stated that "chemical wastes may now be polluting South Valley wells. . . . As many as three thousand open fifty-five-gallon barrels were dumped into the arroyo, which drains most of the rain and snow runoff from the Sandia Mountains into the Rio Grande."[59] No agency that I'm aware of ever linked this story with the 1986 reports of explosive chemicals in the Mountain View aquifer. But Hester reported that ACF, working at its plant on Woodward near Broadway, was "a classified contractor making nuclear warhead components for what was then the Atomic Energy Commission."[60] Hester wrote that none of the barrels contained radioactive waste but did not attribute the statement.[61]

No one would have had a clue about the dump and its potential dangers if it hadn't been for a man named John Beal, who called Hester at the *Journal* and told him the story. Beal worked as a part-time truck driver at ACF. He and other drivers "would back their trucks into shallow trenches carved into the Tijeras arroyo bottom land. Eventually, the trenches covered eight acres," Hester reported.[62] The trenches were unlined, and the water table was about a hundred feet below the surface of the arroyo,[63] which can convey water at tremendous speeds and with unpredictable force in a downpour in the mountains.

"We didn't think anything about it at the time," Beal told the *Journal*. "We were just workers. We thought they (ACF) knew what they were doing."[64]

The deputy director of the state Environmental Improvement Division at the time, Cubia Clayton, said the dumping was "potentially . . . very grave."[65] Clayton told Hester that ACF "should have known better than to use the arroyo for a dump." Clayton added, "Even as a small boy growing up in Tularosa, I was taught you don't dump things in the arroyo. Every one of them is subject to flash floods, and sooner or later it ends up downstream."[66] Once, in the 1990s, a flash flood sent water whipping through the arroyo with such force that it tore out a sewer line coming from the Four Hills residential area to the sewage treatment plant, dumping large quantities of raw waste into the arroyo, through Mountain View, and into the river.

It was impossible for the state environmental health department to learn the actual contents of those fifty-five-gallon drums between 1955 and 1967. GE refused to allow its former ACF employees to be interviewed, and the Atomic Energy Commission had turned its records over to the Department of Energy, which won't reveal the contents. "Without a specific list of chemicals dumped at the site, state officials said it is impossible to predict exactly what the health effects of the wastes might be," Hester wrote.[67]

It's equally impossible to tell, apparently, if such waste is related in any way to the explosive chemicals found in groundwater under Mountain View. The timing of the discovery of the explosives is suggestive. The state estimated that it would take about twenty-five years for the pollution from Tijeras Canyon to migrate into the Mountain View water supply.[68] The waste dumped in the late 1950s should have started to appear in the water supply in the early 1980s and continued into the 1990s.

In 1984, the *Albuquerque Journal* ran a piece on the Mountain View nitrate corridor, with no mention of any other contaminants.[69] In 1987, press coverage of the discovery of nitroglycerine and other chemicals used in making TNT did not mention John Beals's revelations about the Tijeras Arroyo industrial waste dump. The next questions, of course, are: What other instances were there of military dumping into Tijeras Arroyo? Was it a regular practice? And if it was, how much material has settled into the South Valley, and how much has been transported to Elephant Butte and beyond?

Groundwater Sacrifice Zone

The history of groundwater pollution in minority neighborhoods remains largely undiscovered, even after many decades of concern. Perhaps the most interesting place to start such investigations is at Kirtland itself, following leads by reporters like Nolan Hester, who in 1982 mentioned that Kirtland base officials, concerned over the Tijeras Arroyo dump, were investigating four landfill sites on base, "including one where heavy metals and radioactive test animals were buried."[70] Ten years later, the *Albuquerque Tribune*'s Tony Davis reported that Kirtland Air Force Base officials agreed to parlay with Mountain View "activists" about nitrates in their water: "Neighboring residents and community groups have long suspected it comes from Kirtland. The base has heatedly denied the allegation," saying there is no evidence of "contamination off site."[71] No mention was made of "explosive chemicals" or of the industrial solvents and liquid plastics dumped in the arroyo by truckers working for the Atomic Energy Commission's subcontractor, ACF.[72] The arroyo runs through Kirtland land, also the site of Sandia National Labs, the major nuclear defense laboratory in central New Mexico, second only to LANL for suspected industrial and nuclear waste pollution. With truckers in the 1950s and 1960s hauling liquid wastes from Broadway and Woodward up the arroyo, one has to wonder what else found its way into the arroyo and ask: Where did those 170,000 gallons of solvents go?

Focusing on nitrates in the water, instead of other pollutants, was obviously in the base's interest. Nitrates do not come from defense contracting, but rather from chemical fertilizers, septic systems, wastewater plants, feedlots, and the like. Focusing on nitrate pollution distracted attention from the Tijeras Arroyo as a possible conduit for decades of Cold War military waste.

Even without reading between the lines of all these newspaper stories, we can see that Mountain View and the rest of the South Valley have been for decades the city's major groundwater sacrifice zone. And not much has changed with the arrival of the twenty-first century.

Dodging responsibility as agilely as other suspected contamina-
tors, the Public Service Company of New Mexico (PNM) tried unsuccessfully to ward off state regulators in 1991, maintaining it didn't
have to clean up the groundwater at its power plant at Broadway
and Rio Bravo, the northern edge of the South Valley, because the
pollution was dissipating.[73] From 1951 until it was demolished in
1986, the PNM Delta-Person generating plant provided power for
the city. PNM argued that the plume of toxic solvents emitted by the
Delta-Person plant, which expanded considerably between 1987 and
1990, was not a threat to any population. In his 1991 story, Tony
Davis quoted utility officials who asserted that the contamination
was dissipating and would continue to decline "because solvents tend
to vaporize as they age and will seep up as vapors from the ground
water through the soil."[74] In the end, PNM bowed to federal and state
authorities and did the right thing. It was involved in an extensive
cleanup of the groundwater plume and soil toxicity until the New
Mexico Environment Department signed off on its efforts in 2005.[75]

New Mexico's $4 Billion Environmental Lawsuit

The PNM issue was minor compared to the massive pollution of
groundwater near the GE site, which generated a $4 billion lawsuit.
This court fight to get compensation for the destruction of groundwater did not end satisfactorily for the people of New Mexico. The
story is a complicated one, leaving many unanswered questions, chief
among them, how does a major nuclear R&D effort in the middle
of Cold War not produce radioactive waste at an industrial site used
for experiments in the creation and feasibility of nuclear-powered
engines? The lawsuit was marred by what are often known as techni-
calities and by a decidedly sour tone on the part of a federal judge and
the Tenth Circuit Court of Appeals—a tone that some might regard
as flagrantly disrespectful to New Mexico and to Albuquerque's
South Valley.

In the 1950s, New Mexico had three major nuclear defense
facilities, one in Los Alamos, one at Sandia National Laboratories in
Albuquerque, and a third facility down the bluff from SNL known
as the South Albuquerque Works. All three facilities were operated
by the Atomic Energy Commission and its subcontractors. In 1967,

the South Albuquerque Works was purchased by the air force, which contracted with GE to make jet engines there. The air force sold the facility to GE in 1984, well after the contaminant plume was discovered. To begin at the beginning, the South Albuquerque Works was started in 1952 when ACF, "which had been operating a secret project for the Atomic Energy Commission" there, according to the *Albuquerque Tribune*,[76] took over the Eidal Manufacturing plant on the Woodward Avenue site. "Details of the work are 'fully classified under restrictions of the Atomic Energy Act of 1946,'" officials told the *Tribune*. Five years later, in July 1957, the *Tribune* reported that the ACF plant did "super-secret manufacturing."[77] The *Tribune* cited a stockholders report listing the major products ACF made for the Atomic Energy Commission at the plant in Albuquerque, two sites in Buffalo, New York, and one in Riverdale, Maryland.

The South Albuquerque Works worked on "nuclear reactors, missile components, airframe machine tools, classified Atomic Energy Commission products, detection devices and countermeasures, flight simulators and training devises, ordinance and components of radioactive materials, handling systems, and weapons handling equipment," the *Tribune* reported.[78] The plant had about a thousand employees at the time. In 1958, the ACF plant was involved with the development of Project Rover. According to Brigadier General Alfred D. Starbird, director of the Atomic Energy Commission's division of military applications, the ACF plant was "fabricating a portion of an experimental reactor for nuclear propulsion under a subcontract to the Los Alamos scientific laboratory."[79] Interviewed at the *Tribune's* Washington, D.C., bureau, Brigadier General Starbird characterized the South Albuquerque Works as "one of three major New Mexico facilities of the [Atomic Energy] Commissions weapons complex. . . . Naturally there is an extremely close coordination between activities of the South Albuquerque plant and the other two major . . . facilities."[80] ACF was fabricating the "structural components for the pre-flight experimental reactors and has done the mechanical work in connection with the Kiwi-A device, which is designed for testing a nuclear rocket engine at the [Atomic Energy Commission's] atomic test grounds in Nevada."[81] The Kiwi device, using radioactive materials to superheat gases to provide thrust, was one of three stages of nuclear-fueled Project Rover engines designed at Los Alamos for long-distance space travel, perhaps to Mars, and as an alternative to chemical engines for intercontinental ballistic missiles. Although Project Rover rockets were tested successfully in Nevada, the project closed down for good in 1973 because of "shifting national priorities," as one scientist put it. An engine using radioactive fuel, plutonium-238, was used in 1997 on a mission to Saturn.[82]

It's impossible to be sure from Brigadier General Starbird's account whether radioactive materials for Project Rover were used directly at the ACF South Valley Works. Stockholder reports and newspaper accounts say that radioactive materials were on-site, but their specific use was cloaked by Project Rover's top-secret status. From what I can tell, no mention has been made of radioactivity in the contaminated groundwater under the ACF-GE Superfund site, nor does the state's suit against GE mention radioactivity in the groundwater. Yet as a reporter, I've always been stunned by how little actual investigative reporting and even less normal coverage was given to the state of New Mexico's $4 billion dollar suit against GE and its codefendants. The largest environmental lawsuit in the state's history[83] should have been covered by several reporters at both the *Albuquerque Journal* and the *Albuquerque Tribune*. The expert testimony alone should have supplied multiple stories a week. But this suit was the most poorly covered major litigation that I can recall. I covered the federal courts when I was a newspaperman in the 1960s, and had such a suit been brought in the 1960s, I know it would have generated dozens of stories in both papers instead of the rather paltry coverage of the state's initial loss[84] and its subsequent failure in 2006 at the Tenth Circuit Court of Appeals in Denver.[85] Why the miserly coverage? Were the newspapers somehow restrained from on high? Did the business community deem the state's suit a precedent that would lead the public to demand expensive accountability on the part of all polluters, large and small? Did such a group get to editors and publishers? Although I don't believe that happened directly, I can imagine phone calls to editors' offices from members of New Mexico's congressional delegation. They've done it before and since on far less substantial matters. But without succumbing to conspiratorial fantasy, I'll simply reiterate that the most expensive and sensational environmental lawsuit in New Mexico's history was given little attention by local media.

Chapter and Verse

Expert testimony for the state of New Mexico was provided in November 2000 by Jack V. Matson, professor of environmental engineering at Pennsylvania State University. In support of the state's case that the defendants had ruined the groundwater at the Superfund site forever and that the defendants (which he referred to as ACF/GE) owed the state damages for despoiling an irreplaceable natural resource, Matson set out a series of opinions that included the following:

> ACF/GE historically did not exercise reasonable and prudent care with respect to environmental practices. . . . ACF/GE should have known that hazardous chemicals spilled, released, or discharged into the environment could contaminate surface [water and] ground water. . . . ACF/GE practices were in conflict with statutory regulations and common law protecting watercourses. . . . ACF/GE did not respect the importance of preserving and protecting natural resources in their community. . . . GE's industrial practices have contributed to environmental contamination in other parts of the United States [and] Defendants' groundwater remediation systems have the potential to release toxic chemicals into the atmosphere.[86]

The contamination was first discovered in 1978. Not until September 1983 was the GE site, at the request of the New Mexico Environmental Improvement Division, placed on the National Priorities List as a Superfund site. It took five more years, until 1988, for the EPA to define the nature and severity of the groundwater contamination and to come up with a plan to clean it up. The plan was a mix of "soil vapor extraction" and "pump and treat systems."[87]

During manufacturing, according to Matson's report, not only did ACF and GE release heavy metals and acids into the groundwater, but they also permitted spills, leaks, and outright discharges of chlorinated and nonchlorinated hydrocarbon solvents. The New Mexico Office of Natural Resources trustee identified fifty-nine separate chemicals that had been released into the groundwater.[88]

"Based on my experience working in the chemical industry," Matson observed, "it was common practice for companies to have in place mechanisms and controls that kept releases to a minimum and procedures to promptly clean up any accidental spills. . . . Many companies that did not employ proper mechanisms, procedures, and controls for minimizing their toxic chemical emissions acquired Superfund status."[89]

In the June 2007 edition of *Chemical Engineering Progress*, authors from the University of New Hampshire wrote that over the "past few decades, pollution prevention and control has assumed a prominent role in the chemical engineering profession." The authors concluded, "From an ethical standpoint, pollution prevention is no doubt the best route to follow in preliminary design" of factories.[90]

In an industry that has dedicated itself over the last thirty years to pollution prevention, it is shocking that two government contractors, both major corporate players, were lax in pollution control, especially in an urban neighborhood. Did the poor neighborhood that surrounded the factory appear to corporate cold warriors to be so rundown as to be virtually deserted? I can only conclude that their callousness was an expression of their values. Surely such behavior epitomizes environmental injustice.

Matson's report contended that inspections of the South Albuquerque Works site by "regulatory agencies and consultants all noted that GE improperly covered over previous spill areas without sampling or any subsequent remedial actions. . . . GE either paved with asphalt or covered with sand chemical storage areas. Stained pavement and stained sand were strong indicators of past releases that were not remediated. The consultants further noted that these acts were perceived as a potential concealment of past chemical mishandling."[91]

To get rid of their toxic waste, ACF and GE stored liquid waste in underground tanks, "discharging effluent to the San Jose Draining Ditch, spraying oil mixed with solvents on the ground for dust control, and burning oil mixed with solvents in open pits. Most of these disposal techniques," Matson observed, "have been identified as causing surface and groundwater contamination."[92]

Matson argues that "considering the abundance of literature on the effect of disposing wastes into ditches and into or onto the ground, ACF/GE should have known that many of their disposal methods could negatively impact the environment. . . . Chemicals such as solvents and oils are easily recoverable, and the technology has been available since at least the early 1920s. Industrial wastewater treatments, whereby wastes are treated to minimize their effects prior to releasing them into the environment, have been employed for almost 100 years."[93]

New Mexico law has been clear on the subject of water pollution since 1915, when a law was passed that made it illegal to "cast refuse matter" into any water or conduit of water, particularly if that water is used "for drinking or domestic purposes."[94] When ACF/GE dumped chemicals on the ground and poured them into the San Jose Drain, which empties out into the bosque and Rio Grande, it must have been clear to company executives that they were potentially polluting the aquifer that provided drinking water to thousands of South Valley residents. As Matson observed, "The relation between industry and the surrounding community can be either cooperative or abusive, depending upon the perception of the industry as to their [sic] role within the community."[95] He continued, "GE shared the aquifer beneath the Albuquerque plant with the residents of the city, specifically the city drinking water wells and surrounding private wells. Ground water in the Albuquerque area is the only source of public water supply."[96] GE, Matson pointed out, was involved in many other Superfund sites around the country, including three in New York State, two in Massachusetts, two in Kentucky, and sites in Washington State, North Carolina, Philadelphia, and Kansas.[97]

On its website, the New Mexico Environment Department gives some indication why prevention is the only acceptable way to deal with pollution near vulnerable groundwater supplies. The reply to its rhetorical question, "Can ground-water pollution be cleaned up?" is "Not always. Once contaminated, ground water is difficult, or in some cases, impossible to return to its original quality.... Restoration of ground-water quality often takes decades to accomplish, and can be very expensive."[98]

Madrid's Case

That description gives the context for the multibillion-dollar suit brought by New Mexico Attorney General Patricia Madrid in October 1999 against GE, ACF, Chevron, Texaco, Phillips Pipeline Company, Phillips Petroleum, Texaco Pipeline, West Emerald Pipe Line, Diamond Shamrock, the ATA Group, Giant Industries Arizona, Duke City Distributing, Whitfield Tank Lines, the DOE, DOA, the U.S. Air Force, "and John Doe Companies 1 through 100 inclusive."[99]

The intersection of Prosperity SE and Prosperity Avenue SE, the main street through the neighborhood of Mountain View. September 2006.

A well that monitors water quality, a flood canal that drains to the Rio Grande, and petroleum holding tanks next to GE. October 2006.

Scrap metal yard. Junk lots of all kinds pepper the neighborhood. October 2006.

The cement lining of the South Diversion Channel (called the Tijeras Arroyo further up) ends here as it nears the Rio Grande. October 2006.

Agricultural land in south Mountain View. October 2006.

Mountain View is zoned both industrial and residential, leaving the citizens with little recourse to fight contaminating neighbors. October 2006.

Train track heading west near the Tijeras Arroyo. November 2006.

Dirt bike tracks up the Tijeras Arroyo. November 2006.

One of the many types of junkyards in Mountain View. December 2006.

The state's allegation against all defendants was that "remediation of the contaminated soil and groundwater will take many years to complete and will never return the natural resources including the impacted groundwater to its pre-polluted or uncontaminated state.... Further, even after . . . remediation, the natural resource will remain in an impaired state, unpotable, and unfit for human consumption."[100]

U.S. federal judge Bruce S. Jenkins didn't buy any part of New Mexico's argument. The state dropped its claims against federal agencies in order to take the case out of his jurisdiction and move it to New Mexico district court. Judge Jenkins blocked that move. The EPA and the state Environment Department concluded that the groundwater contamination spreading out from the GE plant could be treated and made potable, so the judge could see no reason to change venues. GE started cleaning up the plume in 1989. By 2002, GE had spent nearly $30 million on remediation, with many decades of expenditures remaining.[101] The attorney general's lawsuit was obviously at odds with earlier state Environment Department views, views generated during the tenure of Republican governor Garrey Carruthers. Attorney General Madrid was a prominent Democrat.

In 2004, Judge Jenkins gave a summary judgment to the defendants on all charges. The case had been in New Mexico U.S. District

Court for more than five years. Although the suit made barely a ripple in New Mexico, it had a sobering effect on other states. The *New Jersey Law Journal*, for instance, in its May 31, 2004, issue, ran a story under the headline "New Mexico v. General Electric: A Cautionary Tale."[102] The state of New Jersey was pressing a similar kind of lawsuit at the time against what it claimed were major groundwater polluters. The *New Jersey Law Journal* said the "trial judge concluded that [New Mexico] cannot prove its claimed damages because the state did not show an actual loss of ground water services and could not show that remaining contaminated ground water has lost all beneficial use. . . . The court simply could not accept the state's paradigm that contamination equals injury and injury equals damages."[103] The court ruled the "state could not recover [damages] simply because the groundwater was no longer 'pristine.' The availability of groundwater for drinking water purposes depends upon whether the drinking water standards are met, not whether the water 'remains in its primordial state.'"[104] "Even contaminated groundwater, the court found, had beneficial uses, e.g., for agricultural, industrial, fire protection, or other uses."[105] I have to ask the obvious questions here. Would the federal judge draw the same conclusions if the neighborhoods affected by the pollution had been affluent and Anglo, or near his own house? Doesn't the closing of two municipal wells, supplying water to some seventy thousand residents in minority neighborhoods, constitute the loss of all beneficial use? The uses that the judge suggested, such as fire protection and agriculture, are patently unrealistic. How would New Mexico convert that particular pool of contaminated groundwater into water used for fire protection? Would they siphon it off with a separate pump and somehow spray it on fires? Or agriculturally, would the state thirty years from now, when the water meets EPA's changing political standards, pump the water into the ditch system, sullying the rest of the water with it?

Jack Matson believes the case was thrown out on a "technicality." The technicality was "interesting," he said, "in that many types of solvents were contaminants; none of which exceeded drinking water standards, but as a sum total made the water undrinkable. . . . The water was legally drinkable even though no one in their right mind would ever drink it." He called the court's decision "a legalism, not justice."[106] The defendants in the case were never proved innocent of polluting the groundwater. They just could not be held individually liable for the pollution. Was the state of New Mexico wrong to bring this lawsuit in the first place? I would venture to say that the portion of the groundwater contaminated by GE and their codefendants will never be drinkable by anyone other than people who can't afford to refuse it. Imagine the trouble you might have trying to bottle that water and sell it to residents of well-to-do neighborhoods.

The Tenth Circuit Court of Appeals in Denver agreed with the trial judge that New Mexico had proved no factual injury to its natural resources. The circuit court quoted the New Mexico federal district court ruling at length, giving us a sample of the satirical and even flippant nature of the original ruling.

> In effect, then, Plaintiffs rely upon specific facts showing the existing EPA remedial system *is* detecting further contamination and *is* addressing it by adding additional extraction and monitory wells as support for an inference that the system is *not* detecting and *not* treating contamination, an inference that there yet exists undetected "deep, deep" contamination that the system does not and will not treat. Viewed through the Plaintiffs' eyes, direct evidence of the system's remedial efficacy becomes inferential proof of its deficiency.
>
> Much like Scotland's famed Loch Ness monster, the Plaintiffs' "deep, deep contaminant plume" is believed to be "down there somewhere," and has not been conclusively proven *not* to exist, but its proponents have yet to come forward with significant probative admissible evidence of specific facts affirmatively demonstrating that it *does* exist.[107]

These sentences, and the scorn they exude, make it painfully clear how easy it is to ignore health dangers in poor states and poor neighborhoods, especially if the behavior of large corporations is called into question. The fact that the ACF/GE site had been occupied, polluted, and covered up for nearly thirty years is at the very least strongly suggestive of further contamination at deeper levels. But to the federal court, it was merely a joking matter. Inference is, sometimes, the only logical avenue that leads to a "probable cause," if you will, for further investigation and remediation of soil and water pollution. Imagine if a national defense laboratory, long into the business of handling, storing, and manufacturing radioactive components for nuclear weapons, were to assert that its operation was lily pure, free of all polluting, and certainly of no threat to public health. One would be justified in arguing from inference and asking, "Is it possible that this is the only nuclear research facility in the nation that has no pollution problems? Do you mean to tell me that, unlike Hanford, Rocky Flats, Savannah River, and other facilities, yours is the only clean and healthy one?" Such an assertion would be as ludicrous as dismissing with the wave of a bad joke the notion that deep aquifers under a plume of pollution accumulated over more than thirty years might also be also polluted and, irrespective of a current EPA remediation plan, might quite possibly have been destroyed for future use by the plaintiffs in the case. The possibility is so great that the court should have ordered the EPA and the defendants to investigate the possibility and fund its cleanup, if such a cleanup is even possible.

A Tiny Win

Eventually, in January 2006, some ten months before the circuit court dismissed all allegations against other defendants, the state of New Mexico did win a small portion of its lawsuit against two of the defendants in the case, Chevron and Texaco. The court ordered a mediation process between the state and Chevron and Texaco, which resulted in a $7.5 million award, nearly $3 million of which went to the attorneys. Although Attorney General Patricia Madrid was ebullient, seeing this as a significant victory,[108] New Mexico was compensated only $7.5 million out of the $4 billion it had sought, not much of a victory against global corporations with resources in the hundreds of billions.

The New Mexico Natural Resources Trustee, former Albuquerque city councilor Martin Heinrich, held a public hearing in December 2006, looking for ideas on how to use the $4.8 million left of the settlement after legal fees. Among the proposals were to create a wetlands in the uncontaminated areas around the GE site to recharge the aquifer, working to clean up the septic system in the area, collecting household hazardous wastes, and creating water conservation strategies.[109] Albuquerque activists have learned to be skeptical about such planning processes. The sewage treatment plant in Mountain View was still stinking up the neighborhood as late as 2001, after numerous public hearings, so Superfund site residents were wary of the public process in 2006. As early as 1992, the notion of creating wetlands to help with the city's sewage and its odors in the South Valley was recommended by University of New Mexico professor Paul Lusk, the eminent planner who authored the progressive Albuquerque/Bernalillo County Comprehensive Plan. Lusk even created a demonstration wetlands in his own garden to compensate for his leaking septic system.[110] As yet, a drive down Second Street to the sewage treatment plant does not reveal a massive wetlands project, though one can find the small pits that were used briefly as a wetlands experiment until the loss of funding. In 2007, New Mexico's acting Natural Resources Trustee, former Albuquerque mayor Jim Baca, ruled that the $4.8 million be spent not on the Superfund site but rather on cleaning up Mountain View's plume of nitrates, a problem in the area since the 1960s.

Railroad Superfund

Not far from Mountain View, a second Superfund site is being cleaned up at an old yard of the Atchison, Topeka, and Santa Fe Railroad (AT&SF) near Second Street. Cleanup could probably go on until 2025 and cost the new site owner, the Burlington Northern–Santa Fe Railway, upwards of $64 million.[111]

The AT&SF site, about two miles north of Mountain View and about a mile and a half south of San Jose, was used from 1908 to 1972 as a "wood pressure treatment plant . . . and primarily used creosote and oil mixtures for the manufacture of pressure treated wood products, including railroad cross ties, bridge ties, switch ties, bridge timbers, [and] road crossing materials."[112] The plant was "totally dismantled" in 1972, "and the only physical feature remaining on-site is the wastewater reservoir/wastewater sump."[113] The site was designated a Superfund site in 1994. The EPA estimates that between 59,300 and 70,000 gallons of what it calls "dense non-aqueous phase liquid," or as it's known in less exalted circles, "toxic sludge," had slowly dissolved into the ground and has been found sixty-five feet down into the groundwater and its gritty matrix.[114] The EPA created and signed off on a plan for cleanup in 2002, over the objections of neighborhood groups who didn't like the EPA's plan to impound contaminated soil on-site and cap it with a mixture of soil-bonding additives and dirt. Neighbors wanted the dirt removed and incinerated. As one woman told the *Albuquerque Journal*, "We don't want to dig a hole and put the stuff back. We want it out of our community."[115]

According to the October 2006 EPA Fact Sheet on the site, a compromise was reached. Soil with sludge in it would be removed and incinerated off-site; contaminated soils with no sludge would be capped. The groundwater itself, much like the groundwater at the GE Superfund site, is being pumped out, treated, and reinjected into the aquifer.

Jibberish Fact Sheets

Reading the EPA Fact Sheet, it must be said, is rather like reading undeciphered military code. The jargon, syntax, and obfuscation are wonders of gobbledygook. So much for rational interactions between environmental bureaucrats and educated nonspecialists. For instance, it's next to impossible to find out what is meant by "pump and treat," other than that contaminated water is pumped out, treated, and pumped back in. But how is it treated, what are the processes used, how safe are they in themselves, and, most importantly, how effective is the treatment? Treatment varies from "air stripping" and "activated carbon treatment" to "bioremediation" and "chemical oxidation."[116] But to make polluted water, like treated sewage, drinkable, expensive reverse osmosis is needed, a form of dialysis used in desalination and water recycling. Presumably, it is expense that keeps such a process from being used in polluted drinking water in poor neighborhoods, and the effect is to redline a populated area as a sacrifice zone.

The Business of Air Pollution

Not only do the Mountain View neighborhood and other South Valley sites have to contend with junkyards, various brownfield sites, groundwater hazards, and gasoline storage tanks and their leaks and spills, but air pollution is a problem in the area, as well. In March 2005, five small industries were applying to the Albuquerque Air Quality Division for air-emission permits. "It's like were [sic] besieged by air polluting businesses," the president of Mountain View Neighborhood Association, Patty Grice, told the *Albuquerque Journal*.[117] "On top of having most of the air-polluting businesses, we have 90 percent of the pollution. What are we supposed to do with that?"[118]

The *Journal* reported that the "city has said the permits of the industries in the Mountain View area are protective of residents' health, and the city's air quality overall is good."[119] It's the air quality in Mountain

View, however, that Mountain View residents are worried about, not the city's as a whole.

As late as September 2006, yet another industry was seeking an air quality permit. Vulcan Materials, a cement plant, was to be built in an empty lot directly across the inaptly named Prosperity Avenue from the Mountain View Community Center, a place where nearly two hundred children come to play in the summer. The permit would allow Vulcan to vent fumes derived from exuding some three hundred cubic feet of concrete an hour, or some thirty truckloads. It would allow the plant to operate twenty-four hours a day, cheek by jowl with a low-income residential neighborhood.[120] The whole area is zoned for industry.

This part of the South Valley, between Broadway and Second Street, feels like a walled-in city. Only two streets, Woodward and Prosperity, connect between Second and Broadway. The rest of the five-mile-long area is not open to through traffic. From Interstate 25, no one could tell at first glance that the area is a residential site at all. Junkyards, gasoline storage tanks, and a huge chicken farm, with numerous long, rank-smelling sheds, dominate the eastern edge of the area. From the interstate, the massive Tijeras Arroyo can be seen channeled through to the river, strangely inconspicuous to passing motorists and all but unknown to the city's residents. On city maps, the arroyo is usually marked by a thin blue line, as if it were a tiny stream rather than the major drainage for two mountain ranges that runs right through what might well be the greatest polluters in the area, Kirtland Air Force Base and its neighboring Sandia National Laboratories. A half mile south of the arroyo and not a mile east of Mountain View are the beginnings of Mesa del Sol, the large, elegantly planned residential and business community currently being built. But like their Mountain View neighbors across the interstate, Mesa del Sol residents will be living in close proximity to, albeit uphill from, major pollution in the groundwater, soil, and air.

This invisibility is shared by all underground pollution and most soil pollution. Along with defensiveness, indifference, and arrogance on the part of polluters, that invisibility is what makes industrial and military toxic waste so difficult to remedy. A classic example is the largest radioactive accident in the nation's history, one that most Americans have never heard of.

Church Rock

It happened in 1979 at a uranium mine in Church Rock, New Mexico. Church Rock is some twenty miles northeast of Gallup. The dam on a huge evaporative tailings pond near a moderate-sized arroyo leading to the Puerco River burst, sending ninety million gallons of radioactive liquid and over eleven hundred tons of radioactive mill waste cascading toward Gallup and Chandler, Arizona. It amounted to a flash flood of radioactive contamination coursing down the Puerco. This wall of bad water and grit contained traces of heavy metals and isotopes of uranium, thorium, radium, and polonium, the nuclear substance thought to have been used in the assassination of a Russian spy in 2004. Ninety million gallons of wastewater suddenly exploding through a dam into the Puerco River was like a twenty-seven-story tower of grit and liquid, an acre square, roaring through the landscape. The force was so powerful, observers recorded, that sewers were backed up and manhole covers lifted in Gallup, some twenty miles away. It was a catastrophe of huge proportions.

"Except for bomb tests, Church Rock was probably the biggest single release of radioactive poisons on American soil," Harvey Wasserman and Norman Solomon wrote in their book *Killing Our Own*.[121] The Church Rock disaster took place some three and a half months after the malfunctioning of the nuclear power plant at Three Mile Island and thirty-four years to the day, oddly, after the first atomic bomb was set off at the Trinity Site, south of Carrizozo, New Mexico. The massive release attracted little attention in the national media. Those immediately affected were three hundred and fifty or so Navajo families who watered their sheep in the Puerco River. Many of their animals had highly elevated levels of radioactivity in their bodies. Children were admonished by public health officials to keep out of the riverbed and not play on its banks. Traces of radioactive debris were found as far as seventy miles down the Puerco, making a vast stretch of the river unusable for years. Navajo families have been waiting ever since for the delayed health reactions that come with exposure to radiation.

The small dam that held the tailings pond in check began to develop cracks almost immediately after it was constructed. "Soon after the spill an angry U.S. representative Morris Udall (D-Ariz.) told a congressional hearing that 'at least three and possibly more Federal and state regulatory agencies had ample opportunity to conclude that such an accident was likely to occur.'"[122]

The tailings pond and the uranium mine, operated by United Nuclear Corporation (UNC), were up and running again five months after the spill. The same pond area was used, Wasserman and Solomon report, resulting in "constant seepage—up to eighty thousand gallons of contaminated liquid per day."[123] UNC closed the mine in the early 1990s.

Heavy Poison

Uranium tailings ponds result from the milling process in which sandstone that contains uranium ore is crushed so the uranium can be leached out using acid or strong alkaline baths. The uranium is then concentrated and dried into a form sometimes referred to as *yellow cake*.[124] The liquid mixed with powdered ore, called *liquor*, is stored in ponds.[125] The rest of the ore is heaped in piles, some of them mountainous, near the mine site.[126] In north central New Mexico, tailings piles have collected from as many as a thousand uranium mines, most of them on Native American lands. These tailings piles are not benign. They contain more than 80 percent, by some reckonings,[127] of the ore's radioactive content, which includes isotopes of thorium, and radium, and many heavy metals. In fact, when the so-called pure yellow cake is processed into usable form for reactors, the isotope U-235 remains.[128] The resulting "depleted uranium," used in armor and ammunition by the military, still contains all of its U-238, a powerfully charged U-236, and "very small amounts of the transuranic elements of plutonium, americium, and neptunium and the fission product technetium-99," according to the World Health Organization.[129]

Mining for uranium has gained an infamous reputation among Native Americans, so much so that the Navajo Nation in 2006 banned all uranium mining in its territories. The Navajo Nation and many others maintain that the epidemic of lung cancer among uranium miners and their families, along with several maladies—including something that the *Denver Post* calls Navajo neuropathy, a degenerative disease[130]—is the direct result of mining during the Cold War. And now in the age of global warming, with the aid of U.S. Senate leaders like New Mexico's Pete Domenici, nuclear power is having a renaissance of sorts, at least in the commodities market, where uranium had gone from an all-time low in the 1990s of $7 a pound to some $31 a pound in 2005 to upwards of $140 a pound in late 2006, settling out in mid-2007 at $70.[131] It's a sky's-the-limit market, as the nuclear industry turns on its lobbying and public relations campaigns, touting the need for energy sources that release no greenhouse gases.

The nuclear and uranium mining industries are probably the only mainstream energy source with strong government backing that actually use global warming as an excuse for their existence. While the coal, oil, and natural gas industries loudly deny that global warming is a major threat and fund all manner of think tanks and propaganda organizations, nuclear power posits itself as the savior of the world from bad carbon companies.

Leaching

The uranium industry, aware of its rotten reputation, has taken to the idea of a so-called new mining method, something called *in situ leaching*, which I'll discuss in greater detail in the chapter on toxic waste. Briefly, companies that use in situ leaching employ the same kinds of chemicals that end up in uranium "liquor" but put them into groundwater to leach out uranium and other radioactive substances and heavy metals, pumping them out, turning the uranium into yellow cake, but this time pouring the liquid, with its now highly concentrated content of radioactive and heavy metal poisons, back into the groundwater.[132] Such an operation was scheduled to open near the Navajo town of Crownpoint in 2007, even though the Navajo Tribal Council and Navajo president Joe Shirley, Jr., had banned uranium mining of any kind on Navajo land and under Navajo jurisdiction. Uranium mining companies were also looking at reopening the mines at Church Rock in 2008. And a major uranium mill, employing some three thousand people, was scheduled to be operational the same year near Grants. The estimated yield from both operations was around forty-two million pounds of uranium over twenty years, which would bring in some $2.5 billion at the going rate in 2006.[133] A major court battle was anticipated.

Uranium mining around Crownpoint has been disputed at least since 1996, when the Eastern Navajo Diné Against Uranium Mining (ENDAUM) opposed U.S. senator Pete Domenici and the Texas-based

Uranium Resources, Inc. (URI).[134] As Chris Shuey of the Southwest Research and Information Center in Albuquerque writes, "The heart of the controversy is URI's plan to use the community's high-quality groundwater as the medium for mining. URI proposes to mine uranium by injecting oxygen and sodium bicarbonate into water-bearing strata, 2,000 feet to 2,400 feet below ground, pumping out the resulting 'pregnant' solution and processing it to remove the uranium, at a plant located within one-half mile of several churches, schools, businesses, government offices, and most residential areas of Crownpoint."[135]

Shuey, of course, was describing in situ leaching. The project was too expensive in 1996, but in July 2005 the Nuclear Regulatory Commission (NRC) endorsed a mining company's plan to use in situ leaching of uranium in northwestern New Mexico.[136] Doug Meiklejohn, a lawyer at the New Mexico Environmental Law Center, summed up the problem: "It's my understanding that this type of mining has never been done in a drinking-water aquifer before, and the aquifer that they're proposing to do this to is the sole source of drinking water for about 15,000 people, almost all of them Navajo."[137]

The enormous profits to be made mining uranium have emboldened mining companies to propose in situ leaching beyond the realm of impoverished Indian country. Because most landowners in Colorado, for instance, like most in New Mexico, only own the surface rights to their lands, companies can buy up mineral rights and pretty much do what they like, especially with a promining NRC and court system. But mining companies run into trouble when they take on relatively well-to-do Anglo ranchers, especially newcomers. Small ranchers and farmers in northern Colorado are putting up a fight over uranium mining, creating an organization called Coloradoans Against Resource Destruction (CARD), which contends that uranium mining threatens not just water supplies but wheat and organic food products.[138]

Apparently trying to short-circuit potential opposition, in 2007 the NRC began to fast-track approvals of in situ leaching by using what came to be called "generic environmental impact statements" (GEIS), skirting public comment, though allowing some informal local review.[139] Opponents argue that there is no such thing as a "generic environment" and that a GEIS is a useless sham designed to benefit uranium mining companies. New Mexico Governor Bill Richardson came out strongly against GEIS.

Opponents of in situ leaching cite troubling histories of cleanup. One in situ leaching well in Wyoming ended up with NRC-approved "restored" water that contained seven hundred times as much uranium as before leaching began. When leaching ended, a USGS study showed that the groundwater had 40,000 micrograms per liter. Restoration, nine years later, had reduced it to 3,500 micrograms a liter. The EPA safe drinking water standard is a mere 30 micrograms.[140] Uranium has an unhealthy history. The Radiation Exposure Compensation Act has already paid out $1.2 billion, mostly to uranium workers, most of whom are Native Americans, and to downwinders.[141]

Witnesses and Watchdogs

Is there anything positive in all of this? I'd have to give an emphatic, if qualified, yes. No longer can companies and their federal cronies get away with murder undetected. Environmental and culturally sensitive law firms and extremely knowledgeable nonprofit advocates are paying attention. Neighborhood associations, along with such advocates as the Southwest Organizing Project, the Southwest Research and Information Center, Ganados del Valle, and the New Mexico Acequia Association, are sophisticated and aggressive opponents of polluters and exploiters. In November 2007, a Toxic Tour sponsored by a coalition of the Mexican American Law Students Association, the Student Chapter of the ACLU at the University of New Mexico Law School, the Association of Public Interest Law, the Native American Law Student Association, Women's Law Caucus, the Environmental Law Society, and the Student Health Law Society at UNM and guided by members of the Southwest Organizing Project took students through "communities struggling with environmental justice issues," including Mountain View.[142]

In December 2006, the Indigenous World Uranium Summit at Window Rock, Arizona, was covered in depth by many alternative and indigenous news sources, including the reliable and informative publication of the Southwest Research and Information Center, *Voices from the Earth*.[143] Acoma and Laguna pueblos, the All Indian Pueblo Council of New Mexico, and the Eastern Navajo Agency Council of the Navajo Nation passed resolutions opposing uranium mining around Mount Taylor, in western New Mexico, which is sacred to the Pueblos and Navajos. The Navajo Nation took resolutions banning uranium mining on its lands to the Sixth Session of the United Nations Permanent Forum on Indigenous Issues held in New York in May 2006. At that meeting, a declaration called for "a world wide ban on all aspects of the nuclear fuel chain."[144] The ban was supported by not only the Navajos, but also by indigenous representatives from Australia, Brazil, and Canada, from the Lakota, Wind River Shoshone–Arapaho, Kiowa, Cheyenne, Alaska, and Pueblo tribes, and from China, Germany, India, and Japan.[145]

Perry Charley, a Navajo educator and researcher at Diné College in Arizona, puts uranium mining in perspective: "New Mexico was one of the largest producers of uranium. Thirty-nine million dry tons of uranium oxide was mined—the majority of it in the Grants Mineral Belt. Currently, the Navajo Nation has over 1,200 abandoned mines on the reservation, and the radioactive waste scattered down the mountainsides. . . . These mines dot the landscape, our lands and our sacred sites, the areas where people work, live, and play. It's in the deserts, . . . the beautiful mountains: Chuska Mountain, Razor Mountain, and Monument Valley. The list goes on and on. These are the things that we had to live with for many years."[146]

The indigenous world is fighting for itself in more and more empowering ways. In 2007, there was strong opposition, for instance, on the Navajo Reservation to a new 1,500-megawatt Desert Rock coal-burning power plant to be built on Navajo land and to burn Navajo coal. Big signs outside Burnham, New Mexico, read "Dooda Desert Rock," which means "No Desert Rock." Even though the Navajo tribal government has sanctioned the power plant, many Navajos don't want smokestacks spewing pollution into their air just to run "air conditioners in Arizona and southern California by burning 5.5 million tons of Navajo coal each year."[147] Desert Rock would be the fourth major smog-producing coal-fired power plant in the area, joining the Four Corners plant, which generates 2,040 megawatts on Navajo land in Fruitland, New Mexico; the 1,800-megawatt San Juan Generating Station in Waterflow, New Mexico; and some 185 miles to the west, the 2,400-megawatt Navajo Generating Station in Page, Arizona. This is a serious matter. "In 2000, the U.S. EPA . . . estimated that existing coal plants produced pollution equivalent to 3.5 million automobiles."[148]

The opposition to Desert Rock might well prove to be an early salvo in a long-term legal war over power generation to produce water. As global warming affects California and Colorado snowpacks and makes it necessary for states in the West to desalinate brackish aquifers and ocean water, as well as to recycle wastewater, they will look to energy-hungry reverse osmosis or dialysis plants. In the arid

Middle East, such desalinization plants come with their own power facilities, sometimes generating upwards of 50 megawatts each. It's possible that over the next fifty years, dozens, if not hundreds, of such dialysis plants would be needed to compensate for heat and drought. And Navajo land is among the first places mining and power companies would try to locate power plants.

In spite of the hardship and abuse suffered by culturally and economically marginalized Americans, successes in the struggle against polluters do occur. In August 2003, after New Mexico's congressional delegation weighed in, a twenty-year battle against an Arizona power company called the Salt River Project ended with victory for Zuni Pueblo.[149] The Arizona firm had proposed a coal mine near Fence Lake, which is close to Zuni Salt Lake, among the most sacred Zuni sites. The congressional delegation sent a letter to the U.S. Department of Interior asking that the coal mining permit for the power company be temporarily shelved. The company's board of directors then broke the deadlock and voted to get their coal elsewhere. Zuni Pueblo governor Arlen Quetawki said the campaign against the coal mine had, according to Ollie Reed of the *Albuquerque Tribune*, "cost his tribe dearly in money, hard work, and anxiety. But I think what we have done will cause a ripple effect in Native American issues."[150] The Zunis and the various environmental groups that called themselves the Zuni Salt Lake Coalition "used a hard-driving publicity campaign and legal maneuvers in court to keep the mine venture at bay," Reed wrote. The Zunis countered the power company's geological experts with experts of their own, establishing the strong possibility that mining and putting a rail line near the Salt Lake would damage underground water flows. Carleton Albert, head of the Zuni council, told Reed that "we as native peoples have a belief that Mother Earth is sacred to us, and we should always keep that in our hearts."[151]

Many more environmental battles lie ahead for New Mexico's poor of every race and culture. There are hopeful signs that environmental injustices are coming to be seen for what they really are—not just expedient cost efficiencies by corporate managers, but brazen crimes against the poorest of America's people. What Zuni Pueblo, the Desert Rock and Crownpoint dissenters, and Acoma, Laguna, and the South Valley protesters have done and continue to do is lift the veil of invisibility from these crimes. Their courage and persistence have given future activists a better chance to carry the day.

CHAPTER FOUR

TOXIC WASTE
"EVERYTHING HAS TO GO SOMEWHERE"

When it comes to reports of toxic spills, leaks, and other poisonous intrusions in our air and water, Americans and New Mexicans have gotten used to hearing the same reassuring and never-changing claim. No matter what has befouled the environment—radioactive material, heavy metals, industrial solvents, mercury, or mining and drilling waste—news releases from government and media portray it as not being a danger to public health and therefore nothing to worry about. Even when a 2006 Santa Fe Water Quality Report accompanying city water bills mentioned traces of plutonium in Santa Fe's drinking water, which is drawn from an aquifer down the hill from Los Alamos National Laboratory (LANL) near the Rio Grande, the official response was, in effect, "Pay no attention, all is under control." This response came in the face of what a national investigative blog

◀ Tony Hood shows me around the United Nuclear ("United Unclear," he jokes) mine site in northeast Church Rock. When he was a kid, his grandparents grazed about a hundred goats and two hundred sheep on this land. This canyon is a natural pen—his uncle could let his horses run free but confined here. It is now dotted with different colored flags signifying testing locations, ore deposits, or hot spots. April 2007.

said were numerous "detections of LANL radionuclides in Santa Fe drinking water wells" that have been "published by the Department of Energy in environmental reports since the late 1990s."[1]

Typically, months later another report, this time in the *Santa Fe New Mexican*, said the plutonium finding might have been a scientific mistake after all, "a false positive," LANL officials called it.[2] If one goes by official accounts, no toxic substance, it seems, is ever a danger, and its appearance was probably an illusion to begin with. This all suggests George Orwell's Ministry of Truth. Analyses like the 1995 *Toxic Sludge Is Good For You: Lies, Damn Lies, and the Public Relations Industry* by John Stauber and Sheldon Rampton[3] offer important but largely impotent corrections to official and corporate spin. Environmental accidents allow the media to titillate the public with fearful headlines, then calm everyone down with sober-sounding "reality checks" that deny their own initial reporting. No matter what might have happened, the reasoning goes, if it's said not to be a danger, then no one has to worry about it. And if you do worry about it, you're something of a fool or an alarmist. In fact, you may even be branded a traitor to the economy or worse.

This pervasive pattern has gone a long way toward distracting even the proenvironment voting public from what could well become a major economic and public health calamity in the making. If it becomes a common suspicion that, say, Albuquerque's aquifer is not as pristine as home buyers and new businesses have always been told, then New Mexico's protracted drought makes every drop of clean water we have a communitywide treasure to be preserved at all costs. And dirty water becomes a fateful drain on the prosperity of the region.

Poisonous Reality

It's difficult for many people to get a handle on how serious toxic wastes and other pollutants have become to our physical health and economic well-being. News accounts are scattered around the back pages of the papers and rarely, if ever, appear on TV news. Perhaps the best summation we have of the magnitude of the problem for the Albuquerque area is a 1995 report from the U.S. Agency for Toxic Substances and Disease Registry (ATSDR), according to which Bernalillo County has had "over 150 documented ground-water contamination events" that have polluted "vast amounts of groundwater, its quality degraded to an extent that it affects its usefulness as drinking water."[4] More ominous is the report's assertion that more than "20 of these cases" may reach the EPA's Superfund National Priorities List. Albuquerque–Bernalillo County still had only three Superfund sites as of 2007. The ATSDR says "as much as 30 square miles of land area" here may "overlie" groundwater supplies polluted from "septic tanks, underground storage tanks, landfills, industrial facilities, and releases of hazardous materials."[5] As far as I can tell, this alarming assessment has never been a factor in discussions of water and urban growth in the region nor in general growth planning.

Apparently the military-industrial complex in New Mexico is such a sacred cow and land speculation such a dominant force in our economy that we'll believe any denial of their potential danger. Only this "What, Me Worry?" mentality could allow the public to overlook a report that plutonium has appeared in Santa Fe's water supply when even hammers and gloves that have merely touched plutonium have to be buried in a salt mine 2,000-plus feet underground in the Waste Isolation Pilot Project (WIPP) near Carlsbad. Public officials in New Mexico have often scoffed at how ignorant citizens are about the nature of radioactive materials. The late Harry Kinney, a Sandia Labs engineer and long-time mayor of Albuquerque, boasted with vaudevillian flair that he could carry around a ball of plutonium in his pocket and have no ill effects.

In photographs I've seen of people actually holding plutonium in their hands, they're always wearing thick, oversized rubber gloves, perhaps the kind stored in WIPP with the other equipment used to make plutonium triggers for nuclear bombs. Plutonium is inherently hard to deal with, not only because it is radioactively potent, but it is also pyrophoric, like processed uranium. In some circumstances, it can oxidize in the open air and become so hot it causes things close to it to burst into flame. If too much of it is stored in close quarters, it can get so hot it causes a chain reaction: not an explosion, but a powerful, random burst of lethal radioactivity.[6]

Radiation comes in many varieties. The five kinds that concern humans most are alpha, beta, gamma, X-ray, and neutron radiation, which can impact humans in nuclear power plants, in industry, and in high-altitude flight.[7] Plutonium, radium, radon, uranium, and thorium emit mostly alpha radiation, a short-lived form that cannot penetrate the skin or even a piece of paper, but can cause lung, liver, and bone cancer if inhaled, ingested, or absorbed through wounds. Much is made in the literature of how only inhalation of alpha particles is worrisome. But if you have ulcers or similar kinds of digestive problems, bladder lesions, or any other kind of internal bleeding like internal hemorrhoids or gingivitis, you surely wouldn't choose to drink plutonium-laced water.

Beta radiation travels farther and faster and penetrates deeper than alpha. That's how strontium-90 and other beta emitters cause cancer. Gamma radiation moves as a wave and penetrates deeply. It has been described as "an invisible bullet that can kill in hours," whereas alpha and beta radiation come in particles that "work as a time bomb."[8] Much of the immediate human damage resulting from the Chernobyl disaster came from releases of gamma radiation. The long-term damage caused by alpha and beta radiation is still not completely known even two decades after the accident and will probably never be completely comprehended, as it's notoriously difficult to track down direct causes of cancer—and politically imprudent in the former Soviet Bloc and the United States. Gamma rays are emitted by such isotopes as cesium-137, radium-226, and cobalt-60. X-rays, of course, should be used with caution.

El Cobalto

Radioactivity isn't funny, but human clumsiness and deceitfulness sometimes are. A 1984 accident involving gamma radiation emitted by cobalt is a case in point. If it hadn't been for an alert Illinois State police officer and the radiation detector in his car, as well as a Geiger counter at an entrance gate to Los Alamos National Laboratories, folks across the United States and northern Mexico might have been living in radioactive houses or sitting at metal patio tables that were emitting enough gamma rays to kill them off far before their time.

The story begins with more than six thousand silver-colored pellets of cobalt-60 that were used in a cancer radiation treatment machine.

Hauled off, still in the machine, from a hospital in Juarez, Mexico, the pellets were accidentally dispersed around large mounds of scrap metal in a Juarez junkyard called Jonke Finix. The pickup driver who hauled away the cancer treatment machine had tried to salvage some parts for himself, including a metal container that he had no idea contained radioactive poison. He apparently whacked open the container to see what was inside, and the pellets were scattered every which way. The scrap and the radioactive pellets were melted down and then formed into some six hundred to nine hundred tons of radioactive steel that was sold and shipped to the United States in two months at the end of 1983 and the beginning of 1984. Much of that tonnage was in the form of rebar. That's what was being delivered to Los Alamos before it was detected. A significant amount had gone into the manufacture of metal table legs used in restaurant furniture, some of which the Illinois police officer detected. The thief was eventually arrested and spent time in the Juarez city jail, where he was known as El Cobalto.[9] He was not charged with endangering the lives of thousands.[10]

Down Playing

Just like tobacco companies proclaiming the safety of their product, coal mining companies prophesying that clean coal is on the way, or uranium mining firms downplaying the dangers of extraction to miners and their families and neighbors, the nuclear establishment has done everything but scoff outright at people who fear that nuclear power endangers public health. Mainstream media supports this strategy, portraying serious scientists with differing views as cranks. This was the fate of the chief medical researcher of the Atomic Energy Commission in the late 1960s, Dr. John Gofman, described as "one of history's most respected and revered medical and nuclear pioneers."[11] Gofman claimed in public that the nation's network of nuclear power plants could cause lethal diseases in as many as thirty-two thousand Americans a year, even without malfunctions. Whether a reactor melts down "or doesn't melt down," says Gofman, "you've created an astronomical amount of radioactive garbage which you must contain and isolate better than 99.99 percent perfectly. In peace and war, with human error and human malice, guerilla activity, psychotics, malfunction of equipment . . . do you believe that there's anything you'd like to guarantee will be done 99.99 percent perfectly for a hundred thousand years?" Gofman was speaking in a documentary film, *Lovejoy's Nuclear War*, which documented a Massachusetts man's civil disobedience against nuclear power equipment in his hometown.[12]

Whether you're a homeowner in New Mexico, a rationalist skeptical of nuclear power's vast array of lobbyists and government tax breaks and other handouts, a member of the French public that gets 70 to 80 percent of its residential and commercial energy from nuclear reactors, or a born-again, pronuke environmentalist seeing atomic power as the salvation of a world caught in the vortex of global warming, the assessment of a scientist like Gofman cannot be dismissed out of hand. Some might say that scientific debunkers of nuclear power are similar to the scientific minority of climate change deniers and deserve to be dismissed. But there is no worldwide scientific consensus on the safety of nuclear energy, as there is an overwhelming international consensus on climate change. Gofman's views serve as a reminder that skepticism about blanket claims of harmlessness is more useful than gullibility.

Galisteo Basin

The oil and gas industry, of course, is also given to reassurances that strain credibility. At the end of 2007, Santa Fe was in a community firestorm over the possibility that the Galisteo Basin south of the city would be subjected to oil and gas exploration on a considerable scale. This area is rich in archeological sites and is also a budding residential enclave. The drillers, Tecton Corporation, and the New Mexico oil and gas industry in general made remarkable assertions that drilling, and all its waste, had never tainted any of New Mexico's underground water. This improbable claim was undermined by the December 2007 publication in *Parade* magazine of a brief article called "The Dirty Side of Domestic Fuel." This national magazine comes with the Sunday *Albuquerque Journal* and is distributed across the state. In one issue's "Intelligence Report," an article asserted that "extracting oil and gas is known to release toxic chemicals, including mercury, benzene, and arsenic, and harmful chemicals are routinely injected underground to boost output." The article continued, explaining that "such wells are exempt from the parts of the federal Safe Drinking Water Act and Clean Air Act that would control these substances," owing to the oil and gas industry's tremendous clout in Congress.[13]

Santa Fe County government responded to residents' concerns and placed a three-month moratorium ban on oil and gas drilling in the Galisteo Basin in 2007. Tecton abandoned its efforts thereafter. Fearing more attempts to drill in the basin, Santa Fe County enacted strict drilling regulations in 2008. The oil and gas industry in New Mexico considered them "the toughest in the United States."[14]

Despite the culture of denial that surrounds virtually the entire military-industrial complex, all extractive industries, and most manufacturing and housing, it's clear to anyone who can put two and two together that poisonous garbage in the air, soil, and water are economic and health disasters waiting to happen. Love Canal, the work of Erin Brokovich in Southern California against Pacific Gas and Electric over carcinogenic hexavalent chromium in the water supply of the town of Hinkley, and the revelations of contamination in Albuquerque's South Valley have alerted us to this issue. They've also fed the healthy skepticism that asks the fundamental question, Do you mean to tell me that in spite of all the pollution in every single nuclear lab and facility around the country, and in spite of all the pollution associated with virtually every other chemical and manufacturing facility in the nation, and in spite of all the poison debris from power plant emissions and mining, New Mexico's facilities are the only ones that are "harmless"? Who could answer that question in the affirmative with a straight face?

Burying the Evidence

Even if a team of reputable investigative reporters explored the New Mexico pollution scene and arrived at solid evidence, you can bet that their findings would be debunked with great vigor. As an Associated Press story out of Dayton, Ohio, reported in January 2007, "Former nuclear weapons workers are questioning why the federal government buried records they say would help determine if exposure to radiation and other industrial toxins made them sick."[15] Some four hundred boxes of records, almost a small roomful, from a nuclear munitions factory that made plutonium detonators for bombs in Miamisburg, Ohio were buried in 2005 at the Los Alamos National Laboratories. The Department of Energy, the AP reported, contended that the records themselves were radioactive. The Miamisburg plant had closed in 1996, and the DOE was still cleaning up nuclear and industrial waste on the site. One of the plant's former workers didn't see how illnesses could be tied to on-the-job exposures without the material in those boxes. "The whole process just has a smell to it," the man said.[16] How many other such boxes, one wonders, are buried at LANL in top-secret precincts?

It Happens Everywhere

Why might one worry about the overall health of New Mexico's soil and groundwater? Isn't it all just paranoid thinking? The state does, after all, occupy the fifth largest land mass in the union. It's the sixth least populated state, and much of it is located in a Chihuahuan desert environment. Surely there's enough room for questionable trash to stay isolated from those residents. Things are more complicated, however. New Mexico's remoteness and size have not exempted it from the Industrial Revolution or from dependence on hard rock mining and oil and gas. Nor, obviously, has it been uninvolved in the arms race since World War II. Quite the contrary. New Mexico has been, perhaps, more central to the arms race than any other state. It is safe to say that what has happened in other areas of the country when it comes to Cold War pollution has also happened in New Mexico, and perhaps even more than elsewhere, partly because the state is remote from the centers of political power. Out of sight, out of mind. And New Mexico's nuclear redoubts at LANL and SNL are near major urban centers and have always been clothed in secrecy.

In other parts of the country, pollution has been more obvious. Surface water in lakes and rivers has been befouled, or shorelines desecrated, or landscapes polluted or destroyed by mining operations. Much of New Mexico's problem, in contrast, involves invisible contamination of water, soil, and air. Groundwater pollution, I expect, will become a major national issue in the next decade. As years of industrial and military dumping and leaking, as well as vast amounts of oil and gas exploration and production—whose technology invariably includes accidents leading to pollution—finally befoul rivers and water tables, such pollution will come to have a major economic impact in chronically water-poor New Mexico. If your state gets only fifteen inches of rain a year on average, has only about two hundred fifty square miles of surface water, and uses rapidly dwindling aquifers to supply more than 90 percent of its drinking water, groundwater pollution of any kind is a potential catastrophe.

New Mexico's clear air has long been one of its leading attractions. The state is built on its reputation for health. In a place that isn't supposed to have any major air pollution problems, the accumulated effect of power plants, oil and gas drilling engines from tens of thousands of pumps, and industrial air pollution in the Middle Rio Grande Valley from urban industries in the South Valley and a gigantic smokestack operation making computer chips—as well as a possibility for dramatic growth in all such pollution sectors—has created the potential for New Mexico to become an environmentally endangered place.

The chances for pollution from accidents and illegal dumping in New Mexico are in keeping with the luck of the draw nationally and internationally, as all places in the world are bearing similar burdens. But like everyplace else, New Mexico's situation is unique to its demography and geographic setting. Much toxic waste is released near cities and city water sources in New Mexico, and much also occurs in seemingly remote places that are, of course, connected to larger populations by weather and underground water flow.

Odds Are Against Good Luck

Not only does New Mexico have massive coal reserves to fire up electric power plants, its reserves are close to big energy users in Arizona and Southern California. The power plants produce smog, mercury releases, and myriad other ills. Coal mining and uranium mining, with their vast amounts of waste in western New Mexico, could make large parts of Indian country uninhabitable. New Mexico is also home to some fifteen thousand oil wells and more than thirty-three thousand natural gas wells.[17] Each well has its own engine or generator usually run on diesel fuel, with attendant smog and pits full of industrial chemicals and other waste. Aerial photographs around the Four Corners area in northwestern New Mexico and around southeastern cities like Roswell and Carlsbad reveal a vast grid of little squares across the landscape, each occupied by an oil or gas pump and connected by roads. In the center of one such web of oil and gas pumps is Eunice, where a massive $1.5 billion uranium recycling plant is being built. In an oceanic expanse of potash mines and oil and gas facilities near Carlsbad resides WIPP and its massive plutonium waste storage vault nearly half a mile beneath the surface. If boosters of Roswell, northwest of Carlsbad, have their way over citizen objections, another uranium recycling and nuclear waste reprocessing plant will be built some forty miles east of town, near oil fields on the western edge of the Llano Estacado, or "the staked plains," the dead flat landscape of eastern New Mexico that spreads deep into West Texas. These three operations have the potential of turning southeast New Mexico into a major player in what some hope will be a world nuclear energy boom.

New Mexico also has some seven thousand miles of gas pipelines, one section of which exploded in a campground near Carlsbad in August 2000, killing twelve members of a family who were on a camping trip.[18] Some 38 percent of all water contamination from oil and gas operations comes from pipeline leaks, 266 of which have been documented.[19]

Like most places in the country, New Mexico is home to many businesses that store and use hazardous materials. Some 120 of them in the state have reported more than ten thousand pounds of dangerous chemicals and materials in their operational sites. These businesses include AT&T, GE Aircraft Engines, Halliburton, Honeywell Defense Avionics Systems, New Mexico Propane, Philips Semiconductor, Industrial Chemical Corporation, Qwest, PNM Gas Services, and Verizon Wireless.[20] One such site, Sparton Technology on Albuquerque's West Mesa, was closed down and underwent extensive cleanup under the Superfund Act and supervision by the New Mexico Environment Department (NMED). Sparton made printed circuit boards for the military and industry from 1961 to 1999. Its 64,000-square-foot factory was perilously close to the Corrales Main Canal and the Calabacillas Arroyo, one of the major aquifer recharge areas on the West Side. Sparton's industrial solvents, stored in cement-lined ponds near the factory that apparently leaked, got into the groundwater some sixty-five feet below the factory.[21] Why the factory was placed so near major water resources is anyone's guess. It seems likely to me that neither Sparton nor city and county governments had bothered to understand the geology and danger of the location.

Downwinder issues also plague New Mexico. Largely because of two major power plants in the Four Corners region, the Four Corners Power Plant and the San Juan Generating Station, the state, according to New Mexico attorney general Gary King, "has the highest atmospheric concentration of airborne mercury in the nation."[22] King made the remark in joining more than a dozen other state attorney generals in 2006 to protest an EPA ruling creating a "cap and trade" system for mercury control that would allow some plants to actually increase their mercury emissions.[23] Mercury emissions, usually calculated in tons, can cause severe neurological damage in fetuses and children, as well as adults. Mercury from smokestack emissions settles on lakes, rivers, and soil and can be taken up, most dangerously to humans, by fish.

New Mexico High on the List

It's not possible as of now to calculate which states have been hardest hit by military and corporate pollution. But it is safe to say that states with large nuclear establishments, coal-burning power plants, oil and gas pumping, and heavy mining activity, including uranium mining—even if they don't have massive industrial pollution—will be found in the top ranks.

New Mexico's level of nuclear pollution is not unique. Colossal errors in judgment and procedure hounded highly classified and thoroughly monitored nuclear facilities such as the Rocky Flats plutonium pit manufacturing site outside Denver, shut down in 1992 because of its massive pollution problems, and the plutonium production site in Hanford, Washington, with its leaking underground containers that hold more than fifty-four million gallons of radioactive sludge and nitric acid. In fact, the entire nuclear establishment in the United States and its corporate managers, including Rockwell International, Dow Chemical, Bechtel, and others, all appear to have operated under something close to an "anything goes" philosophy during the Cold War, when losing the nuclear arms race seemed far more dangerous than the risks of disease or death from shoddy waste management of nuclear materials.

It's not just New Mexico's national laboratories that produce radioactive waste. The state has some three hundred other radiation sites, according to state government, and many, many more according to miners and protesters in uranium mining country. The sites the state lists range from abandoned mines and old milling sites to numerous businesses in Albuquerque, hospitals, Kirtland and Holloman air force bases, and White Sands Missile Range. According to the National Park Service in 1996, abandoned mineral lands (AML) or mines all over the Colorado Plateau, including New Mexico, are unregulated by the federal government. There are in fact "no federal regulations addressing the management of AML sites for radioactive emissions or enhanced soil and radiological constituents."[24] One wonders how much airborne and groundwater pollution is actually associated with those abandoned mines and how many cancers they have caused. Samuel S. Epstein, a professor in the School of Public Health at the University of Illinois at Chicago, sees "run-away petrochemical and radionuclear technologies" as the prime cause of cancer rates rising in the United States some 55 percent from 1950 to 1995. In a essay in the *International Journal of Health Services*, Epstein reports that "non-smoking-related cancers" of the prostate and lymph system increased 200 percent in that time period and that brain and nervous system cancers rose almost 80 percent, while breast and male colon cancer jumped 60 percent.[25]

In August 1991, a DOE study of nuclear fallout concluded that Albuquerque had "higher than expected plutonium levels" in its soil, but, predictably, "none high enough to cause health concerns."[26] Of the thirty-three sites examined in older sections of town, twenty-four were determined to have safe levels of plutonium derived from downwinder fallout from Cold War atmospheric testing. Nine of the sites with higher levels of plutonium include the city zoo, major parks in older parts of town, and the lawn of the president's house at the University of New Mexico, all apparently fertilized with sludge that contained plutonium. Cleanup was recommended at all sites. Just exactly how does sewer sludge become laced with plutonium? Were DOE facilities in the Middle Rio Grande Valley flushing plutonium down the toilet?

Malignant Radiation

The relationship between radiation and cancer is described clearly in the 1988 book *Deadly Defense: Military Radioactive Landfills*, a "citizen guide." As with smoking, which increases the probability of coming down with certain diseases, write the epidemiologists and medical researchers who assembled this book, "individuals exposed to radiation may or may not develop cancers, but a population exposed to radiation will see a general rise in the number of genetic effects, cancers, and other diseases. . . . Age is an important factor. For a given radiation dose, the very young and the elderly are more likely to develop cancer."[27] "In low levels, radiation causes lung, bone, and other kinds of

cancer, leukemia, premature aging, birth defects, sterility, blood com-
position changes, and cataracts." The guide contends that there are no
levels of radiation so low as to not trigger the possibility of cancer, and
any that are proposed are "without scientific justification."[28]

"Since a single alpha, beta, or gamma ray can initiate the process
of uncontrolled cell multiplication, there can be no lower limit." And
accidents do happen. In 1957, a fire at Rocky Flats released plutonium
contamination into the area around Denver. And "truck accidents"
involving nuclear materials "are fairly frequent."[29] The DOE reported
173 accidents from 1972 to 1988 involving trucks carrying plutonium
between Los Alamos, Hanford, and the Savannah River and Rocky
Flats plants.[30] As of 2008, the health impact of low-level radiation
exposure is still asserted to be nonexistent by nuclear power advocates.
But plenty of contemporary health experts contend that assessing a
dangerous dose remains largely "arbitrary." Current scientific standards do not take into consideration anything other than a medical
model known as the "standard man." Dangerous levels of radiation
doses are not judged against the sizes and ages of men and women,
fetuses, infants, or young children, just against the body type of a
healthy male in his prime. Mary Fox Olson and Kay Drey, writing for
the Nuclear Information and Research Service in 2003, said, "The late
Dr. Donnell Boardman, a physician with many years of medical observation of nuclear workers, explained that no two radiation exposures
are ever the same, even to the same individual. [The] nuclear industry
minimizes the dangers of radiation and does not admit to the many
uncertainties in monitoring and calculating the amounts of radioactivity to which workers and the public are exposed."[31] Olson and Drey
call on "authorities to make it clear that the health consequences of
any resulting exposure cannot be standardized or accurately predicted.
Therefore any claim to 'no damage to the public' has no credible basis
except as one more convenient myth."[32]

Cancer was unknown on the Navajo Reservation before uranium
mining started in the 1950s. "While the increase in Navajo cancer is
still below the national average," then–U.S. representative Tom Udall,
Democrat from New Mexico, said at a uranium roundtable discussion in Washington in December 2007, "that increase is due to outside
forces on the Navajo Reservation. That's important for us to understand. . . . They were a cancer-free population until they came into
contact with the industrial forces of our society."[33] Dr. Douglas Peter,

director of the Navajo Indian Health Service, agreed with Udall, pointing out that since "the presence of smoking among Navajos is far lower than the U.S. population . . . there would be essentially no lung cancer had there not been uranium mining among Navajos."[34] The uranium mines on the Colorado Plateau are not federally regulated, and physician Doug Brugge, professor at Tufts University School of Medicine, contends there has been "too little research on the health impacts of uranium mining in Navajo communities. . . . Clearly, uranium ore is a toxic brew of numerous nasty hazardous materials. Uranium, itself highly toxic, gives rise to a series of other radioactive decay elements. . . . Hence, uranium mill tailings and mill tailings effluent are not only highly radioactive, but they are acutely hazardous."[35] The Nuclear Information and Resource Service cites a 1,500 percent increase in testicular and ovarian cancer in children living on Navajo lands near uranium mines, a 500 percent increase in bone cancer in children exposed to uranium, and a 250 percent increase in leukemia among people of all ages on the Navajo Reservation.[36]

New Mexico—with its powerful congressional delegation headed for decades by nuclear advocate Senator Pete Domenici, its nuclear laboratories, and the world's only underground nuclear waste storage site—could have been a leading advocate for nuclear health safety research. But that is not the case. No state or government entity, apart from the Navajo Nation and Laguna and Acoma pueblos, has even evinced any interest in examining the effects of persistent low- to moderate-level radiation exposure or the health impacts of drinking radioactive water and breathing radioactive atmospheric dust. After its contribution to victory in World War II, New Mexico could have demanded serious, ongoing, well-funded health studies controlled, not by the Nuclear Regulatory Commission (NRC), but by other federal agencies and the state health department. But state and federal agencies have chosen to simply ignore the health effects of exposure to radioactive substances.

WIPP

Radioactive material, however, is considered dangerous enough to be stored at the Waste Isolation Pilot Project (WIPP) nearly half a mile underground in a place that must seem like the end of the world to most Americans, in potash mining country, twenty-six miles from the small city of Carlsbad. WIPP has been controversial and passionately contested since Sandia Labs started planning for the facility in 1974 and Congress authorized WIPP in 1979. It has survived thirty years of legal battles and numerous blockages by state elected officials and the New Mexico congressional delegation and will in all probability persist until its expected closure date of 2070. Since it began accepting Cold War nuclear waste in 1999, it had stored by 2008 some seventy-seven hundred shipments of what's called transuranic radioactive waste (waste heavier than uranium) contained in metal barrels, the kind of waste that workers can apparently handle without extra shielding. After Congress revised its permit in 2006, it began preparing to store "remote handled" transuranic material, waste that is so radioactive it needs special shielding and special trucks and is moved by remote-controlled machinery. By January 2008, the DOE reported, WIPP had already accepted one hundred such remote handled shipments.[37] LANL sent its first remote handled shipment to WIPP in June 2009.

The controversy over WIPP derives from differing views of risk and differing interpretations of fact. The government considers the salt beds in which WIPP is buried to be ideally suited for storing long-lived nuclear waste, including plutonium, which has a half-life of twenty-four thousand years, and all the radioactive isotopes into which such waste decays. The government and its scientists contend that the Carlsbad area salt beds have been stable for two hundred thousand years. But salt, they say in the same breath, has a tendency to move around and fill up openings in itself, including a cavernous, human-made nuclear waste deposit, thereby sealing it off for all time. Because WIPP was dug in an extremely profitable potash mining region, and the area is also rich in natural gas and oil deposits, plans have been made to cover the WIPP site with ultra-long-lasting warning signs and markers to keep miners and drillers from accidentally tapping into the radioactive cyst that WIPP will one day become. No one knows how the government plans to construct markers than can last ten thousand years or more or what language it might use.

The government considers WIPP a vital storage facility. The site can handle approximately 6 million cubic feet of transuranic waste, only about 2 percent of what is currently scattered dangerously around the country. Opponents of WIPP have argued variously that the site is inherently unsafe and could even be used, covertly or legally with changes in its permit, to store other kinds of highly dangerous, hot nuclear waste, should emergency situations occur in the years ahead. They also have contended that WIPP's football-field-sized storage rooms leak salty water that compromises the reliability of the metal drums holding the waste. Fissures and fractures in the salt layer, they say, provide openings to a brine aquifer below and to other drinking water supplies, including the Pecos River and its water table some twenty-five miles west of the WIPP site. WIPP detractors have also worried about the safety of the special containers and trucks that carry the waste on the state's and nation's highways, from Los Alamos, Savannah River, the Hanford site, Lawrence Livermore National Laboratory, the Nevada Test Site, Argonne National Laboratory, and even Rocky Flats to WIPP. The DOE maintains that the WIPP transportation system has an exemplary safety record, that its drivers are "superbly trained," that they are continually monitored by a "state of the art computer-based satellite-linked tracking system, and that drivers are always updated on weather conditions.[38]

But despite the WIPP transport system's near-immaculate safety record, opponents contend logically that it takes only one fiery accident to send aerosolized plutonium into the atmosphere. The uncertainty of bringing nuclear waste over thousands of miles and through some densely populated areas has caused many people to consider WIPP bad for everyone's business and property. In March 2008, the driver of a fully loaded WIPP-bound truck became ill outside Las Vegas, New Mexico, and the truck veered off the road. Luckily, the truck stayed upright and nothing spilled or leaked, according to the state police.[39] WIPP opponents point out that it's almost impossible to get riders on homeowner insurance to cover nuclear contamination. And they argue that real estate values along WIPP routes are severely diminished.

WIPP continues to be a catalyst for controversy. The Bush administration's DOE suggested that some of the millions of gallons of radioactive nitric acid leaking into the Columbia River from Hanford plant storage tanks in Washington State might be relabeled as suitable transuranic waste so it could be stored at WIPP. But even the Bush people eventually realized what a political dust devil such a notion would stir up in New Mexico. In 2008, the suggestion was removed from potential WIPP inventory lists. That it was considered a legitimate possibility is shocking but not surprising.

In October 1991, eight years before WIPP accepted its first shipment of transuranic waste, then–U.S. energy secretary James Watkins
decided that more than eight thousand barrels of transuranic waste
had to be moved into WIPP immediately for experimental reasons,
even though the facility was acknowledged, even then, to be years
away from being operational. Jack Ehn, editor of the *Albuquerque
Tribune*'s editorial page, wrote at the time, "Imagine: New Mexico's
congressional delegation has been squabbling since 1987 over legislation that would permit WIPP to open. Never mind that the waste
will have to remain safely buried for at least 10,000 years before it
loses most of its harmfulness. Never mind that WIPP is unlikely to
fully meet Environmental Protection Agency safety standards, old or
new, until 1994 at the earliest." As Ehn went on to note, Watkins and
the DOE maintained that, despite all the safeguards that would have
been swept away by such a move—a move, incidentally, approved
by New Mexico's Manuel Lujan, who was secretary of the interior
at the time—"WIPP will be safe. 'I guarantee that we won't do anything unsafe down there, and we are not going to be rushing things,'
Watkins chirped. 'Trust me.' But the nation for years trusted DOE's
protestations that its weapons research and production facilities were
safe. Lately studies have shown that facilities such as Los Alamos
and Rocky Flats are loaded with environmental problems. Trust an
agency with a legacy like that?"[40]

The controversy raged until then–New Mexico attorney general
Tom Udall sued the DOE, spurred on by support from then–New
Mexico congressman Bill Richardson, Governor Bruce King, and
many activist organizations, including the influential Albuquerque-
based Southwest Research and Information Center and its tireless
WIPP watchdog, Don Hancock. In 1992, a U.S. district court judge
issued an injunction against shipping waste to WIPP until safety
and legal issues were settled. As Sandia Labs described it, "With the
repository under legal scrutiny, Sandia and DOE needed to ensure
their technical work was defensible in both the legal and regulatory
environments, and 'quality assurance' (QA) became more than a
buzzword at the WIPP site. . . . QA required much more rigor in how
Sandia and [WIPP contractor] Westinghouse planned, carried out,
and documented their work. . . . In October of 1996 DOE submitted
to EPA a Compliance Certification Application (CCA), 80,000 pages
of documentation representing more than 20 years of scientific study.

. . . The CCA was DOE's request to officially certify the repository."[41] The EPA approved the CCA by 1999, and the injunction lifted soon after. But even SNL acknowledged that, after opening in March 1999, "a lingering controversy brews over whether mixed waste—transuranic waste that also contains . . . hazardous constituents such as lead and solvents—can also be shipped to WIPP."[42]

Despite the blemish-free safety record of Carlsbad potash miners who dug and almost sculpted WIPP's massive underground storage chambers and despite the all-but-blemish-free transportation history of toxic nuclear waste going to WIPP, to this day not everyone agrees that WIPP is fundamentally safe. And I don't believe these ongoing opponents are merely spiteful obstructionists. With something that's supposed to be as highly regulated as nuclear transport, accidents and strange mistakes are made. And, much to everyone's dismay, state and federal oversight is not consistent or all that focused.

Early in 2006, for instance, the New Mexico Environment Department "tentatively approved" a DOE request to allow nuclear waste drums going to WIPP to leave their site of origin uninspected by direct observation. The DOE, instead, wanted to base its judgments about drum contents on paperwork and what they called "acceptable knowledge." That notion was being seriously considered in February 2005, less than three months after two drums containing plutonium waste exploded and burst into flames while they were being unearthed at the Idaho National Laboratory. Plutonium is unstable in certain situations and prone to igniting. Such flaming explosions have happened before. Some barrels of waste have been known to contain not only plutonium-contaminated materials but also explosives, flammable and corrosive industrial waste, and materials that can generate potentially explosive gases like methane and hydrogen. The DOE standard of "acceptable knowledge" forced citizen activists and the state of New Mexico to swallow early concerns about mixed-waste storage. There was no stopping it, as almost no records were kept on what went into the garbage-can-like barrels.[43] The state's tentative approval came less than sixteen months after it was discovered in October 2004 by the EPA that more than six hundred drums of plutonium-contaminated materials had been sent to WIPP, apparently from the Hanford site. According to the Associated Press, the shipment violated "a directive against shipping waste when questions were raised about whether it was properly tested. . . . It was the second time in 2004 and the fourth since WIPP opened in March 1999 that a shipment had been sent to WIPP without proper testing."[44] State oversight had ended in 1996, three years before the first shipments appeared, because of cuts in federal funding. The state's response to the mistakes uncovered in 2004 was to reopen its oversight bureau at the site and staff it with four inspectors. In 2006, despite these infractions and violations, the state was again proposing to back out from its inspection responsibilities. The NMED eventually dropped the idea and continues to inspect shipments as of this writing.

No Bar Codes

Still, accidents happen, and some of them are almost built into the inventorying and inspection mechanisms used in nuclear facilities across the country. Most waste drums have to go through a preliminary X-ray procedure for inspectors to see what's in them, as no external list exists. If they are found to contain liquid, they are set aside, as liquids cannot go to WIPP. In June 2007, however, a drum of prohibited liquid radioactive waste from the Idaho National Laboratory made it into WIPP unnoticed because the label was misread, causing what Don Hancock called "a serious violation."[45] It's not that the Idaho facility was trying to sneak one over on New Mexico. It was a systemic mistake, one tied up with equipment and procedures. In a world where every pencil, every container of breath mints, and anything else you can think of has a bar code to identify it, the fifty-five-gallon drums containing nuclear waste, hot and moderately hot, had no bar codes.[46] One more "serious violation" like that could cause the entire system to shut down in order for regulators to address issues of technical backwardness. Liquid nuclear waste in metal fifty-five-gallon drums can eventually leak and perhaps even escape into underground water to be carried to who knows where.[47] The DOE eventually was forced to ship the offending drum back to Idaho.

Underfunding of basic identification technology, as well as accidents and incidents of poor judgment, all seem to confirm initial worries by New Mexicans over WIPP's fundamental safety. The political and public pressure to remove the astronomical amounts of transuranic waste from weapons factories around the country led to an improvident haste on the part of DOE officials to solve the waste storage problem. Before the proposed Yucca Mountain repository for highly radioactive waste was conceived, early planners thought WIPP might be the place for such deadly materials. But the geology of the site was not studied thoroughly enough in the beginning. Salt beds, it was later found, would melt under the intense heat of hot nuclear waste. Nor did the early planners at SNL know that a rich pool of oil and natural gas lay directly under WIPP's storage rooms, prompting the site's opponents to worry about drilling going directly into WIPP. WIPP planners did not foresee that by 2007 the entire site would be ringed with oil and natural gas drilling and pumping rigs. Nor did it occur to them that injecting water under great pressure into near-empty wells to flush out the last drops of profit could send flooding water into WIPP from as far as two or three miles away.[48] Planning for both WIPP and Yucca Mountain seems to have been plagued by the kinds of blind spots caused by overspecialization. Physicists and military-industrial bureaucrats, not able to do their geological home-work, hired experts who gave them the opinions they wanted.

For instance, why would a nuclear waste repository be placed 2,150 feet below the surface when a freshwater aquifer called the Rustler is on top of it and a brine aquifer is only few hundred feet below it? It probably wasn't stupidity that set such a plan in motion. It appears to have been incompetent geologic analysis spurred on by undeflected political pressure. The Rustler apparently contains fractures and caverns that might be compromised should a gas explosion occur in WIPP, and such an event could contaminate drinking water. What happens if a drill accidentally taps into WIPP or somehow structurally compromises its salt formations, sending fluids moving for miles through the shale formations and fissures that are layered on top of WIPP's storage chambers?[49] Early planners did not know of the six-mile-wide sinkhole between WIPP and the Pecos River, which could funnel nuclear waste very quickly from the site to the Pecos water table. Inevitably the thousands of fifty-five-gallon drums in WIPP will rust and corrode, at some point releasing gas. What isn't known is how long it would take for groundwater users to realize that an underground cataclysm had compromised their drinking water and what, if anything, they could do about it.

Not only is WIPP potentially dangerous, it is also relatively useless. As massive as WIPP is, it will only handle 2 percent of existing nuclear weapons production waste from across the country. It will probably never contain any of the arms industry's really hot waste. The site is scheduled to hold five million curies of radioactivity, enough to cause considerable damage, but only one-tenth of a percent of the nuclear industry's existing radioactivity stored at its various sites.

Nuclear watchdog Don Hancock feels that all the existing above-ground radioactive waste should be temporarily stored on-site at the various laboratories and facilities that generated it. Waste could be placed in hardened and shielded buildings and constantly monitored, until a geologically stable, secure, and politically feasible site can be found. As far as future generations are concerned, Hancock says, "It's better to have a contained problem to deal with rather than an uncontained problem to deal with."[50]

It Wasn't Supposed to Happen That Way

One of the problems with nuclear material is that radioactivity can be surprisingly difficult to contain under any circumstances. The two underground nuclear explosions in the Project Plowshare Atoms for Peace programs in New Mexico in the 1960s are classic, and almost ludicrous, examples of the unintended consequences of nuclear adventures.

The projects were called Gnome and Gasbuggy. Both involved the detonation of huge nuclear explosions underground. The intended consequences of these experiments were thoroughly altruistic. They were efforts to use human ingenuity to come up with something positive to do with atomic explosions, something that would redeem the whole Cold War arms race. The schemes had a Rube Goldberg feel to them. Bombs were going to be used to widen the Panama Canal, build tunnels and harbors, and create huge subterranean storage vaults for water and gasoline storage. When the Plowshare projects were actually tested, however, they all shared a common drawback—radiation.

In 1961, Project Gnome, the first experiment in the Plowshare program, fired off a 3.1-kiloton nuclear blast 1,184 feet down in the karst fields of the Salado Formation around Carlsbad, some ten miles from what would eventually become the WIPP site. The plan was to excavate a huge underground hole that would be filled with steam and heat that could be used for synthetic geothermal heating. The city of Carlsbad was delighted with the publicity such a program would bring the mining town, and some think that Gnome primed Carlsbad politicians to actually offer the town and environs to the Atomic Energy Commission when the AEC surveyed sites for what would become

WIPP. The *Carlsbad Current-Argus* described the citizenry as being "quietly jubilant" when Gnome received the final go-ahead from President Kennedy, historian Ferenc Szasz reports.[51] The explosion went off without a hitch, except for one result. Because the geology of the area was insufficiently known, the experimenters hadn't counted on any release of heat or radioactivity into the atmosphere. But two or three minutes after the explosion, some three hundred officials and the press saw steam and smoke rising from the elevator shaft that scientists had expected to be closed by the blast. The plume, of course, was highly radioactive and was moving toward the town of Artesia. The deadly gamma-ray-saturated steam was released for the better part of a half an hour in a highly visible cloud and continued to peter out until the next day. Apparently, the shaft had been excavated through a fault line in the karst.[52] Karst fields are riddled with fissures and sinkholes. To this day, opponents contend that WIPP itself is in a karst field and highly unstable because of it, while the DOE maintains the karst field starts at least a mile away. After the Gnome plume started drifting in the direction of both Artesia and Carlsbad, the state police closed down the roads to both towns. Cars that had inadvertently driven through the smoke and steam had to be thoroughly cleaned, and area ranchers couldn't graze their cattle on land in the path of the plume for several weeks.

Even after Gnome's unintended consequences, the Atomic Energy Commission wasn't perturbed by the geology of the area. Karst fields didn't trouble them, even though such land has so many sinks and fissures that what little rain falls in the area never stays on the ground, funneling instead into the salt beds and aquifers below. It wasn't until 1998 that Congress came up with the funds to allow New Mexico Tech in Socorro to plan for a nearly $5 million facility for the National Cave and Karst Research Institute in Carlsbad. The institute, which broke ground in 2003, associates itself with Carlsbad Caverns but not, publicly at least, with WIPP.

The second nuclear "oops" experience in New Mexico was near the Jicarilla Apache Reservation in Dulce, New Mexico, in natural gas fields sixty miles east of Farmington. In December 1967, Operation Gasbuggy exploded a huge 29-kiloton nuclear blast at the bottom of a shaft 4,222 feet deep. The idea was to do with a nuclear charge what natural gas drillers used to do, in a small way, with nitroglycerin explosions—create a cavern in natural gas shale beds that would allow the gas to seep and collect so as to be pumped out easily and efficiently. Sponsored by El Paso Natural Gas, Gasbuggy resulted in some 295 million cubic feet of gas, well over the amount expected. The only problem was that the gas was radioactive. And no matter how much the government and El Paso Natural Gas tried to convince the public that putting small amounts of the gas into the main gas streams over time would so deplete the radioactivity as to render it harmless, they could find no buyers. Apparently, all 295 million cubic feet of the contaminated gas was flared off over a six- or seven-year period, releasing radioactive tritium, which would combine with oxygen and make contaminated rain that showered downwind of the Gasbuggy site.[53]

Amazingly, the Atomic Energy Commission fired two other similar nuclear explosions in natural gas fields after Gasbuggy's debacle, one in 1969 and another in 1973, both in Colorado. In 1969, near Rifle, Colorado, Project Rulison set off a 43-kiloton bomb (more than three times the size of the bomb that flattened Hiroshima) 8,420 feet below the surface. Gas, as expected, seeped into the gigantic hole. But once again the gas was too radioactive to sell. The second Colorado explosion had similar results. As late as 2006, Texas-based natural gas companies were getting permits to drill for gas close to the Rulison site, to the extreme discomfort of many area residents.[54] To people who aren't vested in the success of the nuclear industry, Project Plowshare seems as inexplicable as putting weapons waste in salt caverns sandwiched between two bodies of water in a karst area known for its geologic instability.

Waste Roulette

That SNL played "a primary role in the development of WIPP and its eventual permitting by . . . the EPA"[55] sheds light on a problem that SNL also had its hand in—the Mixed Waste Landfill (MWL) in the sand hills above the South Valley in Albuquerque. While the DOE designated SNL as the WIPP's scientific advisor—with principal responsibilities in site selection and characterization, in analyzing the interaction of certain nuclear wastes with "the disposal environment," and in performance modeling "of the repository for the 10,000-year regulatory time frame"[56]—SNL was dumping toxic and radioactive waste into a huge unlined pit of about two and a half square acres. By the time it closed in 1988, the site held about seven hundred thousand cubic feet of industrial and nuclear waste. The site is so hot, SNL officials contend, that the contents would be too dangerous to move.[57] What worries officials most is the highly radioactive cobalt-60 that was dumped there. That's the same stuff that ended up in those tons of hot rebars from Juarez that were almost used in home and office construction in Los Alamos.

The Mixed Waste Landfill worries just about everyone. It sits, like everything else in the Middle Rio Grande Valley, right on top of Albuquerque's aquifer, the city's major, if not only, source of drinking water. Even SNL admits that some of the contents of the MWL will leak into the groundwater, and some say it already has. Located south of the Albuquerque airport, the MWL is pretty much cheek by jowl with Albuquerque's ambitious and progressive Mesa del Sol development. Realtors were so nervous about the MWL that the most prestigious organization in the profession, The Elite 25, the top moneymakers in the business in Albuquerque, wrote a letter to Governor Bill Richardson in August 2003 urging him to do everything in his power to clean up the mess in the MWL, which meant either digging it up and carting it off or putting it into a hardened aboveground storage area. The Elite 25, representing, as they said, "Albuquerque's best interests," was taking sides in a long-standing debate between SNL and a local activist group called Citizen Action, which urged the cleaning of the MWL and removal of its waste. The statement of The Elite 25 was straightforward; they worried over "the potential environmental contamination from the Mixed Waste Landfill . . . . Knowing that there is potential environmental contamination at Mesa del Sol is quite disconcerting as that is one direction in which Albuquerque could grow."[58] Until that letter, the New Mexico environmental community had rarely, if ever, been supported by major players in Albuquerque's mainstream growth economy.

The letter, unhappily, has had no practical impact. I'm sure its signers were told by their peers, however subtly, to shut up and get on with business. Still, the concerns the letter expressed validated one of the state's more courageous examples of citizen moxie in the person of Sue Dayton, founder of Citizen Action, who was joined by numerous other concerned New Mexicans in calling for the cleanup of the MWL, including nuclear expert Paul Robinson of the Southwest Research and Information Center.

Subsidized Radioactivity

In a 2004 op-ed piece in the *Albuquerque Tribune*,[59] Robinson commented on the evasion of government responsibility championed by longtime nuclear industry defender Senator Pete Domenici. The federal Omnibus Appropriation Bill of December 2003 included a provision that forbids the state of New Mexico or "any other entity" from forcing SNL to post bond or "any other financial responsibility requirement" guaranteeing the cleanup of any of its various waste sites, but most directly the MWL. Even if SNL were to close, the state could still not require a financial guarantee to clean up its messes. Robinson and other members of Citizen Action asked, "Why is this provision needed for Sandia and not the rest of the Department of Energy complex?" Domenici's office said such bonding wasn't necessary, as SNL was backed by the "full faith and credit" of the federal government. "A fundamental reason for concern," Robinson wrote, "is the very mixed record of 'full faith and credit' related to nuclear waste management. Taxpayers are spending upward of $200 billion to clean up waste from federal nuclear weapons production during the unregulated Cold War."[60]

Imminent Endangerment to Health: Sandia National Labs

Domenici's provision came in partial response to the 2002 determination of an imminent and substantial endangerment to health and the environment leveed against SNL by the New Mexico Environment Department. The state concluded that SNL endangered the population of Albuquerque with radioactive and industrial hazardous wastes they had dumped over the years on land that is perilously close to the aquifer and city and Kirtland Air Force Base water wells.[61]

In April 2004, NMED issued a consent order signed by SNL and DOE with "corrective action requirements" for SNL to follow in order to clean up its wastes. The requirements, however, did not pertain to radionuclides, a curious and telling omission. In negotiating and signing the consent order, the state and SNL acknowledged that it was not "an admission of liability, or an agreement with any Findings of Fact or Conclusions of Law." If it weren't for certain "findings of fact," the consent order, from my perspective, would be a fundamentally useless gesture, mediating a path of least resistance between powerful federal forces and the state of New Mexico on one side and the people of the Middle Rio Grande Valley on the other. The fact that the order does not deal with nuclear contamination in the MWL or in other dump sites in the Sandia Labs precinct renders it all but neutered in the long run, though it does draw attention to PCB contamination.[62]

Fact Finding

Located on a 2,830-acre precinct within the 81.6 square miles of Kirtland Air Force Base just south of Albuquerque and stretching to the Cibola National Forest in the Manzano Mountains, SNL operates five "technical areas" that are used for testing on the base. In its findings of fact, the state contended that DOE and SNL "have disposed of materials, including hazardous waste and hazardous constituents, in pits, trenches, landfills, and waste piles throughout the Facility." By 2008, most people in Albuquerque were unaware of the MWL, despite prolonged coverage in the daily papers, and almost no one, I'm sure, had any idea that there is much more than one massive dump to clean up. The state also says that SNL "discharged industrial waste water from outfalls into the Tijeras Arroyo water course and through numerous septic systems located across the facility."[63] Mountain View Elementary School on Second Street is not ten yards from Tijeras Arroyo, near where it empties into the Rio Grande. Much of the waste was also discharged into "unpermitted land fills, septic system leach fields and seepage pits, outfalls, waste piles, and test areas."[64] The unpermitted landfills include "Classified Waste and Radioactive Waste Landfills."[65] The use of the plural, here, might raise an eyebrow or two at the meetings of The Elite 25.

SNL never really pretended to be sensitive to concerns about its history of toxic dumping. Its 2004 *Annual Site Environmental Report for Sandia National Laboratories, New Mexico*[66] listed management's practices for its hazardous and chemical waste, its radioactive and mixed waste, and its cleanup and site closure activities. It did not allude to the legacy nuclear waste that accumulated since 1945, which is at the heart of the problem. To my knowledge, neither the daily papers nor broadcast news media covered the 340-page, jargon-filled report, thereby missing a chance for some useful investigative reporting.

SNL has a reasonably successful history of cleaning up its waste, but New Mexico media has failed to report both the best and the worst of the lab's cleanup practices. A Chemical Waste Landfill (CWL), occupying nearly two acres at SNL and full of chemical and potentially explosive waste deposited from 1962 to 1985, was cleaned up starting in 1998. The process was elaborate and painstaking, involving high-tech soil separations. A portion of the site with an "unknown disposal history" was examined closely for a "hypothetical explosion" caused by sodium-potassium materials that might have been on-site.[67]

In December 2007, SNL came up with another plan to clean up its waste in a way that would mollify the NMED and comply with the federal Resource Conservation and Recovery Act (RCRA). In response to the mandatory public notice inviting comments, Citizen Action New Mexico, which focuses on SNL, filed a forty-page document in January 2008.[68] The response analyzed SNL's plan and reached many eye-opening conclusions. SNL was seeking to take "no further action"[69] on what Citizen Action charged were "dozens of dump sites of legacy waste containing cyanide, mercury, volatile solvents, and radionuclides."[70] In the same news release, Citizen Action contended that one of those dumps, "called SWMU-4 [Solid Waste Management Unit] operated for thirty years from 1963 to 1992, dumping 12,000,000 gallons of radioactive effluent into ditches from where the contamination could enter groundwater. Not far from SWMU-4 is the Mixed Waste Landfill with over 700,000 cubic feet of radioactive and toxic waste intended for permanent burial in unlined pits and trenches."[71] Waste was dumped there from 1959 to 1988.

Citizen Action also contended that "the Sandia permit request fails to address the 'Yardholes.' These were more than thirty primitive open holes dug deep into the ground to contain wastes from experiments simulating nuclear meltdowns that involved nuclear reactor fuels that had been shipped in canisters to Sandia during the mid-1980s 'from reactors around the world.' Sandia claims the Yardholes are vulnerable to terrorist attack and refuses to describe or remediate the toxic wastes in these dump sites that are a great danger to contaminate the groundwater."[72] Dave McCoy at Citizen Action wrote in the press release, "Sandia wants to get away with only an 'industrial' standard of cleanup rather than the residential standard which is stricter."[73] The group considers air and groundwater monitoring at SNL as wholly inadequate.[74]

Early in 2006, after NMED had OK'd Sandia Labs' plan to cap the MWL with a yard of dirt, SNL itself released the findings of one of its new studies, concluding that some industrial waste from the site would, indeed, reach Albuquerque's aquifer, perhaps as early as 2010. While the study's findings made the papers, it did not grab the headlines it deserved. The study calculated that a carcinogenic industrial chemical known as PCE (perchloroethylene) would reach the groundwater, a finding that overturned the claims SNL had made for years that nothing in the unlined waste site would ever contaminate groundwater. And Paul Robinson from the Southwest Research and Information Center said matters were much worse than that. "Sandia's study only models for the movement of one chemical (PCE) to the groundwater, even though previous investigations by Sandia have shown that at least a dozen various chemicals have escaped the dump."[75]

In 2006, a geologist and groundwater expert who used to work at LANL said in a report to the EPA that monitoring wells around the MWL reminded him of the basically useless monitoring of wells stationed at various sites around LANL, sites that he'd also reported on to the EPA. The geologist, Robert H. Gilkeson, told SNL and the media that the wells were not only "deficient" but that they could actually "hide" pollution in groundwater, instead of detecting it.[76] The NMED took Gilkeson's report seriously and fifteen months later, in August 2007, ordered the replacement of two of the monitoring wells and also told SNL that it would have to change a background monitor that they had ordered to be replaced earlier in the year.

Secrets and Coverups

This looks like progress. But progress was thwarted in a bizarre twist of legal fate. The NMED in late 2007 claimed "executive privilege" in refusing to release a study it had undertaken at the MWL. When Citizen Action sued the NMED, it countersued to keep its report secret, even after New Mexico attorney general Gary King told NMED that the report was a public document and not subject to executive withdrawal from public view. What did the report contain? Was it an even more dire warning about the MWL polluting the groundwater? Had it already happened? Were there nuclear wastes in the water? Even the conservative *Albuquerque Journal* editorialized against NMED's claim of executive privilege: "Thanks to the Bush administration, the public has become better versed in this principle [of executive privilege] than at any time since Watergate and should be able to spot its use as a legal dodge." The *Journal* laid on its criticism with unusual severity, concluding that "instead of 'executive privilege' this smacks of executive coverup. It would be much better policy to produce the pubic document than to spend more tax money to argue against the public interest."[77] Perhaps the state worried the report might put a damper on Mesa del Sol, a massive public-private partnership that had just announced two major new businesses were moving into the project, a European-based solar panel manufacturer and a sizable office of Fidelity Investments that promised to bring Albuquerque many thousands of relatively high-paying new jobs.

Lethal Landfills

One wishes that every landfill in New Mexico received the scrutiny devoted to the MWL at Sandia Labs. There are potential long-term hazards in all of them. The tragic death of an environmental scientist working for the city of Albuquerque brought home how dangerous and unpredictable public landfills can be. On August 3, 2007, fifty-two-year-old Mary Carnes was monitoring methane in a pit dug in the old Los Angeles landfill just west of where tens of thousands of enthusiasts and international competitors convene for the annual Albuquerque Balloon Fiesta. An experienced researcher, Carnes was nonetheless overwhelmed by the gas. *Albuquerque Tribune* reporter Peter Rice wrote that while "a medical examiner's report lists the cause and manner of Carnes' death as 'undetermined,'" another report for the city's insurance company determined that she died "due to lack of oxygen." The city was fined by the New Mexico Occupational Health and Safety Bureau on the grounds that the city had failed to classify the pit as "a hazardous confined space."[78] The city contested the cause of death to avoid paying compensation to Carnes's husband.

For anyone who studies landfills, the dangers of being exposed to hazardous gas are common knowledge. The landfill industry nationwide has been concerned about methane and other toxic gases escaping. Some cities, like Albuquerque, have tried to harness the energy potential of the gas. Others have sought to burn the gas through flaring processes, lighting gas as it escapes, but have found that, at times, other deadly substances like dioxin have appeared in the flare.[79] Along with the many legacy landfills in Albuquerque, including the Los Angeles and the San Antonio landfills and Montessa Park, the city's "state of the art" modern landfill on the southwest edge of the city, called Cerro Colorado, takes up to four hundred fifty thousand tons of household and business waste a year. But all landfills, whether or not they are lined with plastic like Cerro Colorado, pose long-term dangers to groundwater because of what experts refer to as *leachate pollution*, which is simply the leaching of any one of hundreds of dangerous substances into the water table over time. It's estimated that nationwide some 75 to 80 percent of all inactive landfills are currently polluting groundwater with various kinds of leachate. In California, with more than twenty-two hundred active and inactive landfills, the State Water Resources Control Board found that 83 percent of those landfills are polluting groundwater.[80]

New Mexico has an inordinately large number of municipal landfills, according to a 1996 EPA listing. Sparsely populated New Mexico has seventy-nine of them, compared to sixty-seven in Florida, fourteen in New Jersey, forty-two in New York State, fifty-nine in Arizona, and seventy-two in Colorado, all states with immensely larger populations than New Mexico.[81] In 2001, a hazardous waste facility called Triassic Park was proposed for the western part of Chavez County, near the city of Roswell. The proposal was strongly challenged by local residents and conservation groups, who cited "the understated hydrologic impact, lack of emergency response preparations, and inadequate closure plan and associated financial assurance."[82] Near the town of Chaparral, New Mexico, on the Texas–New Mexico border around El Paso, another imported landfill was proposed in 2001 by a company called Rhino Environmental Services out of Anthony, Texas. It would hold solid and "special waste" and was also opposed by the community leaders. Both Triassic Park and the Rhino dump would bring in wastes from other states and even Mexico in large volumes. "New Mexico is a target for new waste disposal sites due to its status as one of the poorest states in the nation and as a state where people of color are in the majority," representatives from the Southwest Research and Information Center wrote.[83]

The residents of Wagon Mound successfully fended off efforts by Herzog, Incorporated, of Missouri to bring out-of-state waste to the Northeastern New Mexico Regional Landfill, located a short distance from the community. A court fight in 2004 blocked a permit to bring in imported waste, and Wagon Mound won again in 2007 when the NMED denied Herzog's second permit request, "which would have allowed the landfill to accept asbestos-contaminated materials, packing house and killing plant offal, ash, petroleum-contaminated waste, and treated waste formerly characterized as hazardous," according to the *New Mexico Business Weekly*.[84] In August 2000, the sheriff of Mora County, John Sanchez, threatened to block highways leading to the Wagon Mound landfill to keep out debris trucked in from the Cerro Grande fire in Los Alamos. "I'll turn them around and send them right back," Sanchez told the *Albuquerque Journal*.[85]

New Mexico has always suffered from its image as an empty place. That the national labs in New Mexico have deposited problem waste here, along with WIPP, seems to have set the tone for private firms who see New Mexico as a suitable place to dump a variety of crud.

E.T. Graveyard

One curious incident of out-of-state waste landing in New Mexico took place well before WIPP's opening, but during its construction. In 1983, an El Paso manufacturing plant had to get rid of an unsalable product. The Atari video game called *E.T. the Extra-Terretrial*, after the movie character of the same name,[86] was a legendary flop; it couldn't even ride the Spielberg movie to success. In September 1983, Browning Ferris Industries, which managed the Alamogordo Landfill, allowed the manufacturer to dump what columnist Mike Smith characterized as "literally millions of unsold and returned copies" of Atari's *E.T.* game, and other games, into its landfill. The load was carted nearly a hundred miles from Texas in fourteen standard and very large dump trucks. As the landfill's city permit mentioned nothing about that kind of waste, no laws or contractual arrangements were broken. Alamogordo's city manager at the time told the *Alamogordo Daily*, "We had never planned for anything like this—to become an industrial dump site for Texas."[87] The dump immediately used its own trucks to drive over and crush the millions of videocassettes and eventually capped the whole mess in concrete.

National Security Trash on the Loose

It appears that hot trash from LANL has been regularly dumped into New Mexico landfills. In May 2007, the Nuclear Information and Resource Service (NIRS) contended that "radioactive materials from nuclear weapons facilities are being released to regular landfills and could get into the commercial recycling streams. Radioactive scrap, concrete, equipment, asphalt, plastic, wood, chemicals, and soil are placed in ordinary landfills, researchers learned."[88]

The DOE has been working to remove radioactive debris from most of its weapons sites. "One of the largest and most technically complex environmental cleanup programs in the world, the effort includes cleanup of 114 sites across the country," the Environmental News Service reports. Once contaminated debris leaves a DOE site, the contractors, apparently, can dump it anywhere they please. "By permitting radioactive materials to go directly to unregulated destinations and to licensed processors who subsequently release it, DOE is enabling man-made radioactivity to get out into the open marketplace, landfills, commercial recycling, and into everyday consumer projects, construction supplies, equipment, roads, piping, buildings, vehicles, playgrounds, basements, furniture, toys, zippers, personal items, without warning, notification, or consent, NIRS researches discovered." NIRS contends that "this dispersal of radioactive material is being done without comprehensive complex-wide tracing, [and] without routine public reporting of the releases from each site."[89] The NIRS report examined seven DOE sites "with varying levels of detail." The sites were Oak Ridge, Tennessee; Mound, Ohio; Fernald, Ohio; Rocky Flats, Colorado; Los Alamos, New Mexico; Paducah, Kentucky; and West Valley, New York. Although Los Alamos was not one of the major case studies, considerable information was revealed.

Diane D'Arrigo, director of the NIRS's Radioactive Waste Project, said, "As long as DOE and other nuclear waste generators can slip their contamination out . . . there really is no limit to the amount of additional radiation exposures members of the public could receive."[90]

In July 2000, just as the final term of President Clinton was wrapping up, then–secretary of energy Bill Richardson suspended the release of what DOE said was "potentially contaminated scrap metals for recycling from DOE nuclear facilities. The suspension is part of a new policy aimed at ensuring contaminated materials are not recycled into consumer products and at improving the department's management of scrap materials at its nuclear weapons production sites."[91]

In his memorandum announcing the suspension, Richardson acknowledged that the DOE had been "reviewing ways to improve our management of materials which might be released from department control"[92]—in other words, given to contractors to dump wherever they pleased.[93] Richardson's ban on the commercial recycling of radioactive metal was still in effect in 2007.

According to NIRS's May 14, 2007, report entitled *Out of Control—On Purpose: DOE's Dispersal of Radioactive Waste to Landfills and Consumer Products*, the moratorium must have had some impact on the Bush administration, but only as far as metals are concerned. Still, NIRS concluded that, although "the ban leaves several loopholes for radioactive metal to get out, and there have been efforts within DOE to circumvent these bans, nonetheless, it is likely that much less radioactive metal is making it into the marketplace than otherwise would have absent the moratorium and suspension. But this could change without notice."[94]

No Record Keeping

But in asking rhetorically, "How much radiation gets out?," the authors of the report responded, "We don't know. Apparently DOE doesn't know. There is *no cumulative* tracking, measurement, quantification, record keeping, or reporting *on all of the DOE's radioactive releases* in terms of volume, weight, type of material, or radioactive amounts or concentrations. . . . There is no estimate or compilation of radioactivity or radionuclides released."[95] This does not mean that the DOE is simply opening the gates. DOE does have criteria for how much radiation can be released but apparently no records with which to check it. Basically, according to NIRS, if within an entire site, the totality of its recyclable debris—from concrete to pipelines—meets the basic radiation exposure standard that the Nuclear Regulatory Commission has set based on its health risk models, then material can be released from the site and carted off to public landfills. But there's an odd glitch in the process. The same radiation exposure standard that applies to an entire site also applies to "to each piece of a site in the form of released waste material."[96] This waste can go to an alarming number of outlets and uses, including "municipal and other solid waste landfills on site or off site of DOE, incinerators . . . recycling into raw materials for consumer goods, building supplies, industrial and public works, waste brokers . . . for storage or shipment to processing, recycling, reuse, disposal, or direct release . . . schools, community organizations, and nonprofit charities."[97]

Does the DOE dump such material in New Mexico? It depends on what source you check. There's indication, according to NIRS, that contaminated soil from LANL "went to a golf course in the area."[98] According to the LANL News and Communications Office, since 2001, LANL has been sending "clean fill," not contaminated soil, to the Los Alamos County Golf Course. As usual, there is no ready way to verify the assertion that the fill is clean. It's all a matter of whom you believe. OMB Watch, an online community-based watchdog blog, for instance, contends that LANL "sends potentially contaminated metal to Rio Rancho landfill in Albuquerque [*sic*], New Mexico, which is regularly canvassed by Habitat for Humanity for supplies. The landfill does not ensure that the potentially contaminated material is not taken by Habitat for Humanity. Instead, the burden is placed on Habitat for Humanity to know which supplies not to choose."[99]

Radioactive Recycling

While the dumping of radioactive materials into common landfills seems inherently immoral, it has special significance at a time when recycling of petroleum-based and construction materials is growing in importance. What a disaster it would be to the whole notion of recycling as a cornerstone of conservation if recycled materials are suspected of being contaminated by radiation, in whatever amounts. That would be a legacy of the Cold War that could never be put right.

Wealth from Waste

In 2006, the city of Albuquerque announced its intent to be the first city to eliminate its landfill through recycling.[100] As fuel prices rise and the costs of materials skyrocket, landfills around the country will become sources of a potentially vast and renewable income stream for financially strapped cities. Albuquerque hopes to recycle glass, paper, cardboard, plastics, and aluminum, in effect emptying its land-fill of the residue of the American packaging and marketing indus-tries. The city "wants to find alternative uses for literally everything people throw away, according to Leonard Garcia, the director of the solid waste department. While he concedes that a few things will always stay at the dump, the inspiration is still there. 'That's a goal that we're going to strive for,' he said."[101] Potential profits, even in the early stages, are considerable. Waste newspapers bring more than eighty dollars a ton, and plastic milk jugs go for thirty-two cents a pound or more as oil prices rise.[102]

Most of Albuquerque's trash is still being buried, and the recycling effort lost money in 2006. It brought in some $700,000 at a cost of $1 million to process less than 3 percent of the garbage stream. The more consumers get used to recycling and sorting their trash before it hits the landfill, the better the city's return will be. Although recycling has its detractors, who cite transportation, processing, and manufac-turing costs, industry figures show that processing recycled aluminum saves 95 percent of the energy it takes to mill and process new alumi-num, and recycling plastics saves some 70 percent of the energy needed to manufacture new material. Problems of consumer morale and the believability of the program, though, persist. In February 2007, an enterprising news team from a local television station discovered that more than 150 tons of recyclables had been dumped into the landfill, apparently by dump truck drivers who were unclear on various recy-cling directives. But the city made good on the mistake, excavating and recovering most of the tonnage and processing it through its recycl-ing department.[103]

Grass and Sludge

One of the more dangerous aspects of landfills, and probably the cause of the methane that contributed to the death of Mary Carnes at the old Los Angeles Landfill, is the dumping of yard and agricultural waste. Putting yard waste in landfills is squandering a valuable fam-ily resource. Yard waste takes up some 15 percent of all residential debris[104] and could be used, instead, as compost and water-saving mulch. Sewage sludge that is put in landfills is even more dangerous in terms of methane gas buildup and release, as well as the potential for its carrying biotoxins and other materials, possibly radioactive, that were flushed into the sewer system. Remember the plutonium associated with the sewer sludge that was used as fertilizer in Albuquerque and on the University of New Mexico president's lawn? That had to come from somewhere.

Across the United States, about 25 percent of sewage sludge is dumped in landfills. In New Mexico, it's a staggering 73 percent, second only to Nevada.[105] The city of Albuquerque in the early twenty-first century "treats over 5 million gallons of mixed residential and industrial wastewater daily, producing about 22 dry tons of stabilized biosolids a day." Sludge tends to liquify faster than other waste matter in landfills and can be a danger to fresh groundwater if the water table is too high. Most treated sludge could be used as fertilizer for nonfood crops, such as turf, or to help in mining restoration without causing much danger to human health, as long as industrial and pharmaceutical poisons have been removed.[106] Two New Mexico State University civil engineers, Z. A. Samani and Adrian Hanson, are experimenting with organic landfill waste as a renewable source of energy to generate electricity. A "two phase bio-fermentation process" that "can digest even such tough substances as paper, generating high quality natural gas," also leaves a "usable compost as a residue."[107] The fermentation process first mixes solid waste with cattle manure. Water is added, and eventually bacteria in the animal waste converts the solids into "volatile fatty acids." Those acids are leached into the water and transferred to a second container, where a different kind of bacteria in the mixture turns it into methane. Albuquerque and Las Cruces have started to use landfill methane to run some of its generators, and the economic potential of the New Mexico State University process could produce sizable amounts of commercial energy. If Albuquerque culled the thirty-one thousand tons of solid organic waste dumped annually into its landfill, the inventors estimate that some ninety-three billion BTUs of energy could be produced a year. Various sources show that a single home uses an estimated one million BTUs of natural gas over five to six days. The thirty-one thousand tons of organic waste deposited each year in Albuquerque's major landfill would produce enough methane to run about fifteen hundred houses for a year. All the organic waste in America's innumerable landfills could go a long way in supplementing natural gas production.

Lethal Pits

While lethally dangerous in the worst circumstances, methane is relatively benign compared to the plutonium triggers being produced at LANL for thermonuclear bombs. LANL was the site of plutonium pit manufacture in the early days of the Cold War, until the Rocky Flats facility near Denver opened in the early 1950s. Recently, LANL scientists, metallurgists, and machinists produced some eleven plutonium triggers, or pits, between July 2007 and the beginning of 2008.[108] When Rocky Flats stopped its thirty years of plutonium pit production in 1989 amid FBI raids and horrendous pollution scandals, the DOE needed another national lab to produce the pits. The department feared that triggers in old bombs might need to be replaced. It turned to LANL, which is located, like Rocky Flats, close to major population centers and the hub of state government. Rocky Flats had made nearly every plutonium pit for the American nuclear arsenal, estimated at some twenty-five thousand warheads at its peak (fewer than ten thousand are still in use).[109] Beginning in 1997, according to the Alliance for Nuclear Accountability, DOE "attempted to establish 'limited' and 'interim' production of up to ten pits per year" at LANL. But in 2002, "the National Nuclear Security Administration [NNSA], the semi-autonomous nuclear weapons agency within the DOE, unsuccessfully pushed Congress for a massive facility to produce some 450 pits at LANL again. NNSA now plans to raise interim production at Los Alamos to as many as 80 pits per year."[110] Some writers, including Len Ackland, an associate professor at the School of Journalism and Mass Communication at the University of Colorado–Boulder, writing in the Southwest Research and Information Center's *Voices from the Earth*, call this new LANL pit facility "Rocky Flats II." Before the real Rocky Flats was built in the early 1950s, however, LANL was the site of plutonium pit manufacture during the early days of the Cold War. These pits were used both in weapons and in the research and development of more advanced thermonuclear devices. The new plans, however, met a formidable hurdle. In March 2008, when the head of the New Mexico Environment Department, Ron Curry, said that it was "unconscionable" for the DOE and other agencies to propose making more pits at LANL before the labs cleaned up its "legacy waste" of plutonium "while at the same time refusing to put the required funding toward clean up. Before it looks to new missions," Curry said, "the lab must meet its clean up commitments to the people of New Mexico. . . . Addressing and correcting LANL's legacy of pollution should be job number one for the lab."[111]

Infernal Power

Just what does a plutonium pit actually do? It is the triggering mechanism for the hydrogen bomb. A plutonium pit is covered in explosives that cause it to implode and create a chain reaction that generates another reaction in a large quantity of uranium-235, producing a massive explosion. The Hiroshima atomic bomb Little Boy was filled with 130 pounds of uranium-235, enough to create a blast with the equivalent force of 13 kilotons of TNT. The Nagasaki bomb, nicknamed Fat Man, with 14 pounds of plutonium-239 as the explosive element, yielded a blast equivalent to 21 kilotons of TNT. The explosive yield of hydrogen bombs, however, is figured in megatons, or millions of tons of TNT. The Nagasaki explosion created heat estimated at 7,000 degrees Fahrenheit, with winds of some 620 miles per hour.[112] Imagine what infernal power was released when a device that yielded 10.4 megatons of power was dropped on Enewetak Atoll in 1952. Called Sausage, it was more than 450 times as powerful as the Fat Man. It contained a plutonium pit that ignited a uranium core.[113]

When Rocky Flats closed in 1989, it had stored up some fourteen tons of plutonium that had to be moved, some of which ended up in Los Alamos. Making pits is an inherently dirty business, in more ways than one. In 1992, the DOE reported that plutonium residue—some sixty-one pounds of it, enough to make a powerful bomb—lined the ductwork of six buildings at Rocky Flats. If it was lining the ductwork, it must have been in the air in those buildings. Inhalation is one of the three major ways that the low-penetration alpha rays emitted by plutonium can cause cancer, accessing the lungs as it does. I'm tempted to say, as goes Rocky Flats, so goes Los Alamos. But who's to say if new classified technology and a state-of-the-art new production facility will actually contain plutonium dust and debris in the twenty-first century—though I do have to say that a nuclear establishment that can't afford the funds to provide bar codes and their reading devices to stored nuclear waste containers on the way to WIPP doesn't seem a safe bet for new ecofriendly bomb-making technology.

Demon in the Jemez Mountains

Los Alamos, of course, was the home of the Manhattan Project, the holy of holies in the romantic history of the United States' scientific and military cultures, where the first atomic bombs were developed in World War II. Known early as Site Y, the lab eventually became the design studio and testing field, along with competitive partner Lawrence Livermore National Laboratory in California, for components of the hydrogen bomb. The University of California, Berkeley (UCB), managed the Los Alamos labs for more than sixty years, until 2006, when a consortium of UCB, Bechtel Corporation, Washington Group International, and BWX Technologies won a seven-year contract to operate LANL after a series of dicey security breeches and a catastrophic wildfire in the surrounding forest, known as the Cerro Grande fire, threatened to destroy the lab.

The health of the natural and human environments in the Jemez Mountains where Los Alamos is located, and in much of northern New Mexico from Santa Fe to Taos, has been intertwined with nuclear science since the Manhattan Project was launched in 1943. But downwinders from "the hill" in Santa Fe, in the Española and Chama valleys, and at the pueblos of Santa Clara, San Ildefonso, San Juan (now called by its original name of Ohkay Owingeh), Tesuque, Nambé, Picuris, Pojoaque, and Taos are all affected by LANL. For some, the lab has the smell of death to it.

In University of Chicago anthropologist Joseph Masco's ethnography *The Nuclear Borderlands*, New Mexicans of many walks of life, including antinuclear activists, reveal their fears about living in the aftermath of the Manhattan Project in "Post–Cold War New Mexico," as Masco puts it.[114] As one Santa Fe activist said, "The lab seems to be reasonable, and in a microcosm, usually is the more reasonable party when it comes to health and safety. But somehow macroscopically the citizens are more right, the hysterical people to which the lab always says, 'It's safe, it's safe, it's safe' are more right because the laboratory never wants to talk about the big picture."[115] The big picture he describes is that LANL is a "toxic archipelago that will never be cleaned up."[116] Masco observes that surrounding communities "worried that they may have been physically sacrificed to the Cold War national security project"[117] and what Masco calls the "plutonium economy."[118]

Public awareness of LANL's physical realities was substantially heightened and expanded during and after the terrible Cerro Grande fire, which scorched some forty-three thousand acres in the Jemez Mountains around Los Alamos and nearly seventy-five hundred acres on LANL property. A December 2000 report from Concerned Citizens for Nuclear Safety and the Nuclear Policy Project about the "environmental, safety, and health impacts of the Cerro Grande fire"[119] contended that "the fire released radioactive and hazardous airborne contaminants from LANL and from burning vegetation and debris. In the fire's aftermath, the magnitude of its destruction significantly changed environmental conditions and has increased the risks of flash floods, surface and groundwater contamination, and large amounts of LANL contaminants entering the Rio Grande."[120] While the report lauded the DOE, LANL, "other federal agencies," and the state of New Mexico for taking "prompt actions to mitigate risks" and noted their "progress in providing the public with prompt and detailed information pertaining to the risks from the fire aftermath," still "cleaning up the contaminant burden at LANL warrants a high priority."[121]

The revelations of the magnitude of LANL's hazardous and nuclear waste problems after the fire shocked many New Mexicans, who mostly had only rumor to go on in judging congressional funding and oversight behavior of the labs. LANL is located on top of the Pajarito Plateau, a windswept forest high in the Jemez Mountains. Like so many other large mesas in New Mexico and Arizona, the plateau channels its runoff into canyons. In the sixty-five years of LANL's existence, its employees and scientists have dumped incalculable amounts of radioactive and hazardous liquid waste into major canyons in the area, including Mortandad Canyon, which empties out near Santa Fe's Buckman aquifer wells; Acid Canyon, known for its heavy concentrations of plutonium; Water Canyon; Pueblo Canyon; Los Alamos Canyon; and others. Topographical maps show that these canyons all empty into the Rio Grande, an alarming thought for people downstream in Albuquerque and beyond who planned to start drinking river water in July 2008.

From a lay citizen's perspective, it seems that LANL scientists and administrators, the Atomic Energy Commission, and the Department of Energy have all taken what might generously be called a cavalier attitude toward atomic and industrial waste. Not that there was a conspiracy to contaminate New Mexico, or a conscious plan to consider the northern part of the state a so-called sacrifice zone, but rather the big brains at LANL, like those at SNL and the other 114 DOE weapons sites around the country, had convinced themselves that nuclear waste, while lethal in certain situations, was basically harmless when under their control. At every site, nuclear and hazardous waste was mischaracterized and its dangers underestimated. This seems to be the result of two mindsets. First, the corporate and academic managers who run the weapons sites for the DOE bring the same view of hazardous waste to nuclear weapon manufacture as they have toward their own businesses and waste. They evaluate risk by a cost-benefit model that results in their using the environment as a trash can. I believe that attitude results from the second mindset, which has to do with the professional arrogance and nonchalance of nuclear scientists, technicians, and bureaucrats, most of whom believe the public's fear of radioactivity and the response of some of the public's elected representatives is not only ignorant, but willfully so, and therefore dangerous to the integrity of science and to national security interests. This attitude suggests that nuclear technocrats have created a culture of denial. The risks of cancer, disabilities, and developmental crippling from environmental contamination, according to this worldview, are not serious enough to be concerned with, certainly no more than background radiation risk.

The LANL facility, some thirty-six square miles, contains about 2,120 chemical and nuclear waste sites, called by the DOE "potential release sites." Concerned Citizens for Nuclear Safety contends that contaminants—including oils, sludge, solvents, PCBs, and the debris from manufacturing and research endeavors, many laced with transuranic radionuclides such as enriched and depleted uranium and isotopes of plutonium and americium—"were regulated at the point at which they reached the site boundary, not at the point of discharge—creating significant and irreversible contamination and concentrations in soil, sediment, and water."[122] And Los Alamos residents beyond formal lab boundaries suffer from time to time from odd oversights on the part of LANL officials. In the early 1990s, as many three hundred homes and some condominiums were built on inactive LANL landfills and waste sites. The DOE reported that neither its people nor LANL's notified "Los Alamos homeowners in a timely manner that they were located on or near inactive waste sites, nor were these homeowners given an opportunity to comment on or provide early input into the corrective action process."[123]

Nuclear Nonchalance

In 1997, a high level of radioactive pollution made its presence known in the south fork of Acid Canyon, which had been turned into a city wilderness park in the late 1960s. "This fork of Acid Canyon was the main point for treated and untreated radioactive and hazardous discharges from the 1940s to the early 1960s" released from a waste processing facility at a major technical area on LANL grounds.[124] On the urging of the NMED, LANL issued a report on the site, showing much higher concentrations of plutonium than expected in the canyon soils, as high in some places as those at the condemned Rocky Flats site. The south fork of Acid Canyon, located within the Los Alamos city limits, is surrounded now by housing. Perhaps the best indication of LANL's attitude about places like Acid Canyon can be seen in a September 4, 2001, issue of LANL's *Daily News Bulletin*. In reassuring PR prose, the *Bulletin* describes how "personnel with the Laboratory are using a giant vacuum to clean up contaminated sediments" from Acid Canyon. The *Bulletin* acknowledged that the NMED has found "several isolated 'hot spots' along the stream channel about 30 feet away from the closest hiking trail" but reassures readers that there's nothing to worry about. "Laboratory scientists comprehensively studied Acid Canyon's south fork and confirmed that the potential risk to people using the canyon was low. The study determined that children playing along the stream channel one hour a day, 200 days a year, would receive a minimal radioactive dose that is below limits established for members of the public under [EPA] guidelines." In short, a polluter studied its own plutonium waste and found it harmless even to children.

In February 2008, LANL, home of "environmentally blithe scientists,"[125] as a *Santa Fe New Mexican* editorial called them, was sued in federal court by the Western Environmental Law Center on behalf of Amigos Bravos, Concerned Citizens for Nuclear Safety, and the Southwest Organizing Project, along with two northern New Mexican acequia associations, charging that LANL wasn't living up to its agreements with the state of New Mexico, wasn't monitoring or cleaning up its immense piles of pollution, and was seriously endangering groundwater and the health of the Rio Grande.

The *New Mexican*'s editorial claimed that LANL had long been "resistant to the idea of cleaning up the mess it made ending World War II and waging the Cold War."[126] And even in 2008, three years after signing an agreement with NMED to do a "fence to fence" housekeeping job on all its immense volumes of industrial and radioactive waste by 2015, LANL's cleanup funding from the Bush administration was woefully far behind schedule, and the lab's scientists continued to downplay the dangers of its wastes. If the lawsuit gets to open court, it will inform the general public of situations that would be shocking to many people. Though the *Santa Fe New Mexican* has long done an outstanding job covering LANL's top-secret operations as best it can, the rest of the state has taken a three-monkeys approach to nuclear science, refusing to see anything wrong, refusing to hear anything but the rosy "no danger" pronouncements of the lab, and generally saying nothing themselves. For instance, the *Albuquerque Journal* carried a ludicrously brief story about the Western Environmental Law Center suit on page D2, as if it were as important to New Mexicans as a small earthquake in Java. The *Santa Fe New Mexican*, on the other hand, assigned science writer Sue Vorenberg to the story and put it on the front page. Near the end of the piece, interestingly, appears a typical LANL attempt at staving off the pressures of the suit. The lab's web pages reported on fish studies it has done looking for PCBs, radionuclides, and heavy metals, claiming no difference between upstream and downstream levels of pollution, inferring it must be coming from somewhere farther up the river than the lab. One wonders where that might be. Dixon, Taos Pueblo, Questa, Alamosa, Creed? Take a look at maps of northern New Mexico and southern Colorado. I doubt you'll find any big defense contractors or industrial works north of Los Alamos. Spokespeople for the labs often refer to higher background radiation in northern New Mexico geology.

LANL issues reports responding to the concerns of the media and the voting public on the dangers its hazardous waste poses to the community. These documents report the institution's own studies, conveying the reassuring findings of nameless LANL scientists whom the media considers the only bona fide experts. LANL, SNL, DOE, DOD, and other national labs around the country are masters of this genre. In February 2002, the *Santa Fe New Mexican* reported on a hydrological study by LANL scientists that announced, reassuringly, that groundwater below LANL and its 2,120 waste sites would "take thousands of years" to reach the Santa Fe drinking water aquifer known as the Buckman well field. LANL scientists used to believe that its wastes would never migrate into those wells because they wouldn't be able to cross under the Rio Grande. The 2002 story confirmed that such a view was wrong, attempting to deflect worries by moving dangers into the distant future. The *New Mexican* reported that wells near San Ildefonso Pueblo, which is much closer than Santa Fe to LANL, might be contaminated by LANL groundwater in perhaps a century. And Los Alamos County has already detected "trace amounts" of a chemical known as perchlorate as well as tritium in one of its wells in Pueblo Canyon. The *New Mexican*'s story ran under the headline "Report: Santa Fe's Water Is Safe." Two years earlier, in 2000, an Associated Press story following the Cerro Grande fire reported that "radioactive contaminants and other chemicals have been found in storm water"[127] flowing onto LANL property, but with no threat to health, as experts predictably opined. "The worst of the contaminated material," the AP reported, "seems to be coming from the forest above the lab, officials said."[128] While the cyanide found in the runoff could well have come from the fire retardant used to combat the Cerro Grande fire, the lab figured that the cesium-137, strontium-90, and plutonium didn't come from the lab but more "likely came from the fallout from the 1950s and 1960s because the contaminated water was coming from headwaters above lab canyons in the mountains,"[129] the AP said. This information was in the last paragraph of the piece, far from the lead that made it clear that such waters were running onto lab property. Nowhere did the story say that LANL was monitoring storm waters before they reached their borders. This story and others like it in 2000 caused considerable concern in Santa Fe. The credibility of LANL's scientific authority was being stretched thin. To shore up its expertise in the public mind, LANL ran computer models for groundwater contamination, which was reported in the *New Mexican* two years later, in February 2002.

LANL and the State

In May 2002, LANL ran into difficulty harder to dismiss than the worries of Santa Fe voters, businesses, and householders. NMED issued an administrative order demanding cleanup of laboratory wastes, characterizing LANL practices as being of "imminent and substantial endangerment" to the people of northern New Mexico. LANL went ballistic. At no time in the past had the practices of the labs been called into question by a state agency, not even after a 1993 study on Los Alamos cancer rates was issued by the Division of Epidemiology, Evaluation, and Planning of the New Mexico Department of Health and the New Mexico Tumor Registry at the UNM Cancer Center. The study, free of any hyperbole, had eye-opening information, all of which was underplayed in the media. The most alarming finding, which was not included in the summary, was that "Los Alamos County ranked first among all New Mexico counties for childhood cancer death rates during the period 1953–1987."[130] The study reported that incidents of childhood cancer, not deaths from cancer, fell off after "an initial two-fold elevation" during 1970–72 and fluctuated slightly higher or slightly lower through 1990. As far as LANL was concerned, it was as if that study had never been carried out.

The *Los Alamos Monitor* reported in August 2002 that the "laboratory's multi pronged reply" to the NMED's charges "attacked the endangerment determination as misleading, unlawful, and defectively obtained. Answering blow for blow, the lab dismissed the state's information as inconsistent and called its solutions burdensome. In conclusion," the *Monitor* observed, "the laboratory asked for the finding to be withdrawn and the prospective cleanup order to vanish."[131] It wasn't until 2005 that the state and the lab signed an agreement to clean up LANL wastes.

The history of the dispute over cancer in Los Alamos is as much a matter of interpretation as it is of fact. A high incidence of cancer on "the hill" would be inconvenient, to say the least, for the lab and the government to deal with. Early studies that should have led to further studies didn't. LANL, which for years was privileged to police its own activities and hazardous waste storage practices, saw fit at every turn to downplay health risks to surrounding towns and counties. The press focused on one sensational kind of cancer, that of the brain, played up the possibilities, and then all but banished the whole cancer question from its attention when brain cancer incidents were found to be small, though elevated. Commonsense health concerns on the part of surrounding communities were portrayed as alarmist. But plenty of solid data support the contention that LANL is the source of considerable health endangerment in communities that surround it.

The brain cancer issue attracted national attention in September 1991 when the *New York Times* ran a story under the headline that read "Study on Cancer Rates Splits Home of A-Bomb."[132] The *Times* piece legitimized what had been considered in New Mexico to be something close to mass hysteria. At issue was a "cluster of cases of brain tumors" in a Los Alamos neighborhood catalogued by Tyler Mercier, a resident of the area who thought he was performing a public service. He reported that many residents had stories of cancer illnesses and premature deaths among their friends and relatives. An artist and longtime resident of the area, Mercier didn't consider himself an antinuclear activist, but after he compiled his list of cancer deaths and illnesses and made his findings known at a public meeting, not only did the DOE not agree to fund an investigation, but Mercier became the target of anger and threats. When a state epidemiologist with the New Mexico Department of Health (NMDH) confirmed that the brain cancer rate in Los Alamos from 1984 to 1988 was twice the national rate, he summed up the implications with the near-mystical pronouncement that the difference between the national rate and the Los Alamos rate was "not statistically significant," as it was assumed to be the result of chance alone. Moreover, the brain cancer rate for New Mexico from 1976 to 1991, according to the New Mexico tumor registry, was very close to the same as the national incidents of brain cancer for the same time period. This, of course, left many people scratching their heads and caused the local media to turn their attention elsewhere. It wasn't until 1993 that the NMDH and UNM study reported high incidences of cancers other than those of the brain, especially childhood cancers.[133]

Bothersome Data

There's considerable confusion in the public press about the meaning of the phrase *statistically significant*. If a finding isn't statistically significant, it doesn't mean it's unimportant. It means incidences are probably random, with no clear cause. In this case, no cause-and-effect relationship could be proved. But lack of statistically significant proof doesn't mean there is no cause-and-effect relationship. Absence of evidence is not evidence of absence. For a cluster of seven people in a single neighborhood in Los Alamos to have brain cancer is not epidemiologically insignificant. Working under a grant from the

National Institute of Environmental Health Sciences, Catherine M. Richards, MS, conducted a study of twenty-four cancer types in Los Alamos appearing on the New Mexico Tumor Registry from 1970 to 1996. She found that while many cancers were not considered statistically significant, they "were elevated" in comparison with New Mexico State reference populations that include people with cancers of the brain, colon/rectum, esophagus, and urinary bladder and Hodgkin's leukemia.[134] And mortality rates were higher in Los Alamos County than in the rest of the state for cancers of the colon/rectum, kidney, liver, ovary, pancreas, and others, including non-Hodgkin's lymphoma.

Missed in the hoopla over brain cancer was the alarming truth that there were elevated cancer rates in Los Alamos County that were considered statistically significant, including breast, ovary, prostate, testis, and thyroid cancers. Breast cancer deaths in Los Alamos were "significantly elevated" compared to the state overall. As Richards points out, "Cause and effect is difficult to establish when examining a group of people. For example, not everyone who smokes gets lung cancer. . . . Other variables may enter into the scenario. The same can be said of radiation exposure and cancer. . . . However, a lack of clear information on cause and effect does not mean that there is no risk to the surrounding population from low levels of radiation."[135] Among her many recommendations, Richards urges LANL or the state to "conduct dose reconstruction studies by accessing LANL documents to determine potential exposures for the community" of Los Alamos County. A ten-year study of LANL published in 2009 by the Centers for Disease Control and Prevention concluded that the labs had significantly underplayed its long history of releases of plutonium, polonium, and other radioactive isotopes into New Mexico's air, soil, and water. A study by F. Benjamin Zhan at Southwest Texas State University published in 2001 showed "that a statistically significant cluster of childhood cancer existed in Los Alamos County from 1973 to 1997 and in the six counties west and southwest of Los Alamos."[136] New Mexico also suffered from another area of childhood cancer clusters in Bernalillo, Cibola, Valencia, Socorro, and Doña Ana counties, all of which have some downwind exposure to either nuclear defense contracting, uranium mining, hazardous and radioactive waste dumping, or missile and explosive testing.

Low Level Dangers

A sobering report by the Washington State Department of Health makes it clear how dangerous low levels of radiation exposure really are. Washington has a particular interest in low level radiation because of the staggering amounts of nuclear waste at DOE's Hanford site. Alice M. Stuart, MD, a senior research fellow at Birmingham University in England since 1974 and at the Oxford Survey of Childhood Cancers, wrote in the Washington State report that "constant, low levels of radiation are relatively more harmful than higher levels of exposure over a short period of time. . . . There is increasing evidence that the risk of cancer is proportionately greater at low doses. . . . Internal radiation doses from contaminated food and water over a long time appear to damage the body much more than the same doses from short external exposures. . . . Whether internal exposure will result in a cancer that spreads to other parts of the body depends on the ability of the immune system to detect and destroy the cancer cells."[137] In the same report, Gregg S. Wilkinson, a professor of epidemiology at the University of Texas Medical Branch in Galveston, reports that "exposure to radiation can harm the immune system."[138] A person with a weakened immune system "might also have developed a cancer from the radiation exposure. By not accounting for deaths from weakened immune systems, current risks of cancer deaths from radiation exposure underestimate the harmfulness of radiation."[139] Apparently at Hanford and other DOE nuclear sites, releases of iodine-131 have a direct effect on elevated incidents of thyroid cancer. According to Wilkinson, the high incidents of embryonic cancers around the world, discovered by the Oxford childhood cancer study, might well increase even further by the addition onto background radiation of long-term, low-level radiation released by nuclear defense facilities.

Polluted Dust

Another troubling story of LANL's fallout appeared in June 2007 with relatively muted media fanfare, considering its implications. An independent environmental testing lab, Boston Chemical Data, Incorporated (BCD), found significant plutonium, uranium-235, uranium-234, and strontium-90 levels in dust, wood ash, and soil samples in and around Los Alamos. When inhaled or ingested in other ways, plutonium's short-traveling alpha radiation has the greatest chance of upping a person's probability of developing cancerous tumors and lesions. BCD was brought in to do its testing by Government Accountability Project (GAP), an NGO out of Washington, D.C. The samples were collected in November 2006 with the cooperation of tribal governments, the state of New Mexico, the *Los Alamos Monitor*, and NGOs concerned about nuclear contamination from the labs. Indoor dust was gathered from air filters, vacuum cleaner bags, space heaters, fans, and refrigerators. Here's a short list of what BCD discovered. An interior dust sample collected from NMED's LANL Oversight Bureau offices in White Rock, near Los Alamos, found the highest amounts of radioactivity of the whole research project. The sample was taken from fan dust in a washroom. It contained strontium-90, uranium-234, and uranium-238—all in quantities exceeding background and state reference levels. Wood ash taken from an interior woodstove in San Ildefonso Pueblo, just downhill from LANL, had double the reference level of plutonium. A soil sample from downtown Los Alamos near the parking lot at the Los Alamos Inn had two hundred times the safe level of plutonium in the soil. The highest doses of strontium-90 came from a dust sample taken from Picuris Pueblo, some forty miles northeast of Española. An earlier dust and soil sample study by LANL and NMED on the LANL site, using a much larger sample, showed that off-site "concentrations of radionuclides necessarily are below on-site radionuclide concentrations, since LANL is the source of the bulk of uncontrolled contamination."[140]

True to form, LANL scientists in December 2008 concluded that the radioactive dust, collected largely from indoor samples, did not come from the labs, but rather from nuclear fallout during worldwide atmospheric nuclear testing in the 1950s or from naturally occurring radiation levels in northern New Mexico. Private scientists counter by pointing out the extremely "hot"[141] waste in certain dust samples, implying they originated in experimentation and manufacture. The argument is sure to linger on for years.[142]

In February 2008, the EPA required LANL to monitor, and in some cases clean up, storm water that flowed over many of its waste sites, carrying "contaminants toward the Rio Grande or into the groundwater. Contamination has been found at 25,000 times the New Mexico water quality standard for human health in these flows," a Concerned Citizens for Nuclear Safety news release reported.[143] If we accept this view, we have to assume that storm runoff has carried similar doses down the canyons and into LANL groundwater on the Pajarito Plateau for decades.

Nuclear Nerves

By 2006, more and more New Mexicans were beginning to worry that the Cold War and the nuclear arms race might be starting to poison them. No one pretended to know for sure, but the uncertainty and nervousness in Albuquerque and Santa Fe were reflected in a major front page piece on LANL in the *Santa Fe New Mexican* by environmental reporter Andy Lenderman in September 2006. "Uphill," he wrote in the lead, "there's 1.38 million cubic yards of nuclear and chemical waste. Downhill, there's the Rio Grande, one of the state's main water supplies."[144] Both Albuquerque and Santa Fe were scheduled to begin drinking river water by 2008, water that has the potential of being polluted by LANL runoff, if it already hasn't been for years. No one really knows whom to believe anymore. LANL's refutations of charges by the state environment department seemed self-serving. The NMED, while using strong language, seemed to some to be deferential to the labs. Information from citizen watchdog groups seemed the most believable, but no one really wanted to think about the implications of their findings until they had absolutely no other choice. Had LANL's radioactive tonnage and incompetent storage practices finally started to affect the deep aquifer around Santa Fe? Had its practices of pouring radioactive effluent into canyons that drained directly into the Rio Grande been polluting surface water for years? Had storm runoff gathered up nuclear detritus from subsurface pits and washed it down the canyons, churning up sediments already contaminated with "legacy" radioactivity and dumping it all in the river? What if Cochiti Lake, a major flood control reservoir where Rio Grande water collects before being sent down to Albuquerque, were to dry up, a distinct possibility in view of New Mexico's drought conditions? Would the dust at the bottom be so full of plutonium that it would cause a radioactive dust bowl? What began to haunt people in northern New Mexico was the thought that mutually assured destruction (MAD), the driving concept behind the nuclear arms race, might take on a deadly afterglow in their state, as it had near other bomb-making facilities around the country and the world.

Old-Fashioned Septics

Old fashioned waste dangers like septic tanks and leaking underground gas station storage tanks seem so normal as to be almost harmless compared to the magnitude of a full-scale, ongoing nuclear waste disaster undermining the health and economy of northern and central New Mexico. And in fact, they are—both normal and ubiquitous, and a massive ongoing problem that's endemic to a largely rural state like New Mexico and to the semirural neighborhoods of its major cities and suburbs. Some quarter of a million septic tanks and cesspool systems operate in New Mexico, putting nearly eighty million gallons of wastewater a day into the subsurface soils above water tables. Most septic systems work successfully, without contaminating groundwater, rural residents say. But many do not. The NMED considers septic tanks to be the greatest source of water pollution in the state. Not only have such systems polluted some twelve hundred drinking water wells, but they've ruined nearly 355 miles of New Mexico streams and waterways from Española to Doña Ana County.[145] The state of New Mexico considers septic systems such a risk that, as of September 2005, an owner of a piece of land smaller than three-quarters of an acre was required to install a precleaning filter in a septic system before allowing it to go into the ground.[146]

Underground Leaking

Some environmentalists concerned with water pollution from nuclear defense facilities in New Mexico see the state's emphasis on septic systems as a cover for its inaction in protecting water from nuclear contamination. But no one questions the severity of leaking underground storage tanks (USTs) in New Mexico and around the nation. The Sierra Club in 2005 estimated some 680,000 USTs existed in the United States, with 130,000 backlogged for cleanup and repair and 9,000 new leaks appearing each year. "In 2004, UST cleanups declined by 22 percent compared to 2003," the Sierra Club observed. "Chemicals in USTs can quickly move through soil and pollute groundwater. One gallon of petroleum can contaminate one million gallons of water. One pin-prick-sized hole in a UST can leak 400 gallons of fuel a year. More than 100 million people drink groundwater in states where delayed cleanups threaten groundwater quality."[147]

USTs were seen to pose such a serious threat to health that 71 percent of all known UST releases had been cleaned up by 2005, owing to state and federal environmental laws and funding. By 2004, however, according to the Sierra Club and the EPA, New Mexico joined twenty-four states that had failed to meet the 71 percent national cleanup average. While some states like Florida had only undone the damage to 31 percent of known leaking USTs, impoverished New Mexico had cleaned up 62 percent of its leaking USTs.[148] What leaks from those tanks is a witch's brew of poisons from gasoline, including benzene, MTBE, xylenes, naphthalene, ethylbenzene, PCBs, and lead. New Mexico still has far too many USTs that need repair. And no matter if all of the USTs in the state were under corrective control, the groundwater that they've poisoned would still be poisoned.

In 1994, Ralph Odenwald in the *New Mexico Business Journal* wrote that the state was "clearly emerging as a national leader and model in the hazardous business of cleanup from leaking underground storage fuel tanks."[149] Most of the USTs with problems were buried in the late 1940s and '50s. In 1985, when it became clear that insurance companies wouldn't write policies to cover USTs, the EPA and the Resource Conservation and Recovery Act allowed states to raise money and police themselves. That year, the New Mexico legislature passed the Petroleum Storage Clean Up Act, and five years later, the legislature came up with more funds under the Groundwater Protection Act. In 1994, more than five hundred bad UST sites were under cleanup regulations, and thirty to forty new leak sites were being found a month.[150] By 1998, the EPA had mandated that all states require new USTs be made of materials that do not corrode, like fiberglass, or be wrapped in noncorrosive materials, or be made of steel with protective coatings.[151] In 2008, the NMED Petroleum Storage Tank Bureau put out a request for proposals for emergency services, drilling services, and investigations of abandoned storage tank leak sites.

To my knowledge, no data exists as to actual health problems associated with USTs in New Mexico. We don't know how many illnesses have been directly or indirectly caused by exposure to gasoline byproducts. The national Superfund law itself was enacted in the early 1980s in response to health issues directly related to the Love Canal crisis in 1978. Birth defects, miscarriages, nervous disorders, and cancers were tied to the pollution in the area. A survey of children in the Love Canal area showed that 56 percent of those born from 1974 to 1978 had birth defects. To my knowledge, no studies, other than those on cancer in Los Alamos and surrounding communities, have been carried out by epidemiologists on the health of people living in the vicinity of New Mexico's eighty-nine Superfund sites. Seventeen of those sites are on the EPA National Priorities List. The Agency for Toxic Substances and Disease Registry did survey the health implications of such National Priorities List sites as the Atchison, Topeka, & Santa Fe railyard site in the South Valley, LANL, the Molycorp mine in Taos County, and the Fruit Avenue groundwater plume in downtown Albuquerque. But the ATSDR only conducts what it calls "public health assessments primarily to determine whether people are exposed to contaminants and whether this exposure might be of health concern to them."[152] It does not do medical histories of the neighborhoods around the sites.

The Center for American Progress estimates that "the rate of annual Superfund cleanups" across the country fell "more than 50 percent under the Bush administration. One in four Americans live within three miles of one of the 12,400 Superfund sites awaiting cleanup, and approximately three or four million children, who face developmental risks from exposure to environmental contaminants, live within one mile."[153] The primary reason for the slowdown is the Bush administration and Congress's corporate tax cuts, especially the "polluter pay" tax that used to accumulate as much as $1.5 billion annually for Superfund cleanup of so-called orphaned sites, those that polluters refuse to remedy at their own expense. In the absence of this corporate tax, and after the depletion of the fund itself, taxpayers have been forced to pay as much 30 percent of the cleanup costs at orphaned sites, up from 18 percent when the fund was flush. The beneficiaries of the end of the corporate Superfund tax are the big polluters, including oil companies and petrochemical corporations.[154] But corporations aren't the only big polluters. A massive plume of percholoroethylene was found near Main Street in Las Cruces. The plume, discovered in 1995, will take some fourteen years of cleanup and more than $13 million to do it. It ruined nearly seven billion gallons of water in the Mesilla Bolson and caused the closing of seven wells. The plume apparently came from the city of Las Cruces fleet maintenance yard and the Doña Ana County transportation department maintenance yard.[155]

Navajo Superfund Law

The federal Superfund financial situation and foot-dragging have become so grievous that the Navajo Nation announced in early 2008 a Superfund law of its own. Like the original national Superfund law, the Navajo version calls for polluters to pay for the cleanup. The law would allow the Navajo Nation to clean up contaminated sites that, for one reason or another, don't meet federal EPA standards, including the thousand or so abandoned uranium mines on the twenty-seven thousand square mile reservation, the Associated Press reported.[156] Clear assessments of the health dangers of uranium mill tailings, piled up mountainously around old mines, is only slowly emerging from the responsible public health community. The Canadian-based Community Coalition Against Mining Uranium reported in November 2007 that uranium "mine workers are exposed to the highest radiation doses of any workers in the nuclear industry."[157] The coalition says that the "most serious health hazard associated with uranium mining is lung cancer due to inhaling uranium decay products" like radium-226 and radon gas. Mill tailings are full of radium and dangerous heavy metals like manganese and molybdenum, which can leach into the water table. Radon gas, however, is the most dangerous byproduct, second only to tobacco as a cause of lung cancer. The coalition asserts that when "Radon-222 gas is released from a uranium mine, it deposits solid radioactive dust on the ground for hundreds of miles downwind from the mine site. The Radon-222 and all of its radioactive decay chain products release twelve times as much radiation as is in the uranium-238 itself. These solid particles that form Radon-222 decay quickly [to] become Lead-210, which has a half-life of 22.3 years." Add the radon gas hazard to the radium-226 and the thorium-230 in the tailing sludge pumped into ponds and released accidentally, and it is clear that downwinders must deal with radioactivity that will be measurable for "more than 100 years after a mine is closed."[158] Uranium itself, of course, is a heavy metal and as such can be highly toxic. It is not natural to the body even in trace amounts, as copper, zinc, cobalt, manganese, and molybdenum are. But they, too, can be dangerous in excessive doses. Mercury and lead, even in trace amounts, undermine health, sometimes catastrophically. Inhaling or ingesting uranium over long periods of time, irrespective of its radioactive impact, may lead to serious, often incurable kidney disease. As the federal government and the uranium mining companies won't take this seriously, the Navajo Nation is.

Ned Yazzie—who was relocated from his home near the detritus of the mill—stands on the state highway that runs through Church Rock. He looks toward the now-abandoned ion exchange building. October 2006.

At the Church Rock Chapter House. October 2006.

United Nuclear Corporation ion exchange building. The company has changed
hands over time, and now no one takes responsibility for cleanup. November 2006.

Fence around the UNC ion exchange building with a sign that reads, "Restricted
Area" in English and "Keep Out" in Diné. November 2006.

Scotty Begay outside his home in Church Rock. He worked here for more than twenty years, doing everything from underground mining to mill work to reclamation; he is now a community activist. February 2007.

The Church Rock spill moved through this wash off of State Highway 566 to the Puerco River. February 2007.

Indicating the abandoned structures—a floor is all that remains of this building—
and industrial trash, Tony Hood says, "They were supposed to restore the land to
its original state." April 2007.

This gray dirt is low-grade ore, which is waste. April 2007.

The Biggest

The *Navajo Times* in July 2009 commemorated the thirtieth anniversary of the disastrous Church Rock uranium spill with the banner headline "Poison in the Earth." On the morning of July 16, 1979, the tailings pond dam at the United Nuclear Corporation uranium mill gave way. A great wall of radioactive, foul-smelling yellow water and tons of grit roared down an arroyo and into the dry Puerco River, churning for some seventy miles, past Gallup and into Arizona. It sounded to local residents like the frightful rumbling of an approaching flash flood, a nightmare of inundating force well-known to New Mexicans. This time, though, it wasn't rain water from faraway mountains. It was all generated by the leavings of a uranium mill and constituted "the single largest release of radioactive material in U.S. history," Marley Shebala wrote in the *Navajo Times*, "and its effect on the health of the area's people and animals has yet to be measured by any government or private entity." Immediately after the flood, thousands of sheep died, and many hundreds of Navajos were sickened. Area sheepherders and miners and their families believe that flood of radioactive water, along with radiation from hundreds of other uranium tailings sites on the Navajo and Laguna reservations, to be the principal causes of cancers, kidney failures, and birth defects that have plagued the Native peoples.[159]

"The name 'Poison Canyon,'" the Associated Press reported in 2009, "offers a hint of what's faced by those trying to clean up abandoned uranium mines in the West." Poison Canyon is near the town of Milan, west of Grants, and contains many of the 259 uranium sites in New Mexico that were scheduled for cleanup with federal stimulus funds from the Obama administration.[160]

Church Rock, like Poison Canyon, is not only geographically isolated, but remains politically isolated even now. The Church Rock community "doesn't have the political and economic clout" to get its uranium leavings cleaned up like "the community of Moab" in Utah, said Chris Schuey of the Southwest Research and Information Center in Albuquerque. Schuey has been working for decades on Navajo uranium issues. Moab's cleanup of its uranium tailings "has the support of people and legislators in Southern California concerned about the effects of the tailings . . . on the Colorado River and, therefore, their water supply. . . . We shouldn't forget that the Puerco River is a tributary of the Little Colorado, which is a tributary to the Big Colorado River," Shuey warned.[161]

Native American Activism

The Navajos' antagonism to uranium mining was one of the reasons the Navajo tribal government joined Zuni, Acoma, Leguna, and Hopi pueblos to petition the New Mexico Historic Preservation Division to designate Mount Taylor as a traditional cultural property. Mount Taylor is a massive volcanic mountain west of Albuquerque that's sacred to virtually every Native American tribe in the region. At its southwestern base is what could be one of the largest uranium veins in the world. During the fact-finding process for the designation, old political and cultural animosities were brought to the surface in heated public meetings. Despite bitter, and often racially abusive, exchanges that pitted the tribes against the city of Grants, private landholders on the mountain, and mining companies, the tribes prevailed in June 2009 in a unanimous vote by the state's Cultural Properties Review Committee. Private lands are unaffected by the decision. Uranium companies must now inform tribes and the state where and when they plan exploratory drilling in traditional protected areas. The victory makes it more difficult for mining companies to defile archaeological ruins, medicinal plant habitats, spiritual centers, and grave sites as they have in the past.[162] Mining companies and nonindigenous landowners on Mount Taylor have appealed the Cultural Property Review Committee's designation in New Mexico state court. In November 2009, the National Trust for Historic Preservation along with the pueblo of Acoma filed a motion to intervene in the case, supporting the committee. And in what is considered a virtually unprecedented move, the New Mexico commissioner of public lands has intervened in the case, joining the plaintiffs. The matter remains in litigation as of 2010.

Native American activism against uranium mining and milling and radioactivity released from the Cold War atmospheric testing of more than two hundred nuclear bombs grew in intensity 2009. Navajos and others sought major changes in the federal Radiation Exposure and Compensation Act (RECA). The most comprehensive changes seek to give official federal downwinder status to New Mexico, Arizona, Utah,

Colorado, Nevada, Idaho, and Montana. "As the coverage area now stands," writes Kathy Helms of the Diné Bureau, "radioactive fallout . . . appears to have traveled across the state of Arizona and a portion of Utah before hitting a wall and dropping at the borders of Colorado and New Mexico."[163] U.S. senators from Idaho and Montana introduced a bill in June 2009 recognizing that all the states in and around the Four Corners were exposed to nuclear fallout. The bill would not only make residents of the region eligible for federal compensation for radiation caused diseases, it would expand coverage to uranium miners working in the industry past the old 1971 cutoff date. The Navajo Nation outlawed uranium mining on its lands in 2005, citing the epidemic of cancers its people had suffered during and after the last uranium boom. RECA has already paid out some $625 million to compensate miners and their families for radiation-caused diseases directly related to uranium extraction.

Here Today, Gone Tomorrow

Despite labor struggles, political controversies, and environmental accidents, mineral and energy extractions have been the hard-earned mainstays of New Mexico's economy for centuries, surviving countless boom-bust cycles. The economic instability of mining and drilling have caught many New Mexico towns off guard over the years. The town of Grants suffered an economic depression when the uranium boom of the Cold War era came to an end in the 1980s as prices fell to $7 per pound of processed uranium ore. Nearly six thousand jobs were lost. High hopes for another uranium boom filled Grants again in the early years of the twenty-first century when prices soared to $175 a pound. But the market stagnated, and prices dipped to $50 a pound by early 2009. With new nuclear power plants costing an estimated $7 billion to build, and with their fourteen-year construction time, the nuclear industry failed to inspire the kind of private investments required for start-up ventures.

The health risks that come with uranium mining have been kept from public view for decades. Uranium is a stealth mineral. It has what amounts to national security status. Most Americans, and the miners themselves, were kept in the dark about how dangerous it might be even to live close to a mine or a tailings pile. To this day, the federal government and academic research institutions in New Mexico have failed to create and fund studies examining the mining-related health issues of Acoma, Laguna, and Navajo miners. Many in New Mexico harbored some hope that the Obama administration would beef up mining regulations and challenge the 1872 Mining Act, which practically gives away public lands to mining interests at $5 an acre, even in 2009, and charges no federal royalties on minerals taken from federal land. Ample precedents exist, however, for charging royalties on extractions from federal land. Coal miners, for instance, pay federal royalties, and most mining and drilling operations pay a variety of state taxes in New Mexico.

Hard-rock mining, and coal mining, too, release "more toxic substances—such as mercury, arsenic, lead, and cyanide—than any other industry in the United States," reports the Center for Biological Diversity.[164] "The 1872 law grants an absolute right to mine but sets no standards for prudent mine operations, mine site cleanup, reclamation or restoration, or financial responsibility. Despite being the largest U.S. producers of hazardous waste, mining companies have used their political clout to exempt themselves from most federal hazardous-waste laws."[165]

State officials in New Mexico were lobbying the Obama administration in the fall of 2009 for more economic stimulus money to clean up environmentally hazardous hard-rock mines. The U.S. Government Accountability Office estimates that over a quarter of the more than eight hundred abandoned hard-rock mining sites in New Mexico are a threat to the environment and to public health from industrial chemicals and radioactive waste.[166]

Obsolete Mining Act

Despite New Mexico senators Jeff Bingaman and Tom Udall's introduction of the Hard Rock Mining and Reclamation Act in April 2009, changes to the 1872 mining law have been blocked for years by congressional leadership from mining states in the West and East. Although fears remain that extractive industries would be damaged by fundamental changes in the law, a poll conducted from May to June 2009 showed that 67 percent of New Mexicans in the oil-rich Second Congressional District in the southern part of the state "favored modernizing the 1872 Mining Act."[167] Among Bingaman and Udall's proposed changes are measures requiring mining companies "to pay their fair-share for clean-up of the land and water pollution created from their activities."[168] Others worry that New Mexico's economic base could be eroded by what they consider overregulation. The state depends on revenue from a wide range of minerals and energy sources. The mining of copper, potash, perlite, silver, gold, lead, pumice, molybdenum, vanadium, salt, turquoise, uranium, coal, oil, and natural gas has supplied a major number of jobs and sources of state revenue. At the time the uranium boom ended in the Grants Mineral Belt around 1982, the Jackpile-Paguate uranium mine, a 2,800-acre mine on Laguna Pueblo land, was the largest open-pit uranium operation in the world. Run by Anaconda Minerals Corporation, the gigantic hole was filled in and "reclaimed" in the late 1980s, though people living west of Albuquerque still worry about uranium dust blowing from the site.

Sentiment is growing across the West that the 1872 Mining Act is giving away the store by allowing American and foreign-owned companies to prospect and mine on public lands at virtually no charge. The Pew Charitable Trusts' Campaign for Responsible Mining has called this a "fire sale" of public lands and lobbies for reforms that establish "strong public health, environmental, and cleanup standards." Pew argues that because "metal mining emits more toxic pollutants than any other industry, it should be required to meet the same environmental and cleanup standards that other sectors of the economy do."[169]

Mining damage to the ecology and public health comes from a variety of sources. Streams and other waterways, including private and public drinking wells, can be contaminated by mining waste. The once popular Red River, near Questa, for instance, has been ruined for fishing by runoff from mountainous wastes produced by a molybdenum mine there. Acid drainage is another cause of much water pollution. When the sulfides in ores are exposed to water and air, they form sulfuric acid. Acid mine drainage can be many hundreds of times more acidic than acid rain and can not only kill fish but burn skin. Some copper mining draining ponds are so acidic that birds are killed when they land on them. Sulfuric acid is used in automobile batteries. Cyanide poses a danger to freshwater when it is used to separate gold from ore. Mercury is a deadly byproduct of coal-burning power plants that settles onto waterways, killing plants and animals and endangering public health. It also has been used like cyanide to separate precious metals from ore and can linger for decades in the environment.[170]

With mercury posing such a danger, especially to children and vulnerable seniors, it's strange that as of 2007, the EPA didn't regulate airborne discharges of mercury from coal-burning power plants, considering it "special waste" that has "been exempted from federal hazardous waste regulations." The EPA does, however, regulate "coal combustion wastes" that are "disposed in landfills and surface impoundments."[171] The illogic of this situation speaks to the power of the coal mining lobby in Washington, D.C. According to Green America, "Coal is the absolute dirtiest of all energy sources."[172] Coal-fired power plants send mercury, cadmium, arsenic, sulfur dioxide, hydrogen chloride, and other toxic substances into the atmosphere. Coal mining itself generates "enormous amounts of liquid toxic heavy metals" in slurry that is "stored in large lagoons that sometimes leak or break, resulting in slurry floods and water contamination."[173]

Clean Coal, Clean Oil and Gas?

Coal in contemporary New Mexico is mined mostly in the northwest and northeast portions of the state. Coal mining and oil and gas drilling are ranked as the number one users of water in the extractive industries in New Mexico.[174] In the nineteenth and early twentieth centuries, coal was mined in north central New Mexico, as well. The paradoxes of rural coal mining are glaring. While the political and economic clout of all extractive industries make regulating them almost impossible, New Mexico, or anyplace else in the country, could not operate as an informed technological civilization without the elbow grease of rural miners and oil and gas field workers, the tax revenues they generate, and the products and energy that would not be produced without them. Even the atomic age depended on the coal extracted from the soon-to-be ghost town of Madrid, near Cerrillos on the back road to Santa Fe from Albuquerque. At the beginning of the Manhattan Project in the early 1940s, the installation at Los Alamos was powered by coal excavated from old mines in Madrid and shipped by rail and truck to Los Alamos. Michael Jenkinson in his book on New Mexico ghost towns, *Playthings of the Wind*, observed that using coal in Los Alamos was like the "ewe giving suck to the wolf pup."[175]

The enduring paradox of dirty coal is that it is burned in America's 614 coal-fired power plants and produces 31 percent of the nation's electricity. The same kind paradox exists with oil and gas around the nation and in New Mexico. The oil and gas industry, according to the New Mexico Oil and Gas Association, is the "largest civilian employer in the state." It is ranked second in the country in natural gas production and natural gas reserves, sixth in production of crude oil, and fourth in crude oil reserves. The association estimates that 70 percent of New Mexico's homes are heated by natural gas.[176] Despite its impact on New Mexico's economy, the oil and gas industry persistently locks horns with state regulators and water activists over its hazardous waste problems, which it consistently denies it has, and over the practice of hydraulic fracking.

The State Oil Conservation Division established a rule in 2008 requiring oil and gas drillers to use lined pits to store their toxic waste on-site. Before the rule, all pits were simply unlined holes in the ground. The drillers complained that the new rules were punitive and costly and would cause small drillers to move to other states. Supporters of the rule, including ranchers and homeowners in semirural areas, worried about their water supply. New Mexico's state government documented from the 1980s to 2003 more than seven thousand cases of storage pits spilling or leaking into soil and surface water and some four hundred cases of outright polluting of aquifers. During the hearing process for the new pit rules, the state sampled the contents of pits and found not only many carcinogens but heavy metals as well.[177] Hydraulic fracking produces other kinds of waste. In difficult soils and rock formations where oil and gas are trapped, a concoction of water, sand or ceramic beads, and chemicals is pumped into the blockages to fracture the formations and release the oil or gas. In a process called *acidizing*, hydrochloric acid is pumped into the rock to dissolve it and soften it up for more fracking. Along with huge amounts of water, sometimes as much as 350,000 gallons in a single well, chemicals that can cause cancer even in trace amounts are also used to loosen up the flow. They include diesel fuel and its poisonous mix of benzene and benzene derivatives, along with ethylene, formaldehyde, various hydrocarbons, methanol, and hydrochloric acid. When fracking is used to unlock methane in coal beds that contain drinkable groundwater, pollution is very difficult to contain. But according to clean water activists, successful fracking does not require a carcinogenic brew of chemicals and diesel fuel. Oil and gas production in New Mexico and elsewhere in the mountain West can use the same techniques used in offshore drilling. Fracking into seabeds uses sand, water, and nontoxic additives to protect marine wildlife.[178]

Spurred on by citizen activists since the 1970s, government agencies are coming to take hazardous mining and drilling wastes seriously, despite industry lobbying to preserve the status quo. But even now, more than thirty-five years since the first Earth Day, hazardous waste and contamination of drinking water are not a red flag issue in the popular culture and mainstream media of the United States. Even though contaminating practices are commonplace throughout the mining and drilling business, most people are shocked when they find out such callous practices are part of the normal way of doing business.

The enlightened concern of the Navajo Nation about uranium mining's poisonous tailings and effluents is a rare example of local mainstream government—in this case the Navajo Nation—coming to grips with the long-denied realities of the magnitude of public health hazards of mining and drilling. The Navajos believed their own experience when they bucked corporate and military public relations imagery of the benignity of radiation and forbade any more uranium mining on tribal land.

Eunice

But who's going to take the uranium waste issues seriously in southern New Mexico around the town of Eunice, where Louisiana Energy Services (LES) has opened the first gas centrifuge uranium enrichment plant in the nation? Many environmental and watchdog groups already have, but largely to no avail. The Eunice enrichment plant, five miles northeast of town, close to the Texas border, was under construction in 2008 and a year away from completion. It will "generate 8,000 tons a year of radioactive and chemically hazardous depleted uranium waste, which would be stored in steel cylinders at the plant site," according to John Fleck, the science writer for the *Albuquerque Journal*.[179] LES is a consortium of corporations, including the Dutch firm URENCO, which is itself a consortium comprised of the Dutch government, British Nuclear Fuels, and German firms. URENCO operates other gas centrifuge uranium enrichment plants at Capenhurst, England; Almelo, Holland; and Gronau, Germany. President Jimmy Carter, a former nuclear scientist and officer in the U.S. Navy, banned centrifuge enrichment in the United States, preferring the more costly gas diffusion method. He believed the lower costs could lead to nuclear arms proliferation and terrorist thievery of production secrets. URENCO itself was the victim of perhaps the greatest nuclear secrets theft and sale since the Soviets cracked the top-secret world of the American nuclear establishment. The thief was Pakistani scientist and engineer A. Q. Khan, the father of Pakistan's nuclear program, who in 1972 was working for a subcontractor of URENCO that ran a uranium enrichment plant, like the one being built in Eunice, at Almelo in the Netherlands. Dr. Khan stole details of the gas centrifuge technology and gave it to Pakistani intelligence a year after India exploded its first nuclear bomb, the Smiling Buddha. He then became the prime scientist in Pakistan's version of the Manhattan Project, catching up with India. Dr. Khan confessed to having engineered the passing of the gas centrifuge technology to North Korea, Iran, and Libya. Al-Qaeda operatives and agents for the Taliban were also vying for the technology, though it's doubtful they secured it before Pakistani proliferation schemes were stopped. This is not to imply that little Eunice, New Mexico, sixty-one miles northwest of Odessa, Texas, will necessarily become the site of nuclear espionage. It simply means that this technology is not as benign as many people make it out to be if it falls into the wrong hands. Its sordid history makes one worry about security as well as waste.

President Carter was not as concerned about the expensive gas diffusion process the United States exclusively used to enrich uranium before the Eunice plant opened. The process is basically a kind of nuclear reverse osmosis, in which uranium hexafluoride, or UF-6, is pumped through molecularly fine filters that allow lighter U-234 and U-235 to pass through but keep the bulkier U-238 behind. U-235 is the fissionable isotope of uranium and is used not only to power nuclear reactors but as the major explosive agent in hydrogen bombs. It was also used in the bomb that destroyed Hiroshima. Enriched uranium for reactors can have as much as 5 percent U-235. Bomb-grade enrichment has more than 90 percent U-235, though a powerful bomb can be made of an explosive element of uranium enriched to only 20 percent U-235.[180] UF-6 waste from gas diffusion plants has already piled up to nearly three-quarters of a million tons, all stored in metal containers at closed plants in Oak Ridge, Tennessee, and Portsmouth, Ohio, and at the only operational gas diffusion plant in the country, at Paducah, Kentucky. Now more will be stored in Eunice, New Mexico, from the LES plant's gas centrifuge enrichment process. This is a nuclear waste gamble that so-called green nuclear energy and new reactors will make a dramatic comeback in the face of global warming, causing an ongoing boom in uranium prices. Another way of looking at the uranium boom is that we're being asked to trade dangerous hydrocarbon waste for even more dangerous radioactive waste.

When LES was struggling to get its Eunice license, the tone of the discussion of the dangers of nuclear waste was typically blasé. A Dutch engineer from the Almelo plant run by URENCO told a New Mexico radio audience that the radioactive waste from the gaseous centrifuge process was so safe, he'd store it in his own backyard garden shed. The waste is UF-6. The U.S. Nuclear Regulatory Commission (NRC) says the principal hazards from such waste are "chemical hazards in handling UF-6."[181] When any moisture comes into contact with UF-6, the highly corrosive and toxic substance can explode. And while radiological hazards exist, the chief dangers come from inhalation of the gas in handling, the NRC says.[182] During the Eunice debate, I never heard a proponent of the project refer to a deadly accident involving UF-6 that took place in 1985 in Gore, Oklahoma, at Kerr-McGee's Sequoyah nuclear facility. One Native American worker, James Harrison, twenty-six, was killed in a release of UF-6 that hospitalized forty or more other workers and some one hundred area residents. The Sequoyah plant was notorious for "uranium spills, airborne discharges, excessive disposal of contaminated material into wells underlying the plant."[183] The releases of radioactive matter had been going on at Sequoyah for more than a decade. After the accident, the *New York Times* reported in April 1986 that "measurable levels of uranium and fluoride" were found southeast of the plant, adding, of course, that they "may not be a health hazard." When the chairman of the NRC, Nunzio J. Pallandino, testified before a House subcommittee in March 1986, according to the *New York Times*, he said the Sequoyah accident "suggested the Government was not concerned enough about chemical safety problems at nuclear facilities."[184] None of this sordid history was reported in the mainstream press in New Mexico while the Eunice LES plant's fate was being decided. And no mention was made, either, of another such accident involving radioactive uranium fluoride (UF-4) gas in 1977 at the COMURHEX plant in Pierrelatte, France. The plant converted UF-4 to UF-6 and used roughly the same kind of gaseous materials and processing equipment that are associated with Sequoyah. No major injuries were reported there.

The gas centrifuge plant in Eunice, while safe in principle, will be as prone to human error, laziness, lax regulation, faulty equipment, and corporate arrogance as any other nuclear operation. The UF-6 gas is spun at very high speeds in thousands of cylinders, using centrifugal force to separate out the U-235 from the gas concentrating it in the center. This enriched material is processed, usually nearby, and bonded with ceramic substances that form radioactive pellets used to fill nuclear fuel rods. According to the Nuclear Information and Research Service in Washington, D.C., the LES plant in Eunice "does not have a meaningful or realistic UF-6 disposal strategy. . . . And there are currently no facilities available in the United States for disposal of the massive quantities of UF-6 the LES plant would generate," refuting the statement by LES that once the on-site storage limit is reached, the overflow will be shipped to a "licensed disposal facility."[185] As many as four hundred fourteen-ton metal canisters of UF-6 will be shipped into the plant by truck for processing every year. The prospect of all that dangerous waste and transport worried New Mexico governor Bill Richardson, a former federal secretary of energy himself. He initially opposed the proposed Eunice LES plant. But in June 2005, he signed an agreement with LES stipulating that it could keep no more than a maximum of ten years of waste on-site, still a massive amount, perhaps eighty thousand tons of UF-6. Any excess would have to be stored outside of New Mexico. Where the material would actually go is anyone's guess, though a facility almost exactly on the New Mexico–Texas border, not five miles from the plant, is a possibility.

Depleted Uranium

Some of the more than 750,000 tons of UF-6 depleted uranium (DU) around the country has been converted into what's known as *DU ammunition and armor plating.* The ammo and armor have become basic equipment for U.S. ground forces in the Middle East. Quite a lot of those munitions have been tested in New Mexico since the early 1970s. The polarizing nature of nuclear science is maximized in the debate about the risks and benefits of using DU munitions in battlefield conditions. Government scientists at national labs, at universities, and in the military contend that DU munitions work with superb efficiency, destroying tanks and ripping apart the opposition, leaving the environment messy, to be sure, but safe from any meaningful contamination. Physicians, soldiers, and others say the Gulf War Syndrome that afflicts many U.S. and British military personnel is directly related to the vast tonnage of DU shells and bullets fired in Iraq, Afghanistan, and Kosovo. The civilian populations of these battlegrounds, they contend, have been made lethally ill by DU contamination, suffering cancers of all sorts, kidney diseases, and genetic abnormalities. The entire population of Iraq, they say, has been the victim of a kind of genetic holocaust, compromising the well-being of countless future generations.

Which is it, a useful weapon with neither civilian side effects nor unintended consequences, or the instrument of an atrocity of near-genocidal proportions? It's not hard to tell where the smell of hogwash is coming from. All one ever has to ask in these matters is who benefits and who suffers. Clearly, it is in the interests of the nuclear and military-industrial complex to spin a view of depleted uranium munitions as having little or no negative environmental and public health consequences. Is it in anyone's interest to link depleted uranium to a growing public health crisis in the Middle East and to Gulf War Syndrome? Is this interpretation somehow a financial boon to the public health community or to independent physicians unfunded by the government? That would be absurd.

A "no harm" scenario clearly benefits those who are responsible for making depleted uranium and those who use it. But what is not clear, in my mind, is how such a disparity in interpretation could take place at all. What could account for such violently opposing views? And ultimately, how does one know who is telling the truth and who is to be believed? The government's position on depleted uranium falls into the standard category of civil but adamant denial—almost the exact opposite strategy of, say, that of the Department of Homeland Security, which cried wolf so often and put out so many red and orange alerts that people no longer pay attention. We know a few things for sure. Depleted uranium munitions have been tested in New Mexico since 1972 at LANL, Kirtland Air Force Base, White Sands Missile Range, and New Mexico Tech in Socorro. Starting in 1985, the tests were increased on a six-thousand-acre site near Socorro Mountain behind the New Mexico Tech campus. So many rounds of ammunition were fired there that eventually the site became too contaminated with DU residues to be used for any other testing purposes.[186] New Mexico Tech, during a twenty-one-year testing run from the early 1970s to the early 1990s, fired off about forty tons of DU. The bulk of it, Tech researchers say, was shot into "catch boxes" made of wood with metal targets and packed with sand. Tech denies ever doing open-air DU testing. The sand catches the DU particles, aerosolized and pyrophoric as they are, Tech maintains, and keeps them away from Socorro.[187] New Mexico Tech is concerned, however, with cleaning up DU debris, even as it says there is none. A school researcher, according to Defensetech.org, has shown that tumbleweed, an invasive species New Mexico has in abundance, absorbs DU from contaminated soils. DU-laced tumbleweed is carted off and then disposed of somehow, perhaps by burning, as is the practice in New Mexico, sending the DU airborne, of course.[188] Why, one wonders, if DU is so harmless, would one go to the trouble of growing tumbleweeds to clean it up?

DU munitions testing continues in other locations, too. At LANL, it's estimated some 220,000 pounds of DU munitions were fired off, with some 10 percent of the residue reaching the watershed.[189] Open-air testing has been conducted there for years. Bunker Buster missiles were tested at White Sands Missile Range in the 1990s, with heavy DU warheads simulating the weight and size of the nuclear bombs that the real Busters would employ. One Buster went into the water table sixty meters down and was never recovered, leaving the surrounding aquifer heavily contaminated.[190]

Such testing in New Mexico, around the country, and in the Middle East in battlefield conditions has shown that DU munitions offer enormous firepower. DU was used by the Israelis in the 1973 Yom Kippur War, by the British in the Falklands War, by the U.S. in the invasion of Panama, and in both Iraq wars. In Desert Storm in 1991 alone, some 851,000 rounds of DU munitions were fired. And millions of rounds have been fired during and since the invasion of Iraq that began twelve years later.[191] The U.S. military-industrial establishment apparently believes that the residue left by DU weaponry is harmless. A Sandia National Laboratories report by respected researcher Albert C. Marshall released in 2005 contends that "the health risk to all downwind civilians is predicted to be extremely small."[192] He goes on to write that "claims of observable increases in leukemia and birth defects from DU exposure are not supported by this study. External radiation doses from DU are generally very small."[193]

Sandia Labs' view of DU is in direct contradiction to that of Damacio Lopez, a longtime resident of Socorro and the founder of the International Depleted Uranium Study Team (IDUST). In its mission statement, IDUST portrays DU as an "internationally recognized . . . health hazard . . . a suspected environmental contaminant in more than 50 sites across the U.S. and on battlefields and test sites throughout the world. Affected communities experience health problems similar to those of U.S. Gulf War veterans and Iraqi soldiers and civilians."[194] Perhaps the most convincing evidence supporting the claim that the residue from DU munitions is highly dangerous comes from an official 1991 report from the United Kingdom Atomic Energy Authority (UKAEA), a corporate body overseeing nuclear energy in Great Britain since 1954. It cites research from the International Committee of Radiological Protection claiming that DU munitions in the Gulf War could cause death from cancer for more than half a million civilians in the Middle East. While UKAEA modulated its view by writing that "obviously this theoretical figure is not realistic," it then reinforced it by saying, "However it does indicate a significant problem."[195]

Writer, scientific researcher, and anti-DU activist Leuren Moret asserts that this significant problem has led to the "genetic future of the Iraqi people for the most part [being] destroyed."[196] Moret writes that DU "trashes" the body. The rapid appearances of cancers in soldiers in the second Iraq war is darkly significant. "Soldiers developing malignancies so quickly since 2003 can be expected to develop multiple cancers from independent causes. This phenomenon has been reported by doctors in hospitals treating civilians following NATO bombing with DU in Yugoslavia in 1998–1999 and the U.S. military invasion of Iraq using DU for the first time. Medical experts report that this phenomenon of multiple malignancies from unrelated causes had been unknown until now and is a new syndrome associated with internal DU exposure."[197] Dr. Helen Caldicott has reported that pediatricians in Basra, Iraq, have seen "a sevenfold increase" in childhood cancers and a "sevenfold increase in gross congenital abnormalities" since the beginning of the use of DU munitions.[198]

A useful description of DU munitions like those tested for years in New Mexico comes from the International Atomic Energy Agency (IAEA), which was created in 1957 by the United Nations to serve, in its words, as "the world's center of cooperation in the nuclear field." The IAEA, the international version of the pronuclear Atoms for Peace program started in the United States in the 1950s, has a staff of twenty-two hundred from more than ninety countries. In a 2000 document, the IAEA describes what happens to a DU "kinetic energy penetrator," or shell, when it hits a target like a tank: "On impact with targets, DU penetrators ignite, breaking up into fragments, and forming an aerosol of particles ('DU dust') whose size depends on the angle of impact, the velocity of the penetrator, and the temperature. These fine dust particles can catch fire spontaneously in air."

The IAEA confirms what many DU opponents contend about the "purity" of U-238 depleted of fissionable U-235. Uranium itself is dangerous as a source of low-level radiation and as a heavy metal, but DU is not pure. According to the IAEA, it contains "small amounts of transuranics (elements heavier than uranium, such as neptunium, plutonium, and americium) and fission products such as technetium-99 . . . at very low levels. During the enrichment of reprocessed uranium [between the 1950s and 1970s], the inside surfaces of the equipment also became coated with these anthropogenic radionuclides which later contaminated the DU processed from the enrichment of natural uranium as well. The exact amount is not known." The IAEA cites studies that show statistically significant increases in mortality rates among veterans having served in DU-contaminated areas. But, it says, "this cannot be linked to any exposures to DU." Published in 2000 from data gathered before the second Gulf War, in which millions of rounds of DU ammunition have been fired, the IAEA report on DU cannot be construed as antinuclear or even anti-DU. It still, however, cautions against the potential hazards of inhaling the aerosols, both because of their low-level radiation and because of uranium's toxicity as a heavy metal. There's also the danger of those aerosolized particles moving up into the atmosphere during windstorms, and "depleted uranium present in the soil can migrate to surface and groundwater and flow into water streams."[199]

A year after the IAEA DU report surfaced, an opposite view appeared from an international body. Writer Piotr Bein, in Vancouver, Canada, both praised and took to task a report entitled *Depleted Uranium Weapons and Acute Post-War Health Effects* from the International Physicians for the Prevention of Nuclear War. Bein agreed with the report's view that training U.S. military to "take precautions" in handling DU munitions, "while issuing blanket denials of health risks to the public, strikes us as hypocritical at the very least and reinforces our judgment that these weapons should be withdrawn from service." But he was critical of the report's lack of "much advocacy . . . on behalf of the soldiers and civilians who are sick and dying of DU." Bein focused on the transuranic impurities in the DU munitions, citing a 1976 UK Royal Commission report affirming that "a person inhaling a few micrograms of plutonium" is "likely to develop a fatal lung cancer in 10 or 20 years after exposure." Bein argued that if all the "'impure' specks of DU dust were ingested or inhaled, they alone could kill millions of people."[200] It's numbers like these, along with bald statements one hears from time to time—such as the rumor that half the residents of Socorro have cancer—that compromise the DU opposition's principled positions. Still, for all the official denials of risk, the state of New Mexico did start testing soldiers returning from Iraq and Afghanistan for DU in their urine and tissue in 2007. No report has been forthcoming as of this writing.

As recently as July 2010, veterans advocacy groups brought to light a "little known 1993 Defense Department document written by then–Brigadier General Eric Shinseki, now secretary for the Department of Veterans Affairs (VA), [which] shows that the Pentagon was concerned about DU contamination and the agency had ordered medical testing on all personnel that were exposed to the toxic substance. . . . The VA, however, never conducted the medical tests, which may have deprived hundreds of thousands of veterans from receiving medical care to treat cancer and other diseases that result from exposure to DU."[201] At a July 2010 House Veterans Affairs subcommittee hearing, Veterans for Common Sense urged the VA to take action on DU-caused illnesses, citing a recent Armed Forces Health Surveillance

Center report confirming that "service members tend to have higher rates of certain cancers compared to civilians."[202]

Hot Waste Hotly Disputed

How is it possible to find even cautious optimism regarding toxic waste in industrial and nuclear America when the basic data and analysis are so hotly disputed? This polarization is so extreme that progress can't be accomplished by reason and persuasion, but only through the force of politics and increasingly sophisticated activism. And that, as in other situations, is the cardinal cause for hope—sophisticated activism. Communities and organizations in New Mexico and across the country who oppose the indiscriminate dumping of hazardous waste or of industrial, energy-based, and military production of such waste have been around so long now, nearly forty years in many cases, that they are acquiring an alternative history based on their memories and their extensive files and networks. This base of knowledge makes it increasingly troublesome for the powers that be, despite being armed by their science for hire, to stonewall the public. And it will be increasingly tough to lie and obfuscate when Washington, D.C., is inhabited by an administration even marginally more competent that those we have been burdened with in the past. Courageous groups like the Los Alamos Study Group, the Southwest Organizing Project, the Southwest Research and Information Center, Citizen Action, Amigos Bravos, New Mexico Environmental Law Center, Concerned Citizens for Nuclear Safety, and dozens of land- and neighborhood-based communities of dissent around New Mexico have been laying the groundwork with careful, long-term research and reasoned argument for a cultural turnaround in the future. One day voters will come to understand the enormous economic damage that indiscriminate waste, lax enforcement of laws, and minimal penalties for polluting bring to their own cities and towns and pocketbooks. It will take a while yet to make the connections between massive pollution, contaminated water, real estate downturns, rising health care costs, and the debt crisis that predatory lending, inadequate insurance, and chronic forms of environmental illness can cause. But when your environment is the source of sickness, when you can't with assurance drink local water, when you can't sell your home, not only because of national banking crises but because no one wants to buy a house in a field of poison, maybe the connection between well-being, clean land and water, a safe home, and a strong economy will become clear. Soiling your nest is like losing your income and losing your health, with no rescue in sight.

CHAPTER FIVE

URBAN/RURAL STRUGGLES
THE BROADER HABITAT

In the early 1990s, New Mexico land commissioner Ray Powell heard alarming tales of refrigerators washing down Tijeras Arroyo into the South Valley after heavy rains in the Manzano Mountains. He knew the state owned a parcel of land near the top of the arroyo and went to look around. What he found amazed and baffled him. There at the edge of the arroyo was an open landfill covering some forty acres. Arroyos are dry most of the time, but the water they carry can move with dangerous force. And if the arroyo is huge, like the Tijeras, and comes out of a mountain, running downhill for many miles, the force of floodwater can be devastating, even near the top. The landfill he found was relatively old, unlined, and full of all the debris and chemicals that you'd expect in a dump. The city of Albuquerque had been dumping there for years. It had a lease with the state to

◄   Cimarron. As the irrigation system on the ranch dates from the late 1800s, this ditch has become lower than the field; Gayle McBrayer digs an outlet so that the crop will receive water. June 2007.

do so. The city had been "dumping in a manner that extended the refuse into the arroyo," Ray Powell told me. When "it rained hard and the arroyo ran, the water began to erode into the side wall of the extension of the landfill in the bottom of the arroyo." The State Land Office's consulting engineers determined the landfill "had not been closed out properly. It had been a very serious unresolved problem for years," Powell said. A mobile home park north of the landfill had run its sewer line into a larger line that ran down the arroyo. "Because of the instability of the landfill, the lines would often break and release raw sewage in the area," Powell said. After extensive consultations with experts, who thought it was too large and dangerous to move, Powell decided to cap it with dirt and concrete.[1]

The state of New Mexico owns thirteen million acres of land from which it generates revenue for higher education. Much of this trust property is checkerboarded across the state. The State Land Office, Powell told me, has a longstanding problem with people using its more remote properties as dumping grounds. The situation is impossible to police. In the case of Tijeras Arroyo, which links a wild mountain watershed with the Rio Grande, moving through a military base and a highly polluted and industrial part of the city, it's also impossible to hide. Tijeras Arroyo is a metaphor for the bond a city has with its natural and rural surroundings.

Cities in Hostile Context

It's a common enough myth that cities are isolated, self-contained entities, that where they stop civilization ends, that what's beyond them is of no consequence to those who hold the sophisticated, competitive worldview they represent. But cities exist in contexts. What happens to the wild world around them portends their fates. What happens to other cities who compete with them for natural resources foreshadows their futures. What happens to distant watersheds that supply their water determines their lives and deaths. And what happens to farmers, rural communities, and ranchers has more to do with the intricacies of cities' existences than urbanites can imagine. If their rural neighbors are in trouble, it's likely they are, too.

But as is true in most rural states, New Mexico's cities have always been in competition with their rural neighbors. Small towns, ranchers, and agriculturalists have seen Albuquerque, Santa Fe, Rio Rancho, and Las Cruces as goliaths to be battled, stalled, waylaid, and diverted at every session of the state legislature. Albuquerque is the most glaring target for rural legislators. Its water use and economic development are perennially blamed for draining wealth and resources from the rest of the state. The longstanding animosity between rural and urban New Mexico came to a head in the January 2009 legislative session. At issue was a 1995 amendment to an obscure state statute that allowed municipalities to condemn, through eminent domain, water rights far beyond their boundaries. The bill to abolish those powers passed both houses in the legislature unanimously and was signed into law by Governor Bill Richardson in April 2009. Organizations representing virtually the entire rural world in New Mexico supported the bill—including the New Mexico Farm and Livestock Bureau, Conservation Voters New Mexico, the New Mexico Cattle Growers Association, the New Mexico Acequia Association, La Montanita Co-op, and the Middle Rio Grande Conservancy District. Only the powerful New Mexico Municipal League opposed the bill. Lisa Robert, a farmer south of Albuquerque and one of the state's most acute observers of water issues, said that once rural property owners and regional water planners realized that "the wealthiest urban centers could, if they wished, simply confiscate all water rights for hundreds of miles,"[2] they came together to form an unbeatable political alliance.

The unanimous victory shows that while the split between urban and rural New Mexico is still alive in political rhetoric and on editorial pages, even urban legislators would not vote against the anticondemnation bill, realizing not only its unfairness, but that rural hostility might grow so intractable that purchasing water rights in the future could be stymied. Governor Richardson said, in signing the bill, that municipalities "already enjoy extraordinary preferential powers under state water law. Most significant is the power to hold water rights unexercised for up to forty years without fear of forfeiture."[3]

Perhaps the subtlest conflict between urban and rural businesses occurs when urban growth is fueled on the mere promise of water, not the actual wet stuff. Such promises are known as "dedications." Lisa Robert articulates the rural perspective:

> The Albuquerque Basin has a hydrologic deficit of at least 70,000 acre-feet a year, and that figure does not include 30 years worth of dedications, those state-issued permits that allowed groundwater appropriators to postpone the purchase of offset rights. Countless developments . . . have all been promoted on the assumption that sufficient agricultural water will be available for transfer when the time comes to repay the river/aquifer system. In the last several years, however, back of the envelope computations have proven less than reassuring: the pledges add up to more water than can credibly be wrung from retired farmland.

In order to honor those "dedications" with real water, however, "90 percent of the remaining agricultural lands in the middle valley will have to be dried up, including what belongs to six Middle Rio Grande Pueblos. Outrageous as it seems, private assets have been committed without the approval—or even the knowledge—of the relevant owners," Robert concludes.[4] To actually honor those dedications would be physically, legally, and morally impossible. But the strain on rural businesses of coping with urban growth and water use is much more severe than city dwellers realize.

The Troubling Diversion

The greatest worry of rural irrigators is Albuquerque's use of its San Juan–Chama water. In December 2008, the city began diverting what could be as much as ninety-six thousand acre-feet a year, water that had been flowing into the Rio Grande since the mid-1970s and artificially supplying rural and Pueblo farmers' irrigation needs. (The city has rights to use only forty-eight thousand acre-feet of San Juan–Chama water but must divert double that to move the flow through miles of new pipes and the drinking water treatment plant.) What might this diversion mean to people living south of the city? What about its impact on the cherished cottonwood forest that lines the Rio Grande in Albuquerque? The greater Albuquerque area has grown so much and so fast that the middle valley's aquifer is shrinking dangerously. The new residents who are using so much water, many of whom know little about New Mexico's rural life, probably didn't even know that a switch was made from aquifer water to river water for drinking.

When you add up the impact of small farmers selling water rights to developers, the Bureau of Reclamation's water needs for endangered species like the silvery minnow, increasing drought, climate change, the dwindling snowpack in the Colorado River Basin and Rio Grande watershed, and massive population growth up and down the river, the antagonism felt by rural agricultural businesses toward urban expansion makes sense.

Janet Jarrett, chair of the Middle Rio Grande Conservancy District (MRGCD), which regulates irrigation up and down the valley, has said that "the Middle Rio Grande was like a kind of breadbasket" during its prewar peak of agricultural production. But as "you start having water rights transfers," she said, "it isn't just about water rights. It's the land that goes with it."[5] With less land, less agriculture, and less recharge of the aquifer from unlined conservancy ditches, there is less hope for creating a new self-sustaining agricultural and ranching base, which would provide more locally grown food, to counteract the future impact that rising costs of gasoline and diesel fuel will have on inflating prices of trucked-in food. Currently, New Mexico grows only 3 percent of what it eats.

Water hasn't been running smoothly or plentifully south of Albuquerque since the mid-2000s. In April 2009, irrigators complained bitterly to the MRGCD board that water just wasn't flowing to their fields. One farmer said, "There have been times when I've called the district office, and they tell me the computer says there's lots of water in the ditch. But I'm standing on the ditch bank, and there's no water."[6] The flow, farmers feel, doesn't have enough momentum to fill their fields.

Amblers versus Farmers

Symbolic of the struggle between urban and rural citizens of the Middle Rio Grande Valley was a fight between an Albuquerque state senator and the MRGCD board over the Ditches with Trails project, which was intended to turn the highly trafficked walking paths along the conservancy's ditches and drains into a designed and landscaped suburban recreation site. The board abruptly withdrew from the project at a meeting in July 2008, angering the senator and her suburban constituents who pay taxes to the MRGCD without getting direct use of its water, though they benefit from its flood control system. The focal point was a $200,000 pedestrian bridge over one of the MRGCD's drains in the North Valley. The board, in a public meeting, disavowed any knowledge of authorizing such a sum for a footbridge and unanimously withdrew its support of the project. Apparently one of the conservancy's employees had OK'd the bridge without informing the board. The political repercussions were extraordinary. Rural users of the ditch system told the board they "preferred the ditches to remain as they are: accessible and unspoiled." The dispute ended up in the legislature, where numerous bills designed to do away with the conservancy altogether were proposed. None of them prevailed. During the MRGCD elections of 2009, suburban candidates, supported by the senator, won seats on the board. As of this writing, the ditches and trails issue remains unresolved, though the election may make future communication between rural and suburban constituencies more productive.[7]

Water Provocations

What seemed to many to be a preposterous proposal to pipe water a hundred and fifty miles from Fort Sumner to Santa Fe was an even more telling example of the tensions between urban and rural New Mexicans. Emotions ran high in early 2009 when this unprecedented plan began to take on an aura of reality. Here we see the real nature of the struggle for water rights. In 2008, five farmers from eastern New Mexico filed an application with the Office of the State Engineer to sell water rights for around two billion gallons (or sixty-six hundred acre-feet) a year to Santa Fe and other cities. No one took them very seriously until Citibank of New York made substantial loans to the pipeline developer. The reaction of the plan in other towns and small cities in the south was reflected in an editorial in the *Roswell Daily Record* entitled "Draining Our Future."[8]

"Should this pipeline be built," the editorial declared, "what's to stop a second one from being set up alongside it? A third? Why not 20? With 150 miles of pipe already in place, why not tack on another 80 miles and start pulling water out from under Roswell?" The editorial warned that "residents in this part of the state should be gravely concerned about creating a precedent of having our water piped away for the benefit of residents living far to the west of us."

The Roswell paper said what is on the minds of rural New Mexicans much of the time as they contemplate the impact of drought conditions and the rapacious needs of their urban neighbors. "That Santa Fe is willing to use a 150-mile pipeline to get more water is an extremely ominous development. . . . If a city populated with affluent and influential residents finds itself in danger of running out of water and that city has the means to get it elsewhere, that's very bad news for people living in that 'elsewhere.'"

The *Roswell Daily Record* editorial concluded with a classic description of water wars in the future as climate change keeps New Mexico's deserts dry. "Eastern New Mexico is an arid region which has managed to grow only through the careful management of its water. It would be a travesty if all that progress were to be lost because the other side of the state is unable to similarly manage its water and then plunders ours. Agriculture is a vital industry in our region, but if water starts disappearing from our area because of city dwellers a couple of hundred miles away, you can bet farmers and ranchers will be the first to feel the pinch."[9]

Other southeastern New Mexico towns joined Roswell's outrage. The Carlsbad Irrigation District filed a protest with the Office of the State Engineer, as did both the water agencies in Roswell and Artesia. And later in 2009, the formidable New Mexico Interstate Stream Commission filed a protest with the state engineer opposing the pipeline. The Interstate Stream Commission's protest is significant, since the state engineer himself is the secretary of the commission, and the commission's director is the deputy state engineer. It almost goes without saying that citizens of Santa Fe and Albuquerque are fundamentally clueless when it comes to the formal and practical roles that water plays in the lives of rural citizens and their businesses. The struggle for water, the most precious of resources and one that is frighteningly scarce, will render the relationship between cities and the countryside they inhabit increasingly more dysfunctional as drought, peak oil, climate change, and the global financial crisis stresses the state.

The Disappearing Colorado River

Rural water planners have a view of the future not shared by urbanites and their city papers. People who live off the land are growing more and more concerned about the condition of the Colorado River, its dwindling water flow, and the cascading impact that will have on farm and ranch water supplies as Albuquerque, Rio Rancho, and Santa Fe desperately look for water. Curtailment of New Mexico's use of the Colorado River is a real possibility.

Like all things having to do with water in the West, coping with shortages will be legally and politically complicated. Every major city in the region has been preparing for the worst since 2005 or earlier, some more than others, and Albuquerque perhaps least of all. Albuquerque mayor Martin Chavez campaigned in his unsuccessful 2009 reelection bid on Albuquerque's rosy environmental reputation and its "bright" water future. The mayor told voters he remained "unabashedly" a growth advocate who saw the city's development extending many miles west to the Rio Puerco. That made him look to some like an old guard, 1950s booster, despite his and the city's many environmental awards. In 2007, the city won the U.S. Conference of Mayors inaugural Climate Protection Award. A year earlier, Albuquerque won a World Leadership Award for its work to secure "sustainable water supply," meaning, of course, the San Juan–Chama Diversion Project. In 2008, the Siemens Sustainable Community Award went to Albuquerque, along with other green awards.[10] Chavez did take important steps in conservation, ordering a pilot project for gray water to be used on city parks and golf courses. But Chavez's Democratic opponent in the 2009 mayoral race, Richard Romero, was the first candidate to even mention water in the election, claiming that "no mayor can honestly claim that our water future is secure." Romero said that Mayor Chavez's confidence in the city's water supply was "political spin." As mayor, Romero said, he would focus on rigorous conservation. "We cannot secure our water supply independent of our neighbors. . . . God forbid that the Colorado River dries up."

That's exactly what has everyone in the West worried about the future of growth and even the ability to maintain present populations in the years ahead. The Colorado River is experiencing what the Bureau of Reclamation calls a "protracted multi-year drought which began in October 1999."[11] Ten years later, both Lake Powell and Lake Mead, the river's major reservoirs, were at 43 percent capacity. If population levels hadn't skyrocketed in virtually very state that uses Colorado River water, the drought wouldn't be quite as threatening. And if those same states weren't in drought conditions themselves, the state of the Colorado River would be troublesome but not potentially catastrophic. But in 2009, the state of California was three years into a severe drought itself. Worries were heightened by concerns about global warming. In February 2009, Governor Arnold Schwarzenegger moved California steps closer to mandatory water restrictions, the first since 1991. "This drought is having a devastating impact on our people, our communities, our economy, and our environment," the governor said. "Last year we experienced the driest spring and summer on record, and storage in the state's reservoir system is near historic lows."[12] It takes only two years for California's huge population of nearly thirty-seven million people to drain its reservoirs. Los Angeles mayor Antonio Villaraigosa told Angelenos in February 2009 that "water shortages are becoming permanent realities."[13]

In 2009, it started to dawn on New Mexicans that if the general drying and specific droughts continue in the West and mountain West, access to Colorado River water could be in temporary or long-term jeopardy. If the Colorado River watershed continues to dry up and western drought becomes a perpetual hazard—as current predictions have it—Las Vegas, Nevada's million or more inhabitants could be facing a crisis of Katrina-like severity, not from flooding, but from running dry. Some 90 percent of Las Vegas's water comes from the diminishing Colorado River. Denver, Los Angeles, Phoenix, and Tucson are in different boats, but their ponds are shrinking, too. For New Mexico, everything hinges on the Colorado Compact of 1922. New Mexico, Colorado, Utah, and Wyoming are the "upper basin" states. When it comes to drought, the upper basin has inferior status to the lower basin states of California, Arizona, and Nevada. That means in a crisis, upper basin states won't get their Colorado River water until lower basin states have theirs. Western water planners are painfully aware of what happened to Atlanta, Georgia, during the hundred-year drought that hit the region in late 2006. Atlanta was caught off guard when the drought, with the speed of a blitz, almost emptied Lake Lanier, Atlanta's only water supply. Atlanta got some of the rain and snow it needed, but its drought still hadn't entirely lifted by 2009. New Mexico's drought became serious in 2003. It doesn't look like it will lift for a long, long time, either, owing to climate change.

If the Colorado River—which supplies New Mexico with about 110,000 acre-feet of water a year and has been counted on to give Albuquerque about 70 percent of its drinking water—continues to dwindle, New Mexico might be deprived of its Colorado water when it needs it the most because of its status as an upper basin state. Should the drought continue, this could happen before 2020. New Mexico's water loss would be triggered by key elements in what's known as the Law of the River, the most important of which is Article III, Section (d), of the Colorado Compact of 1922. It stipulates that the states of the upper basin "will not cause the flow of the river at Lee Ferry [in Arizona] to be depleted below an aggregate of 75 million acre-feet for any period of ten consecutive years." Even though both the upper and lower basins are guaranteed the use of 7.5 million acre-feet of water each year in "perpetuity,"[14] in a long-term drought, the lower basin gets its water first, should the conditions outlined in Article III be reached. Another part of the Law of the River, the Upper Colorado River Basin Compact of 1948, stipulates how the upper basin states will compensate for the shortfalls at Lee Ferry. Exactly how that's done would be determined by a commission composed of representatives from upper basin states. Compensation might be adjusted according to how the 7.5 million acre-feet of the river guaranteed to the upper basin are apportioned—51.75 percent to Colorado, 11.25 percent to New Mexico, 23 percent to Utah, and 14 percent to Wyoming. Cities across the West are praying such a situation never happens, but it grows more likely with each year of drought.

Junior Status

The administration of Governor Bill Richardson has raised the alarm about drought and climate change in New Mexico. Richardson has created numerous committees of experts to survey the range of potential problems. But the complications of water law and the sounds of lawyers in California, Nevada, Arizona, and Colorado strapping on their armor and sharpening their swords have many New Mexicans jumpy and nervous. We just don't have the money to hold the other states off. And when it comes to the Law of the River, even powerful places like Los Angeles have had to bite the bullet. Even though California, as a lower basin state, cannot be denied its share of the Colorado River, the Metropolitan Water District (MWD) of Southern California, which supplies 60 percent of the water to nineteen million people in the Los Angeles area, has a junior, or lesser, status than California itself because it made its claim on the Colorado after the

Colorado River Compact divided up the water in 1922. Effectively, Los Angeles is last in line for water in California by the prevailing rule of prior appropriation. In 2003, the MWD and its customers got a glimpse of the future when California had to curtail, somewhat, its water portion. The MWD had to take the hit and reduce its water usage after the state's agricultural regions got theirs. California's water needs affect every state in the Colorado River Compact. As the MWD states on its website, "For many years, California has depended on surplus water to meet its water needs—and to supplement its basic apportionment of 4.4 million acre-feet a year."[15] That surplus water comes from Arizona and Las Vegas, Nevada, which in the past didn't use their full allotments. But population growth and climate change will take that surplus out of play. Arizona's drought and the Colorado River's desiccation are already squeezing Phoenix and Tucson, with their shallow and depleting aquifers. The Colorado River supplies more than half the annual water used by both cities. Arizona was expecting a potential shortfall from the Colorado River as early as in 2011.

In July 2009, the *Denver Post* summed up the situation from the viewpoint of Coloradans: "A 10-year drought along the Colorado River, which runs 1,450 miles from the Rocky Mountains to the Gulf of California, has created anxiety. Lawyers are looking into how downriver users such as Californians might assert water rights if reservoirs [Lake Mead and Lake Powell] dried up. Denver residents rely on water from both the South Platte River and the Colorado River Basin."[16] A study by a University of Colorado (CU) scholar has predicted that global warming and overuse could cause all the reservoirs along the river to dry up. The *Post* quoted CU civil environmental engineer Balaji Rajagopalan: "In the short term, the risk is relatively low. But after that, the risk escalates enormously, if you do nothing, and you have no policies in place, even drastic measures such as cutting people off will not help from staving off catastrophe."

A far more dire warning came from researchers at the University of California in 2008 who found a "one-in-two chance that overuse and warming could deplete reservoirs much sooner—by 2021."[17]

Unpredictable Vulnerability

New Mexico's statewide drought task force issued a major report and warning in 2006. That year, the unpredictability of weather conditions in a time of global warming came home to New Mexicans. The first six months of the year were the driest in 112 years, while the last six months were the wettest in 112 years. Despite such fluctuations, the state is still drier than ever, and our increase in population "has dramatically increased the state's vulnerability to drought," according to the *New Mexico Drought Plan.*[18]

Even though the political debate in Albuquerque's 2009 mayoral race shied away from water issues, local scientists and thinkers were driving home how vulnerable the city was. In an anthology of articles produced by the New Mexico Bureau of Geology and Mineral Resources for a "decision makers field conference" on water, natural resources, and the urban landscape for the Albuquerque region in 2009, State Geologist Peter A. Scholle wrote in the introduction that a "doom and gloom" scenario for the Middle Rio Grande Valley is not warranted, if we have the desire to make certain changes. Scholle acknowledged that "increasing population, increasing development, and climate change will all add to the stress on natural ecosystems," not to mention increasing sources of pollution. But he argued that

> if we have the will to do what the environmentalists have urged for decades—act locally but think globally—we can control the slide toward future crisis. . . . We change our energy use patterns to ones that are more sustainable, if we have the desire to do so. . . . We can set positive examples at the local level, in Albuquerque and other New Mexico communities. We can pioneer cities run predominantly off renewable or sustainable energy. . . . We can build far more energy-efficient homes, offices, and transportation systems. We can emulate other communities that already recycle most of the products and materials they use. We can do far more to reduce consumptive water use. We can pioneer ways of reducing evaporative water losses. We can put our heads together and come up with a thousand more things to do to affect the trajectory of future change, and then we can conjure up the will to do them.[19]

It's finding the will, of course, that is the problem. Unprecedented change seemed to be on its way in the West, like it or not, as a new decade approached. And cutting-edge thinkers in cities around the country were trying to drum up the will among the citizenry to embrace the possibility of doing what the *New York Times* advocated in a piece called "Reinventing America's Cities: The Time Is Now." Nicolai Ouroussoff wrote that though the country had "fallen on hard times," those "who love cities know we have been living in the dark ages for a while now. We know that turning things around will take more than just pouring money into shovel-ready projects, regardless of how they might boost the economy. Windmills won't do it either. We long for a bold urban vision." Ouroussoff contended that cities "are also vastly more efficient than suburbs. But for years," he writes, "they have been neglected, and in many cases forcibly harmed, by policies that favored sprawl over density and conformity over difference."[20]

Making Cities Work

Reinventing cities in the West is not the same as retrofitting rust-belt metropolises in the Midwest and Atlantic coast. Western cities are not downtown cities to speak of: they have nothing to build up or reclaim that bears any relationship to the population ratio in the traditional city. Los Angeles is its sprawl, and so is Albuquerque, largely. Retrofitting Albuquerque requires first of all stopping building on the fringes and, until basic water and fuel issues get solved, perhaps stopping building altogether. What would a "bold new vision" look like in western cities? In Albuquerque and Santa Fe? It wouldn't be about building anything new. It would have to embrace the radical idea of slowing down, even stopping growth for a while, until basic plans are in place for new water distribution and conservation systems, a hybrid-fuel economy, and extended public transportation networks and technologies. Proponents of such a vision would also have to begin the politically difficult task of ending the antagonism between urban and agricultural economies in the region.

Visionaries are hard to come by, particularly tough-minded, pragmatic ones. They don't tend to be planners or architects, anymore, with grand designs, but rather grassroots thinkers who know how the world actually works. Lisa Robert, a farmer from Tomé, New Mexico, is such a visionary. For Albuquerque to begin reinventing itself in a time of drought and global warming, she says, it has to do four very difficult, untraditional, but conservative things—conservative in the old sense of the word. First, the city and surrounding counties must place a moratorium on new development, "at least until the aquifer stabilizes—if indeed that's possible. (You'll never convince me that the metro area will run out of houses!)" Robert is appalled by "wall-to-wall subdivisions under construction. When I see them, all I can think of are ghost towns. Who will bear the responsibility when unsuspecting families mortgage their lives to move in and discover one day that the tap delivereth not?"

Second, "Revoke all dedications for non-completed subdivisions." That would require the state engineer to tell new subdivisions that their promises of finding water rights in the future will no longer be honored. That's a radical move, indeed, but in a time of severe water shortages, the last thing you want is new housing stock to attract new residents fleeing drought-stricken cities in Arizona or on the West Coast. For new developments to acquire water rights, they would have to buy or lease them from farmers. (And in a transition economy undermined by high fuel prices, localities like Albuquerque will need to grow a much greater percentage of their food.)

Third, "Institute some sort of expedited adjudication process to assess what we have left in the way of senior rights, and then set about protecting historically irrigated lands by every possible means, with the understanding that they can and should be used to absorb flood flows, or to lie fallow in extremely dry years. The state would, in effect, subsidize the hydrologic function of agricultural land, which is far more crucial here than what's grown on top. Crops are, of course, a bonus, but the bottomland is foremost the conduit to the aquifer." Robert points out here that even though "prior appropriation"—who got it first gets it first—is the definitive water rule of New Mexico and the West, most water rights still have not had their historical claims tested in legal proceedings. Adjudication of those claims would determine who gets water first in a drought. While residential and commercial use of water in New Mexico has almost always had a junior status to Native American, Hispanic, and other agricultural rights, aquifer-dependent cities like Albuquerque must have agricultural lands to absorb water back into their aquifers. If Albuquerque should lose, even temporarily, its San Juan–Chama water from the Colorado River, it would have to return to relying exclusively on the aquifer. If the city continues to grow and more junior users in cities take more water from farmers, the aquifer will deplete even faster than it has. Growth is a lose-lose situation.

Fourth, "Any sort of development should require real water rights, a stringent water conservation plan, and careful attention to natural drainage patterns." Robert lays out a list of critical do's and don'ts for construction regulations in a water-efficient Albuquerque of the future. "Don't move dirt to disturb vegetation any more than is absolutely necessary. Don't relocate or re-engineer arroyos. Don't pave roads with impermeable materials. Don't funnel flows from natural drainages through inadequate corrugated culverts. Don't allow non-native landscaping. And don't condone fountains, pools, or sprinklers." But "do design for rainwater harvesting and passive irrigation. Do combine natural recreational areas with natural drainage features—let mother nature water our parks, and when she doesn't, too bad."[21]

Historical Trend Dead-Ending

Robert's view is a sharp departure from the historical trend in the Albuquerque metro area since World War II. A generic pattern of automobile-dependent growth, heedless of local landforms and weather conditions, was imposed upon the Middle Rio Grande Valley, as it was all over the suburban United States and the arid Southwest. The pattern was formulated by developers in the water-rich east in New York, Pennsylvania, and New Jersey initially. The pattern of development functioned adequately in the arid Southwest as long as it was fueled by plentiful low-cost water and petroleum. Any external stresses on basic resources from weather and overuse show immediately how vulnerable and fragile that eastern suburban pattern is in the West, where the water they demand has to be bought, stolen, or cajoled from other regions. The suburbanization of the United States is a post–World War II phenomenon. With the pressures of climate change, it's possible that the suburbs of the West will have blossomed, thrived, and been largely abandoned in the span of less than seventy-five years.

Most planners and politicians in the Middle Rio Grande Valley would consider such a grim scenario pure rubbish. In 2007, for instance, the public works director of Sandoval County echoed an age-old refrain when he told a reporter, "We can try to prevent growth, but there's nothing we can do to stop it. . . . The city of Albuquerque has policies to try to rein that in, but they don't work. Everyone has the right to use their land as they please—we can't prevent development."[22] As late as 2009, most area planners and politicians were still expecting the Albuquerque metro population to reach one million by 2021 and to grow in the same way it always had—in "a diffuse low-density, low-intensity, sometimes planned, mostly not, low-rise quasi-sprawl," according to the Brookings Institution. Brookings found that out of the 100 largest metro areas in the country, Albuquerque ranked 36th for the most miles traveled per capita by drivers (10,620 per vehicle) and 99th in density, with 88 people per square mile. The national average for the 100 largest metro areas is 467 people per square mile.[23]

As fuel costs are predicted to rise throughout the century, Albuquerque sprawl and annual miles traveled per automobile severely undermine the city's capacity to sustain itself in hard times. Nevertheless, transportation planners at the Mid-Region Council of Governments (MRCOG, formerly the Middle Rio Grande Council of Governments) are following the same patterns they championed forty years ago, patterns that created the low-density, long-distance vulnerability of Albuquerque today. If the MRCOG-planned thirty-nine-mile loop road through empty spaces north of Rio Rancho is ever built, it will be a sprawl magnet worthy of Albuquerque's most profligate growth booms in the 1970s and '80s. Connecting Interstate 40 at the Rio Puerco with U.S. 550 out of Bernalillo, the loop road has been criticized as "a corporate welfare give-away" to big developers in the area. Some planners say it would serve as a "relief valve for traffic congestion" and also be the conduit to a desalinization plant and an expanded airport on the West Mesa.[24]

MRCOG, the only traffic engineering entity in the region, did everything it could to stimulate new growth on the city's West Side. Its engineers and statisticians gave substance to the city's boom or bust mentality. But even into the early 1990s, Albuquerque was still struggling with itself over the kind of city it wanted to be, and it seemed to be choosing not to become an out-and-out Phoenix-like reproduction of Los Angeles. Then the real estate bubble began to expand at the turn of the twenty-first century. The stock market soared. Developers and land speculators up and down the Middle Rio Grande Valley proposed more than a dozen large, upscale, Phoenix-like community developments and probably would have built them if the great recession of 2008–9 hadn't caught them in its grip. Development projects stopped dead in their tracks. Even Mesa del Sol, the huge industrial and residential development planned by Forrest City Covington, slowed to a virtual standstill. Even though it had already constructed solar manufacturing facilities and soundstages for filmmaking and attracted companies like Fidelity Investments to its business park, Forrest City couldn't start residential building in 2009 because it couldn't find enough bondable contractors who'd survived the recession in even modestly good shape.

It was as if Albuquerque were looking in a mirror and seeing an image almost exactly opposite to that of post–World War II prosperity. Then, the boom was on, with the new interstate highway system, military-industrial corporations and national laboratories, and the soon-to-be-debunked tall tale of Albuquerque's limitless underground water supply. In the great recession, the city saw itself in the mirror as haggard and drawn. Construction had come to a halt. The national laboratories had been revealed as major polluters of groundwater, and national chains and local businesses folded, including the *Albuquerque Tribune*, leaving the Duke City with only one newspaper. And in the backs of the minds of environmentalists and rural, land-based businesspeople was the growing worry of global warming and a permanent drought.

Leopold the Prophet

Boosterism, as it used to be called in the 1950s, has helped for years to force Albuquerque's growth beyond sustainability. The Lake Superior metaphor was absurd on its face, but no one other than hydrologists had any idea what the aquifer within the Rio Grande trough was suspended in, or how big it was, even though at least one hydrological report in 1967 refuted the Lake Superior metaphor.[25] It wasn't until the administration of Mayor Louis Saavedra in the late 1980s that Albuquerque began monitoring its aquifer through its water wells. As early as 1919, however, Aldo Leopold, the great champion of wilderness and ethical land use, told Albuquerque how dangerous the hooey of boosterism could be. Leopold was the secretary of the Albuquerque Chamber of Commerce at the time. In a speech to the Ten Dons, an early economic development group, Leopold called boosterism "one of the great political and economic forces of our time." He went on to comment that the "only thing about Boosterism that is not expounded to us daily is its abuses and fallacies," which he proceeded to list. The "creed" of boosterism, he told the Dons, was based on the conviction that the way "to grow big is to advertise advantages and ignore defects, thereby abolishing them. Self-criticism is akin to treason." Boosters see "growth by labor, frugality, or natural increase" as being "slow and old fashioned." "Earned increment," boosters say, "may indicate industry, but unearned increment proves vision and brains." Then Leopold asked the question of questions: "Can anyone deny that the vast fund of time, brains, and money now devoted to making our city big would actually make it better if diverted to betterment instead of bigness?"[26] Only a booster could deny it. And in most respects, Albuquerque has been run by the booster spirit, much more than Santa Fe and even Las Cruces have been.

Moving People

The push for "bigness" was made possible by immense tracts of empty land and the means to commute back and forth from it. With twenty-first century gasoline prices near $4 a gallon, rural residents of New Mexico and other southwestern and mountain West states are suffering profoundly as gasoline consumes as much 13 percent to 16 percent of their total monthly incomes.[27] Because of the distances traveled, New Mexico ranks number six in the nation for annual miles driven per driver, or some 18,500 miles a year. Even urban and semiurban distances are becoming prohibitively expensive. It's quite easy to drive 50 miles a day if you commute from Rio Rancho to the center of Albuquerque. It's a 120-mile round-trip commute to Santa Fe. Compare New Mexico's 121,593 square miles to Great Britain's 93,026 square miles, heavily urbanized, with a sophisticated mass transit system. No one in England drives the commutes that we do here, not at $5 to $6 per liter of gasoline.

Rising gasoline prices have debunked two venerable mass transit myths in Albuquerque. During the gasoline crisis of 2008, the old notion that mass transit depended on high urban densities was soundly debunked. As gas prices skyrocketed, so did bus ridership. In April 2008, the city bus system had 916,169 boardings for the month, up 18.8 percent over the same month in 2007. And because of an expanding Rapid Ride bus system over several years, ridership had increased every month since mid-2006. Owing to gas prices, as well as to increasingly crowded driving conditions on the interstates, the state's first commuter train, the New Mexico Railrunner Express, logged 43,634 passengers in April 2008, a 35 percent increase over 2007, from Bernalillo through Albuquerque down to Los Lunas and Belen.[28] Such high usage pretty much put an end to crank letters complaining about Governor Bill Richardson building a rail line to Santa Fe rather than adding and repairing more roads. The train's long-awaited link to Santa Fe was completed at the end of 2008. The cost comparison caught everyone's eye: approximately $20 per round trip by car versus $6 per round trip by train. The Albuquerque–Santa Fe Railrunner will become the anchor of the state's Regional Transit Department plan to link communities in north central New Mexico through a comprehensive transit system.[29] The Albuquerque–Santa Fe line connects the two cities into the configuration of a super metroplex with an integrated economy, similar to the Phoenix–Tucson corridor.[30]

Without a solid mass transit system, the size of Albuquerque's metropolitan area will increasingly burden its residents as energy prices rise. Along with greatly expanding its mass transit capacity and route system, Albuquerque will have to undergo the engineering and fiscal rigors of retrofitting itself to survive the long transition from fossil fuels to more sustainable energy sources. Can it be done? And can it be done fast enough to avoid financial ruin for hundreds of thousands of financially strapped New Mexicans? Urban retrofitting could transform the city, with its distances and low densities, into a more compact, cosmopolitan, and sociable place. But the costs in dollars and time and labor and social disruption will be immense.

The politics of engineering such a change will go beyond the primitive power plays and maneuvering that Albuquerque and New Mexico are used to. Virtually every phase of public, business, and private life will be altered. Sprawl will be stopped; infill will be incentivized, despite the fury of the residents of current neighborhoods. Sadly, areas in the city without regional, sector, and neighborhood plans will become the new West Mesa, where developers and their interests supercede rational public planning, creating developments without adequate public services or adequate roadways. But mass transit will no longer be an afterthought, instead becoming the major means of transport, which, despite the incalculable public expense that it will bring, will ultimately save massive amounts of money for residents no longer dependent on private vehicles.

Too Big for Its Own Good

Sprawl has damaged New Mexico cities in both gross and subtle ways, as it has most other major cities in the country. University of Miami professor George Gonzales described sprawl's destructive power in clear terms when he said that U.S. cities are "particularly configured to maximize consumption" of fuel, goods, and services. He told the International Conference on Environmental, Cultural, Economic, and Social Sustainability in 2005 that this concentration of urban American buying habits was due to our cities being of a "highly sprawled form. U.S. cities," he said, "are so sprawled because of the influence of local growth coalitions, made up of large land holders and developers, as well as local economic interests that benefit from an expanding local consumer base." Urban sprawl, he said, was a means to absorb excess capital and production of durable goods, like automobiles from the 1920s on. Gonzales says this sprawling response to gorged inventories, even after the Great Depression, is "consistent with the business dominance view of public policy making."[31]

The task of making Albuquerque's and New Mexico's growth policies coherent and true to their context is a daunting one and is all the more confusing when one tries to separate local issues from national trends. It is safe to say, however, New Mexican cities engulfed by the national postwar trend to sprawl were those largely invented by two New Mexican Democratic politicians—Senator Dennis Chavez and Governor Clyde Tingley. Both responded to New Deal opportunities for chronically impoverished New Mexico. Serving mostly at the same time, Tingley and Chavez, both friends of President Roosevelt, brought as much New Deal funding to New Mexico as possible. Tingley concentrated on hospitals across the state, as well as supporting Santa Fe and Albuquerque's artistic economies. Chavez focused on higher education and university capital improvements, as well as water conservation and control of the Rio Grande, with the creation of Cochiti Lake north of Albuquerque and the Navajo Irrigation Project. In 1949, Chavez was joined in the Senate by another New Mexico Democrat, Clinton P. Anderson, whose work as secretary of agriculture under Truman had aided the rural United States, including New Mexico. The New Deal cities of New Mexico, especially Albuquerque and Santa Fe, would begin their journeys to sprawl with

Anderson's tenacious support of the nuclear weapons and energy industries. Anderson was one of the creators of the Price-Anderson Nuclear Indemnity Act, which effectively subsidizes, with massive government insurance, the nuclear power industry and, by extension, military research and development, key operations of which are carried out in Albuquerque and in Los Alamos, northwest of Santa Fe.

Doubled and More in Fifty Years

Postwar growth politics in Albuquerque didn't materialize until the late 1960s and early 1970s. Although hopes were high, no one really foresaw the massive boom that would more than double New Mexico's population in fifty years. But Albuquerque was trying hard to look like the next Phoenix or Denver. It wasn't until 1953 that long-serving Clyde Tingley was ousted as the chair of the city commission and ex-officio mayor of Albuquerque by more business-minded politicians, including the first engineer from Sandia Labs to serve in city government, Richard Bice. The decade of the 1950s saw the creation of a city planning department and the first groundbreaking of a major West Side development, Paradise Hills. By the mid-1960s, issues of Albuquerque urban development had already crystallized. Property interests had split into two factions, one representing the northeast heights, where I-40 and I-25 had stimulated tremendous growth, and the other representing downtown and the West Mesa, downtown serving as the capital of traditional Albuquerque, while the West Mesa sold reasonably priced housing to fill downtown with customers. A third interest that no one in the early days expected to be competitive was what would become the city of Rio Rancho.

When the Model Cities Program and urban renewal came to town during the Johnson and Nixon administrations in the late 1960s and early '70s, this major turf struggle was building. It came to a head in the city election of 1974, which not only changed the city charter to a mayor/council form of government, but also promoted suburban sprawl development both on the West Mesa and in the northeast heights. Advocates of more urban-centered infill development and mass transit were shoved into the role of backbenchers for the next thirty-five years. Infill often found itself opposed by historic preservationists, open space advocates, and the growing neighborhood movement, which as a matter of principle distrusted any zoning change that upped density. As one planner long ago told me, developers and planning bureaucrats look upon zoning as a holding device, to be changed at will when something better comes along. Neighborhoods and householders look at zoning as protection against unwanted intrusions that would profit developers while burdening local residents. The battle has never stopped, not to this day. And the future holds more conflict, owing largely to boosterish denial of real problems.

Water quality in Albuquerque, as is true everywhere in the country where there are defense manufacturing plants, major military bases, and Cold War nuclear R&D laboratories, is growing into a major twenty-first century issue. Had the EPA not deemphasized Superfund cleanup during the Bush administration, the city's water supply might have become officially suspect. For elected officials and bureaucrats, however, to question the cleanliness of the city's water supply was beyond the pale. But in July 2008, Kirtland Air Force Base announced that a major jet fuel leak of two to eight million gallons had been polluting the groundwater around the posh southeast heights neighborhood known as Ridgecrest since the 1970s.[32] The air force refrained from telling the citizenry and even elected officials, not wanting to frighten them, until 2008, according to the *Albuquerque Journal*. Predictably, Albuquerqueans were told not to worry about the spill because the pollution would take a quarter of a century to reach city wells. The major media failed to report that the spill was slightly more than a mile and a half away from the city's major water source in the aquifer near Gibson and Eubank, in the vicinity of the base. That site's vast cone of depression, a vortex of enormous power, sucks water to it from all over the Middle Rio Grande Basin. What happens if the Kirtland base plume gets sucked in, too (not to mention other contamination from sites around Sandia Labs)?

Water quality became a politically troublesome topic in 2009 when Albuquerque and Santa Fe began drinking river water from the San Juan–Chama Project for the first time. In June 2008, the University of California, Berkeley, which administered LANL until 2006, confirmed what most people suspected. "The university said in court filings . . . that 'non-dangerous quantities' of waste were released into Acid Canyon at [LANL] during the development of the atomic bomb during World War II, continuing until 1951."[33] The university had never owned up to dumping "solvents, metals, plutonium, and other radioactive materials" into the canyon before. But this information was part of a disposition of the university in a lawsuit by the family of Lowell Ryman, who accused LANL and its managers of causing the fatal cancer that Ryman contracted while playing in the canyon as a child. The lawsuit increased concern in Albuquerque and Santa Fe over the potability of Rio Grande water into which the runoff from those canyons flows.

Smith and Kinney

Sprawl and the need for new drinking water might have been abated in Albuquerque if the city election of 1974 had gone another way. Herb Smith, a professional planner who had been fired as the city manager in 1973 for advocating controlled growth, lost a tight contest to Sandia Labs engineer Harry Kinney. Running under the banner of "The Right Kind of Leadership," Kinney, his major supporter, Senator Pete Domenici, and their business lobby portrayed Smith as a radical challenger of the free market. Smith attracted progressive Democrats, advocating sustainable, planned growth that would balance expansion with water conservation, increased density, and mass transit. Smith, who understood the implications of the OPEC oil crisis, realized that the sprawling city would have to manage its growth if it hoped to prosper in an age of dependence on foreign oil. But neither the severe stagflation of the period nor OPEC embargoes on supply and rising prices at the pumps helped Smith make his point. It was the pivotal election of the last quarter of the twentieth century in Albuquerque, and I still wonder what the city would be like today if Smith had won that election and created a strong, goals-oriented planning perspective for future mayors to build on.

In 2008, Smith's worries were belatedly proving correct. A new oil crisis sparked by speculation in the market and Middle East insecurity sent gas skyrocketing to over $135 a barrel, and in New Mexico to over $4 a gallon by midsummer. Uncontrolled growth in a desert town experiencing what could be a twenty-five-year drought was starting to look less attractive. And the news from other drought states wasn't cheering to New Mexico's traditionally aggressive building industry. Although no city in the West had ever regulated development according to the availability of water, state government in California, after two decades of drought, was postponing and even denying new developments in Riverside County, east of Los Angeles, because developers couldn't demonstrate the presence of sufficient water.[34] Utah was considering a law that would stop the transfer of paper water rights from farms to cities on the grounds that there was already vastly more paper water than wet water around Salt Lake City.[35] The transfer of water rights from New Mexico farms to cities, especially to water-poor Rio Rancho, became increasingly difficult as acequia associations, market-sophisticated farmers, pueblos, and others resisted the short-term rescue offered by buyers, holding out for the long-term benefits of maintaining a way of life that might even add up to profitable farming in an era of localized food distribution.

Development Tied to Water

Until the twenty-first century, it was heresy to suggest that Albuquerque's supply of drinking water might not support development. But since 2002, water planners have been exploring new options, along with regulation, to make the most of the state's scarce water supplies. These include groundwater banking or storing excess surface water in depleted aquifers; recycling and other conservation methods; and a more aggressive policy toward transferring agricultural water rights to cities.[36] In 2002, both Colorado and New Mexico passed laws that made counties take water supplies into consideration when they ruled on the desirability and public cost of new subdivisions. While state officials can consult on county water supply assessments, counties retain decision-making power.[37] But even as late as 2008, in the depths of a decade-long drought, New Mexico counties and their urban centers are loathe to rein in any kind of development.

Cities can't sprawl without water. They can't grow intelligently without it, either. As tempting as desalinization is in California, with the Pacific at hand, and in New Mexico, with its copious amounts of deep brackish water, the enormous expense remains prohibitive, even with innovations in the membranes used in reverse osmosis, the most efficient desalinization method at this time. And sprawl just makes matters worse—for everything and everyone, from the consumer of gasoline to a world population facing the chaotic weather of global climate change. The Sierra Club estimates that infill development, or putting new subdivisions in already built-up places, can reduce the vehicle miles traveled in a city by as much 60 percent and cut the carbon dioxide emissions by half.[38]

If sprawl is allowed to continue, the nonprofit Smart Growth America (SGA) estimates that driving miles could increase across the country by 48 percent between 2005 and 2030. "Even if the most stringent fuel-efficiency proposals under consideration are enacted," SGA maintains, quoting Steve Winkelman, coauthor of *Growing Cooler: The Evidence on Urban Development and Climate Change*, "'vehicle emissions will be 34 percent above the 1990 levels in 2030—entirely off track from reductions of 60–80 percent below 1990 levels by 2050 required for climate protection.'"[39] "Sprawling cities have driving related energy consumption rates that can be three times that of better planned, more compact cities," the Sierra Club asserts. Such statistics "conceal a startling truth: the hidden costs of sprawl require us to pay for the destruction of our environment from our own bank accounts whether we want to or not."[40]

Burdens of Growth

Both sprawl and infill tend to burden existing residents. Santa Fe is a case in point. Growth has put a heavy burden on the city's water supply. Huge golf courses and swank gated communities have not only raised property taxes and put housing costs well above a level affordable by the middle class, but also have required heavy water rationing since the 1990s. Santa Fe will be able to divert 5,605 acre-feet of water from the Rio Grande under the San Juan–Chama Project agreement, but industrial and radioactive contaminants from LANL are showing up in the water from its major wells near the river, so water and Santa Fe maintain a precarious relationship. Water, in fact, was the issue that put a halt to oil and natural gas drilling in the Galisteo Basin southwest of Santa Fe. Tecton Energy, a Texas firm, had proposed exploration drilling in the area until residents raised an alarm and the state intervened. A report from the state's Energy, Minerals, and Natural Resources Department pointed out that the "Galisteo basin is not only a major source basin for the Rio Grande, but is also the only water source of domestic water for much of the recent population growth of Santa Fe County."[41]

In Albuquerque, the burdens of sprawl have also fallen on existing residents. The iconic example is the Montaño Road Bridge in the semirural North Valley. Construction on the two-lane bridge started in 1995 after twenty years of bitter opposition from residents of the North Valley and the village of Los Ranchos, who claimed that their part of the city was being victimized to provide a conduit for sprawl development on the West Side. In spite of claims by advocates of the bridge that it would alleviate traffic congestion on the West Side, eight years after the bridge opened, what North Valley residents feared the most had come to pass. Their own traffic problems were worsened to an intolerable extent, while the West Side's congestion grew worse from the increased traffic. For five years, the city did nothing to improve the intersections. Cars and trucks could be piled up half a mile back from the light. When the bridge was opened, "the impact on the immediate North Valley residences was dramatic and worsened steadily over time,"[42] writes planner Mikaela Renz-Whitmore.

The situation became so damaging that the unnamed neighborhood surrounding 4th Street and Montaño coalesced around finding ways to get the city to repair the damage to their part of town. The bridge and its approach had sliced through the Valley. Old roadways and paths through neighborhoods were severed, "separating these residents physically, politically, and culturally from each other and the rest of the Valley."[43] To make matters worse, Mayor Martin Chavez, a longtime advocate of West Side development, riled everyone up by threatening to go back on a deal the North Valley had made with the city years before, the capstone deal that would have kept the bridge to two lanes. In the early 2000s, Chavez had new lines painted on the bridge, turning it into a four-lane bridge, with all the added traffic and misery that came with it.

Forcing river crossings in Albuquerque has always been a controversial practice. Long before West Side development had taken off, the city tried to force a bridge across the river at Candelaria Road, a mile south of Montaño. The street was widened to four lanes, trees were uprooted, and houses were suddenly cheek by jowl with heavy traffic. But neighborhoods in the area successfully warded off the bridge and its potential congestion with the arguments that sizable populations didn't live on the West Mesa yet and that the Candelaria bridge would be a feeder for West Side developers at the North Valley's expense.

Open Space

Amid the struggle among landowners, speculators, developers, and residents across the city, struggles that were never addressed or defined by the local media, the progressive forces in the city staged a stupendous victory. If sprawl could not be controlled and directed for the city's good, then Albuquerque's amazing natural beauty could at least be protected from complete depredation and even conserved in a relatively pristine state for the future. In the mid-1970s, the West Mesa volcanoes were preserved from development. The effort was spearheaded by the wife of a retired doctor—Ruth Eisenberg—who went back to school to get her degree in urban planning from the University of New Mexico's School of Architecture and Planning. Eisenberg described herself as a "little old lady in tennis shoes" to keep the powers that be off guard. She was meticulously organized, charismatic, and relentless, the leader of a team of activists, largely women, who saw that they could enlist a farseeing city council with strong representation from the University of New Mexico faculty. The volcanoes define the western skyline of the city and sit squarely in the middle of the most sprawling development in the region—and they remain untouched. That same city council in 1975 approved a building moratorium in the Sandia Mountains above a ten-foot grade, which preserved the mountain's wilderness visage for the whole city to enjoy.

The historical momentum that made such preservation possible originated in 1969, when a remarkable moment in ecological politics set Albuquerque on its divided pathway as a car town and developer haven that also conserves its open spaces and breathtaking vistas. That year, the Bureau of Reclamation proposed to cut down all the cottonwoods, Russian olives, willows, and salt cedars up and down the Rio Grande to stop them from taking up river and groundwater. The thought of ripping out the river forest caused a tremendous uproar among the populace.

As the spirit of the first Earth Day approached fruition across the nation, environmentalists from all over New Mexico, along with state legislators and city council, Mayor Harry Kinney, and David Rusk, who later became mayor, all opposed the Bureau of Reclamation's plan, focusing public attention on the bosque. The cottonwoods that line the Rio Grande as it runs through the city had survived the creation of levees in the 1930s and the creation of dams along the upper reaches of the river. Even managed as it was, the bosque kept the semblance of a wild river running through the heart of town. And there's a good chance that the bosque is among the largest cottonwood forests in the world.

In 1983, more than a dozen years after the Bureau of Reclamation's proposal, the state legislature passed a bill creating the sixteen-mile-long Rio Grande State Park. The park featured a nature center designed by architect Antoine Predock at the end of Candelaria Road, where a bridge had once been planned, and preserved forty-three hundred acres of floodplain cottonwood bosque stretching from Sandia Pueblo in the north to Isleta Pueblo in the south. Up to then, the bosque was a "patch work of overgrown forest, transient camp sites, hunting blinds, fishing spots, and a massive informal dumping ground with everything from sofas and refrigerators to household trash and old tires scattered around."[44] The Bureau of Reclamation thought no one would mind if all the trees were uprooted. Today, the bosque is the pride of the city.

Antisprawl Movement Fizzled

The preservation of the bosque and the policy of open space acquisition were largely the work of citizen activists, a growing constituency of hikers, nature lovers, and bikers who turned into advocates. Citizen activism when it comes to sprawl, however, has been blunted and atomized right from the start. City, county, and state governments have given so many economic subsidies and tax incentives to sprawl developers—many of them involving expensive infrastructure in the form of roads and bridges that every taxpayer in the region has to pay for—that opposition was simply swept away. And until the sudden appearance of $4-plus gasoline and the growing alarm over global warming, sprawl was largely unimpeded by rational argument. Open space is directly tied to the personal and cultural associations of land. Sprawl, in contrast, is by its very nature an amorphous enemy.

Fragmenting Plan

The process of developing a comprehensive plan that embraced neighborhood goals and visions had the unintended consequence of balkanizing the city. Neighborhood activists struggled for their rights of place while the city splurged into open land east and west of the major population center. Then, hard-won plans in place, neighbors found that city officials and bureaucrats often simply forgot the agreements that had been made, the historic overlays that had been hammered out, and the concessions that had been reached. As a result, development initiatives went forward even if they were blatantly disallowed in the plans. The city has seen atrociously large and ill-designed buildings allowed in historic overlay zones. Massive apartments parading as green buildings have tried to sneak into well-zoned neighborhoods on the bogus grounds of helping to ward off global warming. As late as 2007, well before the gas price crisis, Albuquerque and Bernalillo County were seriously considering at least eight major new sprawl developments. On the West Mesa, SunCal was aiming for some hundred and thirty thousand single family lots, Rio West planned for twenty-three thousand homes, and Mariposa expected to build seven thousand high-quality homes on the far northern edge of Rio Rancho abutting Santa Ana Pueblo, twenty miles from downtown. On the east, Campbell Ranch in Torrance and Bernalillo counties was contemplating more than four thousand homes, and Mesa del Sol, south of the airport, had plans for thirty-seven thousand houses by 2057. The bursting of the housing bubble in 2009 made such projections moot. Many environmentalists had argued that Mesa del Sol, with its industrial base and close proximity to downtown Albuquerque, was not strictly sprawl development. But far south of Albuquerque, in Valencia County, the Rancho Cielo, Sierra Madre, and Huning Ranch developments were classic sprawl developments, destined, many worried, to clog traffic on I-25 and east across the river.

TIDDS

Like most other cities in the United States, Albuquerque, Rio Rancho, Santa Fe, and Las Cruces were in 2008 on the verge of facing a reversal in the way they have expanded—from freewheeling centrifugal growth to a restrained, calibrated, but rapid centripetal movement of people from the outskirts into the center city, with its major commercial nodes and neighborhoods. At least three Albuquerque city councilors in 2008, Isaac Benton, Michael Cadigan, and Ray Garduño, seemed to have a clue. In a joint editorial in the *Albuquerque Journal*, they attacked Tax Increment Development Districts (TIDDs) that they say are being used, not to "incentivize urban infill development where revitalization would not occur otherwise," but to subsidize sprawling "'greenfield' development on the city's fringes." Benton, Cadigan, and Garduño were working to refocus TIDD policy at the writing of this book. "By subsidizing the growth of development on the city's edges," they wrote, "economists estimate that even more home buyers and businesses will be lured out of the existing community and into the fringe developments, cannibalizing our urban core and increasing hazardous automobile emissions."[45]

Retreating Cities

Just before gas prices turned into a serious economic impediment to growth in mid-2008, a development epitomizing sprawl was proposed by an Arizona entrepreneur who envisioned thirty thousand new homes on the Rio Puerco some thirty miles west of the urban core along I-40. The developer had no water rights but planned to drill deep wells and desalinate brackish water from the Rio Puerco aquifer. The process would produce massive amounts of salt that would have to be removed. If thirty thousand homes equals seventy thousand new residents, I-40 would endure even worse traffic than it already has.[46] As 2008 slipped by, the downturn in housing starts and sales that accompanied the subprime mortgage crisis spelled the apparent end of this unfortunate project.

There's a chance that the major cities in New Mexico will retreat from the frontiers and compact into denser, more efficient environments and that cities with definite edges might reappear. This could have a positive influence on decreasing light pollution, but would probably increase the harshness of noise pollution. In Albuquerque, retreating from sprawl into the desert might also, however, put a strain on agricultural lands, where affluent infill developments already cramp the North Valley, with its semirural zoning codes. The still sparsely developed areas in the South Valley could suffer the same diminution. Unless mass transit, European-style bicycling culture, and/or a nonpollution car technology takes hold, air pollution is likely to increase, as well. But air pollution is hard to track, especially with the modest and spotty successes of the Clean Air Act around the country. It's still an ongoing major problem, but in many places, like New Mexico, it tends to be a piecemeal phenomenon associated mostly with cities and certain kinds of manufacturing. Even so, I've come to think of all CO_2 and other greenhouse gas emissions as being a subset of traditional smog. If that is so, then air pollution remains the overwhelming environmental contaminant.

Dirty Air

Oddly, though, the state's largest city has cleaner air than one of its major rural areas. The American Lung Association gives Albuquerque an A rating as one of the country's least polluted cities when it comes to ozone, joining Ames, Iowa; Austin, Texas; Eugene, Oregon; Honolulu, Hawaii; and a score of others.[47] Ozone is the major component of smog and is particularly dangerous to children, the elderly, and people with chronic lung problems.[48] In contrast to heavily populated Albuquerque, the Four Corners area, which comprises part of the Navajo Reservation and huge oil and gas fields, as well as the small cities of Farmington, New Mexico, and Durango and Cortez, Colorado, periodically has the worst air in the state and some of the worst in the country, owing to twenty-three thousand or so natural gas and oil wells pumping away with their internal combustion engines and the two biggest coal-fired power plants in the region.

The irony, of course, is that clean-aired Albuquerque gets almost all of its electricity from those plants, built in the 1960s and '70s in the golden era of environmentalism in New Mexico. The Four Corners Power Plant in Fruitland, New Mexico, owned by Arizona and New Mexico utility companies, is "among the 50 dirtiest power plants in the nation based on its emission of nitrogen oxide, carbon dioxide, and mercury."[49] A few miles away in Farmington, the San Juan Generating Station, operated by Public Service Company of New Mexico, "was the nation's No. 21 emitter of total nitrogen oxide in 2004" and was number 34 in the release of carbon dioxide, according to the Environmental Integrity Project in Washington, D.C.[50] The *Durango Herald* declared in a front-page headline in June 2008 that the Four Corners Power Plant's emissions were "among the worst in the U.S."

Four years earlier, the *Durango Telegraph* charged that the power plants were "two of the most polluting in the United States" and quoted a member of the San Juan Citizens Alliance that the "second highest airborne mercury reading in the country was at Mesa Verde

National Park," north of the San Juan Basin but in its air shed.[51] The
Telegraph raised the alarm in 2004 that three new coal-fired power
plants might be coming into the region, "and one of these would be
among the largest ever built in the United States."[52] That plant was to
be built by a subsidiary of a German power company near Shiprock.
Two other, smaller plants were proposed south of Farmington, near
Grants. One was called the Mustang Project, to be run by Peabody
Coal as an experimental clean technology plant. The other, on
the Navajo Reservation just southwest of Farmington, called the
Cottonwood Energy Center, withdrew its application in 2007. None
of the plants that Four Corners residents feared would worsen air
quality in their region came on line. They all were replaced, in effect,
by Desert Rock, another highly controversial coal-fired plant on the
Navajo Reservation.

Desert Rock

Desert Rock would sell power outside New Mexico, perhaps to Phoenix and Las Vegas, while contributing, opponents thought, to New
Mexico's rural air quality crisis. Owned by Sithe Global Power of New
York through its local subsidiary Desert Rock Energy Company, the
plant would operate under an agreement with the Navajo Nation's
Diné Power Authority. Opposition to the plant started with local
Navajos who were already suffering health effects from the air pollution in the region. In opposing their own tribal government, the Diné
residents of Burnham, New Mexico, where the plant would be built, ran
up against Navajo president Joe Shirley, Jr., who supports coal power
while opposing uranium mining on Navajo land. Shirley was widely
quoted as saying critics should stop picking on "the little Navajo" as
long as India and China are allowed to produce hundreds of new coal-
fired power plants a year. Seventy-six-year-old Alice Gilmore, a Navajo
resident of Burnham, told reporters, "We want the smoke to stop."[53]
But it isn't just locals who oppose Desert Rock. As of June 2008, the
plant had been granted none of the necessary permits for the project
to begin. In July 2007, New Mexico governor Bill Richardson joined
the opposition, saying that the facility would "adversely impact air
quality, exacerbate existing environmental problems, and negatively
impact scarce surface and groundwater resources."[54] And a year later,
New Mexico's attorney general Gary King opposed a lawsuit against

the EPA filed by Sithe Global Energy and the Navajo Nation protesting how long it's taken the EPA to approve an air permit for the proposed power plant. King argued that the EPA had to allow the U.S.
Fish and Wildlife Service to rule on whether the plant's massive water
use would harm endangered species. "New Mexico cannot afford
to sit idly by as attempts are being made to skirt the legal requirements for a new coal-fired power plant to be built in the state," he
said. The air permitting process is "truly putting the cart before the
horse."[55] In the summer of 2008, citizens of Durango, Farmington,
Cortez, and the Navajo Reservation were worried about air pollution from the power plants violating federal air quality standards,
particularly ground level ozone, a major element of smog.[56] In August
2008, however, the EPA approved an air quality permit for Desert
Rock. Proponents of the plant said it's the most stringent permit of
its kind ever issued by the EPA. Opponents claimed the plant would
emit massive quantities of CO_2 and ozone-created smog. They immediately appealed the EPA decision.[57]

Intel Air

In 2008, Albuquerque's clean air was in stark contrast to that of
its rural neighbor, the village of Corrales. Many residents there had
been suffering from what they considered an air quality crisis since
Intel Corporation opened what would become the largest computer
chip manufacturing operation in the world in Rio Rancho, on the
bluffs above the village. Corrales is a semirural community along the
Rio Grande northwest of Albuquerque. The dispute between Intel
and residents of Corrales who live in neighborhoods downwind and
under the immense plant is better documented than even the state
of New Mexico's South Valley Superfund suit. But it remains, like
so many other major environmental conflicts, underreported by the
mainstream press and has not become part of the state's popular culture as, say, WIPP has.

The controversy has spawned a detailed and hard-hitting print-
on-demand book entitled *Boiling Frogs—Intel vs. the Village* by New
Mexico writer Barbara Rockwell. It's been covered in agonizing detail
by Jeff Radford, editor of the *Corrales Comment*, a small weekly that
has done a prizewinning job of covering the story the big boys wouldn't
touch. It's generated a large, networked, sophisticated citizens' group

and has engaged state and federal government in dramatic ways. It's spawned Intel whistle blowers and occasioned the community's purchase of its own laser spectrometer, at great expense, to analyze smokestack emissions. It's also caused a clash among scientists who represent Intel, the New Mexico Environment Department, the federal Agency for Toxic Substances and Disease Registry, the community with its retired chemists and engineers from the national laboratories in New Mexico, and various experts for hire.

Intel and Rio Rancho

The city of Rio Rancho has grown up around Intel's massive plant. And Sandoval County issued one of the largest industrial revenue bonds in national history to lure and keep Intel in New Mexico. The conflicts involve not only air pollution but water use, water contamination, and the role major industry plays in a poverty-stricken, water-poor state like New Mexico, where many residents, old and new, still consider the state's environment a part of their healthful way of life. The air pollution issue, as hidden from the broader public as it is, strikes me as the sour note in an otherwise illustrious enterprise, a sour note that might cause some to doubt the worth and virtue of the whole project.

Intel's multibillion-dollar plant sits at the south entrance to Rio Rancho on the bluffs above the southern part of the village of Corrales and the Rio Grande and its bosque. It employed some fifty-six hundred people in Rio Rancho as of 2007, making the city a high-tech business haven, with some fifty technology companies and their subcontractors, many of whom sell products to Intel. The Southwest Organizing Project (SWOP) in Albuquerque's South Valley, a longtime Intel opponent, claims that only a third of the twenty-five hundred Intel hires in 1997 had lived in New Mexico for more than a year.[58]

Here's what the Central New Mexico Economy Guide had to say about Intel in March 2008: "From the air, the vastness of Intel's manufacturing plant in Rio Rancho is most visible. It stretches more than a mile long and a half-mile wide. Dominating Rio Rancho for nearly 30 years, the Intel facility is among the most famous facilities of its type on the globe—a symbol of the digital revolution itself."[59] Intel opened operations in Rio Rancho in 1981. As the blog FACEIntel (Former and Current Employees of Intel) tells the story, "In those early days, the only vague concern was for potential contamination of domestic wells that served each home in the still largely agricultural Corrales Valley below Intel. The microchip manufacturer was, after all, responsible for at least one 'Super Fund' clean-up site in Silicon Valley."[60] Toxic solvents used in semiconductor manufacturing facilities were found in the groundwater around three Intel plants near Highway 101 outside San Jose, California, in 1981. They weren't isolated incidents. The whole Santa Clara Valley, from San Francisco to San Jose, was polluted. What once was an agricultural paradise became Silicon Valley, with twenty-nine Superfund sites, including Intel's. "In 1981, south San Jose residents were stunned to learn they had been drinking contaminated water laced with chemicals such as trichloroethene and Freon, toxins that they later suspected were the cause of birth defects in many of their children."[61] Such companies as IBM, Teledyne, Raytheon, Westinghouse, and Fairchild Semiconductor were also serious Silicon Valley polluters.[62] The major culprits were leaking underground storage tanks. *E: The Environmental Magazine* explained the problem: "The electronics industry revolves around one minuscule yet important component: the semi-conductor chip. . . . The most complex and expensive part of the computer, this chip also requires the most chemicals for production. . . . On average, the production of one eight-inch wafer requires 3,787 gallons of waste water, 27 pounds of chemicals, 29 cubic feet of hazardous gases, and nine pounds of hazardous waste. . . . When 220 billion chips per year are taken into account, the electronic frontier looks like a dangerous place indeed."[63] And around the world, the number of semiconductor manufacturing plants is growing by leaps and bounds.

Intel and Deregulation

Intel's massive growth and industrial dominance stems from deregulation starting in the Clinton administration in 1996, when the EPA granted "the world's largest semiconductor manufacturer the right to change production processes without continually applying to the government for new permits designed to control toxic emissions. This gave Intel a competitive advantage over the rest of the semiconductor industry, where the latest, fastest technology is constantly evolving and the winner breaks the market first."[64]

Intel's take on its Silicon Valley pollution problems and its response go like this:

Volatile organic compounds (VOCs), commonly used chemicals in the semiconductor industry, were first discovered in shallow groundwater from industrial operations in Silicon Valley in 1979. About half of Silicon Valley's water supply comes from a deep groundwater aquifer which is located several hundred feet below the valley floor. . . . In early 1982 concern about widespread contamination in the area's shallow groundwater led the California Regional Water Quality Board to send chemical use questionnaires to over 2,000 facilities regarding the use of hazardous materials. Intel Corporation was among the few questionnaire recipients that responded proactively by installing groundwater monitoring wells adjacent to their underground chemical storage tanks. . . . By early 1986, all site source areas [of pollution] had been removed and groundwater extraction and treatment systems . . . had been installed and were operating to clean up and contain residual VOCs in groundwater.[65]

At just about this time, Intel first appeared in Albuquerque. While local opponents of the company's presence expressed alarm almost from the start at the thought of a massive semiconductor plant sucking up water from the aquifer and perhaps interfering with Corrales residents' wells, questions of water contamination from the gigantic plant had not surfaced. Although Intel uses the equivalent of about 3 percent of the city of Albuquerque's annual water use, even the Silicon Valley Toxics Coalition, a local citizens' group morphed into a semiconductor industry watchdog, expressed no concern about Intel potentially contaminating the Middle Rio Grande aquifer near its site.[66]

Solid State Technology, a trade publication for semiconductor manufacturers, says that "75–85% of the water Intel uses in manufacturing is eventually returned to the Rio Grande River (the remainder is lost to evaporation). First, the wastewater is pretreated, and then piped directly to Albuquerque's sewer system and treatment facility" in the South Valley. "None of Intel's waste water is discharged on the ground or reinjected into the aquifer." Intel also uses reverse osmosis to clean its wastewater and recycles nearly half the water it pumps.[67] Intel's in-house documents tout the company's award-winning ways. The company received eleven "pretreatment awards" from 1996 to 2008, recognizing Intel's recycling, reclamation, and "waste minimization" efforts "that have gone above and beyond the wastewater discharge permit's regulatory requirements."[68]

Intel and Toxic Air

Intel's problem in New Mexico doesn't involve water or any pressure from the government. As many as six hundred residents of Corrales, depressingly ill for years with what they describe as full body rashes, or adult onset asthma, or endocrine and reproductive disorders, chronic headaches, memory loss, even violent stomach ills, blindness, and periodic unconsciousness, battle against the biggest and most powerful company in the semiconductor high-tech world. They accuse Intel of poisoning their air and ruining their health. Of all the arguments Corraleseños have mustered, one defies the efforts of Intel's public relations department to discredit it. Residents who claim Intel's emissions made them ill experienced no symptoms before Intel started manufacturing operations sometime around 1993.

In April 1998, the *Weekly Alibi*'s Brendan Doherty put the ongoing David and Goliath struggle in perspective. At that time, Intel was applying for a "minor source" permit for its smokestack emissions that would exempt Intel from paying fees for pollution over certain limits, including the release of acetone. The company was successful. "It is the latest in a string of enormous breaks the chip maker has been given by the state government," Doherty wrote. "In the world of private-public partnerships, Intel is playing with the store's money. Intel made news all across the country when it received a record $8 billion in Industrial Revenue Bonds [IRBs] from Sandoval County in September of 1995. It was the largest bond of its kind in the history of the United States. . . . For a state 47th in the United States in per capita income, New Mexico did everything but build Intel for itself. Depending on who's talking, Intel is the state's greatest hope for jobs and preventer of social ills, or it's the loathed destroyer of the rural beauty of The Village of Corrales, the industrial drinker of precious water and polluter."[69]

Writer Barbara Rockwell, longtime Intel opponent and one of the founders of Corrales Residents for Clean Air and Water (CRCAW), described the moment when she and her husband decided it was time to leave the Intel air shed and move into the mountains. The breaking point came in 1995. They had just come back from a camping trip, managing "to put the nightmare we were living on hold for a few days. As we unpacked I got a whiff of something sour and within a few minutes I could feel the headache coming on. It was the typical Intel headache . . . along the sides of the head above the ears. I have never had headaches like that before in my life. I didn't say anything to Dave, not wanting to break the mellow mood. However, an hour or so later, Dave asked me if I had gotten a headache in the driveway unpacking the truck. I slowly said yes, and he said he had too, and as we looked into one another's stricken faces, we both knew it was time to move."[70]

Slanted Playing Field

CRCAW and Intel are not evenly matched. Intel has had, and continues to have, the full support of state government and a legal right to keep corporate and technological proprietary secrets. "You have a company that big, with that big a stake, it's hard to get the truth," as Jeff Radford, editor of the *Corrales Comment*, said to the *Weekly Alibi*.[71] And Intel fights every foray against it, often with barbs of sarcasm. "We've done a lot about the complaints we've received," Intel PR man Richard Draper said. "I think with some of these people, their problem is that we exist."[72] CRCAW conducted the health survey that gave credence to its argument that "Intel's air pollution . . . includes hundreds of tons of federal-listed Hazardous Air Pollutants and state-listed Toxic Air Pollutants." It also helped ill residents to obtain "bio-medical analysis . . . of illnesses thought to be linked to Intel's emissions."[73] CRCAW opposed Intel's requests for air permits and was deeply involved in Intel's year 2000 expansion. In January 2001, the *Albuquerque Journal* reported that Intel's "air emissions" did not violate its permit, despite CRCAW's claims. Barbara Rockwell viewed the Associated Press story as Intel PR spin to the effect that "yes we have had excess emissions but we're honest and we reported it and we're still within limits." The headline, Rockwell said, "was calculated to soothe the average reader, a reader who skims through the headlines and only sees 'Permit Not Violated,' and thinks 'all is well there.'" The reality, she wrote, "was that Intel neighbors were sickened by toxic Intel emissions at a rate not seen since 1993 before the incinerators were installed."[74]

The frustrations and conflicts between Intel and Corrales residents became a matter of extreme scientific, and metaphoric, disagreement when retired LANL scientist Fred Marsh became active in CRCAW early in 2000 after Intel told the press it planned to add more than a million square feet to its Rio Rancho plant. Admitting that there would be a "slight increase in emissions," but claiming that they would remain below the "limits of the new permit," Intel's public affairs office said that "emissions would equal those from two and one half average size gas stations and the permit allows for three." The metaphor struck Fred Marsh as totally wrong. He reported that in terms of "relative toxicity, it was more like 300 gas stations from just chromium trioxide, the chemical that poisoned residents of Hinkley, California, as documented in the movie *Erin Brockovich*."[75] Residents and CRCAW had always worried that Intel's pollution control devices would and did malfunction. Just after the company announced plans to upscale the Rio Rancho plant, an *Albuquerque Journal* reporter revealed that one such device had been down for three and half months before Intel knew of it, owing to a mix-up with its computer sensing equipment.

A Drastic Step

The political atmosphere in Corrales became rancid with accusations, countercharges, deft dodging of issues, and not-so-subtle attacks and putdowns. Residents were furious with the state of New Mexico and what they saw as its cozy relationship with Intel, with state lawyers joining Intel lawyers at the same end of the table during the countless public meetings on various subjects relating to permit applications and health findings. In 2002, Fred Marsh, CRCAW, and SWOP decided to take a drastic step to find out exactly what was in smokestack emissions, as Intel refused to say what mixture of chemicals were being used at a given time, claiming proprietary privilege. Marsh and the two grassroots organizations raised $93,000 to purchase a Fourier transform infrared spectrometer (FTIR) to monitor Intel's emissions day and night. In a very short time, the Corrales area went from having no FTIRs, as Barbara Rockwell wrote, to "all of a sudden" having three "dueling FTIRs"—one bought and paid for by Intel's opposition, one bought by Intel's ally the state of New Mexico, and one bought by Intel itself. According to Barbara Rockwell, the "community FTIR's location was kept secret, fearing sabotage. Our FTIR would run continuously."[76] The state and Intel's would run for only a month. At the end of August 2003, the state's FTIR and the community's showed the same findings regarding the load of chemicals coming from Intel: ammonia, hydrogen chloride, acetone, carbon tetrachloride, hydrogen fluoride, phosgene, hydrogen cyanide, isopropanol, carbon monoxide, and methane "in very low concentrations."[77] There were days in August when nothing from Intel was in the air. Fred Marsh reasoned that the air was so clean because of low production at Intel in August, seasonal winds that were not factored in, "strenuous efforts by Intel to minimize their emissions during the monitoring period," and the narrowness of the plumes close to the plant."[78]

State investigators analyzed all the toxic emissions sources for the area around Intel and came up with three crematoria, two landfills, eleven gas stations, eight auto body shops, four wastewater treatment plants, and continuous car and truck traffic.[79] Even though the FTIR and other testing devices found multiple chemicals in the air near Intel, no smoking gun could be identified. Residents made the argument that chemicals in combination, according to their scientific research and consultants, even in low doses, can cause serious health issues in those who breathe them. But that argument wasn't enough to establish definite cause and effect. Nonetheless, as Barbara Rockwell wrote, "Weren't the residents still getting sick? Wasn't that proof enough that even low levels of these chemicals were hazardous?"[80] The answer was no.

Then something very curious and telling happened. A well-respected New Mexico Environment Department chemist, Dr. Brinda Ramanathan, stopped by the home of a Corrales resident with chronic health problems to check the FTIR that had been secreted away in the area. In a note she wrote to CRCAW, she reported that she smelled a faint odor, then her "throat became constricted and I had difficulty swallowing. I was nervous and I just wanted to get out of there. But I checked the FTIR monitor and discovered concentrations of acetone and . . . dichloroethylene in hundreds of parts per billion. I also noticed there were a couple of sudden peaks [in emissions] that could not be identified. I have walked along the hills behind [this home] several times and have detected faint odors but this is the first time I have become sick like this. It took a couple of days for the symptoms to subside. I am a very healthy person, and I do not get sick like this. Intel's response was as follows: 'This anecdotal information is certainly of concern to us and we'll work to find out more about this situation.' We all knew that 'anecdotal' was the code for 'not to be taken seriously.'"[81]

Confusion Spells Defeat

The upshot of the confusing data from the three FTIRs and conflicting evidence from numerous consultants, experts, and surveys was frustrating, if not to say maddening, to Corrales residents. At what turned out to be a final meeting, an expert for the New Mexico Health Department testified that, contrary to the department's official version, she found sufficient evidence to suggest Intel's emissions might well be implicated in the health problems of Corrales residents. "When you have a chronically exposed population to multiple chemicals for multiple periods of time, with minimal data available to characterize risk, it would be highly appropriate to take a conservative approach. It is difficult for the environmental health epidemiology unit to make a conclusion that there are not acute health effects when we know that people seem to be experiencing them." Her boss, the secretary of health, contradicted her own employee in the open meeting, and the case was closed for good when Ron Curry, secretary of the New Mexico Environment Department and a staunch environmentalist, told the meeting, "We believe there is no conclusive evidence that connects emissions from Intel to health effects in Corrales," asserting that the real problems were from septic tanks and auto emissions.

Whistle Blowers

When furious residents countered with questions regarding the testimony of whistle blowers and other experts with opposing views, no one responded. One Intel whistle blower, George Evans, in a letter from his attorney, expressed concern about his company's smoke-stack emissions, claiming that "the scrubbers and cooling towers may be emitting hydrochloric acid, hydrofluoric acid, ammonium fluoride, ammonia salts, free ammonia, and chloramines in unknown quantities." The chemicals, Evans observed, are "respiratory irritants even at very low levels for those with prior medical conditions."[82] Evans was employed by Intel as a professional industrial hygienist.

In 2004, Jim Shively, described in the *Albuquerque Journal* as a recently retired senior state official who supervised air permits for the state, called Intel's "minor source" air permit "a mistake." Four years earlier, Shively had labeled it an "unenforceable sham" and described the bureaucratic process that produced it as "a farce." He charged that the permit allowed "greater amounts of pollutants to be emitted than the previous major source permit." When he was involved with the permit as a state employee, he said, he had recommended that Intel be required to continuously monitor its emissions, but that "Intel strongly objected and the department acquiesced. The way the permit is written, Intel will never be able to violate their permit," Shively told the *Albuquerque Journal.*[83]

Corrales residents rallied twice more. In February 2005, residents asked the Agency for Toxic Substance and Disease Registry (ATSDR) to do a health consultation on air quality risks associated with Intel's manufacturing processes. As of August 2008, the agency had not released its report. Jeff Radford of *Corrales Comment* noted in May 2008 that the report had been "delayed yet again." Fred Marsh, the retired LANL chemist representing Corrales residents, said he "suspects the repeated delays are intended to ease pressure on Intel. 'The longer ATSDR delays its report, the more I expect they're being pressured to produce another Intel exoneration.'"[84]

Smokestack Size

The final episode to date in Intel's relationship with residents of Corrales involves the height of its new smokestacks. After negotiations with Intel's own citizens technical advisory board, the company rejected the board's recommendation to raise the stack from twenty-three to forty meters, contending in the press that it was concerned with the "esthetic" implications of smokestacks of that size.[85] They decided instead to raise them to thirty meters, a height residents maintained would not channel off the emissions into higher wind patterns and away from their homes. Barbara Rockwell contends in her blog, "Intel feels that the higher stacks will lead the public to perceive that this may indeed not be the 'clean industry' that it pretends to be."

Is there anything positive to be gained from all this? Intel versus the Village has been, and will continue to be, a textbook case of corporate and grassroots warfare. My bias is always with the grassroots, which I think is justified by the imbalance of power. One could say that Intel won fair and square because it is very hard to attach cause and effect to air pollution and health issues. One might also say that Intel could have ended the whole matter by behaving with genuine empathy for the afflicted and by fixing its emissions—in other words, by being a genuinely good neighbor and deserving some of the billions it's gotten from Sandoval County IRBs and all of its other perks, tax breaks, and laurel wreaths. Intel knew it would never face a suit in open court. What private individual or nonprofit entity could go up against the world's largest semiconductor company and hope to stay the course, let alone win?

Grassroots Thorns

These kinds of battles, even if lost, leave in their wake many activated, sophisticated, and highly skeptical members of grassroots organizations that can, and often do, have major impacts on public policy in New Mexico. I see the CRCAW as a local variant of a national environmental NGO. All they need is capital, and they become a potentially behavior-changing thorn in the side of private, and even military, polluters. The battles they endure in one arena toughen and educate them for other conflicts. The continuing struggles among local governments, neighborhoods, farmers and ranchers, local and national NGOs, the military, multinational corporations, and local businesses over issues involving global warming, chronic drought in the West, and urban planning are only going to intensify as the weather continues its chaotic new directions and the costs of vital resources rise.

Imagine the constructive uproar and watchdogging that might take place when New Mexicans come to realize that their already scarce water supply has been compromised in many places in the aquifer, making their livelihoods ever more precarious and difficult. When New Mexico cities finally come to terms with the reality of their carbon footprints and the magnitude of the efforts it will take to reduce them, citizen activists of all areas of interest and expertise will provide the political energy to get the work done.

Cities and Countrysides

The antagonisms and misunderstandings between rural and urban-based New Mexicans are often highlighted by struggles over endangered wilderness and species, a cause usually championed by urban environmentalists, who often find themselves at odds with small farmers and ranchers eking out a living on the land, far from urban perspectives. But city and countryside are in a symbiotic relationship. They can't do without each other. The direct impacts are clear. Rural areas need urban centers for basic goods and services, for cultural and educational opportunities. Cities need the countryside and its people for the care they take of the land, the watershed, and the bottomlands that recharge the aquifer. And soon, as energy prices drive up trucked-in food costs, cities will need the countryside to grow and harvest more of their basic food supply.

The indirect impacts are just as important. The Jeffersonian countryside still nurtures the fundamental American values of self-reliance, efficiency, conservation, and savvy about how the real world works. Rural politics are split along liberal and conservative lines, like politics everywhere. But the conservation ethic American society needs to embrace crosses party lines in the countryside. And city dwellers need to hear and learn the lessons of what it takes to survive and even flourish in a world ever more dominated by weather and other natural cycles. The urban world is a world of information. One of the indirect benefits that cities bring to rural areas is the broadening and deepening of the knowledge base, which contributes to rural residents' personal enrichment and economic viability. As long as rural farmers, ranchers, and their local governments can avoid a water war with big cities in their region, the common need to adapt to climate change might hold out hope for the kind of cooperation that survival requires.

Otero Mesa

The preservation of Otero Mesa and its pristine aquifer is a case in point. It's one of those "everybody wins" situations—everybody, that is, except the petroleum industry. Wilderness advocates win, farmers and ranchers in southern New Mexico win indirectly because cities in the southern part of the state will win, having access to a massive new supply of water—not enough to solve all their problems, but enough to keep all but the most ravenous developers from buying up water rights. The wild desert grasslands of Otero Mesa extend over 1.2 million acres. But the wild habitat is equaled in importance by that vast supply of clean, ancient potable water in the Salt Basin aquifer. By some reckonings, there are more than a million acre-feet of water under the surface, perhaps a century's worth of drinking and irrigating water. It's enough to rectify, with careful conservation, much of the water scarcity suffered recently by Las Cruces, El Paso, and Juarez. The Salt Basin has more than two-thirds of its water in Texas and beyond.

The political conflict around Otero Mesa pitted wildlife and water conservationists against the Bush administration's Bureau of Land Management, which supported the oil industry in its pursuit of what is thought to be a small petroleum deposit below the aquifer. The BLM created what it considered a stringent management plan for the area, but one that allowed oil and gas exploration. The agency held that drilling operations would not harm the grasslands and would not be a substantial risk to the aquifer. The New Mexico Wilderness Alliance sued the BLM, contending that the development of oil and gas wells on the mesa "would result in fragmentation of the land, with roads, pipelines, power lines, drill pads, dust, invasive species, [and] topsoil depletion." The Wilderness Alliance also contended that Otero Mesa's "oil and gas resources are small and that its hydrocarbon resources are scattered throughout the area in isolated pockets," requiring "intense infrastructure as well as dense development, which, as demonstrated in southeastern New Mexico near Carlsbad, does not constitute 'environmentally friendly' drilling," as the oil industry argued.[86]

In April 2009, the Tenth Circuit Court of Appeals sided with the Wilderness Alliance, holding that the BLM had to give weight to an alternative plan that would close Otero to oil and gas leasing. "Development is a possible use, which BLM must weigh against other possible uses—including conservation to protect environmental values."[87] In the San Juan Basin, longtime ranchers who have had to deal with oil and gas drillers with mineral rights to their land know how "environmentally friendly" such operations really are. The roads, the poisonous unlined waste pits, the general disturbance of the landscape that comes with coal methane extraction have all led many ranchers in the area to close down their cow and calf operations altogether. Too many of their cattle, attracted to the sweet taste of antifreeze and other pollutants, were dying from drinking drilling waste.

Watersheds: The Unseen Salvation

When Barry Commoner in his 1971 book *The Closing Circle* out-lined his laws of ecology, he was describing the complex interactions and processes at work in natural and human systems, particularly watersheds, which, like the air we breathe, are an overarching net-work that binds us all together, town by town, landscape by land-scape, region by region.[88] In the West, where water is channeled and moved thousands of miles from its sources, we are all each oth-er's watersheds—using, recycling, transmitting, recharging, selling, treating, and discharging the common waters we need to survive. Commoner's first law of ecology describes watersheds precisely: "Everything is connected to everything else." The forested high mountain watersheds of the Colorado River Basin, for instance, con-nect cities and farms large and small in seven states. And the pro-duce and commerce that rely on that water stimulate the economy of the country and beyond. In accordance with Commoner's second law, "Everything must go somewhere," our human, commercial, and industrial wastes end up either in our air or in our water, almost without exception, and often the dust from our mines, dirt roads, and developments darkens snowpacks hundreds of miles away, caus-ing them to melt faster at the wrong times of the year. The Colorado River receives the treated effluent from as many as a dozen towns before it reaches Lee Ferry in Arizona. The Rio Grande receives effluent from Rio Rancho and Albuquerque, as well as pollution from Sandia Labs via the Tijeras Arroyo. And before it reaches those cities, the river has, in all likelihood, been polluted over the last sixty years by radioactive and industrial waste from Los Alamos National Laboratories in the Jemez Mountains.

Everything must go somewhere, and nothing goes away. From power plants in the Four Corners region and chip factories at Intel, whatever can't be contained goes into the environment. Most waste ends up in water humans need. "There's no such thing as a free lunch," Commoner says. "Every gain is won at some cost." And it's water and our health that pay the price: the degradation of rivers and streams by mining waste, the risk to drinking water from waste treat-ment plants breaking down and sending raw sewage into waterways, unrestrained housing development and population growth sopping up water needed for agriculture, overlogging and overgrazing and illegal dumping tearing up the mountain watersheds so they no longer slow runoff or filter natural waste.

Watershed thinking should apply wherever water is generated or treated and discharged as "clean" effluent into a waterway. The city of Albuquerque in 2010, for instance, was scheduled to treat and then to "extra clean" wastewater at its South Valley treatment plant and divert it to twenty-six city parks in southeast Albuquerque. The playing field at the Isotope Baseball Park will get the city's treated gray water to keep its outfield green. This long-awaited use of gray water by the city could be the beginning of a citywide water recycling effort.[89] The sewage treatment facility has been a regenerating watershed, of sorts, for irrigators south of the city. Now it becomes a regeneration agent for parks and sports fields inside the city. Everything goes somewhere. Las Campanas, a large upscale development near Santa Fe, uses vast amounts of water for its two Jack Nicklaus Signature 18-hole golf courses, called Sunrise and Sunset.[90] The development has used 9.53 million gallons of water a day from Santa Fe's Buckman well "to sprinkle irrigate its two private golf courses located outside of the city limits," according to the website SantaFeWaterCrisis.org.[91] Members pay an initial $90,000 membership fee and dues of about $700 a month. But in September 2009 the recession caught up with Las Campanas. The development's sports facilities, including the golf courses and the equestrian center, were closed by Lloyds Banking Group of the UK, which owns the note on Las Campanas.

The aquifer that Santa Fe's Buckman well taps into has been the object of intense scrutiny and concern; its watershed on the Pajarito Plateau is dominated by LANL, with its more than twenty-one hundred waste sites and its record of dumping industrial and radioactive waste into canyons that drain into the Buckman aquifer and the Rio Grande. Santa Fe residents are so concerned about the risk to their drinking water from Los Alamos pollution that the Santa Fe County Commission officially requested the National Nuclear Security Administration (NNSA) agree to a set of provisions including funds for an early warning system. If river water from the San Juan–Chama Project flowing down the Rio Grande headed for Santa Fe should experience an emergency pollution event, water authorities could close down the diversion system and send the water south to Albuquerque, which presumably would stop diverting river water into its drinking water system as well. The Santa Fe County Commission and the NNSA couldn't reach an accommodation in more than nine months of wrangling. According to Julie Ann Grimm of the *Santa Fe New Mexican*, "Both local planners and the secretary of the state Environment Department have said they want the lab and the federal government to pay their fare [*sic*] of the cost of making the diversion project more impervious to nuclear pollution. High levels of plutonium and other radionuclides were detected in runoff from the lab" as recently as 2008.[92] The release of $212 million in federal stimulus money in the fall of 2009 to clean up a contaminated dump from the Manhattan Project did not relieve the anxiety of residents of northern New Mexico about radioactive poison in their water. The dump, near office buildings in downtown Los Alamos, is being excavated by workers in full protection gear, including respirators. This doesn't quite fit with the constant flow of PR from LANL about the safety of the lab and the lack of risk to the public.[93]

Rio Grande Watershed

The Rio Grande watershed is complicated enough without such worries. It flows through multiple terrains in multiple states and is fed by numerous river systems and augmented by discharges of treated effluent from many towns. Water planners are worried about the Rio Grande maintaining its flow because it originates in the southern Colorado San Juan Mountains near Creede, an area with roughly the same climate and drought conditions as the Colorado River Basin. Should the Colorado River and the Rio Grande continue to diminish owing to climate change, New Mexico would face a double jeopardy, losing not only drinking water from the San Juan–Chama Project (the San Juan is a tributary of the Colorado) but also suffering a loss of agricultural and aquifer-recharge water up and down the New Mexico Rio Grande. The big river is fed in New Mexico by the Rio Chama, its most significant tributary; the Jemez River, which empties into it near Bernalillo and Santa Ana Pueblo; and the San Jose and Rio Puerco drainage, which are intermittent streams. The Rio Grande's watershed is made up mostly of federal and other public lands. Less than 10 percent of the watershed is cultivated, though agriculture is intense around Española, from Cochiti Lake to Elephant Butte in the Middle Rio Grande Valley, and around Las Cruces in the Mesilla Valley. Even with the Middle Rio Grande Valley's heavy population, its most beautiful habitat, the cottonwood bosque along its banks, has been preserved by both urban and rural New Mexicans. Yet despite these and many other efforts, in March 2007 the World Wide Fund for Nature placed the Rio Grande on its list of the ten most endangered rivers in the world, most notably its southern reaches, separating Texas from Mexico; there the river flow is sometimes so low that salt water floods up the riverbed, killing native freshwater species.[94]

The Urban Habitat

As the Middle Rio Grande teaches us, humans, animals, and plants occupy local overlapping terrains that directly and indirectly impact each other. The urban habitat influences all life in its vicinity, using up water, polluting existing waters, creating heat sinks, and providing flood control with concrete-lined waterways that shoot water to the river without recharging the aquifer. Cities also establish highly manicured parks and parking lot forests for urban wildlife and feral domesticated species. All habitats, large and small, adapt to the general weather patterns of their geographical milieu. When small habitats and their animal and plant residents are struggling, chances are the overarching habitat and its human residents are on their way to trouble, too. The Comprehensive Wildlife Conservation Strategy for New Mexico, created in 2006 by the state's Department of Game and Fish, gives a complete rundown on the Rio Grande's endangered and invasive species and its numerous aquatic habitats, including large reservoirs, marshes, cienegas, springs, seeps, and various sizes of streams and waterways. The river is in trouble and so are the more than seven hundred thousand people who live in the more than three thousand square miles of the semiarid Middle Rio Grande Basin. The basic problems are that the area is too hot, it has too little water, too much water is consumed, and there's not enough water staying in the river and surrounding farmlands to recharge the aquifer.[95]

In 2000, the Middle Rio Grande Endangered Species Act Collaborative Program created breeding sanctuaries for the endangered silvery minnow, a fish that has become infamous among farmers and water planners who contend that its preservation drains water from more important agricultural and even industrial uses. The minnow was once wild in the river and was a prodigious consumer of insects and algae, helping to keep the river waters clean. Now that the river can no longer support the minnow and the species has been sequestered in safe hatcheries, it is still too early to tell if insect populations have increased or if algae have damaged other species. Restoration work on big burned areas near Los Lunas and around the Alameda Bridge south of Corrales cleared out invasive plant species and replaced exotic with native species. Isleta Pueblo has worked on studies of the endangered Southwest willow flycatcher. Santa Ana and Sandia Pueblos have restored their bosques to more traditional vegetation and removed invasive species.

Invasives

In 2004, the state won an $800,000 settlement against Sparton Industries for the damage it did as a Superfund site to aquifers on the West Side of Albuquerque. The money was used to help in what Governor Bill Richardson said was "protecting ground water and restoring the Rio Grande Bosque to a pristine state."[96] Although dozens of invasive exotic species cause trouble in New Mexico, keeping the bosque "pristine" means, in most people's minds, removing the water-hungry salt cedar, or tamarisk, from the riverside. The fluffy trees with their pink blossoms are sprayed with poison (causing much controversy) or sometimes ripped out of the ground with giant machines. Plans to use grazing goats or tamarisk-eating beetles are also in the works. Tamarisk is universally blamed for water loss and for crowding out native species like the much admired desert willow, which was named Albuquerque's official tree in 1964. Tamarisk has an extremely high evaporation rate, and groves of it have been likened to huge straws sucking water from the aquifer.

Two other exotic species have overwhelmed the Rio Grande bosque and its valley—the Russian olive and the Siberian elm. Like the tamarisk, the Russian olive was purposefully introduced into the United States in the nineteenth century as an ornamental tree and windbreak, but escaped from domestication and moved into the wild. Unlike the tamarisk, the Russian olive is not a complete social outcast. Its blossoms have a fragrance that many New Mexicans equate with spring. And the tree's small but plentiful olives keep many bird populations alive. Russian olives are fine guard trees, with long, sharp thorns that make them virtually impenetrable when planted defensively. But in riparian environments, their ability to thrive in terrible soil makes them a scourge to native vegetation, as they take hold and spread thickly. And they also drink up groundwater.

The Siberian elm, a native of China and Korea, is, like the Russian olive, considered a weed and can overrun parts of the bosque habitat. But elms, too, have supporters as well as their vehement detractors. Planted widely around the West as windbreaks and as shade trees in cities, these exceptionally hardy trees are drought tolerant and have root systems that make them almost impossible to eradicate. No one has ever seriously suggested trying to completely remove elms and Russian olives in the way they have the tamarisk. Albuquerque mayor Clyde Tingley gave Siberian elms away to city residents in the late 1930s, and they provided high desert Albuquerque with relief-giving shade. Siberian elms are hated, however, for their seeds, which are released in such abundance they can drift over steps and curbs in good winds. Called sometimes Tingley's Dandruff or Tingley Flakes, the seeds sprout up anywhere there is water. A vegetable garden near an elm tree can be literally covered in elm seedlings almost overnight. Legend has it that the mayor bought twenty thousand Siberian elms for twenty dollars and stored them in the bosque until residents could pick them up and plant them around their houses.

If you want to kill off trees, including the cottonwood, and destroy the bosque itself, all you really have to do is pollute the groundwater. The effect is disastrous. In 2004, nearly forty-five acres of the bosque in Rio Rancho died off—everything from cottonwoods to Russian olives and willows. Hydrologists from the U.S. Fish and Wildlife Service tested a number of wells near the die-off and found higher than normal concentrations of uranium, strontium, lithium, ammonia, potassium, and calcium, among other chemicals. The source of those chemicals remains unknown. But the affected area, just east of the River's Edge development, is upriver from Intel, but downriver from Los Alamos, as is all of the Middle Rio Grande Valley.[97]

Human Threat

The greatest proven threat to the river and its wildlife so far—overuse by humans—involves a controversy with a nasty urban-rural twist. Two lawsuits opposing, in different ways, Albuquerque's massive drinking water project found urban environmentalists and rural water users in conflict. One suit involves strategies to protect the endangered silvery minnow and the other a challenge to the state engineer's permit, granted in 2004, allowing Albuquerque to divert 48,200 acre-feet of Colorado River Basin water flowing down the Rio Grande through the tunnels and channels that comprise the San Juan–Chama project. City residents started drinking river water for the first time in modern history in December 2008. Silvery minnow advocates wanted the Bureau of Reclamation to put aside San Juan–Chama water for the preservation of the minnow, arguing that curtailing agricultural use by reining in the Middle Rio Grande Conservancy District (MRGCD) would supply more than enough water for the fish. They were opposed by not only the Bureau of Reclamation and the state of New Mexico but also by the MRGCD, representing area farmers, and by the city of Albuquerque. Despite wins for minnow advocates in federal court, eventually Senator Pete Domenici put a rider on the appropriations bills funding the Department of Interior that exempted San Juan–Chama water from being used to protect the minnow or other endangered species.[98] Nearly simultaneous to the minnow case, a coalition of agricultural and environmental groups were protesting Albuquerque's permit from the state engineer to divert San Juan–Chama water in the first place, arguing that San Juan–Chama water has been flowing down the river since 1972, when the tunnels and channels of the Bureau of Reclamation project were first completed, artificially keeping the river wet and bottomlands irrigated with some 109,000 acre-feet a year. Because surface flows and groundwater are intimately connected, San Juan–Chama water, in the early 1970s, appeared to supply a surplus, despite the massive pumping of groundwater for drinking purposes during the city's peak period of growth. Opponents of the permit contend that not only will diverting the flow from a thirteen-mile stretch of the river through Albuquerque damage vital habitat in the cottonwood bosque, but it will also exacerbate groundwater depletion. Pumping aquifer water has a delayed reaction, and over time its effects will begin to diminish river flows. Some studies contend that the pumping is draining the surface water of the river itself by as much as 70,000 acre-feet a year. In granting the Albuquerque permit, the state engineer denied the needs of those who had used the water before the drinking water project came along, including farmers and thousands of rural owners of permitted wells. Under the rule of prior appropria-tion, Albuquerque has junior water rights, while Native American and most rural water users have senior water rights. Without major water from the depleted river, ditch irrigation farming won't be able to help recharge the rapidly depleting aquifer-river system. It's mostly in the bottomlands that recharging takes place.[99]

The worst stretch of the river for wildlife and the bosque is the 105 miles between the Percha Dam south of Truth or Consequences and the American Dam in El Paso. Few cottonwoods are left; the habitat has been largely denuded; and the river itself looks like a canal. In 2009, the International Boundary and Water Commission released a plan to revitalize 553 acres in thirty locations in the old riparian landscape, allowing flooding to water new cottonwoods and other native plants along the way. Area farmers have bought into the idea and will donate small amounts of their water rights, realiz-ing their interests won't be damaged, and that groundwater reserves might actually be augmented.[100]

Agriculture and Warming

With drought and higher temperatures projected to increase evap-oration,[101] farmers in New Mexico are likely to face a multitude of pressures, just like the cities they surround. City governments sharpen their efforts to buy water rights just when local agricul-ture is called upon to feed more and more of the local population. The convergence of drought and peak oil will put everyone in a double bind, but no one as much as farmers. Even in 2009, way before the full force of the projected decades-long drought hit the region, farmers south of Albuquerque were complaining that the water flow in the ditches didn't have sufficient force to irrigate their lands from top to bottom.

Selling water rights during a recession, especially when those rights have grown in value nearly 1,000 percent in twenty years, is hard to resist. But while selling water rights to cities seems logical to some landowners, more and more produce farmers, ranchers, and dairy farmers put peer pressure on their neighbors not to.[102] It's hard for farmers to do long-range planning. Weather and commodity prices are too chaotic most of the time to permit them to calculate ahead. But as green-minded consumers in New Mexico's big cities seek locally grown food, raising food for profit is becoming more attractive.

A sizable new market is building for niche agriculture that not only provides local restaurants with vegetables, organic beef, pork, and fowl, but also supplies the growing number of area co-ops and farmers' markets. And the Middle Rio Grande Valley has been shown by researchers at the New Mexico State University College of Agriculture and Home Economics to be ideal for the growing of French hybrid grapes that also flourish in northern New Mexico and the European grapes that grow so well in the southern part of the state.[103]

Working the land has always been hard and the profit margin low, but New Mexico was once dominated by agriculture in the river valleys and floodplains. Cattle and sheep have long been mainstays of the New Mexico economy. Though city dwellers in New Mexico think of agriculture and ranching as throwbacks practiced today only by stubborn traditionalists out of tune with modern times, many of us who live in New Mexico's semirural cities also practice small-time agriculture, both to augment our diets and to enact conservation values otherwise missing from urban life. In 2008, out of the state's nearly two million people, 670,403 of them lived, worked, or ran small businesses in rural areas. The New Mexico Farm and Livestock Bureau clearly explains the interdependence of rural and urban life:

> The rural sectors of our State and Nation have need for healthcare that is not readily available to them, education is an ongoing struggle for smaller communities, broadband Internet service is a must for business in rural areas and lags far behind the urban areas, the road infrastructure system and mass freight transportation for our communities is an essential need for agriculture as well as those who live and work in rural sectors. Becoming energy efficient and independent is also a common interest. And all of this is driven by entrepreneurship from people in the urban areas as well as the rural areas.

Urban economies and environmental issues are a context in which all rural people have to operate. Conversely, rural economies and conservation practices model, in many respects, values and skills that global warming and peak oil will force on cities and their residents.

The Dominance of Small Farm
and Ranch Businesses

The intermingling of urban and rural New Mexico is clear at the state fair, held in Albuquerque in September. The glitz of the midway and the general carnival atmosphere all but hide the cattle, sheep, and hog exhibits, the myriad domestic fowl on display, the grain and vegetable competitions, the baked goods contests, the rodeo, and the horse racing. All derive from a huge network of some thirty-three county fairs in rural New Mexico lasting from July to October. Most county fairs last three to five days. All of them feature farm and ranch competitions.

New Mexico is a huge state, the fifth largest in the country, with a very small population, ranked thirty-sixth. Nearly 58 percent of the total land area of New Mexico (more than 43 million acres in 2007) was devoted to agriculture. That's down from nearly 60 percent in 1997, according to the U.S. Department of Agriculture. Some 33 percent of New Mexico's 1,984,356 residents in 2008 lived in rural areas. Of the state's twenty-one thousand or more farms, 87 percent were owned by families or individuals and could be considered small-time operations, with incomes maxing out at $50,000 a year. Dairy products and cattle were the top commodities in 2008, with hay production just below. In its rankings among states, New Mexico's pecan industry was fifth in the country, and we're a big producer of onions. Though most farms have gardens, in 2008, greenhouse edibles remained a small part of New Mexico's commodity economy. Farming is a hard life. Rural living has its appeals, but the rural poverty rate was nearly 21 percent in 2007, almost 5 percent higher than the rest of the state.[104]

Cattle ranching is still big business in New Mexico and a way of life that pervades the politics and the culture of the state. Rodeo and local 4-H clubs are permanent fixtures in most counties, even in the remaining rural parts of Bernalillo County. Ranching is almost always a family business here, with some sixty-eight hundred beef and sheep ranch operations in the state. More than half the grazing land is held by the federal government, the state land trust, or Native American tribal governments. Some fifty-one hundred grazing permits, leases, and allotments are on public lands. In nearly a quarter of New Mexico's counties, ranching is the biggest business. In some, ranching accounted for 40 percent or more of total income.[105]

Roswell. Josh, one of the five Hagelstein kids, all of whom help on the ranch, herds cattle on horseback for the photographer's benefit. The family owns 800 yearlings plus 130 calves. March 2007.

Roswell. Jack Hagelstein fills the watering trough for the cattle. March 2007.

Roswell. Josh, his dad Jack, and his mom Pat (inside the truck). March 2007.

Roswell. Jack sends one animal at a time through the chute to be branded on the left cheek. April 2007.

Roswell. Josh dehorning a cow in the holder. April 2007.

Cimarron. Julia Davis Stafford, one of the six Davis siblings, each of whom manages a part of the ranch, with employee Gayle McBrayer. Between the towns of Springer (named for Charles Springer, as is the ranch) and Cimarron in northeast New Mexico lie the 130,000 acres of the CS Cattle Company. June 2007.

Cimarron. The view to the south from headquarters. In 1873, Julia's great-grandfather came west from Iowa. Upon laying eyes on this view, he purchased the land. To the left is Rayado Mesa, to the right Gonzalitas Mesa. June 2007.

Cimarron. The tack room has been in continuous use for more than a hundred years. June 2007.

Cimarron. Out mending fences. November 2007.

Cimarron. Mike Vigil, a part-time employee here, helps round up the calves in the early morning. CS Ranch is the only cow-calf ranch in the area. The average number of cattle here is 2,500. November 2007.

Open pecan shells still on the branches in the Mesilla Valley, Las Cruces.
March 2010.

Dick Salopeck's family orchards north of Las Cruces; these pecan trees were
planted when he was twelve years old. After the trees are trimmed, the wood
chips are spread in the orchard, then bacteria is sprayed to break them down.
March 2010.

Three-year-old trees in Dick Salopeck's orchards in front of the Organ Mountains of Las Cruces. One cannot expect nuts before a tree's seventh season. March 2010.

Apprentice Michelle Posey transplants in the Los Poblanos greenhouse.
Los Poblanos Organics runs a CSA (community supported agriculture) farm
on the historic Los Poblanos Ranch in Albuquerque's North Valley. There is an
apprentice program for people who want to learn about farming. April 2009.

Shauna Pearson (also an apprentice) lifts the plastic cover to check on new plants and adjust the watering hoses at Los Poblanos. April 2009.

Michelle Posey harvests baby salad greens for the Los Poblanos CSA boxes. April 2009.

Two Kinds of Environmentalists

And yet ranching and environmentalism have been seemingly at odds with each other since the 1970s, with ranchers accused of flagrantly overgrazing public lands and threatening endangered species like the Mexican wolf with the same intensity that urban planners and developers blame farmers for wasting water with inefficient irrigation methods. A deep divide in understanding separates what one might call two branches of environmentalism. One is a form of conservation practiced by the majority of land-based rural people that I'll call, borrowing from Aldo Leopold, a form of "land ethic." The other is advocacy for the natural world, which is seen as threatened by human consumption and overpopulation. Both these positions exist in a context of endangered watersheds, polluted soils, air, and groundwater, the growing chaos of climate change, and a globalized economy that threatens most localities around the world.

The disagreements between those who live a land ethic and those who advocate for nature and clean environments was made especially clear at an Aldo Leopold centennial celebration in Albuquerque in February 2009. Billed as "a cultural conversation," the centennial meeting was designed to examine the evolution of Leopold's "land ethic for the future." The meeting was, to my recollection, the most culturally diverse environmental conference in New Mexico since Earth Day 1970. Native American and Hispanic speakers often remarked, "with respect," that they'd never heard of Leopold but that they had been practicing a land ethic for centuries. Some had choice things to say about the dismissal of traditional and indigenous land-based knowledge by academics and environmentalists. Leopold's version of a land ethic can be summed up in a series of short quotations:

> "A thing is right when it tends to preserve the integrity, stability, and beauty of the biotic community. It is wrong when it tends otherwise."

> "A land ethic . . . reflects the existence of an ecological conscience, and this in turn reflects a conviction of individual responsibility for the health of the land."

> "The land ethic simply enlarges the boundaries of the community to include soils, plants, and animals, or collectively: the land."[106]

The split between rural and urban environmental thinkers was drawn sharply by two speakers of towering reputation in New Mexico who have, nevertheless, felt excluded from mainstream environmentalism. One was poet and writer Juan Estevan Arellano, a farmer and acequia mayordomo in Embudo, New Mexico, acknowledged as a leader in the continuation of Indo-Hispano agriculture in the northern part of the state. The other was Professor Gregory Cajete from Santa Clara Pueblo, who is director of Native American Studies at the University of New Mexico.

Acequia View

Arellano told a large audience that environmentalists had never asked him to participate in such a conference before. Reading Leopold's land ethic, he said, he was surprised that there "was no mention of us, as if we knew nothing, or didn't exist." Leopold, in his view, was a latecomer to New Mexico, arriving early in the twentieth century. New Mexico's land ethic, Arellano pointed out, is ancient. "We've always cooperated, always shared," he said. Cajete echoed Arellano's view and took it one step farther, saying that the land ethic of indigenous people had been trivialized and that he, personally, and other Native American scholars had been "largely excluded" from the conservationist and environmentalist community. "People like Aldo Leopold were actually formed by New Mexico. We've been living that land ethic and have not been recognized," Cajete said. Miguel Santistevan, an agricultural ecologist from Taos who specializes in permaculture, also said that New Mexicans did not learn the land ethic from Leopold. Instead of owning land, people here, Santistevan said, "belonged to the land, struggled for the land." Northern New Mexico, he said, "has always had climate change. It's always feast or famine."

Arellano, in his introduction to the English edition of *Ancient Agriculture: Roots and Application of Sustainable Farming* by Renaissance Spaniard Gabriel Alonso de Herrera, writes about his own farm in Embudo, leaving readers with a sense of what is possible in the future with a local agricultural revival in the rural interstices between the cities of modern New Mexico. *Ancient Agriculture* was first published in 1513, and while no copies from the colonial period exist in New Mexico today, it is likely that pioneering Spanish farmers who followed Juan de Oñate into the north had studied the book's recommendations. Using traditional forms of gardening recommended by Herrera and passed down through the generations, Arellano writes that although he grew up "in a family without much money, our place was a paradise full of glorious vegetables and fruits, including chiles, corn, cherries, pears, peaches, apples, watermelons, and cantaloupes." Following Herrera's advice further, he has terraced all his property. One section has twelve terraces, "which not only simplified my irrigation but prevented erosion. I have grown," he writes, "as many as one hundred twenty-five varieties of heirloom apple trees, ten kinds of pear trees, and about forty peach trees." Arellano made a direct connection between Herrera and traditional agriculture in northern New Mexico and other Spanish colonial realms and contemporary "organic farming, sustainable agriculture, and permaculture."[107]

Herrera, and those who carry on his tradition in the north, may well prove in the future to have laid the foundations for a re-creation of agrarian values and economic pragmatism on a scale that could supply New Mexico residents, in cities and in the countryside, with a sizable portion of their edible needs—if, of course, they can withstand the pressures of growth and the uncertainties of climate change. Agrarian values in the north are embodied in acequia culture, both the political and social entities of acequia communities and the irrigation systems themselves. Some one thousand organized acequias still exist in New Mexico. They belong to an umbrella organization called the New Mexico Acequia Association, founded in 1990. According to the association's website, its "mission is to sustain our way of life, protect water as a community resource, and strengthen the agricultural traditions of our families and communities. We work to define acequia water rights so that current and future generations can grow food and can have a healthy and secure source of water for local community needs."[108]

Water Competition

But as David J. Groenfeldt of the Santa Fe Watershed Association, coordinator of the Indigenous Water Initiative, has written, "Acequia farmers face water competition from two sources: One is the large-scale irrigation districts whose farmers have a more industrial, profit-oriented ethos, as compared to the more traditional acequia ethos of close interaction with nature through . . . growing food for subsistence as well as sale and hunting for subsistence. More urgent, however, is water competition from residential and commercial development. Although acequia associations have strong legal claims to the water they need for agriculture, they are under increasing pressure to sell their water rights to commercial developers." Groenfeldt points out that acequias have established "collective rights to water" that let the entire association community rule on the sale of some of their water to developers. Water used by acequias, pueblos, and small farmers in the Middle Rio Grande Valley "creates an artificial habitat very similar to the natural habitat of the surrounding riverine landscape."

But with overdevelopment, Groenfeldt warns, the "green zone of the river valleys—once expanded through agriculture—decrease and wither, as the water once diverted for adjacent fields is now pumped outside the river zone to meet the demands of housing development many miles away."[109]

In a book published by the National Hispanic Cultural Center, *La Vida del Rio Grande: Our River—Our Life*, Paula Garcia, executive director of the New Mexico Acequia Association, writes, "What we are talking about when we talk about the river is a whole culture, an economy, and a way of life." She cautions that "acequias will play a vital role in future development decisions. At the moment many development decisions are being made that are completely unaccountable to traditional communities."[110] She adds, "In the Western United States they are calling this an era of re-allocation, which is a scary idea for us in agriculture, because re-allocation means moving water out of agriculture into cities. Why are cities needing to do this?" she asks. Because they have mined their groundwater almost dry.[111] "Water is a community resource, not an economic commodity that can be sold, severed from the land and transferred out of the community."[112] Enrique Lamadrid, folklorist and professor of Spanish at UNM, remarked, "I will believe that a drought has hit New Mexico if I see brown golf courses or if I see golf courses with Buffalo Grass. This really is a conflict of values, we are talking about cultural values."[113] Since 2004, the National Hispanic Cultural Center has been conducting a river education and restoration project with high school students, called Jardines del Bosque, in which the NHCC says it works "to support and inspire a new generation of scientists, scholars, and caretakers of our most precious resource—the Rio Grande." The project will create a research station in the bosque near the NHCC, where river ecology will be studied and high school students trained over the summer in bosque restoration and management.

Pueblo View

Gregory Cajete, in *A People's Ecology*, envisions vigorous, humane, and productive land-based living, not only for rural people, but for everyone who depends on the land, city and rural dwellers alike. The formula is "healthy environment, healthy culture, healthy people."[114] In his chapter entitled "Look to the Mountain," Cajete writes that the

"Americas are an ensouled and enchanted geography, and the relationship of Indian people to this geography embodies a 'theology of place,' reflecting the very essence of what may be called 'spiritual ecology.' The land has become an extension of Indian thought and being because, in the words of a Pueblo elder 'it is this place that holds our memories and the bones of our people.... This is the place that made us.'"[115] The environment is not, he said, "separate or divorced from Native people's lives, but rather was the context or set of relationships that tied everything together. They understood the ecology not as something apart from themselves or outside their intellectual reality, but rather as the very center and generator of self-understanding."[116]

After World War II, increased demand for water from growing cities challenged traditional Pueblo agriculture, as did the growth of agribusiness, which almost broke the backs of small farmers all over the country. Many Pueblo farmers risked their lives working for uranium mining companies to raise income. In the mid-1960s, the All Indian Pueblo Council, under the leadership of Domingo Montoya, began refocusing Pueblo agriculture toward high-value crops and sustainable gardening of staple food supplies. With their senior water rights, pueblos and acequia associations are in a position to be pathfinders for the revival of agricultural practices and marketing that could help supplement the diets of tens of thousands of New Mexicans. All over the Pueblo world, from Sandia and Tesuque to San Felipe, Picuris, Zuni, and Isleta, a back-to-the-land movement has picked up momentum since the 1960s, according to James Vlasich, a historian from Southern Utah University. "For many people," Vlasich writes, "the trek back to the past arose from dissatisfaction with social and political conditions that encouraged and allowed them to stray away from their Pueblo heritage."[117] Pueblo farmers are growing sacred blue corn in enough quantity to supply half the nation's needs for blue corn flour for cooking. And farmers all over the Pueblo world are reassessing their families' dependence on processed foods.[118]

Fuel Costs and Local Growing

A constellation of high fuel costs, water conservation, and a deep recession in the housing industry has not only spurred Pueblo and Hispanic farming, but has prompted the world's largest food distributor, Sysco Corporation, to modify a decades-long strategy of national food distribution by regionalizing its operations to save fuel. Part of Sysco's plan is to stimulate local agriculture and get more locally grown products into New Mexico restaurants and grocery stores. When the plan was announced in 2005, the dean of New Mexico State University's College of Agriculture and Home Economics, Jerry Schickedanz, said that it was a "tremendous opportunity" for local growers, particularly for small- and medium-scale producers. Through the program, called Born in New Mexico, Sysco not only has plans to build demand for local goods but to pass that demand onto producers through creating business partnerships with New Mexico growers that will "help sustain local agriculture in the long term."[119] In 2009, one grower in the neighborhood of Taos, Paul Cross, said that Sysco is "working to save middle-sized farms all over New Mexico." He added, "The big industrial farms are doing okay and so are the small gardeners, but farms in the middle like mine are disappearing at the rate of 20 percent a year. It's becoming less and less efficient to truck food across the country, so smart companies build a relationship with local farmers." Cross tends a 3,000 square-foot greenhouse that grows "microgreens," young leaves, shoots, and root crops for garnishes and restaurant fare. His farm is called Charybda, New Mexican Spanish for "between a rock and a hard place," which he characterizes as the permanent condition of most small agriculturalists.[120] Phaedra Greenwood, an optimistic Taos journalist, writing in a newsletter called *Enchantment: The Voice of New Mexico Rural Electric Cooperatives*, believes that New Mexico is only a few generations from total food growing independence," except for "items such as oil, coffee, and sugar."[121]

Quivira Coalition

The best model for a collaboration between urban and rural interests in New Mexico might well be foreshadowed in the efforts of the Quivira Coalition, an organization comprised of ranchers, ecologists, and environmentalists who understand the interdependence of cities and countrysides. The Quivira Coalition works to demonstrate that natural systems and human economies can create a hybrid vigor if humans pay attention to the natural world and cooperate with it instead of working against it for short-term gains and long-term depredations.

Early on, the Quivira Coalition was willing to say that the bickering between urban mainstream environmentalism and people who work the land was a waste of enterprise and precious energy, since both parties were striving in their own ways to keep the land vital and safe from those who would exploit it and ruin not only its beauty but also its enormous productive power. Environmentalists took a long time to see that suburban overdevelopment had become as troublesome in New Mexico as desertification in sub-Saharan Africa, threatening to drain cities of natural resources and subdivide the natural world into a dead zone. As with acequias and their valuable water rights, ranch lands attract developers who will pay top dollar to take ranches out of cattle production and build on them. Cattle prices always fluctuate, and struggles with drought and rural poverty lead some ranchers to see selling off their land as an economic godsend.

One way to enable ranchers to continue raising stock while selling off a small portion of their land to developers is through conservation easements in which the ranchers agree to protect the majority of their land from future development. Bridging the urban and rural divide, Albuquerque architect and author Anthony Anella teamed up with New Mexico State University geography professor John Wright to write *Saving the Ranch: Conservation Easement Design in the American West.*[122] In a case study of a development package and conservation easement on the Montosa Ranch, 150 miles southwest of Albuquerque, Anella employed a site selection technique called *sieve* or *overlay mapping,* in which a sizable parcel of land would be divided for development of one house per 100 acres, preserving the remainder of the land for cattle raising. The overlay maps show the precise place on each parcel of land to build a sustainable house, out of the wind, with good solar access, clear views, and no threat of flooding.[123]

When urban environmental groups concerned about watershed preservation began suing state and federal governments to control or prohibit grazing on public lands, what *Orion* magazine called a "religious war" started up, "a pitched battle between the Church of Zero Cow and the Church of Holy Cow."[124] Such actions, and accompanying rhetoric, angered some ranchers and discouraged many more, prompting them to consider selling their spreads to developers. The Quivira Coalition was created by archaeologist-turned-conservationist Courtney White and others to find a way out of this conflict. A proponent of what's known as the Savory Method of grazing—based on the work of wildlife biologist Allan Savory, who advocates imitating the behavior of wild herds—White became a champion of progressive grazing, a friend to both ranchers and conservationists. Simply put, the Savory Method involves rotational grazing, moving cattle from grazing place to grazing place, allowing them to fertilize the soil, break it up with their hooves, and feed, but not letting them to remain long enough to do lasting damage. White writes that the

> emergence of the progressive ranching model across a wide variety of western landscapes . . . means the goal of public lands environmentalism can no longer simply be to "protect" the land from human activity. Instead, its goal should be the same as the progressive ranchers'—to figure out how to live sustainably in our native landscapes. This is something difficult for the average city-bound Sierra Club member, much less an activist to understand—that our western lands, all of them, need more and better stewardship, not less.[125]

By 2005, the Quivira Coalition had more than nine hundred members, as many as three hundred of them working ranchers. The group collaborates with over forty other entities, including Sandia, Santa Ana, and Santa Clara pueblos, the New Mexico State Land Office, Earthworks Institute, the Rio Puerco Management Committee, the Coalition for the Valle Vidal, the Navajo Nation, and Farm to Table. It conducts workshops in progressive grazing, performs demonstration projects in land health and riparian restoration, and funds and produces numerous publications on such matters as water harvesting from low-standard rural roads, erosion control, public lands ranching, and environmental justice.[126]

Despite the Quivira Coalition's efforts, the battle between ranchers and wildlife conservationists continues with the same intensity as the ongoing struggle between rural water planners and city developers. Paul Larmer, publisher of *High Country News*, argues that public land agencies have "for too long favored livestock over wildlife." Grazing reform has not caught on in any major way, he writes. Larmer asserts that the federal government charges ranchers the equivalent of a cup of coffee to graze a cow and a calf on public land for a month. "How could the country's public-grazing system continue in its eco-unfriendly and financially indefensible state, year after year?" he asks. The answer is politics, of course, the same kind of politics that allows the Mining Law of 1872 to continue to this day. The West's "ranching community continues to hold political power far beyond its numbers in many state legislatures and county commissions. There's also the sheer weight of history itself."[127] Public lands were, in large part, created for grazing and timbering and other extractive uses long before environmentalism became a national passion.

The Quivira Coalition stresses cooperation and problem solving rather than political confrontation. And while its success has been unprecedented, its impact remains small. Still, it is a formidable model for defusing entrenched antagonisms and reconciling deeply conflicting interests. Cities and their housing industries, urban environmentalists, and rural farmers and ranchers need to resolve their struggles over the uses of land and water and find ways to begin to end their entrenched mistrust and often outright hostility. Facing long-term drought, global warming, and the prospects of rising fuel prices, farmers, ranchers, and the cities that are their markets must create a new economic and political accommodation among themselves. With these new conditions becoming the dominant patterns for the future, old-style urban growth won't be coming back in the long term. And the old transportation-based model of nationalizing and internationalizing consumer goods, bypassing local food producers and business, won't last for long either. Just as the Quivira Coalition created a symbiotic relationship between like-minded conservationists and ranchers (the Roswell and Cimarron ranches photographed for this book were both recommended by the Quivira Coalition), a new relationship of interdependence needs to be forged between New Mexico's urban and rural populations. More than ever, in the future, they will not be able to survive without each other.

CHAPTER SIX

CONDITIONS, CONCLUSIONS, NEW PATHS TO FOLLOW

In the early spring of 2010, when this final chapter was written, the United States, New Mexico, and the world were stranded in a trough of economic recession and moral indecision, a trough that separated the past, and its crumbling institutions, from a new global reality that most Americans did not want to face. We did not want to believe that our world was undergoing a long-term, massive transition in which the ongoing failure of systems that had nurtured us might soon give way to something else, probably not of our design, something so different from what we had known that we could not prevent or prepare ourselves to meet it.

Some hoped against hope that the financial security of the old status quo would return to pull us out of the trough. Others, myself included, see the end of cheap oil and inexpensive clean water as new realities that will redefine social, political, and economic systems in the

◀ Pecan orchard in the Mesilla Valley, Las Cruces (see page 282). March 2010.

United States and most other nations. New Mexico will have to cope with the soaring costs of peak oil and the dismantling of the petroleum economy with no alternative energy sources sufficiently developed to replace it in the short term. This one condition alone threatens the global economy that depends on cheap fuel to keep goods and produce flowing. Other threats to the status quo, along with drought and water scarcity, are population growth in the developing world; chaotic climate change; costly struggles between alternative energies like solar and wind power and heavy carbon dioxide–producers like coal and natural gas; the high cost and financial uncertainty of nuclear energy and the continued devastating health consequences on Native American communities of uranium mining and processing; and the inevitable (if largely still hidden) consequences of 150 or more years of never-ending environmental pollution.

A New Future Shock

Americans and New Mexicans are living in a state of denial reminiscent of what sociologist Alvin Toffler described in his 1970 book *Future Shock*. Change is accelerating too fast for our minds to adapt to ever-evolving future conditions. We'd rather pretend that nothing new and momentous is happening to our world. The state of future shock described forty years ago by Toffler is a "real sickness," the "disease of change," he wrote. "In the most rapidly changing environment in which man has ever been exposed, we remain pitifully ignorant of how the human animal copes."[1] Future shock in such a situation is "the dizzying disorientation brought on by the premature arrival of the future. It may well be the most important disease of the future." And it seems more than likely that the future he is talking about is the present we are living in and failing to deal with, one in which societies are composed of human beings who find themselves "increasingly disoriented, progressively incompetent to deal rationally with their environments." Toffler warned that "the malaise, mass neurosis, irrationality, a free floating violence already apparent in the contemporary life are merely a foretaste of what may lie ahead unless we come to understand and treat this disease." He refines this diagnosis, writing that future shock "is a time phenomenon, a product of the greatly accelerated rate of change in society. It arises from the superimposition of a new culture on an old one. It is culture shock in one's own society."[2] For many of us living in this future, his analysis rings true.

New Mexico's drought and clean water problems are a manifestation of a global phenomenon, as is the challenge of a rapidly approaching fuel crisis. Few countries in the world appear to be readying themselves to cope with what's ahead. The dizzying quality of future shock is absorbed to some extent by the abundant technological miracles that the world's developed countries have experienced since World War II—from commercial jets and vast highway systems to computers and the Internet. But a few years after the appearance of *Future Shock*, two other volumes, both produced by a think tank called the Club of Rome—*Limits to Growth* in 1972 and *Mankind at the Turning Point* in 1974—predicted that the end of the growth economy and the beginning of a steady state eco-economy, one that grows through quality rather than quantity necessitated by the depletion of natural resources, especially oil, was at hand. Without reference to the Club of Rome's findings, Toffler predicted that, "in effect, our century represents The Great Median Strip running down the center of human history." That "Median Strip" has turned into the trough of the twenty-first century.

What Might Be Ahead

In these concluding remarks, I'm going to survey existing conditions and project them into the future, trying to foresee what radical changes in energy costs and fuel availability mean for the fifth largest state in the union. I'll try to explore what might happen in arid New Mexico with two million people if the drought of the early twenty-first century should extend into mid-century and what that might mean in terms of competition for water with other parched western states. Assuming that all states in the West have similar water pollution issues as New Mexico's, with ours possibly being the worst, I'll also assess the chances we might have of cleaning up industrial and military pollution of the state's aquifers and curtailing urban sprawl and fostering vibrant in-city communities.

Decentralization

In the long run, the future will be built upon the most enduring political structures of the present, which I consider to be not the institutions of the status quo but rather those associated with burgeoning NGOs, with tribal and local governments, with home-owned banks and credit unions, with rural towns and ranching and agricultural associations whose reasons for existing are to serve the public interest. Decentralization is a keystone to what lies ahead. Why would anyone trust big energy, big insurance, big government, big military, or big finance after the mess they've made? It's up to us—single individuals and groups of like-minded people—to search for local solutions to local problems and to bond across communities, working for the common good.

As it has throughout this book, my thinking operates off two basic assumptions. First, human created or not, the world's climate is undergoing a period of rapid and unpredictable change, one that is causing severe drought in the West. Second, the lifeways that revolve around gasoline and the internal combustion engine are about to be severely altered owing to resource scarcity, poor resource management, market opportunism, and a virtually complete lack of preparation for replacement fuel sources that are carbon and petroleum free.

In addition to these two underlying assumptions, three others inform my summary. First is that the recession that began in 2008 in the United States will not go away quickly. In New Mexico, it will combine with drought and peak oil inflation to create pressures and opportunities for local businesses, undercapitalized though they may be. Second, water pollution in New Mexico could prove to become a major health risk. Though it remains uncertain how much of New Mexico's underground water supply is contaminated—by oil and gas drilling, the military-industrial complex, septic systems, and underground pipelines and storage tanks—it is certain that as water supplies dwindle, a greater percentage of our water will be unsafe. And that leaves New Mexico, and by extension, all other DOE nuclear facility states, in a vulnerable position. Third, the relative chaos caused by the technological, political, and economic transitions ahead will be intensified by corporate intractability and government indecision in the future.

Dirty water and petroleum scarcity will be a common misery suffered by virtually everyone in the world at some point in the future. As the climate change conference in Copenhagen in December 2009 made clear, the world cannot agree in a binding way on almost any aspect of the most serious threat to the well-being of all. With no viable alternatives to gasoline and no consistent plans for water conservation on a massive scale, the transition between scarcity and new fuel and water systems will be daunting. In desert New Mexico and in the generally parched American West, these compounding problems will require huge expenditures of public money and massive changes in public attitudes and lifestyles.

Knowing Our Water

The first major task to get New Mexico prepared for the future will be for the legislature to find the funds to correct enormous holes in our knowledge about water. First, we must find out just how much potable and brackish water our thirty or so aquifers possess. It's a tremendously difficult job and one that in the final analysis might produce only educated guesses. Five of New Mexico's aquifers have been scientifically analyzed so far, all with federal funds supporting efforts by the USGS and geologists at New Mexico Tech. We also need at least a ballpark estimate of how much water can reasonably be conserved through various levels of urban and rural rationing, as well as estimates of total brackish water potentially reclaimable through desalinization and its costs over time, including waste disposal. We cannot plan to adapt to a drought if we do not know how much water we actually have. And we need lawmakers and citizens to be clear as to how those aquifers are recharged by surface water and how quickly they can be drained in a time of water scarcity.

Equally vital is an accurate, unbiased assessment of how contaminated our ground and surface waters actually are, particularly those in our urban areas and their counties and near our military bases and national laboratories. We also need a realistic estimate of how much it will cost, not just to treat that water, but to make it drinkable again. Polluted groundwater might just prove to be one of New Mexico's most expensive problems in an age of water scarcity, when every drop counts. If New Mexico is to compete successfully with other states and cities for high-end tech businesses and the green think tanks of the future, it must have clean water to go along with its uncrowded, wide open spaces, which are a powerful selling point for clear thinking about an environmentally sustainable new world. If we don't know how much polluted water we have, where it is, or what the contaminants are, then we're flying blind. Of course, we have been doing that very thing since the last years of World War II.

When water is plentiful, a state might get away with ignoring pollution for a while, until some horrible tragedy turns poisoned water into a scandal. In a protracted drought, when already depleted groundwater is the major factor of survival in the desert, high concentrations of contaminants become not only more apparent but intolerable. In northern New Mexico in and around LANL, in the heavily urbanized Middle Rio Grande Valley with its industry, heavy agriculture, and military research presence, and along the missile ranges and test sites in southern New Mexico, we know groundwater is polluted, but we're not sure how badly. There is enough information available, however, to cause grave concern.

Updates

Earlier chapters of this book have detailed a number of instances of groundwater pollution in the state's most populous areas. Here is an update about one in particular, regarding waste disposal at Los Alamos National Laboratory.

This information comes from the Centers for Disease Control and Prevention (CDC) in its Los Alamos Historic Document Retrieval and Assessment (LAHDRA) report, started in 1999, finished in June 2009, and made available on the Internet in early 2010. The report describes massive "airborne plutonium releases" from the major site of plutonium and polonium processing at LANL from 1948 until 1978. If releases were as high as records from LANL's own "industrial hygiene staff indicate," from 1948 to 1955, "plutonium releases from LANL could easily exceed the independently reconstructed airborne plutonium release totals from the production plants at Hanford, Rocky Flats, and Savannah River combined, even without the other sources and other years at LANL included."[3] The LAHDRA report confirms that "liquid radioactive waste was discharged to Acid-Pueblo Canyon without treatment or monitoring from 1945 through 1950."[4] But there wasn't a year from 1945 until 1996, and perhaps beyond, that plutonium, strontium-90, and other forms of radioactivity weren't released into the waterways of the canyons coming off the Pajarito Plateau and leading to the Rio Grande.[5]

The CDC's LAHDRA report makes it obvious why future generations of New Mexicans must have honest answers about water, soil, and air polluted by LANL's more than sixty-five years of operation in New Mexico and, by extension, honest answers from all the other polluters, such as manufacturers and ever-present extractive industries, who have "underestimated" or downplayed the health risks of their activities. "Because facilities of the nuclear weapons complex used a wide variety of toxic materials and operated for decades behind a 'cloak of secrecy,' public concern about potential health risks from their operations grew as more was learned about past activities and events. And in New Mexico, suspicions would have undermined public confidence even more if it had been known that between 1979 and 1992, each of the major Atomic Energy Commission sites around the country had undergone 'retrospective evaluations of historical releases and potential health effects . . . except Los Alamos.'" And because DOE contractors closely associated with the nuclear-industrial complex carried out the studies, "a general distrust of the results of the studies developed."[6]

It remains to be seen, of course, if there will ever be enough money to actually, and verifiably, clean up all of LANL's waste. And if it should prove true that a plume of radioactive and industrial waste has gotten into the Rio Grande aquifer from years of LANL pouring who knows how many millions of gallons of liquid waste "treated" and untreated into canyons running into the river, there's very little at the moment to be done about it, despite talk of "early warning systems" alerting Santa Fe and Albuquerque of such an event. Water polluted with industrial solvents, pharmaceuticals, petroleum products, explosive chemicals, and sewage cannot be made drinkable without using reverse osmosis, the principle process in the desalinization of seawater. But even very heavy radioactive elements like plutonium, polonium, and strontium are nuclides, or atoms, and are far too small to be contained by a membrane that allows H_2O to pass through it, as would happen in reverse osmosis. Radioactive molecules, however, are big enough to be detained behind the membrane while water flows through. Nanotechnology may supply a remedy in the years ahead.

If you add to this situation well-documented pollution problems with extractive industries, including oil and gas exploration and production, poisonous tailings from uranium milling, and other leavings from New Mexico's long mining history, our dirty water could prove to be a major obstacle to economic recovery and success in the future. And there remain pollution issues from Sandia Labs and other military installations, from fuel and natural gas pipelines that literally crisscross the state, leaking landfills, septic systems, and deteriorating underground gasoline storage tanks, as well as agricultural fertilizers. Granted, much drinking water in the United States is substandard, according to the *New York Times*. Standards of the Clean Drinking Water Act have been broken by so many communities since 2004 that the water "provided to more than 49 million people has contained illegal concentrations of chemicals like arsenic or radioactive substances like uranium, as well as dangerous bacteria often found in sewage."[7]

The End of Sprawl as a Viable Economic Strategy

In an era of water shortages and steadily rising oil prices, sprawling cities in the West will have to face the challenge of downsizing their range, retrofitting their urban and residential cores to accommodate mass transit and neighborhood shopping, and lessening the necessity of automobile use for short urban trips. Green planners, designers, and activists have contemplated this scenario for many decades. Business and political leaders have been in denial for just as long. This is not just the plight of New Mexican cities, of course. Denver, Las Vegas, Phoenix, Tucson, Los Angeles, and San Diego will all be pushed by market forces or required by the federal government to adapt themselves to diminishing quantities of expensive gasoline. That, combined with the housing bust and the need for construction jobs, will drive cities to expend what incentives they can to create denser urban spaces. This could result, as Timothy Egan said in the *New York Times*, in something he calls "slumburbia," suburbs that are half-deserted already because of bank foreclosures. As Eagan asked, "How can a community possibly be healthy when one in eight houses are in some stage of foreclosure? . . . How can a family dream, or even save, when unemployment hovers around 16 percent?"[8] It will take extraordinary creative initiative to reel cities in from their farthest expansions. But even now, the great recession is causing sprawling suburbs to be penalized with foreclosures and stagnant resale values while turning older, denser areas into rich veins of sustainable housing or areas ripe for upgrading and retrofitting to meet the needs of pedestrian and mass-transit-using urbanites.

It's been more than a decade since the White House has had a forward-looking urban policy instead of one rooted in the 1950s. President Obama grasps the enormity of the urban struggle ahead. He's an advocate of modernizing urban mass transit systems, including rail, and repairing and maintaining transportation infrastructure. He opposes continuing old patterns of urban sprawl because he understands its relationship to fuel prices. "Over the long term, we know that the amount of fuel we will use is directly related to our land use decisions and development patterns, much of which have been organized around the principle of cheap gasoline," he's said, and "we must move beyond our simple fixation of investing so many of our transportation dollars in serving drivers and . . . make more investments that make it easier for us to walk, bicycle, and access [other] transportation alternatives."[9] The president is also an advocate of regional planning, which might mean future funds for serious regional transportation and water planning.

As Lester Brown put it in his 2001 book *Eco-Economy*, "As the new century begins, the world is being forced to reconsider the future role of the automobile in cities in one of the most fundamental shifts in transportation thinking over the last century. It is ironic that the very cars and trucks that made massive urbanization possible are now contributing to the deterioration of cities."[10] In Albuquerque, Santa Fe, Rio Rancho, and Las Cruces, making such a transition might well require a major disruption in how land is sold and subdivided, almost a reversal of postwar patterns since the mid-1940s. The challenges to sustainable development in states with so much land and so few people are the lack of discipline and forethought in development that led to sprawl, disregard for the expense of extending public services, and a pathetic disregard for the preservation of open spaces on the edge of town that used to give urban New Mexicans immediate access to the land and its liberating solitude. These challenges differ from those that face cities whose suburbs have melded together. Climate change, drought, and peak oil prices might require New Mexicans to create dense urban enclaves, ones that mirror in practicality, though certainly not in size or culture, patterns of development in the pre-Pueblo world dating back a thousand years or more. Making such changes would cause a political nightmare but might prove to be the only way to simultaneously preserve agricultural open space and open new land for cultivation, creating fuel- and water-efficient oases of conservation and urbanity.

Should the drought of the early twenty-first century turn out to be the new norm, as such dry spells often have been in the past, it is not inconceivable that we might see Rio Rancho, Bernalillo, Corrales, Albuquerque's North and South Valleys and near heights, and Los Lunas and Belen become discrete, tightly packed, relatively self-sufficient urban enclaves surrounded by agricultural open space with little or no development between them, connected by mass transit and containing perhaps half their current populations.

Local Energy, Local Business

The creation of more compact, conservation-oriented New Mexican cities will be made possible in the future by what seems to be an inevitable trend toward decentralized energy and a renaissance of local businesses. The definitive characteristic of the future is that what was once inexpensive and abundant will soon become expensive and scarce. If international climate change agreements require major and costly adjustments in American coal-fired power plants, coal energy prices will inflate dramatically. If market vagaries and astronomical costs and dangers continue to squash nuclear power, or if a nuclear accident, however minor, should occur, energy from regional nuclear sources will rapidly become unavailable. If solar and wind power solve their various PR problems and make major contributions to the energy grid, decentralized energy will be the ideal investment opportunity for families and small businesses in the West.

It doesn't take a Wall Street genius to see that conservation systems and technologies—of water, electricity, natural gas, and petroleum, such as those long promoted by think tanks like the Rocky Mountain Institute—will be in a boom situation as the technologies of the past fade and the tools of the future are late in coming on line. On a macro scale, New Mexico is paving the way to become a hub for alternative energy passing through the state to sites in the West. The Tres Amigas SuperStation planned outside of Clovis would "help route energy from isolated wind and solar installations to urban centers and other places that consume the most power."[11] Governor Bill Richardson said the proposed transfer station would be "historic" and "the largest power converter in the world, making New Mexico the meeting place for America's electricity needs,"[12] according to the Associated Press. The hub would be a triangle of "underground superconductor pipelines, combined with AC/DC converters that synchronize the flow of power between the interconnections."[13] The project is scheduled for completion in 2013. On a smaller scale, cities, towns, and even counties should be able to get off the grid in a substantial way using local solar and wind energy to augment and eventually replace more centralized energy sources. On a micro level, the use of individualized solar and wind systems, along with advanced fuel cells, will help us make inroads against pollution from centralized coal-fired power plants and the potential catastrophes and huge public costs of nuclear power sources. When coal's contaminants become cost prohibitive and peak oil sends gas prices skyrocketing, the market for clean, highly localized, inexpensive alternative energy sources will soar.

Driven largely by rising fuel prices and consumer desire for service, accountability, and locally tailored products, the trend toward decentralization will move through some sectors of the retail and agricultural economy, as well. The locally owned future could be a bonanza for home remodeling and retrofitting businesses, plumbing and electrical subcontractors, and landscapers. The rise of local agriculture and husbandry will also enable local grocers and co-ops to compete more successfully with corporate supermarkets and expensive health food chains.

The End of Dumbbell Journalism

For New Mexico to thrive in a decentralized economy, it will need the help of a new kind of journalism, heavily localized and focused, not on national scandals and distractions, but on serious local, political, business, and environmental issues, a journalism that understands that New Mexico can't compete for business if parts of its environment are a danger to public health. When science for hire persistently minimizes the health hazards of pollution, when negative tipping points are not contemplated, when government and industry get away with deceiving society, when the precautionary principle is looked upon as an impediment to "progress," it's because the local media establishment has been lax and irresponsible. In our state, pollution from military installations and the national labs have been an open secret for years, hidden in plain sight and largely ignored by the state's major media. This is not to say that newspapers are devoid of environmental news, but it is mostly relegated to the back pages. Local TV news covers next to nothing about environmental issues. Some would argue that television news is not structurally designed to deal with complicated issues that can't be explained by sensationalized oversimplification. Some of the best environmental coverage comes from news organizations outside of Albuquerque, including the *Santa Fe New Mexican*, the *Roswell Daily Record*, and dozens of other local papers. But generally, editors and TV producers are suffering from a case of future shock themselves and opt to whitewash environmental risks and emphasize the economic benefits of virtually any new business that appears. A new generation of journalists and electronic media outlets cannot let that continue.

Radically Unprepared

The bottom line, then, is that ten years into the new century, despite years of warnings, New Mexico has developed no consensus, and certainly no pragmatic strategy, for how to survive the difficult transition ahead. And it is not alone. There are no thriving alternative fuel industries anywhere in the United States as yet and certainly no coordinated water conservation efforts among the western states. Cities still hope to grow along the lines of the model of the 1950s. The notion of prosperity joined to a steady state economic philosophy of growth in quality—as opposed to growth in size—remains little short of heresy. New Mexico's major cities still, even in a backbreaking recession, equate success with growing more, rather than with growing better. We have failed to maximize our environmental, professional, and cultural advantages to compete with the struggling, overgrown, mismanaged, water-poor cities around us. With business decentralization brought on by rising fuel prices inflating the cost of imported goods, New Mexico's leadership still does not equate refining and magnifying our cultural assets with economic prosperity. This shortsightedness also misses the likely coming economic combat among cities and states in the West, which will battle for residents, water, and businesses largely on the grounds of quality of life. New Mexico still hasn't come to terms with its advantages in lifestyle and small population. Although raw population growth and suburban territorial expansion is not supportable, business growth from incubating local high-tech start-ups and attracting innovative green companies to expand their creativity in our environment with our labor force and universities is not seen as a possible engine of new prosperity as the great recession deepens. In New Mexico, where the hard conditions of water and fuel scarcity are so obvious, business, government, and education leaders still have not come together to brainstorm a new business model for the future. The legislature, the governor's office, and city officials around the state are still treating the future as an extension of the recent past, and the recession as a mere economic correction, rather than as the first sign of the perfect storm of corporate corruption, resource depletion, political stalemates, and climate chaos that it surely is. While other cities and states are gearing up for water wars, New Mexico and its major cities remain sitting ducks.

But that's not our fate if we choose to move in a different direction. In an overcrowded world, our isolation, small population, and vast, open landscape could be valued—as they always have been—by people who need to work and think in peace. New Mexico is an ideal place for future-thinking entrepreneurs to flourish. In a fuel-constrained transition, our multicultural heritage and scientific and creative communities could draw to us the talent and spirit we need to prosper without swamping us with populations we cannot support. And if we are serious about cleaning up our groundwater, conserving all the water we have, nurturing an agricultural and ranching business climate that focuses on local and regional needs, and redeveloping our urban areas to be contained, culturally rich, and ecologically self-sustaining, then New Mexico could profit from serving as a model for innovative and pragmatic solutions to the problems facing us all in the difficult times ahead.

NOTES

Preface

1. Kevin Fernlund, *The Cold War in the American West* (Albuquerque: University of New Mexico Press, 1998).

Introduction

1. Chuck McCutcheon, *Nuclear Reactions: The Politics of Opening a Radioactive Waste Disposal Site* (Albuquerque: University of New Mexico Press, 2002), 2.
2. John Fleck, "Mountain Snow More Than Just Beautiful," *Albuquerque Journal*, March 4, 2010, A1.
3. Rachel Carson, *Silent Spring* (Boston: Houghton Mifflin, 1962), 5–6.
4. Barry Commoner, *The Closing Circle* (New York: Random House, 1971).
5. Ibid., 29–44.
6. Peter Montague, Lois Marie Gibbs, and Anne Rabe, e-mail to *Rachel's Environment and Health News* mailing list (Center for Health, Environment, and Justice and Be Safe Campaign), September 25, 2003.
7. Jacques Barzun, *A Stroll with William James* (Chicago: University of Chicago Press, 1983), 73.
8. J. R. McNeill, *Something New Under the Sun: An Environmental History of the Twentieth-Century World* (New York: W. W. Norton, 2000), xxiv.
9. *The Economist: The World in 2003*, December 2002.
10. Project Censored, *Censored 2006: The Top 25 Censored Stories* (New York: Seven Stories Press, 2005), 75–77.
11. Aldous Huxley, *Brave New World*, rev. ed. (1932; repr., New York: Bantam Books, 1958), 66–69.
12. Tania Soussan, "N.M. Industry Toxicity Levels Drop," *Albuquerque Journal*, July 1, 2003, D3.
13. Editors of *Time* Magazine, *TIME Almanac 2003*, 151.
14. Kristen Davenport, "Nuclear Waste Levels Unknown," *Santa Fe New Mexican*, October 27, 2000.
15. Kevin J. Fernlund, ed., *The Cold War American West, 1945–1989* (Albuquerque: University of New Mexico Press, 1998), 211–12.

Chapter One

1. Andrew Goudie, *The Human Impact on the Environment*, 5th ed. (Cambridge, MA: MIT Press, 2000), 36.
2. E. L. Moulton, *New Mexico's Future: An Economic and Employment Appraisal* (Albuquerque: University of New Mexico Press, 1945), 57.
3. Rachel Carson, *Silent Spring* (1962; repr., Boston: Houghton Mifflin, 1994), 5.
4. Ibid., 5–6.
5. Goudie, *The Human Impact on the Environment*, 33.
6. Ibid., 379.
7. Mike Marshall, personal communication with author, 2003.
8. Stuart A. Northrop, *Minerals of New Mexico* (Albuquerque: University of New Mexico Press, 1942), 11.
9. R. G. Matson, "The Spread of Maize to the Colorado Plateau," *Archaeology Southwest* 13, no. 1 (Winter 1999): 10–11.
10. Jerry L. Williams, *New Mexico in Maps* (Albuquerque: University of New Mexico Press, 1986), 77, 79.
11. Northrop, *Minerals of New Mexico*, 11–12.
12. Stephen H. Lekson, *The Chaco Meridian: Centers of Political Power in the Ancient Southwest* (Walnut Creek, CA: Alta Mira Press, 1999), 72.
13. Northrop, *Minerals of New Mexico*, 11–12.
14. Kathleen Hunt, "Horse Evolution," The TalkOrigins Archive, http://www.talkorigins.org/faqs/horses/horse_evol.html (accessed August 29, 2006).
15. Dan Scurlock, *From the Rio to the Sierra: An Environmental History of the Middle Rio Grande Basin*, General Technical Report RMRS-GTR-5 (Fort Collins, CO: Rocky Mountain Research Station, U.S. Department of Agriculture, Forest Service, 1998), 115.
16. Linda Cordell, "Albuquerque's Environmental Story: Heritage and the Human Environment—Hispanic Influence," City of Albuquerque, http://www.cabq.gov/aes/s3hisp.html (accessed May 25, 2008).
17. Ibid.
18. Erna Fergusson, *New Mexico: A Pageant of Three Peoples* (1951; repr., Albuquerque: University of New Mexico Press, 1973), 299.
19. Ibid., 298.
20. R. E. Moore, "Horses and Plains Indians," Texas Indians, http://www.texasindians.com/horse.htm (accessed August 28, 2006).
21. Scurlock, *From the Rio to the Sierra*, 273.
22. Ibid.
23. Ibid.
24. Ibid., 274.
25. Ibid.
26. Ibid.
27. Fergusson, *A Pageant of Three Peoples*, 299.
28. Ibid.

29. William deBuys, *Enchantment and Exploitation: Life and Hard Times of a New Mexico Mountain Range* (Albuquerque: University of New Mexico Press, 1985), 280.

30. Wikipedia, "Mexican-American War," http://en.wikipedia.org/wiki/History_of_New_Mexico (accessed September 8, 2006).

31. Wikipedia, "Lincoln County War," http://en.wikipedia.org/wiki/Lincoln_County_War (accessed September 8, 2006).

32. Everything2.com, "Great Buffalo Massacre," http://everything2.com/index.pl?node_id=945485 (accessed September 8, 2006).

33. Wikipedia, "Passenger Pigeon," http://en.wikipedia.org/wiki/Passenger_Pigeon (accessed September 8, 2006).

34. Fergusson, *A Pageant of Three Peoples*, 325.

35. Ibid., 307.

36. Northrop, *Minerals of New Mexico*, 29.

37. U.S. Fish and Wildlife Service, Arizona Ecological Field Office, "Appendix H: Exotic Plant Species in Riparian Ecosystems of the U.S. Southwest," *Southwestern Willow Flycatcher Recovery Plan*, August 2002, http://www.fws.gov/southwest/es/arizona/Documents/SpeciesDocs/SWWF/Final%20Recovery%20Plan/Recovery%20Plan%20Appendices/ H_ExoticPlants.pdf.

38. Jeff Bingaman, "Conservation Corps in New Mexico," New Mexico Features, http://bingaman.senate.gov/features/ccc/projects.cfm (accessed September 16, 2006).

39. Civilian Conservation Corps Legacy, "Roosevelt's Tree Army," http://www.cccalumni.org/history1.html (accessed September 16, 2006).

40. Jerry L. Williams, *New Mexico in Maps*, 322–24.

41. Ken Wright, "Power Plant Developers Pitch a Coal-Fired Future," *New West Network*, http://www.newwest.net/index.php/main/article/5571 (accessed September 24, 2006).

42. Theodore Jojola, personal communication with author, spring 2004.

43. Harvey Wasserman and Norman Solomon, "Uranium Milling and the Church Rock Disaster," chapter 9 in *Killing Our Own: The Disaster of America's Experience with Atomic Radiation* (New York: Delta Books, Dell Publishing, 1982), http://www.ratical.org/radiation/KillingOurOwn/K009.html (accessed September 24, 2006).

44. Southwest Research and Information Center, "Navajo Nation President Signs Bill Banning Uranium Mining and Milling," Uranium Impact Assessment Program, http://www.sric.org/uranium/index.html (accessed September 24, 2006).

45. World Information Service on Energy, "Impacts of Uranium In-Situ Leaching," WISE Uranium Project, http://wise-uranium.org/uisl.html (accessed September 24, 2006).

46. Calvin A. Roberts, *Our New Mexico: A Twentieth-Century History* (Albuquerque: Univeristy of New Mexico Press, 2005), 116.

47. P. Gilbert, personal communication with author, 2006.

48. Tom Barry, Deb Preuseh, and Beth Wood, *Who Runs New Mexico: The New Mexico Power Structure Report* (Albuquerque: New Mexico People and Energy, 1980), 10.

49. CensusScope, "New Mexico Population Growth," Social Science Data Analysis Network, http://www.censusscope.org/us/s35/chart_popl.html (accessed September 25, 2006).

50. Editorial, "City Deserves Hearing on Nuke-Trigger Plan," *Albuquerque Journal*, September 15, 2006, A12.

51. U.S. Department of Energy, Office of Environmental Management, "South Valley Superfund Site," http://web.em.doe.gov/bemr96/svss.html (accessed September 30, 2006).

52. Laura Paskus, "The Little Wilderness That Could," *High Country News*, November 28, 2005, http://www.hcn.org/servlets/hcn.Article?article_id=15941# (accessed October 1, 2006).

53. Wikipedia, "Waste Isolation Pilot Plant," http://enwikipedia.org/wiki/Waste_Isolation_Pilot_Plant (accessed October 1, 2006).

54. Akira Tashiro, "3: Open Air," Discounted Casualties: The Human Cost of Depleted Uranium, May 16, 2000, http://www.chugoku-np.co.jp/abom/uran/us3_e/000516.html (accessed October 1, 2006).

55. Public Citizen, "LES: Proposed Uranium Enrichment Facility near Eunice, New Mexico," Critical Mass Energy Program, http://www.citizen.org/cmep/energy_enviro_nuclear/newnukes/les (accessed October 1, 2006).

56. Associated Press, "Ground Broken for N.M. Uranium Plant," HelenaIr.com, http://www.helenair.com/articles/2006/08/30/national/a08083006_05.txt (accessed October 1, 2006).

57. Wikipedia, "Depleted Uranium." Primary source for pyrophoric: http://www.eh.doe.gov/techstds/standard/hdbk1081/hbk1081e.html.

58. New Mexico Energy, Minerals, and Natural Resources Department, Energy Conservation and Management Division, "Wind Energy," http://emnrd.state.nm.us/EMNRD/ecmd/Wind/wid.htm (accessed October 1, 2006).

Chapter Two

1. John D'Antonio, "Frequently Asked Questions," New Mexico Office of the State Engineer, http://www.ose.state.nm.us/faq_index.html (accessed May 28, 2008).

2. Union of Concerned Scientists, "Worldwide Nuclear Arsenals," http://www.ucsusa.org/assets/documents/nwgs/worldwide-nuclear-arsenals-final.pdf (accessed May 11, 2008).

3. John Gregory, "Albuquerque's Environmental Story: Population Growth," http://www.cabq.gov/aes/s5pop.html (accessed May 10, 2008).

4. Bob Quick, "City's Housing Market 'Cooling,'" *Santa Fe New Mexican*, October 8, 2005, A1.

5. V. B. Price, "Landscape and Survival: Thoughts on New Urbanism and Ancestral Puebloan/Pueblo Strategies for Designing Pragmatic Desert Built Environments," in *Canyon Gardens: The Ancient Pueblo Landscapes of the American Southwest*, ed. V. B. Price and Baker Morrow (Albuquerque: University of New Mexico Press, 2006), 173–74.

6. Fernando Pessoa, *The Selected Prose of Fernando Pessoa*, ed. and trans. Richard Zenith (New York: Grove Press, 2001), 10.

7. Tania Soussan, "Aquifer Is Lower Than Expected," *Albuquerque Journal*, February 21, 2003.

8. Jennifer McKee, "Water Under LANL Moving: Study Cites Pull of Santa Fe Wells," *Albuquerque Journal*, February 16, 2002, E3.

9. Ira G. Clark, *Water in New Mexico: A History of Its Management and Use* (Albuquerque: University of New Mexico Press, 1987), 675–78.

10. Richard N. Ellis, ed., *New Mexico Historic Documents* (Albuquerque: University of New Mexico Press, 1975), 130.

11. Lisa Robert, "Hijacking the Rio Grande: Aquifer Mining in an Arid River Basin," *Geotimes*, May 2004.

12. Annie Greenberg, "New Bills on San Juan Water Rights Introduced," *Navajo Times*, December 21, 2006, A1.

13. Eric Mack, "Pueblo Water Battle Nears Its End," *High Country News*, October 30, 2006, 5–6.

14. Jane Marx, "They Had Command of the Waters: An Overview of Indian Water Rights," *Water Law Issues in New Mexico* 42, no. 40 (October 2, 2003): 2–4.

15. Ibid.

16. Sacredlands.org, "Taos Blue Lake," http://www.sacredland.org/historical_sites_pages/taos_blue_lake.html (accessed January 1, 2007).

17. G. Emlen Hall, *High and Dry: The Texas–New Mexican Struggle for the Pecos River* (Albuquerque: University of New Mexico Press, 2002), 3.

18. Ibid., 198.

19. Staci Matlock, "Keeping Rivers Flowing," *Santa Fe New Mexican*, January 8, 2007.

20. Hall, *High and Dry*, 222.

21. Matlock, "Keeping Rivers Flowing."

22. Wendy Brown, "Fragile Food Supply," *Santa Fe New Mexican*, January 14, 2007.

23. Ibid.

24. Paula Garcia, "In the Year of Water, Acequias Will Be Crucial," New Mexico Acequia Association, news release, 2007.

25. Paula Garcia, "Community and Culture versus Commodification: The Survival of Acequias and Traditional Communities in New Mexico," *Voices from the Earth* (Winter 2000): 5–6.

26. Janet Jarrett, "Presentation to the Annual Congress of the New Mexico Acequia Association" (lecture, Taos, New Mexico, December 2, 2006).

27. Ibid.

28. City of Deming, "State Water Plan: Frequently Asked Questions," http://www.cityofdeming.org/Tom/Mainframe.html (accessed June 18, 2008).

29. Char Miller, ed., *Water in the West: A High Country News Reader* (Corvallis: Oregon State University Press, 2000).

30. New Mexico First, "Twenty-eighth New Mexico First Town Hall: New Mexico's Water—Perception, Reality, and Imperatives," http://www.nmfirst.org/library/waterexs.htm (accessed February 3, 2007).

31. Ibid.

32. Michael Davis, "Groundwater Tested at the Site of Sick Bosque," *Albuquerque Journal*, August 18, 2004, West Side Journal.

33. Lisa Robert, "Appeal Pending on City DWP Permit," *APA Watermark*, March 2006, 1.

34. Ibid.

35. Ibid.

36. Ibid.

37. Ibid.

38. Ibid., 1–2.

39. Albuquerque–Bernalillo County Water Utility Authority, "2007 New Water Treatment Plant and Water Conservation Calendar," November.

40. Kate Nash, "A Drop in the Bucket: Important Conservation Data," *Albuquerque Tribune*, January 25, 2002.

41. Frank Zoretich, "Mayor: Pipeline Would Have Saved City from Fish Fight," *Albuquerque Tribune*, November 11, 2003.

42. Jim Baca, "Heart of City Water Strategy: Diversified Balance of Actions," *Albuquerque Journal*, October 9, 2000, Op-Ed Page.

43. U.S. Water News Online, "Emergency Water Conservation Measures Implemented in Drought-Stricken Southwest," http://www.uswaternews.com/archives/arcconserv/6swdrou.html (accessed February 25, 2007).

44. Wikipedia, "Desalination," http://en.wikipedia.org/wiki/Desalination (accessed June 18, 2008).

45. The RadioActivist Campaign, "Study Refutes LANL Claim: Radioactivity leaking into Rio Grande Is above 'Background,'" news release, October 27, 2003.

46. James R. Bartolino, "The Hydrologic Reality of the Basin" (presentation to the Tenth Annual Middle Rio Grande Water Assembly, University of New Mexico, Albuquerque, June 18–19, 2004).

47. Ibid.

Chapter Three

1. Conservation Voters New Mexico, *2007 Legislative Scorecard* (Santa Fe: Conservation Voters New Mexico, 2007).
2. Barry Massey, "State Has Stake in Clovis Plant," *Albuquerque Journal*, May 30, 2007, A1.
3. Ibid.
4. Laura Nesbitt, "Biomass Plant Brings Earful," *Albuquerque Journal*, May 22, 2007, C2.
5. Ibid.
6. State of New Mexico, Office of the Governor, Executive Order 2005–056: Environmental Justice Executive Order, November 18, 2005.
7. Louis S. Warren, ed., *American Environmental History* (Malden, MA: Blackwell Publishing, 2003), 322.
8. Ibid., 322–23.
9. Carolyn Merchant, ed., *Major Problems in American Environmental History* (Lexington, MA: D. C. Heath, 1993), 532.
10. Ira G. Clark, *Water in New Mexico: A History of Its Management and Use* (Albuquerque: University of New Mexico Press, 1987), 599.
11. Ibid.
12. Ibid.
13. Ibid.
14. Ibid., 603.
15. Ibid.
16. Ibid., 606.
17. Ibid., 607.
18. Ward Alan Minge, "Epilogue: Toward Self-Determination," in *Ácoma, Pueblo in the Sky* (Albuquerque: University of New Mexico Press, 1991), condensed by Karen M. Strom as "Acoma Opposition to the El Malpais National Monument," http:www.hanksville.org/voyage/geology/acoma_malpais.html (accessed June 11, 2007).
19. Ibid.
20. Indianz.com, "Sandia Pueblo Land Settlement Signed into Law," http://www.indianz.com/news/2003/000798.asp (accessed June 11, 2007).
21. Signpost staff, "Sandia Mountain Agreement Reached in Senate," *Sandoval Signpost*, November 2002, http://www.sandovalsignpost.com/nov02/html/up_front.html (accessed June 11, 2007).
22. James W. Brosnan, "Lobbyist Made 1.17M off Pueblo," *Albuquerque Tribune*, January 3, 2006, http://www.abqtrib.com/albq/nw_national_government/ (accessed June 11, 2007).
23. Signpost staff, "Sandia Mountain Agreement Reached in Senate."
24. Marc Simmons, *New Mexico: A History* (New York: W. W. Norton, 1977), 183.

25. William deBuys, "Separating Sense from Nonsense in New Mexico's Forests," *High Country News*, February 5, 1996, http://www.hcn.org/ (accessed June 10, 2007).

26. Simmons, *New Mexico: A History*, 183.

27. Mario Encinias, "Iratéo: The life of Reies López Tijerina," http://www.unm.edu/ (accessed July 1, 2007).

28. José Armas, "Courthouse Raid Anniversary Observed," *Albuquerque Journal*, May 24, 1992, editorial page.

29. David Colbert, ed., *Eye Witness to the American West* (New York: Penguin, 1998), 231.

30. Paul Larmer, "Sierra Club Foundation vs. Ray Graham III: The Case That Won't Die," *High Country News*, June 9, 1997, http://www.hcn.org/ (accessed July 4, 2007).

31. Annie P. Michaelis, "Priority-Setting Ethics in Public Health," *Journal of Public Health Policy* 23, no. 4 (Winter 2002): 399.

32. Carolyn Carlson, "Neighbors Target Crime, Pollution," *Albuquerque Journal*, April 2, 2004.

33. Ibid.

34. Ibid.

35. Carolyn Carlson, "Cleanup Expected to Take Years," *Albuquerque Journal*, November 19, 2003, West Side Journal, 1–2.

36. William Paul Robinson, "Ground Water Contamination in a Poor and Minority Community: The South Valley of Albuquerque, New Mexico" (unpublished report, Southwest Research and Information Center, 1985), 19.

37. Ibid., 5.

38. Environmental Protection Agency, "EPA Region 6 South Valley (Bernalillo County), Albuquerque, New Mexico, EPA ID no. NMD980745558, Site ID 0600881" (August 6, 2007), 2.

39. Robinson, "Ground Water Contamination in a Poor and Minority Community," 17.

40. Environmental Protection Agency, "EPA Region 6 South Valley (Bernalillo County)," 2.

41. Ibid.

42. Tony Davis, "South Valley Water Pollution Worsens," *Albuquerque Tribune*, July 27, 1988, A3.

43. Environmental Protection Agency, "EPA Region 6 South Valley (Bernalillo County)," 1.

44. Ibid.

45. Ibid., 2.

46. Ibid.

47. Burt Hubbard, "South Valley Group Protests Drinking Water Quality," *Albuquerque Tribune*, 1981.

48. Ibid.

49. Robinson, "Ground Water Contamination in a Poor and Minority Community," 20.

50. Ibid.

51. Ibid.

52. "Water Problem Faces Area South of Albuquerque," *Albuquerque Tribune*, February 4, 1970, A12.

53. Layne Vickers, "Quick Action Urged on Nitrate in Water," *Albuquerque Journal*, n.d., 1970, A1.

54. Tony Davis, "Snafus Plague Pollution Tests," *Albuquerque Tribune*, September 4, 1990, A3, Inset.

55. Ibid.

56. Ibid.

57. Ibid.

58. Nolan Hester, "Forgotten Dump May Be Time Bomb," *Albuquerque Journal*, April 25, 1982, A1.

59. Ibid.

60. Ibid.

61. Ibid., A4.

62. Ibid., A1, A4.

63. Ibid., A4.

64. Ibid.

65. Ibid., A1.

66. Ibid., A4.

67. Ibid.

68. Ibid.

69. Denise Tessier, "Study Indicates 'Nitrate Corridor' Migrating South," *Albuquerque Journal*, February 4, 1984, B1.

70. Nolan Hester, "Base Starts Search for Toxic Wastes," *Albuquerque Journal*, July 30, 1982, C1.

71. Tony Davis, "Mountainview Activists to Meet with Kirtland," *Albuquerque Tribune*, March 7, 1991.

72. Nolan Hester, "Forgotten Dump May Be Time Bomb."

73. Tony Davis, "Closed PNM Power Plant Leaks Pollution," *Albuquerque Tribune*, March 15, 1991, A8.

74. Ibid.

75. Public Service Company of New Mexico, "Fact Sheet/Statement of Basis, PNM Persons Station, Proposals for No Further Action Status for 7 Solid Waste Management Units/Areas of Concern, RCRA Permit No. NMT360010342–1" (May 13, 2005).

76. "American Car Takes over Eidal Plant This Fall," *Albuquerque Tribune*, September 5, 1952.

77. "Type of Work Done by ACF Is Disclosed: Division Makes Reactors, Missile Components," *Albuquerque Tribune*, July 20, 1957.

78. Ibid.

79. "'Project Rover' Is Small Part of ACF Plant's Atomic Role," *Albuquerque Tribune*, May 1, 1958.

80. Ibid.

81. "ACF Conducting Nuclear Rocket Propulsion Study," *Albuquerque Tribune*, May 15, 1960.

82. Bruce Behrhorst, "Nuclear Rocket Power in Space: Generational Legacy," http://www.nuclearspace.com/a_gen_legacy.htm (accessed September 6, 2007).

83. William H. Carlile, "Superfund New Mexico Drops Claim against Agencies in Lawsuit Seeking $4 Billion in Damages," news release, November 2002.

84. Associated Press, "South Valley Pollution Lawsuit Suffers Setbacks," May 5, 2003, http://fulltrial.newsedge-web.com/ (accessed June 2, 2003).

85. Carolyn Carlson, "Superfund Site Settlement Reached," *Albuquerque Journal*, January 12, 2006.

86. Jack Matson, Preliminary Expert Report, personal notes (November 2000).

87. Ibid.

88. Ibid.

89. Ibid.

90. Gael D. Ulrich and Palligarnai T. Vasudevan, "Predesign for Pollution Prevention and Control," *Chemical Engineering Progress* (June 2007): 53–59.

91. Matson, Preliminary Expert Report.

92. Ibid.

93. Ibid.

94. Matson is referring to New Mexico Statute 1742; ibid., 12.

95. Ibid., 14.

96. Ibid.

97. Ibid., 15–16.

98. Ground Water Quality Bureau, "Ground Water: New Mexico's Buried Treasure," New Mexico Environment Department, http://www.nmenv.state.nm.us/gwb/buried_treasure.htm (accessed April 5, 2002).

99. *State of New Mexico v. General Electric Company et. al*, Civ. 99 1118 (U.S. District Court for the District of New Mexico, 1999), 1.

100. Ibid., 22–23.

101. Associated Press, "South Valley Pollution Lawsuit Suffers Setbacks."

102. Michael L. Rodburg and Timothy L. Borkoski, "New Mexico v. General Electric: A Cautionary Tale," *New Jersey Law Journal* CLXXVI, no. 9 (May 31, 2004): Index 720.

103. Ibid.

104. Ibid.

105. Ibid.

106. Jack Matson, e-mail to author, June 4, 2007.
107. *State of New Mexico, et al., v. General Electric Company, et al.*, No. 04–2191 (U.S. Court of Appeals, Tenth Circuit, 2006), 33.
108. Carlson, "Superfund Site Settlement Reached."
109. Carolyn Carlson, "Superfund Site Ideas Offered by Residents," *Albuquerque Journal*, December 1, 2006, West Side Journal.
110. Tony Davis, "Giving Sewage the Treatment," *Albuquerque Tribune*, September 2, 1992, A1.
111. Dan McKay, "Supefund Plan 'Unacceptable,'" *Albuquerque Journal*, April 11, 2002, D1.
112. Environmental Protection Agency, "AT&SF Albuquerque Superfund Site, Bernalillo County, South Valley Area, New Mexico, EPA Region 6, EPA ID no. NMD980622864, Site ID 0600879" (October 2006), 2.
113. Ibid.
114. Ibid.
115. Dan McKay, "Supefund Plan 'Unacceptable.'"
116. Environmental Protection Agency, "A Citizen's Guide to Pump and Treat," EPA 542-F-01–025, December 2001, http://www.epa.gov/superfund/sites.
117. Michael Davis, "South Valley Air Permits Contested," *Albuquerque Journal*, March 22, 2006, West Side Journal, 1.
118. Ibid., West Side Journal, 2.
119. Ibid.
120. Nathan Tafoya, "Plans for Cement Plant Opposed," *Albuquerque Tribune*, July 28, 2005, A3.
121. Wasserman and Solomon, "Uranium Mining and the Church Rock Disaster," 1.
122. Ibid., 2.
123. Ibid., 6.
124. Uranium Information Center, "The Nuclear Fuel Cycle," Australian Uranium Association, http://www.uic.com.au/nip65.htm (accessed October 13, 2007).
125. Wasserman and Solomon, "Uranium Mining and the Church Rock Disaster," 2.
126. Uranium Information Center, "The Nuclear Fuel Cycle."
127. Ibid.
128. Ibid.
129. World Health Organization, "Depleted Uranium Fact Sheet," no. 257, January 2003, http://www.who.int/mediacentre/factsheets/fs257/en/ (accessed October 13, 2007).
130. Dusty Horwitt, "Uranium Boom in the West," *Denver Post*, January 27, 2007, http://www.denverpost.com/opinion/ci_5089268 (accessed October 13, 2007).

131.   Judy Pasternak, "Mining Firms Again Eyeing Navajo Land," *Los Angeles Times*, November 22, 2006.

132.   Uranium Information Center, "The Nuclear Fuel Cycle."

133.   Judy Pasternak, "Mining Firms Again Eyeing Navajo Land."

134.   Eastern Navajo Diné Against Uranium Mining, "Why Navajos Resist New Uranium Mining," Southwest Research and Information Center, http://sric.or/workbook/features/V22_2.htm (accessed March 18, 2004).

135.   Chris Shuey, "Uranium Mining Plan Splits Navajo Communities in New Mexico," Southwest Research and Information Center, http://www.wise-uranium.org/upcrp.html (accessed August 1, 2004).

136.   Ben Neary, "Judge OKs Uranium Mining near Navajo Nation," *Santa Fe New Mexican*, July 26, 2005, A3.

137.   Ibid.

138.   Jodi Peterson, "Underground Movement," *High Country News*, October 1, 2007, 4–5.

139.   V. B. Price, "Murky Waters: Speedy approvals of uranium leaching can harm land, lives," *Albuquerque Tribune*, August 24, 2007, B1.

140.   Ibid.

141.   Ibid.

142.   Southwest Organizing Project, Toxic Tour flyer, November 3, 2007.

143.   Manuel Pino, "Riding the Yellowcake Road," part 2 of the Global Voices Against Uranium Indigenous World Uranium Summit, *Voices from the Earth* 8, no. 2 (Summer 2007): 1.

144.   Ibid.

145.   Ibid., 3.

146.   Perry Charley, "The Navajo Nation: A Uranium History," *Voices from the Earth* 8, no. 2 (Summer 2007): 7.

147.   Peter Montague, "Resistance at Desert Rock," *Voices from the Earth* 7, no. 4 (Winter 2006/2007): 10, excerpted from *Rachel's Democracy & Health News*, no. 889 (January 11, 2007).

148.   Ibid.

149.   Ollie Reed, Jr., "Zunis Give Thanks for Lake Rescue," *Albuquerque Tribune*, August 8, 2003, A3.

150.   Ibid.

151.   Ibid.

Chapter Four

1.   Government Accountability Project, "Media Event: Plutonium, Hazardous Radioactivity Found in NM Water, Plants, Dust as Domenici 'Celebrates' New Plutonium Warhead Certification," Whistleblower.org, July 10, 2007, http://mexiconuevo.wordpress.com/2007/07/10/media-event-plutonium-hazardous-radioactivity-found-in-nm-water-plants-dust-as-domenici-celebrates-new-plutonium-warhead-certification/ (accessed January 1, 2008).

2. Andy Letterman, "Officials Doubt Plutonium Taints City Wells," *Santa Fe New Mexican*, September 17, 2007, http://www.freenew-mexican.com/news/68675.html (accessed January 1, 2008).

3. John Stauber and Sheldon Rampton, *Toxic Sludge Is Good for You: Lies, Damn Lies, and the Public Relations Industry* (Monroe, ME: Common Courage Press, 1995).

4. Centers for Disease Control, "Public Health Assessment AT&SF (Albuquerque), Bernalillo County, New Mexico, CERCLIS no. NMD980622864," Department of Health and Human Services, Agency for Toxic Substances and Disease Registry (February 1, 1995), http://www.atsdr.cdc.gov/hac/PHA/atsf/atsf_p1.html (accessed April 17, 2006).

5. V. B. Price, "Safe to Drink? Government Needs to Give Assessment on Water Quality," *Albuquerque Tribune*, July 20, 2007, http://www.abqtrib.com/news/2007/jul/20/vb-price-safe-drink/ (accessed June 15, 2008).

6. Colorado Department of Public Health and Environment, Technical Topic Papers: Rocky Flats Public Exposure Studies, http://www.cdphe.state.co.us/rf/plutorelease.htm (accessed January 1, 2008).

7. Health Physics Society, "What Types of Radiation Are There?," http://www.hps.org/publicinformation/ate/faqs/radiationtypes.html (accessed December 31, 2007).

8. Elenafilatova.com, "Alpha, Beta, Gama," http://www.angelfire.com/extreme4/kiddofspeed/chapter34.html (accessed December 31, 2007).

9. Window on State Government, "El Cobalto," Bordering the Future, http://www.window.state.tx.us/border/ch09/cobalto.html (accessed July 5, 2007).

10. William Robert Johnston, "Ciudad Juarez orphaned source dispersal, 1983," Database of radiological incidents and related events—Johnston's Archive, November 23, 2005, http://www.johnstonsarchive.net/nuclear/radevents/1983MEX1.html (accessed July 5, 2007).

11. Harvey Wasserman, "The Genius Doctor Who Diagnosed Nuke Power's Deadly Disease," *The Free Press*, September 7, 2007.

12. Ibid.

13. Parade.com, "The Dirty Side of Domestic Fuel," *Parade*, December 20, 2007.

14. Brad Buck, "State, Santa Fe County Tough on Oil, Gas Restrictions," *New Mexico Free Press*, August 4, 2010.

15. Associated Press, "Records Burial Stuns Workers," *Journal North*, January 9, 2007.

16. Ibid.

17. U.S. Energy Information Administration, "New Mexico 2004: Distribution of Wells by Product Rate Bracket," http://www.eia.doe.gov/pub/oil_gas/petrosystem/nm_table.html (accessed June 15, 2007).

18. Eric Billingsley, "NM to Implement New Pipelines Safety Standards," *New Mexico Business Weekly*, January 10, 2003, http://www. bizjournals.com/albuquerque/stories/2003/01/13/story6.html (accessed January 6, 2008).

19. Earthworks, "Groundwater Contamination," http://www.earthworksaction.org/NM_GW_Contamination.cfm (accessed January 6, 2008).

20. New Mexico Environment Department, Groundwater Quality Bureau, "Table 10: Companies That Reported More than 10,000 Pounds of Hazardous Material in NM," Report on Air Quality Data and Health Study Summaries for the Mountain View Area, August 2004.

21. New Mexico Environment Department, "Statement of Basis/Final Decision and Response to Comments Summary, Sparton Technology, Inc.," RCRA Corrective Action, Region VI, ID no. 2332, NMD 083 212 332, June 1996.

22. San Juan Citizens Alliance, "Desert Rock Power Plant," http://www.sanjuancitizens.org/air/desertrock.shtml (accessed June 15, 2008).

23. Ibid.

24. John E. Burghardt, "Effective Management of Radiological Hazards at Abandoned Radioactive Mine and Mill Sites," March 1996, http://www2.nature.nps.gov/grd/distland/amlindex. htm#technicalreports.

25. Samuel S. Epstein, "Legislative Proposals for Reversing the Cancer Epidemic and Controlling Run-away Industrial Technologies," *International Journal of Health Services* 30, no. 2 (2000): 353–71.

26. Rene Kimball, "Study Finds High, but Safe, City Radiation Levels," *Albuquerque Journal*, August 7, 1991.

27. Dana Coyle et al., *Deadly Defense: Military Radioactive Landfills* (New York: Radioactive Waste Campaign, 1988), 126.

28. Ibid.

29. Ibid., 128.

30. Ibid.

31. Nuclear Information and Resource Service, "Radiation: The Myth of the Millirem," http://www.nirs.org/factsheets/mythmilliremfctsht.htm (accessed January 17, 2008).

32. Ibid.

33. Kathy Helms, "Udall (D-NM): Navajo Cancer Free before Uranium," *Native Unity Digest*, November 15, 2007, http://nativeunity.blogspot. com/2007/12/udall-d-nm-navajo-cancer-free-before.html (accessed January 12, 2008).

34. Ibid.

35. Ibid.

36. Nuclear Information and Research Service, "Radiation Chart," http://www.nirs.org/radiation/radchart.htm (accessed March 23, 2008).

37. U.S. Department of Energy, "WIPP Receives 100th Remote-Handled Waste Shipment," news release, Carlsbad Field Office, Waste Isolation Pilot Plant, January 5, 2008.

38. U.S. Department of Energy, "WIPP Transportation System," Carlsbad Field Office, Waste Isolation Pilot Plant, January 2002.

39. David Giuliani, "WIPP Truck Swerves Off Highway," *Los Alamos Monitor*, March 18, 2008.

40. Jack Ehn, "Take a Hike, James Watkins," *Albuquerque Tribune*, October 7, 1991, Opinion, A6.

41. John German, "First Shipment to WIPP Marks End of a 25-Year Era, and a New Beginning, for Sandia," *Sandia Lab News* 51, no. 7 (April 9, 1999), http://www.sandia.gov/LabNews/LN04–09–99/wipp_story.htm (accessed January 16, 2008).

42. Ibid.

43. Janet Greenwald and Don Hancock, "Modification to WIPP Permit Threatens Public Health," *Co-Op Connection*, February 2006, 15.

44. Associated Press, "State Beefing Up WIPP Oversight," *Albuquerque Journal*, November 4, 2004, D3.

45. Don Hancock, personal conversation with author, November 18, 2007.

46. Ibid.

47. John Fleck, "Liquid Waste at WIPP an Error," *Albuquerque Journal*, July 26, 2007, A1.

48. Don Hancock, personal conversation with author, November 11, 2007.

49. Concerned Citizens for Nuclear Safety, "WIPP and Environmental Risks," http://www.nuclearactive.org/wipp/10reasons.html (accessed January 17, 2008).

50. Ibid.

51. Ferenc Szasz, *Larger Than Life: New Mexico in the Twentieth Century* (Albuquerque: University of New Mexico Press, 2006), 160.

52. Ibid., 163.

53. Wade H. Nelson, "Nuclear Explosion Shook Farmington," Special to the *Herald*, 1999, http://www.wadenelson.com/gasbuggy.html (accessed January 19, 2008).

54. Jennie Lay, "Drilling Could Wake a Sleeping Giant," *High Country News*, March 7, 2005, http://www.hcn.org/servlets/hcn.Article?article_id=15321 (accessed January 19, 2008).

55. Sandia National Laboratories, "Waste Isolation Pilot Plant," http://www.nwer.sandia.gov/wlp/factsheets/wipp.pdf (accessed June 16, 2008).

56. Ibid.

57. Ibid.

58. The Elite 25, letter to Governor Bill Richardson, August 20, 2003.

59. Paul Robinson, "Cash for Cleanups," *Albuquerque Tribune*, January 8, 2004, http://www.abqtrib.com/archives/opinions04/010804_opinions_waste.shtml.

60. Ibid.

61. Ibid.

62. New Mexico Environment Department, "Compliance Order on Consent Pursuant to the New Mexico Hazardous Waste Act 74-4-10: The United States Department of Energy and Sandia Corporation, Sandia National Laboratories, Bernalillo County, New Mexico," April 29, 2004.

63. Ibid.

64. Ibid.

65. Ibid.

66. Sandia National Laboratories, *Annual Site Environmental Report for Sandia National Laboratories, New Mexico*, September 2004, http://www.prod.sandia.gov/cgi-bin/techlib/access-control.pl/2004/042813.pdf (accessed June 16, 2008).

67. Sharissa G. Young et al., "New Approaches to Solve Remediation Challenges Using Technological Applications at the Sandia National Laboratories Chemical Waste Landfill" (unpublished paper, Sandia National Laboratories, n.d.).

68. Citizen Action New Mexico, Citizen Action Comments on Sandia Lab's Long-Term Monitoring and Maintenance Plan for the Mixed Waste Landfill, January 18, 2008, http://www.radfreenm.org/pages/lg-2008jan31a.doc (accessed June 16, 2008).

69. Dave McCoy, "Sandia Labs' Permit Request Asks for Toxic Open Air Burning and Leaving Nuclear Dumps above Albuquerque's Aquifer without Monitoring," news release, Citizen Action New Mexico, January 20, 2008.

70. Ibid.

71. Ibid.

72. Ibid.

73. Ibid.

74. Susan Dayton, "Study Predicts Sandia Dump Will Contaminate Albuquerque's Drinking Water," news release, Citizen Action New Mexico, February 9, 2006.

75. Ibid.

76. Susan Dayton, "Deficiencies in Monitoring Well Construction May Mask Contamination at Sandia Waste Dump," news release, Citizen Action New Mexico, June 12, 2006.

77. Editors, "Landfill Secrecy Toxic," *Albuquerque Journal*, October 25, 2007, Opinion.

78. Peter Rice, "Scientist's Mysterious Death while Working at Landfill Stirs Conflict," *Albuquerque Tribune*, May 29, 2007, http://www.abqtrib.com/news/2007/may/29/ (accessed January 26, 2008).

79. G. Fred Lee and A. Jones-Lee, "Overview of Landfill Post-Closure Issues," http://www.gfredlee.com/asceco2a.htm (accessed January 27, 2008).

80. Ibid.

81. Environmental Protection Agency, "Municipal Landfills in the United States and Protectorates," table 1 in *ERG Estimates*, March 20, 1996, http://www.epa.gov/epaoswer/non-hw/municpl/landfill/tab_1.pdf (accessed June 16, 2008).

82. Southwest Research and Information Center, "Problems with Proposed New Landfills in New Mexico," *Voices from the Earth* 2, no. 4 (2001), http://www.sric.org/voices/2001/v2n4/landfillv2n4.html (accessed January 26, 2008).

83. Ibid.

84. "Wagon Mound Landfill Special Permit Denied," *New Mexico Business Weekly*, December 18, 2007, http://www.bizjournals.com/ (accessed January 26, 2008).

85. Dale Lezon, "Sheriff to Halt Loads of Debris," *Albuquerque Journal*, August 15, 2000, B3.

86. Mike Smith, "Alamagordo's Atari Landfill," *My Strange New Mexico*, January 26, 2007, http://www.mystrangenewmexico.com/ (accessed January 26, 2008).

87. M. E. McQuiddy, "Tons of Atari Games Buried: Dump Here Utilized," *Alamogordo Daily*, September 25, 1983.

88. Environmental News Service, "U.S. Allows Radioactive Materials in Ordinary Landfills," May 14, 2007, http://www.ens-newswire.com/ens/may2007/2007-05-14-08.asp (accessed January 29, 2008).

89. Ibid.

90. Ibid.

91. U.S. Department of Energy, "Secretary Richardson Suspends Release of Materials from DOE Facilities," news release, Office of Public Affairs, July 13, 2000.

92. Bill Richardson, "Memorandum for Heads of Department Elements, Release of Surplus and Scrap Materials," U.S. Department of Energy, July 13, 2000.

93. Ibid.

94. Diane D'Arrigo and Mary Olson, "Out of Control—On Purpose: DOE's Dispersal of Radioactive Waste into Landfills and Consumer Products," Nuclear Information and Resource Service, May 14, 2007, 7.

95. Ibid., 43–44.

96. Ibid., 44.

97. Ibid., 36.

98. Ibid.

99. Nuclear Information and Resource Service, "Coming to a Dump Near You: Nuclear Waste," OMB Watch, 2008, http://www.ombwatch.org/article/articleview/3851/1/1?TopicID=1 (accessed January 31, 2008).

100. Peter Rice, "Ramping Up Recycling," *Albuquerque Tribune*, September 25, 2006, A1, A3.
101. Ibid.
102. Ibid.
103. Peter Rice, "City Aims to Dig into Recycling Controversy," *Albuquerque Tribune*, February 17, 2007, A4.
104. George W. Dickerson, "A Sustainable Approach to Recycling Urban and Agricultural Organic Waste," August 2004, http://www.cahe. nmsu.edu/pubs/_h/h-159.html (accessed January 27, 2008).
105. William Goldfarb and Uta Krogmann, "Unsafe Sewage Sludge or Beneficial Biosolids?: Liability, Planning, and Management Issues Regarding the Land Application of Sewage Treatment Residuals," *Boston College Environmental Affairs Law Review* (Summer 1999), http://findarticles.com/ (accessed January 27, 2008).
106. Dickerson, "A Sustainable Approach to Recycling Urban and Agricultural Organic Waste."
107. Jack King, "Professors Study More Efficient Way to Generate Renewable Energy from Waste," New Mexico State University, February 12, 2002, http://www.nmsu.edu/ (accessed January 26, 2008).
108. H. Josef Hebert, "Lab Defends Replacement Plutonium Pits," *Albuquerque Tribune*, January 21, 2008, A2.
109. "U.S. Plutonium Plans: Weapons, Waste, and Proliferation," Alliance for Nuclear Accountability newsletter, http://www.ananuclear. org (Spring 2007).
110. Ibid.
111. Associated Press, "Curry: LANL Should Clean Up before Making Pits," *Gallup Independent*, March 14, 2008.
112. Wikipedia, "Atomic Bombings of Hiroshima and Nagasaki," http://en.wikipedia.org/ (accessed February 8, 2008).
113. Wikipedia, "Teller-Ulam design," http://en.wikipedia.org/ (accessed February 8, 2008).
114. Joseph Masco, *The Nuclear Borderlands: The Manhattan Project in Post–Cold War New Mexico* (Princeton, NJ: Princeton University Press, 2006).
115. Ibid., 236.
116. Ibid.
117. Ibid., 193.
118. Ibid., 202.
119. Robert Alvarez and Joni Arends, "Fire, Earth, and Water: An Assessment of the Environmental, Safety, and Health Impacts of the Cerro Grande Fire on Los Alamos National Laboratory, a Department of Energy Facility," Concerned Citizens for Nuclear Safety and the Nuclear Policy Project, December 2000, http://www.nuclearactive.org/docs/CerroGrandeindex.html (accessed February 6, 2008).

120. Ibid.
121. Ibid.
122. Ibid.
123. Ibid.
124. Ibid.
125. Editors, "Pete, Jeff, Tom: Fight for LANL Cleanup $$$," *Santa Fe New Mexican*, February 8, 2008, Editorial, A9.
126. Ibid.
127. Associated Press, "Cyanide, Other Poisons Found in Los Alamos Storm Runoff," *Albuquerque Tribune*, September 12, 2000, A2.
128. Ibid.
129. Ibid.
130. William F. Athas and Charles R. Key, *Los Alamos Cancer Rate Study: Phase I—Cancer Incidence in Los Alamos County, 1970–1990*, New Mexico Department of Health and University of New Mexico Cancer Center, March 1993, 17.
131. Roger Snodgrass, "Lab Details Substantial Disagreement with NMED," *Los Alamos Monitor*, August 1, 2002.
132. Dirk Johnson, "Study on Cancer Rates Splits Home of A-Bomb," *New York Times*, September 7, 1991, http://query.nytimes.com/ (accessed February 15, 2008).
133. Athas and Key, *Los Alamos Cancer Rate Study*.
134. Catherine M. Richards, "Cancer Incidence and Mortality in Los Alamos County and New Mexico, 1970–1996," *New Mexico's Right to Know: The Impacts of LANL Operations on Public Health and the Environment*, http://www.nuclearactive.org.
135. Ibid.
136. F. Benjamin Zhan, "Childhood Cancer Clusters in New Mexico, 1973–1997," *Southwestern Geographer* 5 (2001).
137. Washington State Department of Health, "Health Risk Viewpoints: Radiation and Cancer," May 2000, http://www.doh.wa.gov/Hanford/publications/overview/viewpoints.html (accessed February 15, 2008).
138. Ibid.
139. Ibid.
140. Whistleblower.org, "Fact Sheet: Citizens Monitoring and Technical Assessment," Government Accountability Project, July 10, 2007, http://www.whistleblower.org/doc/2007/FactSheetFinal.pdf (accessed June 16, 2008).
141. Roger Snodgrass, "Dust Revisited: Hot Particle Study Unresolved," *Los Alamos Monitor*, November 13, 2008, 1.
142. Raam Wong, "LANL: Dust Isn't from Us," *Albuquerque Journal North*, December 11, 2008, 1.
143. Concerned Citizens for Nuclear Safety, "EPA Issues Draft Permit for LANL Storm Water," CCNS News update, February 2, 2008, e-mail to listserv.

144. Andy Lenderman, "Future Water, Part 2: Cold War Cleanup," *Santa Fe New Mexican*, September 16, 2007, http://www.santafenewmexican.com/ (accessed September 17, 2007).

145. "New Septic Tank Rules Approved by State Board," *New Mexico Business Weekly*, April 12, 2005, http//www.bizjournals.com/albuquerque/stories/2005/04/11/daily7.html (accessed February 26, 2008).

146. Ben Neary, "Conventional Septic Systems Ruled Out," *Santa Fe New Mexican*, August 4, 2005, http://www.freenewmexican.com/news/30888.html (accessed February 26, 2008).

147. Grant Cope, "Leaking Underground Storage Tanks: A Threat to Public Health and Environment," Sierra Club, April 19, 2005, http://www.sierraclub.org/toxics/Leaking_USTs/factsheets/national.pdf (accessed June 17, 2008).

148. Ibid.

149. Ralph Odenwald, "Environmental Cleanup—New Mexico," *New Mexico Business Journal*, July 1994, http://findarticles.com/p/articles/mi_m5092/is_n7_v18/ai_16128122/ (accessed February 18, 2008).

150. Ibid.

151. Mark Weidler, "Overfill Protection a Must for Overall Pollution Prevention," New Mexico Environmental Department, *Tank Notes* 9, no. 3 (Fall 1996): 1.

152. Agency for Toxic Substances and Disease Registry, "Public Health Assessment for Los Alamos National Laboratory, U.S. Department of Energy, Los Alamos, Los Alamos County, New Mexico, September 8, 2006, EPA Facility ID no. NM0890010515," *NTIS* (2006), http://hdl.handle.net/123456789/4915 (accessed February 28, 2008).

153. Center for American Progress, "Bush Administration Fails to Clean Up Toxic Waste Dumps, Leaves Communities at Risk," news release, June 15, 2006.

154. BushGreenwatch.org, "EPA Misleading Public on Superfund," March 1, 2004, http://www.bushgreenwatch.org/mt_archives/000063.php (accessed February 27, 2008).

155. Steve Ramirez, "Seven Billion Gallons of Water Foul," *Las Cruces Sun News*, December 11, 2006, 1A.

156. Susan Montoya Bryan, "Navajo Lawmakers Approve Superfund Bill," Philly.com, February 26, 2008, http://www.philly.com/ (accessed February 27, 2008).

157. Community Coalition Against Mining Uranium, "Fact Sheet on Uranium Radioactivity and Human Health," *Uranium Watch* 1, no. 1 (November 2007), http://www.ccamu.ca/fact-sheet.htm (accessed March 2, 2008).

158. Ibid.

159. Marley Shebala, "1979 Tailings Spill Symbolizes Uranium's Dangers," *Navajo Times*, July 23, 2009, A1.

160. Associated Press, "NM Wants Mine Cleanup Funds to Go to Uranium Sites," *Santa Fe New Mexican*, August 7, 2009, C4.

161. Kathy Helms, "Residents: Clean It Up," *Gallup Independent*, July 8, 2009, 1.

162. State of New Mexico Historic Preservation Division, Department of Cultural Affairs, "Collaboration Results in New Mount Taylor State Register Listing," news release, *Voices from the Earth*, June 5, 2009, 11.

163. Kathy Helms, "Proposed RECA Change: Declare Entire States 'Downwind,'" *Gallup Independent*, July 28, 2009, 1.

164. Center for Biological Diversity, "Mining," http://www.biologicaldiversity.org/programs/public_lands/mining (accessed August 2, 2009).

165. Ibid.

166. Sue Major Holmes, "Mine Cleanup a Priority: NM Seeks More Funds for Uranium," *Albuquerque Journal*, August 8, 2009, Metro & New Mexico.

167. Democracy for New Mexico, "Strong Support in NM's 2nd Congressional District for Reforming 1872 Mining Act," June 29, 2009, http://democracyfornewmexico.com/democracy_for_new_mexico/mining/.

168. Ibid.

169. Pew Charitable Trusts, "Mining Campaign," http://www.pewtrusts.org/our_work_detail.aspx?id=172 (accessed August 10, 2009).

170. Alaskans for Responsible Mining, "Mining: Environmental Impacts," http://www.wman-info.org/ . . . /ARM%20Enviro%20 Impacts%20Fact%20Sheet.doc. (accessed August 1, 2009).

171. United States Environmental Protection Agency, "Fossil Fuel Combustion Waste," http://www.epa.gov/osw/nonhaz/industrial/special/fossil/index.htm (accessed August 1, 2009).

172. Green America, "Coal: Why It's Dirty," Climate Action: Economic Action to Stop Global Warming, http://www.greenamericatoday.org/programs/climate/dirtyenergy/coal/whydirty.cfm.

173. Ibid.

174. William J. Stone, "Water for Industry in New Mexico's Future," unpublished paper, New Mexico Bureau of Mines and Mineral Resources, n.d.

175. Quoted in Philip Varney, *New Mexico's Best Ghosttowns* (Flagstaff: North Land Press, 1981), 3.

176. New Mexico Oil and Gas Association, "NM Gas Knowledge Survey," http://www.nmoga.org/about.asp?CustComKey=362091& CategoryKey=362137&pn=Page&domname=nmoga.org (accessed August 11, 2009).

177. Earthworks, "Oil and Gas Accountability Project," http://www.
earthworksaction.org/oil_and_gas.cfm (accessed August 13, 2009).

178. Earthworks, "Hydraulic Fracturing 101," http://www.earthworks
action.org/FracingDetails.cfm (accessed August 13, 2009).

179. John Fleck, "Deal Limits NM Nuke Waste Plant," *Albuquerque
Journal*, June 4, 2005, A1.

180. Mary Byrd Davis, "Natural, Enriched, and Depleted Uranium,"
Nuclear France: Materials and Sites, http://www.francenuc.org/
en_mat/uranium2_e.htm (accessed March 2, 2008).

181. U.S. Nuclear Regulatory Commission, "Frequently Asked Questions
about Gas Centrifuge Enrichment Plants," http://www.nrc.gov/
materials/fuel-cycle-fac/faq.html (accessed March 1, 2008).

182. Ibid.

183. Conger Beasley, Jr., "The Dirty History of Nuclear Power," *High
Beam Encyclopedia*, February 1, 1994, http://www.encyclopedia.
com/doc/1G1-14802758.html (accessed March 5, 2008).

184. Nuclear Information and Resource Service, "LES EIS Comments
to U.S. Nuclear Regulatory Commission," March 18, 2004, http://
www.nirs.org/les/leseiscomments.htm (accessed March 1, 2008).

185. Ibid.

186. Vladimir S. Zajic, comp., "Ammunition Testing," chapter 5 in
*Review of Radioactivity, Military Use, and Health Effects of
Depleted Uranium*, Ratical.org, http://www.ratical.org/radiation/
vzajic/5thchapter.html (accessed March 10, 2008).

187. Akira Tashiro, "Open Air," part 3 in "Discounted Casualties: The
Human Cost of Depleted Uranium," *Chugoku Shimbun*, May 16,
2000, http://www.chugoku-np.co.jp/abom/uran/us3_e/000516.html
(accessed October 1, 2006).

188. Christian Lowe, "Uranium-Sucking Tumbleweeds," Defensetech.
org, November 10, 2004, http://www.defensetech.org/archives/
001202.html (accessed March 14, 2008).

189. Zajic, "Ammunition Testing."

190. Ibid.

191. Marilyn Gayle Hoff, "Los Alamos National Laboratory Is Blowing
Smoke and Sending Deadly Depleted Uranium into the Air We
Breathe," Peace Action New Mexico, http://www.peace-actionnm.
org/issues/du/burned.html (accessed March 14, 2008).

192. Albert C. Marshall, *An Analysis of Uranium Dispersal and Health
Effects Using a Gulf War Case Study*, Sandia Report SAND2005–
4331, Sandia National Laboratories, July 2005.

193. Ibid., 15.

194. Lou Nicholas, "Heavy Metal or Death Metal?" *Alibi Weekly*,
July 3, 2000, http://weeklywire.com/ww/07-03-00/alibi_feat4.html
(accessed March 10, 2008).

195. Lord John Gilbert, "Depleted Uranium Contamination," United Kingdom Parliament, March 2, 1998, http://www.publications. parliament.uk/ (accessed March 10, 2008).

196. Sherwood Ross, "Radioactive Ammunition Fired in Middle East May Claim More Lives than Hiroshima and Nagasaki," *Global Research*, Center for Research on Globalization, November 22, 2007, http://www.globalresearch.ca/index. php?context=va&aid=7410 (accessed March 10, 2008).

197. Leuren Moret, "Depleted Uranium: Dirty Bombs, Dirty Missiles, Dirty Bullets," *San Francisco Bay View*, August 23, 2004, http://www.truthout.org/ (accessed August 22, 2004).

198. Ross, "Radioactive Ammunition Fired in Middle East May Claim More Lives than Hiroshima and Nagasaki."

199. International Atomic Energy Agency, "Depleted Uranium Questions and Answers," http://www.iaea.org/NewsCenter/Features/DU/ du_qaa.shtml (accessed March 12, 2008).

200. Piotr Bein, "International Physicians against DU," February 28, 2001, http://www.stopnato.org.uk/du-watch/bein/physic.htm (accessed March 12, 2008).

201. Mike Ludwig, "Document Reveals Military Was Concerned about Gulf War Vets' Exposure to Depleted Uranium," Truthout.org, July 28, 2010, http://www.truth-out.org/document-reveals-military-was-concerned-about-gulf-war-vets-exposure-depleted-uranium61781.

202. Ibid.

Chapter Five

1. Ray Powell, personal communication with author, September 23, 2009.

2. Assessment Payers Association of the Middle Rio Grande Conservancy District, "Bailout Thinking Pervades Water Economy, Too," *APA Watermark*, February 2009, 2.

3. Office of New Mexico Governor Bill Richardson, "Governor Bill Richardson Signs Bill Protecting Water Rights," news release, April 9, 2009.

4. Assessment Payers Association, "Bailout Thinking Pervades Water Economy."

5. Joel Gay, "The Big H$_2$O transfer," *New Mexico Independent*, July 24, 2008, http://nmindependent.mypublicsquare.com/view/ the-battle-over (accessed July 24, 2008).

6. Julia M. Dendinger, "Irrigators Say Water Flow Is Inadequate," Valencia County News-Bulletin.com, April 29, 2009, http://www.news-bulletin.com/news/88581–04-29–09 (accessed September 13, 2009).

7. Assessment Payers Association, "Bailout Thinking Pervades Water Economy."

8. Editorial Board, "Draining Our Future," *Roswell Daily Record*, April 15, 2009.

9. Ibid.

10. City of Albuquerque, "Accomplishments," http://www.cabq.gov/albuquerquegreen/accomplishments (accessed September 19, 2009).

11. U.S. Bureau of Reclamation, "Drought in the Upper Colorado River Basin," http://www.usbr.gov/uc/feature/drought.html, September 2009 (accessed September 19, 2009).

12. "California Faces Water Rationing, Governor Proclaims Drought Emergency," Environmental News Service, February 27, 2009, http://www.ens-newswire.com/ens/feb2009/2009–27–093.asp (accessed September 19, 2009).

13. Ibid.

14. *Colorado River Compact of 1922*, signed at Santa Fe, New Mexico, November 24, 1922, pursuant to Act of Congress approved August 19, 1921, ch. 72, 42 Stat. 171.

15. Metropolitan Water District of Southern California, "California's Colorado River Allocation," http://www.mwdh2o.com/mwdh2o/pages/yourwater/supply/colorado/colorado04.html (accessed September 20, 2009).

16. Bruce Finley, "CU Study Warns of Scarce Water," *Denver Post*, July 22, 2009, updated July 23, 2009, http://www.denverpost.com/news/ci_12887585.

17. Ibid.

18. New Mexico Drought Task Force, *New Mexico Drought Plan*, December 2006, http://www.ose.state.nm.us/DroughtTaskForce/2006-NM-Drought-Plan.pdf, 4.

19. L. Greer Price et al., eds., *Decision-Makers Field Conference 2009: Water, Natural Resources, and the Urban Landscape, the Albuquerque Region* (Socorro: New Mexico Bureau of Geology and Mineral Resources, New Mexico Institute of Mining and Technology, 2009), 1–2.

20. Nicolai Ouroussoff, "Reinventing America's Cities: The Time Is Now," *New York Times*, March 25, 2009, Art & Design, http://www.nytimes.com/2009/03/29/arts/design/29ouro.html?_r=1&hp (accessed March 29, 2009).

21. Lisa Robert, personal communication with author, March 30, 2009.

22. Marjorie Childress, "Controversial ABQ Loop Road Project Rolls On," *New Mexico Independent*, February 16, 2009, http://newmexicoindependent.com/18117/controversial-abq-loop-road-project-rolls-forward (accessed September 26, 2009).

23. Erik Siemers, "Managing Albuquerque's Growth Poses Challenges with 1 Million People Projected for 2021," *Albuquerque Tribune*,

September 17, 2007, http://www.mrcog-nm.gov/content/view/7/210/ (accessed September 26, 2009).

24. Childress, "Controversial ABQ Loop Road Project Rolls On."

25. Lisa Robert, personal communication with author, June 20, 2008.

26. Aldo Leopold, "A Criticism of the Booster Spirit," in *The River of the Mother of God and Other Collected Essays,* ed. J. Baird Callicott and Susan L. Flader (Madison: University of Wisconsin, 1992).

27. Clifford Krauss, "Rural U.S. Takes Worst Hit as Gas Tops $4 Average," *New York Times,* June 9, 2008, Business section.

28. Lloyd Jojola, "ABQ Ridership on Record Pace," *Albuquerque Journal,* May 7, 2008, C1.

29. Sean Olson, "Regional Leaders Talk Transit Ideas," *Albuquerque Journal,* July 26, 2006, Westside Journal.

30. John Fleck, "New Breed of City," *Albuquerque Journal,* July 19, 2008, A1.

31. George Gonzalez, "Urban Sprawl, Global Warming, and Oil Depletion: The Unraveling of the Modern Economy," International Conference on Environmental, Cultural, Economic, and Social Sustainability, 2005, http://so5.cgpublisher.com/proposals/49/index_html (accessed June 21, 2008).

32. Felicia Fonseca and Paul Foy, "Debate Rages over Reservation Coal Plant," *Albuquerque Journal,* May 25, 2008, A2.

33. Ibid.

34. Jennifer Steinhauer, "California Water Law Curtailing New Development," *New York Times,* June 7, 2008, U.S.

35. Christopher Smart, "Water Policy Could Slow Tooele Development," *Salt Lake Tribune,* June 2, 2008.

36. Ellen Hanak and Margaret K. Browne, "Linking Housing Growth to Water Supply," *Journal of the American Planning Association* 72, no. 3 (Spring 2006): 154–66.

37. Ibid.

38. Sierra Club, "Cooling the Planet through Smart Growth," news release, n.d.

39. Smart Growth America, "Less Auto-Dependent Development Is Key to Mitigating Climate Change, Research Team Concludes," SmartGrowthAmerica.org, http://www.smartgrowthamerica.org/gcindex.html (accessed June 21, 2008).

40. Sierra Club, "Global Warming: Sprawling across the Nation," news release, n.d.

41. Raam Wong, "School Admits Releasing Waste into N.M. Canyon," *Albuquerque Journal,* June 18, 2008, C2.

42. Mikaela Renz, "Identity and Place: An Intersection at 4th and Montaño" (master's thesis, University of New Mexico, Spring 2006).

43. Ibid.

44. Lou Liberty and Margy O'Brien, *Bearing Witness: Twenty-five Years of Refuge* (Albuquerque, NM: La Alameda Press, 2007), 8–9.

45. Isaac Benton, Michael Cadigan, and Rey Garduño, "Subsidizing Growth on Fringes of City Wrong Policy," *Albuquerque Journal*, April 21, 2008, Opinion.

46. V. B. Price, "Same Sprawl," *Albuquerque Tribune*, August 5, 2008, C1.

47. American Lung Association, "Least Polluted: Ozone," *State of the Air: 2008*, http://www.stateoftheair.org/ (accessed July 5, 2008).

48. Todd Zwillich, "Report: Polluted Air Puts Millions at Risk," WebMD, http://www.webmd.com/asthma/news/20080430/report-polluted-air-puts-millions-at-risk (accessed May 1, 2008).

49. Dale Rodebaugh, "Four Corners Power Plant Emissions among Worst in U.S.," *Durango Herald*, June 5, 2005.

50. Ibid.

51. Will Sands, "Three New Power Plants Pitched for Four Corners," *Durango Telegraph*, April 21, 2004.

52. Ibid.

53. Associated Press, "Proposed Coal Plant Pits Economic Growth Against Navajo Belief in Mother Earth and Father Sky," *Chron*, http://www.chron.com/disp/story.mpl/business/5799622.html.

54. San Juan Citizens Alliance, "Desert Rock Power Plant," *Air Global Warming*, http://www.sanjuancitizens.org/air/desertrock.shtml (accessed July 9, 2008).

55. Joel Gay, "NM Attorney General Intervenes in Desert Rock proposal," *New Mexico Independent*, July 11, 2008, http://nmindependent.mypublicsquare.com/view/nm-attorney-general (accessed July 12, 2008).

56. Associated Press, "Regulators: Four Corners Could Exceed Air Pollution Levels," *Albuquerque Journal*, May 31, 2008.

57. Sue Major Holmes, "Plant Air Permit OK Appealed," *Albuquerque Journal*, August 15, 2008, C3.

58. CorpWatch, "SouthWest Organizing Project (SWOP): Organization and Campaign Information," CorpWatch.org, http://www.corpwatch.org/article.php?id=3442 (accessed July 24, 2008).

59. V. B. Price, "Same Sprawl."

60. FACEIntel, "History of Intel's Toxic Chemical Release in Corrales," http://www.faceintel.com/toxicchemicalhistory.htm (accessed July 13, 2008).

61. Benjamin Pimentel, "The Valley's Toxic History," Silicon Valley Toxics Committee, January 30, 2004, http://www.etoxics.org/site/PageServer?pagename=svtc_SFGate_1_30_2004 (accessed July 23, 2008).

62. Ibid.

63. Chris Hayhurst, "Toxic Technology: Electronics and the Silicon Valley," *E: The Environmental Magazine* (May–June 1997), http://findarticles.com/p/articles/mi_m1594/is_/ai_19998019 (accessed July 23, 2008).

64. Ibid.
65. Intel Superfund Sites, "Overview of Intel Superfund Sites in Silicon Valley, CA," Intel Superfund Cleanup, http://intelsuperfundcleanup.com (accessed July 23, 2008).
66. Silicon Valley Toxics Coalition, "Four Case Studies of High-Tech Water Exploitation and Corporate Welfare in the Southwest," *Sacred Waters: Life-Blood of Mother Earth*, http://svtc.igc.org/resource/pubs/execsum.htm (accessed July 24, 2008).
67. "A Relative Newcomer, but Statistics Put New Mexico 10th in Chipmaking," *Solid State Technology*, October 2001, http://www.solid-state.com/display_article/122167/5/none/none/FabSw/A-relative-newcomer,-but-statistics-put-New-Mexico-10th-in-chipmaking (accessed July 25, 2008).
68. Intel, "Intel in Your Community," April 2008, http://www.intel.com/community/NewMexico (accessed July 25, 2008).
69. Brendan Doherty, "Intel Says It Put a Lot into New Mexico's Economy—but What Is It Putting into Our Environment," *Weekly Alibi*, April 27, 1998.
70. Barbara Rockwell, *Boiling Frogs: Intel vs. the Village* (New York: iUniverse, 2005), 127.
71. Doherty, "Intel Says It Put a Lot into New Mexico's Economy."
72. Ibid.
73. FACEIntel, "History of Intel's Toxic Chemical Release in Corrales."
74. Rockwell, *Boiling Frogs: Intel vs. the Village*, 184.
75. Ibid., 163.
76. Ibid., 271.
77. Ibid., 279.
78. Ibid., 280.
79. Ibid., 281.
80. Ibid., 280.
81. Ibid., 283.
82. Law Office of Richard A. Allen, letter to Todd W. Rallison, "Re: Albuquerque Intel Employee George Evans," March 18, 2003, FACEIntel, http://www.faceintel.com/georgeevans.htm (accessed July 17, 2008).
83. Michael Davis, "Official Calls Intel Air Permit a 'Mistake,'" *Albuquerque Journal*, January 24, 2004, E2.
84. Jeff Radford, "Intel Pollution Report Delayed: Decision on Higher Stacks Soon," *Corrales Comment*, May 26, 2008.
85. Jeff Radford, "Intel Rejects Recommended Higher Stacks," *Corrales Comment*, June 9, 2008.
86. Nathan Newcomer, "Courts Rebuke BLM's Otero Mesa Plans," *New Mexico Wild!: Newsletter of the New Mexico Wilderness Alliance*, Spring 2009, 4.
87. Ibid.

88. Barry Commoner, *The Closing Circe: Nature, Man, and Ecology* (New York: Bantam Books, 1972), 29–44.

89. John Fleck, "Stretching Our Water," *Albuquerque Journal*, August 17, 2009, A1.

90. "A Celebration of the Sport," Las Companas Santa Fe, http://www.lascampanas.com/Golf/Default.aspx (accessed October 14, 2009).

91. William J. Salman, "Profligate Waste of Santa Fe Water," SantaFeWaterCrisis.org, http://www.sfwatercrisis.org/discuss/archives/2003/07/profligate_wast.html (accessed September 19, 2009).

92. Julie Ann Grimm, "Officials Raise Buckman Concerns: Agencies Pressure LANL over the Project's Water Safety," *Santa Fe New Mexican*, March 13, 2009, C1.

93. Michael Cooper, "Carefully Cleaning Up the Garbage at Los Alamos," *New York Times*, October 23, 2009, http://www.nytimes.com/2009/10/24/us/24alamos.html (accessed October 24, 2009).

94. MSNBC Staff and News Service Reports, "WWF Lists Ten Most Endangered Rivers Globally," MSNBC.com, http://www.msnbc.msn.com/id/17704190 (accessed October 16, 2009).

95. New Mexico Department of Game and Fish, *Comprehensive Wildlife Conservation Strategy for New Mexico* (Santa Fe: New Mexico Department of Game and Fish, 2006), 341.

96. State of New Mexico Office of Natural Resources Trustee, "Governor Richardson and Natural Resources Trustee Partner with Mid Region Council of Governments for Bosque Restoration Project," news release, September 13, 2004.

97. Michael Davis, "Death of Bosque Trees May Be Due to Groundwater Chemicals," *Albuquerque Journal*, August 18, 2004.

98. Lisa Robert, *Middle Rio Grande Ecosystem Bosque Biological Management Plan, the First Decade: Review and Update* (Albuquerque, NM: Aurora Publishing LLC, 2005), 62.

99. Lisa Robert, "So-called 'Peace Treaty' Won't Save the Rio Grande," *High Country News*, May 2, 2005, http://www.hcn.org/issues/297/15493 (accessed October 31, 2009).

100. Rene Romo, "A River Reborn: New Rio Grande Plan Calls for Periodic Flooding and Restoration of Habitat," *Albuquerque Journal*, July 19, 2009.

101. John Fleck, "Southwest Drying Up," *Albuquerque Journal*, August 30, 2009.

102. Joel Gay, "Clean Water in the News," *New Mexico Independent*, July 24, 2008, http://www.environmentnewmexico.org/in-the-news/clean-water/clean-water/the-big-h2otransfer#idYTwDSJ9gAa1Vm2Ty _qpzsg (accessed November 3, 2009).

103. Jane Moorman, "NMSU's Los Lunas Agricultural Science Center Celebrates 50 Years of Research," New Mexico State University, http://spectre.nmsu.edu/media/news2.1asso?i=1044 (accessed November 3, 2009).

104. United States Department of Agriculture, "State Fact Sheets: New Mexico," http://www.ers.usda.gov/statefacts/nm.htm (accessed November 7, 2009).

105. Cooperative Extension Service and Range Improvement Task Force, *New Mexico Ranching: Utilizing and Managing New Mexico's Rangelands*, College of Agriculture and Home Economics, New Mexico State University, http://aces.nmsu.edu/programs/ritf/documents/new-mexico-ranching-brochure.pdf.

106. Aldo Leopold Foundation, "Leopold's Land Ethic," http://www.aldoleopold.org (accessed October 7, 2009).

107. Gabriel Alonso de Herrera, *Ancient Agriculture: Roots and Applications of Sustainable Farming*, comp. Juan Estevan Arellano (Santa Fe, NM: Ancient City Press, 2006), 15–22.

108. New Mexico Acequia Association, "About the NMAA," http://www.lasacequias.org/about (accessed November 13, 2007).

109. David J. Groenfeldt, "Culture, Irrigation, and Ecosystems in the Northern Rio Grande Basin, New Mexico (USA)," in *Water, Cultural Diversity, and International Solidarity Symposium Proceedings*, ed. Corinne Wacker, *Zurich Working Papers in Social Anthropology* 14 (2004).

110. Carlos Vasquez, ed., *La Vida del Rio Grande: Our River—Our Life: A Symposium* (Albuquerque, NM: National Hispanic Cultural Center, 2004), 27.

111. Ibid., 29.

112. Ibid., 33.

113. Carlos Vasquez, ed., *La Vida de Rio Grande: Our River—Our Life*.

114. Gregory Cajete, ed., *A People's Ecology: Explorations in Sustainable Living* (Santa Fe, NM: Clearlight Publishers, 1999), viii.

115. Ibid., 3.

116. Ibid., 6.

117. James A. Vlasich, "Postwar Pueblo Indian Agriculture: Modernization versus Tradition in the Era of Agribusiness," *New Mexico Historical Review* 76, no. 4 (October 2001): 376.

118. Ibid., 353–82.

119. Kevin Robinson-Avila, "Sysco Breathes New Life into Local Agriculture," New Mexico State University, http://spectre.nmsu.edu/media/news2.1asso?i=745 (accessed November 18, 2009).

120. Phaedra Greenwood, "Savor the Flavor of Locally Grown Foods," *Enchantment: The Voice of New Mexico's Rural Electric Cooperatives*, http://www.enchantment.coop/features/200903.php (accessed November 18, 2009).

121. Ibid.
122. Anthony Anella and John Wright, *Saving the Ranch: Conservation Easement Design in the American West,* Island Press, http://www. islandpress.com/bookstore/details.php?prod_id=793 (accessed November 28, 2009).
123. Ibid.
124. Michelle Nijhuis, "Between Hoofprints," *Orion* (November/December 2005), 53.
125. Ibid.
126. Quivira Coalition, "At a Glance," http://www.quiviracoalition.org, September 4, 2009.
127. Paul Larmer, "Loosening the Grazing Knot," *High Country News,* October 1, 2007, 2.

Chapter Six

1. Alvin Toffler, *Future Shock* (New York: Bantam Books, 1970), 2–3.
2. Ibid., 11.
3. Centers for Disease Control and Prevention, *Draft Final Report of the Los Alamos Historical Document Retrieval Assessment (LAHDRA) Project,* National Center for Environmental Health, Division of Environmental Hazards and Health Effects, Radiation Studies Branch, June 2009, ES-11.
4. Ibid., ES-13.
5. Ibid.
6. Ibid., 301–2.
7. Charles Duhigg, "Millions in U.S. Drink Dirty Water, Records Show," *New York Times,* December 8, 2009, http://www.nytimes. com/2009/12/08/business/energy-environment/08water.html (accessed January 17, 2011).
8. Timothy Egan, "Slumburbia," *New York Times,* February 10, 2010, http://opinionator.blogs.nytimes.com/2010/02/10/slumburbia/ (accessed January 17, 2011).
9. Commonweal, "Obama and Smart Growth," Connecticut Smart Growth, November 10, 2008, http://www.ctsmartgrowth.com/ diary/225/.
10. Lester R. Brown, *Eco-Economy: Building an Economy for the Earth* (New York: W. W. Norton, 2001), 208.
11. Heather Clark, "Power to the People," *Albuquerque Journal,* October 14, 2009, C1.
12. Ibid.
13. Ibid.

Selected Bibliography

Allaby, Michael. *The Concise Oxford Dictionary of Ecology.* Oxford, UK: University of Oxford Press, 1994.

Ausubel, Kenny, with J. P. Harpignies. *Nature's Operating Instructions: The True Biotechnologies.* San Francisco: Sierra Club Books, 2004.

Bakken, Gordon Morris. *The Mining Law of 1872: Past, Politics, and Perspectives.* Albuquerque: University of New Mexico Press, 2008.

Bartolino, James R., and James C. Cole. *Ground-Water Resources of the Middle Rio Grande Basin, New Mexico.* U.S. Geological Survey, Circular 1222, 2002.

Baxter, John O. *Dividing New Mexico's Waters, 1700–1912.* Albuquerque: University of New Mexico Press, 1997.

Benyus, Janine M. *Biomimicry: Innovation Inspired by Nature.* New York: HarperCollins, 1997.

Berry, Wendell. *Bringing It to the Table: On Farming and Food.* Berkeley: Counterpoint Press, 2009.

Brick, Philip, Donald Snow, and Sarah Van de Wetering, eds. *Across the Great Divide: Explorations in Collaborative Conservation and the American West.* Washington, D.C.: Island Press, 2001.

Brown, David E., and Neil R. Carmony, eds. *Aldo Leopold's Southwest.* Albuquerque: University of New Mexico Press, 1995.

Brugge, Doug, Timothy Benally, and Esther Yazzie-Lewis. *The Navajo People and Uranium Mining.* Albuquerque: University of New Mexico Press, 2006.

Bruegmann, Robert. *Sprawl: A Compact History.* Chicago: University of Chicago Press, 2005.

Bullard, Robert D., ed. *The Quest for Environmental Justice: Human Rights and the Politics of Pollution.* San Francisco: Sierra Club Books, 2005.

Burns, Patrick, ed. *In the Shadow of Los Alamos: Selected Writings of Edith Warner.* Albuquerque: University of New Mexico Press, 2001.

Cajete, Gregory, ed. *A People's Ecology: Explorations in Sustainable Living—Health, Environment, Agriculture, Native Traditions.* Santa Fe, NM: Clear Light Publishers, 1999.

———. *Native Science: Natural Laws of Interdependence.* Santa Fe, NM: Clear Light Publishers, 2000.

Carson, Rachel. *Silent Spring.* Boston: Houghton Mifflin, 1962.

Christiansen, Paige W. *The Story of Oil in New Mexico.* Socorro: New Mexico Bureau of Mines and Mineral Resources, 1989.

Clark, Ira G. *Water in New Mexico: A History of Its Management and Use.* Albuquerque: University of New Mexico Press, 1987.

Cobos, Rubén. *A Dictionary of New Mexico and Southern Colorado Spanish.* Santa Fe: Museum of New Mexico Press, 2003.

Colbert, David, ed. *Eyewitness to the American West: Five Hundred Years of First Hand History.* New York: Penguin Books, 1998.

Commoner, Barry. *The Closing Circle: Nature, Man, and Technology.* New York: Bantam Books, 1972.

Couch, Dick. *The U.S. Armed Forces Nuclear, Biological, and Chemical Survival Manual: Everything You Need to Know to Protect Yourself from the Growing Terrorist Threat.* New York: Basic Books, 2003.

Chronic, Halka. *Roadside Geology of New Mexico.* Missoula, MT: Mountain Press Publishing Company, 1987.

Cronon, William, ed. *Uncommon Ground: Rethinking the Human Place in Nature.* New York: W. W. Norton, 1996.

deBuys, William. *Enchantment and Exploitation: The Life and Hard Times of a New Mexico Mountain Range.* Albuquerque: University of New Mexico Press, 1985.

———, and Alex Harris. *River of Traps.* Albuquerque: University of New Mexico Press, 1990.

Dick-Peddie, William A., with W. H. Moir and Richard Spellenberg. *New Mexico Vegetation: Past, Present, and Future.* Albuquerque: University of New Mexico Press, 1993.

Dunmire, William W., and Gail D. Tierney. *Wild Plants of the Pueblo Province: Exploring Ancient and Enduring Uses.* Santa Fe: Museum of New Mexico Press, 1995.

Edwards, Andres R. *The Sustainability Revolution: Portrait of a Paradigm Shift.* Gabriola Island, Canada: New Society Publishers, 2005.

Eichstaedt, Peter H. *If You Poison Us: Uranium and Native Americans.* Santa Fe, NM: Red Crane Books, 1994.

Ellis, Richard N. *New Mexico Historic Documents.* Albuquerque: University of New Mexico Press, 1995.

Etulain, Richard W., ed. *Contemporary New Mexico, 1940–1990.* Albuquerque: University of New Mexico Press, 1994.

Fergusson, Erna, with photographs by Ruth Frank. *Our Southwest.* New York: Alfred A. Knopf, 1940.

———. *New Mexico: A Pageant of Three Peoples.* Albuquerque: University of New Mexico Press, 1973.

Fitzpatrick, George. *This Is New Mexico.* Albuquerque, NM: Horn and Wallace, 1962.

Flores, Dan. *Horizontal Yellow: Nature and History in the Near Southwest.* Albuquerque: University of New Mexico Press, 1999.

———. *The Natural West: Environmental History in the Great Plains and Rocky Mountains.* Norman: University of Oklahoma Press, 2001.

Fernlund, Kevin J., ed. *The Cold War American West, 1945–1989.* Albuquerque: University of New Mexico Press, 1998.

Fox, Steve. *Toxic Work: Women Workers at GTE Lenkurt.* Philadelphia, PA: Temple University Press, 1991.

The Global 2000 Report to the Present: Entering the Twenty-First Century. New York: Penguin, 1982.

Goals for Albuquerque Report, 1983–84, New Partnerships: Quality of Life, Direction of City Growth. Vol. 1, Albuquerque Goals Report. City of Albuquerque, 1984.

Godrej, Dinyar. *The No-Nonsense Guide to Climate Change.* London: Verso, 2001.

Gonzales-Berry, Erlinda, and David R. Maciel, eds. *The Contested Homeland: A Chicano History of New Mexico.* Albuquerque: University of New Mexico Press, 2000.

Gore, Al. *An Inconvenient Truth: The Planetary Emergency of Global Warming and What We Can Do About It.* New York: Rodale Books, 2006.

Goudie, Andrew. *The Human Impact on the Natural Environment.* Cambridge, MA: MIT Press, 2000.

Grambling, Jeffrey A., and Steven G. Wells, eds. *Albuquerque Country.* Thirty-Third Annual Field Conference, New Mexico Geological Society, 1982.

Grinde, Donald A., and Bruce E. Johansen. *Ecocide of Native America: Environmental Destruction of Indian Lands and People.* Santa Fe, NM: Clear Light Publishers, 1995.

Gruen, Lori, and Dale Jamieson. *Reflecting on Nature: Readings in Environmental Philosophy.* New York: Oxford University Press, 1994.

Harte, John, Cheryl Holdren, Richard Schneider, and Christine Shirley. *Toxics A to Z: A Guide to Everyday Pollution Hazards.* Berkeley: University of California Press, 1991.

Hall, G. Emlen. *High and Dry: The Texas–New Mexico Struggle for the Pecos River.* Albuquerque: University of New Mexico Press, 2002.

Hay, Peter. *Main Currents in Western Environmental Thought.* Bloomington: Indiana University Press, 2002.

Hayden, Dolores. *A Field Guide to Sprawl.* New York: W. W. Norton, 2004.

Herrera, Esteban A., and Laura F. Huenneke, eds. *New Mexico's Natural Heritage: Biological Diversity in the Land of Enchantment.* Las Cruces: New Mexico Journal of Science, 1996.

Herrera, Gabriel Alfonso. *Ancient Agriculture: Roots and Application of Sustainable Farming.* Compiled by Juan Estevan Arellano and translated by Rosa López-Gastón. Salt Lake City, UT: Ancient City Press, 2006.

Herron, John F., and Andrew G. Kirk. *Human Nature: Biology, Culture, and Environmental History.* Albuquerque: University of New Mexico Press, 1999.

Hewett, Edgar L. *Ancient Life in the American Southwest.* New York: Tudor Publishing, 1948.

Hine, Robert V., and John Mack Faragher. *The American West: A New Interpretive History.* New Haven, CT: Yale University Press, 2000.

Jenkins, Matt. *A People's History of Wilderness.* Paonia, CO: High Country News Books, 2004.

Johnston, Barbara Rose, ed. *Life and Death Matters: Human Rights and the Environment at the End of the Millennium.* Walnut Creek, CA: Altamira Press, 1997.

Jones, Ellis, Ross Haenfler, and Brett Johnson with Brian Klocke. *The Better World Handbook: From Good Intentions to Everyday Actions.* Gabriola Island, Canada: New Society Publishers, 2001.

Julyan, Robert. *Place Names of New Mexico.* Rev. ed. Albuquerque: University of New Mexico Press, 1998.

Krech III, Shepard. *The Ecological Indian.* New York: W. W. Norton, 1999.

Keiter, Robert B., ed. *Reclaiming the Native Home of Hope: Community, Ecology, and the American West.* Salt Lake City: University of Utah Press, 1998.

Krupp, Fred, and Miriam Horn. *Earth, the Sequel: The Race to Reinvent Energy and Stop Global Warming.* New York: W. W. Norton, 2009.

League of Women Voters. *The Nuclear Waste Primer: A Handbook for Citizens.* New York: N. Lyons Books, 1993.

Leopold, Aldo. *A Sand County Almanac and Sketches Here and There.* New York: Oxford University Press, 1989.

Markandya, Anil, Renat Perelet, Pamela Mason, and Tim Taylor. *Dictionary of Environmental Economics.* London: Earthscan Publications, 2002.

Masco, Joseph. *The Nuclear Borderlands: The Manhattan Project in Post–Cold War New Mexico.* Princeton, NJ: Princeton University Press, 2006.

McCutcheon, Chuck. *Nuclear Reactions: The Politics of Opening a Radioactive Waste Disposal Site.* Albuquerque: University of New Mexico Press, 2002.

McDaniel, Carl N. *Wisdom for a Livable Planet.* San Antonio, TX: Trinity University Press, 2005.

McNeill, J. R. *Something New Under the Sun: An Environmental History of the Twentieth-Century World.* New York: W. W. Norton, 2000.

Meadows, Donella H., Dennis L. Meadows, Jorgen Randers, and William W. Behrens III. *Limits to Growth.* New York: New American Library, 1974.

Meléndez, A. Gabriel, M. Jane Young, Patricia Moore, and Patrick Pynes, eds. *The Multi-Cultural Southwest: A Reader.* Tucson: University of Arizona Press, 2001.

Merchant, Carolyn. *Major Problems in American Environmental History.* Lexington, MA: D. C. Heath, 1993.

———. *Radical Ecology: The Search for a Livable World.* New York: Routledge, 2005.

———. *The Columbia Guide to American Environmental History.* New York: Columbia University Press, 2002.

————. *American Environmental History: An Introduction.* New York: Columbia University Press, 2007.

Miller, Char, ed. *Water in the West: A High Country News Reader.* Corvallis: Oregon State University Press, 2000.

Mineral and Water Resources of New Mexico. Report prepared by the United States Geological Survey in Collaboration with the New Mexico State Engineer Office and the New Mexico Oil Conservation Commission. Washington, D.C.: U.S. Government Printing Office, 1965.

Mogren, Eric. *Warm Sands: Uranium Mill Tailings Policy in the Atomic West.* Albuquerque: University of New Mexico Press, 2002.

Myers, Nancy J., and Carolyn Raffensperger, eds. *Precautionary Tools for Reshaping Environmental Policy.* Cambridge, MA: MIT Press, 2006.

Myrick, David F. *New Mexico's Railroads: A Historical Survey.* Albuquerque: University of New Mexico Press, 1990.

Northrop, Stuart A. *Minerals of New Mexico.* UNM Bulletin no. 379. Albuquerque: University of New Mexico Press, 1942.

Norstrand, Richard L. *The Hispano Homeland.* Norman: University of Oklahoma Press, 1992.

Olson, Robert, and David Rejeski, eds. *Environmentalism and the Technologies of Tomorrow: Shaping the Next Industrial Revolution.* Washington, D.C.: Island Press, 2005.

Peña, Devon G., ed. *Chicano Culture, Ecology, Politics: Subversive Kin.* Tucson: University of Arizona Press, 1998.

Pernick, Ron, and Clint Wilder. *The Clean Tech Revolution.* New York: Collins Business, 2008.

Porteous, Andrew. *Dictionary of Environmental Science and Technology.* Chichester, UK: John Wiley & Sons, 2000.

Price, L. Greer, Douglas Bland, Peggy S. Johnson, and Sean D. Connell, eds. *Water, Natural Resources, and the Urban Landscape.* Decision-Makers Field Conference, Albuquerque Region. Socorro: New Mexico Bureau of Geology and Mineral Resources, New Mexico Institute of Mining and Techology, 2009.

Price, L. Greer, Douglas Bland, Virginia T. McLemore, and James M. Barks, eds. *Mining in New Mexico: The Environment, Water, Economics, and Sustainable Development.* Decision-Makers Field Conference, Taos Region. Socorro: New Mexico Bureau of Geology and Mineral Resources, New Mexico Institute of Mining and Technology, 2005.

Reisner, Marc. *Cadillac Desert: The American West and Its Disappearing Water.* New York: Penguin Books, 1993.

Renner, Michael. *The Anatomy of Resource Wars.* World Watch Paper no. 162. Danvers, MA: World Watch Institute, 2002.

Rhodes, Richard. *The Making of the Atomic Bomb.* New York: Simon & Schuster, 1986.

————. *Dark Sun: The Making of the Hydrogen Bomb.* New York: Simon & Schuster, 1995.

Rivera, José A. *Acequia Culture: Water, Land, and Community in the Southwest.* Albuquerque: University of New Mexico Press, 1998.

Robert, Lisa. *Middle Rio Grande Ecosystem Bosque Biological Management Plan, the First Decade: A Review and Update.* Albuquerque, NM: Aurora Publishing, 1995.

Rockwell, Barbara. *Boiling Frogs: Intel vs. the Village.* New York: iUniverse, 2005.

Rockwell, David. *The Nature of North America: A Handbook to the Continent—Rocks, Plants, Animals.* New York: Berkley Book, 1998.

Rodríguez, Silvia. *Acequia: Water Sharing, Sanctity, and Place.* Santa Fe, NM: School for Advanced Research Resident Scholar Book, 2006.

Sargeant, Kathryn, and Mary Davis. *Shining River Precious Land: An Oral History of Albuquerque's North Valley.* Albuquerque: Albuquerque Museum, 1986.

Sargent, Frederic O., Paul Lusk, José Rivera, and María Varela. *Rural Environmental Planning for Sustainable Communities.* Washington, D.C.: Island Press, 1991.

Schumacher, E. F. *Small Is Beautiful: Economics as if People Mattered.* New York: Harper & Row, 1973.

Scurlock, Dan. *From the Rio to the Sierra: An Environmental History of the Middle Rio Grande Basin.* General Technical Report RMRS-GTR-5. Fort Collins, CO: Rocky Mountain Research Station, U.S. Department of Agriculture, Forest Service, 1998.

Shero, James, ed. *A Sense of the American West: An Environmental History Anthology.* Albuquerque: University of New Mexico Press, 1998.

Simmons, Marc. *New Mexico: A History.* New York: W. W. Norton and the American Association of State and Local History, 1977.

Smith, Mike. *Towns of the Sandia Mountains.* San Francisco: Arcadia Publishing, 2006.

Stuart, David E. *Anasazi America.* Albuquerque: University of New Mexico Press, 2000.

Toll, H. Wolcott, ed. *Soil, Water, Biology, and Belief in Prehistoric and Traditional Southwestern Agriculture.* New Mexico Archaeological Council, 1995.

Tinbergen, Jan, coordinator. *Rio: Reshaping the International Order.* New York: New American Library, 1976.

Vareny, Paul. *New Mexico's Best Ghost Towns: A Practical Guide.* Albuquerque: University of New Mexico Press, 1987.

Vásquez, Carlos, ed. *La Vida del Rio Grande: Our River—Our Life: A Symposium.* Albuquerque, NM: National Hispanic Cultural Center, 2004.

The WPA Guide to 1930s New Mexico. Foreword by Mark Simmons. Tucson: University of Arizona Press, 1989.

Warren, Louis S., ed. *American Environmental History.* Malden, MA: Backwell Publishing, 2003.

Welsome, Eileen. *The Plutonium Files: America's Secret Medical Experiments in the Cold War.* New York: Delta Books, 2000.

Who Runs New Mexico? The New Mexico Power Structure Report. Albuquerque: New Mexico People and Energy, 1980.

Williams, Jerry L. *New Mexico in Maps.* Albuquerque: University of New Mexico Press, 1986.

Wolfe, Mary Ellen. *A Landowner's Guide to Western Water Rights.* Boulder, CO: Roberts Rinehart Publishers, 1996.

Zeman, Scott C., and Michael A. Amundson, eds. *Atomic Culture: How We Learned to Stop Worrying and Love the Bomb.* Boulder: University Press of Colorado, 2004.

INDEX